Sumner R. Mason

Truth Unfolded

Sermons and Essays

Sumner R. Mason

Truth Unfolded
Sermons and Essays

ISBN/EAN: 9783337160418

Printed in Europe, USA, Canada, Australia, Japan

Cover: Foto ©Thomas Meinert / pixelio.de

More available books at **www.hansebooks.com**

Truth Unfolded.

SERMONS AND ESSAYS

OF

REV. SUMNER R. MASON, D. D.

SELECTED AND EDITED

BY

REV. ALVAH HOVEY, D. D.,
PRESIDENT OF THE NEWTON THEOLOGICAL INSTITUTE.

WITH A SKETCH OF THE LIFE AND CHARACTER OF DR. MASON,

BY

REV. O. S. STEARNS, D. D.,
PROF. OF BIBLICAL INTERPRETATION O. T. IN NEWTON THEOL. INST.

CAMBRIDGE:
Printed at the Riverside Press,
AND PUBLISHED BY
MRS. SUMNER R. MASON.
1874.

Entered, according to Act of Congress, in the year 1874, by
MRS. SUMNER R. MASON,
in the office of the Librarian of Congress, at Washington.

RIVERSIDE, CAMBRIDGE:
STEREOTYPED AND PRINTED BY
H. O. HOUGHTON AND COMPANY.

CONTENTS.

BIOGRAPHICAL SKETCH vii

SERMONS.

SERMON I.
THE PERMANENCE OF THE WORD 1

SERMON II.
THE ONCE DELIVERED FAITH 11

SERMON III.
CONTENDING FOR THE ONCE DELIVERED FAITH . 17

SERMON IV.
THE OBEDIENT ABLE TO KNOW THE WILL OF GOD . 27

SERMON V.
GOD THE SAME IN THE OLD TESTAMENT AS HE IS IN THE NEW . 36

SERMON VI.
THE OLD TESTAMENT REVEALS SALVATION 46

SERMON VII.
THE WORTH OF MAN 55

SERMON VIII.
SIN NECESSARY IN A MORAL SYSTEM 65

SERMON IX.
THE IMPUTATION OF ADAM'S SIN 72

SERMON X.
THE LAW OF PROVIDENCE TOWARDS THE WRATH OF MEN . . . 82

SERMON XI.
THE DUTY OF SINNERS TO MAKE THEM A NEW HEART . . 94

SERMON XII.
THE SINNER'S INABILITY TO COME TO CHRIST . . . 103

SERMON XIII.
CHRIST IN THE OLD TESTAMENT 113

SERMON XIV.
Christ the Object of Worship 123

SERMON XV.
Christ the Object of Worship 134

SERMON XVI.
Only the Name of Jesus saving 146

SERMON XVII.
How Jesus spake 158

SERMON XVIII.
The Resurrection of Jesus Christ the Ground of Hope . 168

SERMON XIX.
No Condemnation to Believers 176

SERMON XX.
The Trial of Faith 185

SERMON XXI.
The Service of Christ not hard 195

SERMON XXII.
Christ's Sympathy with his People 205

SERMON XXIII.
The Truth the Instrument of Sanctification . . . 215

SERMON XXIV.
The Fact of Regeneration 223

SERMON XXV.
The Nature of Regeneration 230

SERMON XXVI.
The Fruits of Regeneration 239

SERMON XXVII.
What is the Holy Spirit? 247

SERMON XXVIII.
The Convincing of the Holy Spirit 257

SERMON XXIX.
Resisting the Holy Ghost 267

SERMON XXX.
On Grieving the Holy Spirit 276

SERMON XXXI.
Danger of Falling 288

Contents.

SERMON XXXII.
The Two Great Certainties of the Gospel . . . 298

SERMON XXXIII.
The Parable of the Pounds 308

SERMON XXXIV.
The Lost Condition of the Heathen and God's Method of saving them 320

SERMON XXXV.
What is that to thee? 366

SERMON XXXVI.
Mansions in Heaven 346

SERMON XXXVII.
The Perpetuity of the Sabbath 357

ESSAYS.
The Penalty of Sin 369
Griffin on Divine Efficiency 385

BIOGRAPHICAL SKETCH.

Sumner Redway Mason was born in Cheshire, Berkshire County, Massachusetts, June 14, 1819. His ancestry was English. Three families of the original stock, representing three distinct religious tendencies, immigrated to America, at three different times. John Mason, the Puritan, came to this country in 1630. He settled at first in Massachusetts, and subsequently in Connecticut. George Mason, or, as he was better known, Colonel George Mason, was a member of the English Parliament; but after the battle of Worcester in 1651, when Cromwell defeated the royal army, he escaped in disguise, came to this country, and settled in Virginia. From him sprang the southern Masons. "None of them," says Hon. John M. Mason, "ever settled north of Mason and Dixon's line." Samson Mason, the direct lineal ancestor of our sketch, left England for America about 1650. He was an officer in Cromwell's army, a radical and a Baptist. He settled in Dorchester, Mass., then removed to Rehoboth, and ultimately, for "conscience' sake," to Swansea. According to Baylies, he was one of the original settlers of that town, but Backus puts his settlement there at a later period. Before his removal from Rehoboth, he had assisted in building the Baptist meeting-house in Swansea, for which he was summoned before the authorities of Plymouth Colony, fined fifteen shillings, and warned to leave the jurisdiction of the colony. So far as these families were concerned, the old issues of Roundhead and Cavalier brought by George and Samson to the country of their adoption, continued to exist in their descendants. Two hundred years passed away, with the moulding and modifying influence of republican institutions, but in the recent struggle between freedom and slavery, the seeds sown in Norfolk and Rehoboth bore their legitimate fruit in the antagonisms of the South and the North.

The family of which Samson Mason was the head, was quite eminent in the early history of the Baptists in New England. Of his sons, Isaac was a deacon of the second Baptist Church in Swansea; Joseph, during his ministerial life, was its pastor, and three of his grandsons, sons of Pelatiah Mason, were pastors of the same church at different times. "When all North America," says Backus, "was ceded to Great Britain, a church was formed out of this church, with Nathan Mason as their pastor, and they went and settled at the head of the Bay of Fundy, but after some years they removed back to New England, and most of them went and settled in Berkshire, in the Massachusetts." It is here we find Pelatiah Mason, the immediate ancestor of the subject of this sketch, and the head of the clerical branch of the family. In the quaint and scriptural family record, the line of descent runs thus: "Sumner Redway Mason was the son of Eddy Mason, the son of Brooks, the son of Russel, the son of Pelatiah, the son of Samson."

His father, Eddy Mason, was a deacon of the Baptist church in Cheshire, a church formed from Elder John Leland's church, "principally on account of his open communion views." He was a farmer, with a good general education, a close student of the Bible, and a man of decided convictions. While possessing a large measure of that charity which "suffereth long and is kind," no consideration of expediency could turn him aside from principle. He was always ready to avow and to defend. He was an exemplary Christian, and commanded the esteem of the church and of his fellow-citizens. He married Matilda Redway, daughter of Deacon Joel Redway of Lanesboro', a man who himself suffered much for conscience' sake. She was a woman of earnest piety from her youth, but being exceedingly perplexed with doubts and fears, she did not publicly profess Christ until the meridian of her life. The issue of this marriage was ten children: five sons and five daughters. Freeman E., now dead, became a physician and a Professor of Anatomy and Surgery in the Medical College of Ohio. Jane, now Mrs. James M. Haswell, has been for many years a beloved missionary in Burmah. Alanson P., now District Secretary of the American Baptist Home Mission Society, and Sumner R., entered the ministry. Of the ten, Alanson P. and Mrs. Has well alone survive.

For a memoir of the early life of Mr. Mason, the material is very scanty. In April, 1826, his parents removed from Cheshire to Penfield in the western part of New York. In August 1828, his father died, leaving a widow with a large family in a land of strangers. Her purpose was to keep the family together and train them up under her own care. "From this purpose," writes her son Alanson P., "she could not be turned, though it cost her many a severe struggle. In 1830 it pleased God to bring four of the children into his kingdom, thus adding helps to our mother's religious influence. But unforeseen changes followed this happy event. I felt it my duty to leave home and study for the ministry. My oldest brother who had been studying medicine for a number of years, settled in Cincinnati, and Sumner, who was much given to reading and study, decided to secure a liberal education. His oldest brother invited him to make his home in his family, and push forward his studies as best he could. He accordingly taught in Cincinnati some years, and pursued his classical studies under Rev. Prof. Asa Drury, as a private teacher. His brother, the physician, being skeptical in his tendencies, exerted at this period an influence upon Sumner, which in respect to religion was anything but favorable."

Having made the requisite preparation, Mr. Mason entered Yale College in 1838, and pursued the studies of his class about two years, leaving New Haven in 1840. This sudden break in his collegiate course was caused by the change in his life-purpose, which occurred at this time. Hitherto, he had been aided pecuniarily by his brother, the physician, but in the year 1840 he became a new creature in Christ Jesus, and decided to give himself to the ministry, in consequence of which the support of his brother was withdrawn. The circumstances attending this change are exceedingly suggestive, as an index to the character of the man he became. He had been accustomed to worship with the Baptist church in New Haven. The pulpit of that church, at that time, did not please his taste, nor satisfy his intellectual cravings. He was poor; and the slightest pressure upon his purse could be used as an excuse for changing his place of worship. He accordingly wrote to his elder brother Alanson, a brother to whom his soul was ever knit like that of Jonathan to David, for advice in the matter. He said, "If I go to the Congregationalist meeting, I can have a free sitting and hear sound sense from the pulpit. If I attend the Baptist meeting, I must hear the brawling Roberts. I have no money to spend thus." This Mr. Roberts had been his pastor at Penfield, N. Y., and was an earnest, successful revivalist. His brother wrote back a kind letter, advising him to remain where he was, and promised to defray the expense. A few weeks elapsed, when he wrote to the same brother, "I have followed your advice, and the 'brawling Baptist' has led me down into the water." He united with the First Baptist Church in New Haven, March 1, 1840. "While with us," says the clerk of that church, "he was active in the church and in the Sunday-school, and our recollection of him is that of a brother beloved by all who enjoyed his acquaintance." The act, however, and the decision in the act, all his friends will recognize as characteristic of the man. Nevertheless, it was an act which involved a sacrifice which none can appreciate except those who have been suddenly dashed in their intellectual aspirations. He was obliged to leave college, and supply the deficiencies in his education as best he could. He accordingly taught a year or more in Cincinnati, and six years in Nashville, Tenn., pursuing at the same time, so far as possible, the studies of his class. How hard he wrought in this direction, is well explained in his own language. In a letter to his sister, Mrs. Haswell, referring to a period shortly after his marriage, he says, "You ask me what I am doing? I reply that I am a teacher of Greek and Latin, have two schools, male and female. Yet I preach, or rather talk occasionally. My ideas of a teacher, especially of advanced pupils in the classics, are such, that he who discharges them faithfully, has but little time for anything else. I now have classes in Nepos, Virgil, Ovid, Cicero's Philosophical Works, Homer, Xenophon, etc. Add to these, classes from Colburn's Mental Arithmetic to Conic Sections, and you will see that I must prove recreant to my trust, not to be all the time laboring for my school, directly or indirectly. This has increased my desire to throw off every trammel, and give myself wholly to the ministry; and now I have this end in view, and the prospect of its speedy accomplishment." The letter from which we have quoted has no date, but it seems to have been written from Huntsville, Alabama, where he went to teach after leaving Nashville, and after the greatest crisis in his life was passed, — his determination to enter the ministry. He had previously been married to Miss Mary Jane Dibble of Buffalo, N. Y. This event occurred November 10, 1844. She was the daughter of Colonel O. H. Dibble, a native of Bennington, Vt., an enterprising, energetic citizen of Buffalo, who amassed an immense fortune prior to the financial crisis of 1837, when he suffered, with so many others, a terrible reverse. In 1852, leaving his family in Buffalo, he went to California, where he spent the remainder of his days, dying at the age of 77. " He died in the fullness of time, and not unprepared for the great change. He was no ordinary man. His long life was illustrated by many high evidences of ability, and his talents were rewarded with distinctions of which any man might be proud." He occupied many prominent positions in civil and political life. He was specially interested in the Theological Institution at Hamilton, N. Y., giving it a fund, the interest of which has aided many poor students who are now preaching the gospel, or have been "called up higher." His wife, the mother of Mrs. Mason, was born in New Brunswick, N. J., and was "a woman of strong practical sense and of ardent love for her children."

To his wife Mr. Mason owed, not only the happiness of a Christian home during the years of their wedded life, but very emphatically the decision he reached at this critical juncture of his history. When the question of devoting himself entirely to the ministry pressed itself upon his conscience, his early skepticism returned with unwonted energy. Doubts respecting the reality of his piety, doubts as to the divine authority of the Scriptures, doubts tending to materialism, plunged him into their miry pit, and brought him to the verge of despair. The body could not resist the mental agony. He was seized with a dangerous fever, and came down to the border of the grave. But God, through the ministry of his wife, "cured him," as he was wont to say, "entirely cured him." "To her," he says, "I owe my restoration from the toils of infidelity." "Who knows," he writes to her some years afterwards, "what might have been the result of my reckless skepticism, but for the gentle yet firm remonstrance of such a wife; for her guardian watchfulness and prayerful entreaties during that dark, *dark* night of bitterness and woe which surprised me in Huntsville! I was already on an awful precipice, ready to stumble headlong to destruction at any moment. Recklessness, skepticisms, and an utter isolation from every human being in interest and sympathy, were driving me with fearful rapidity over the most fearful breaker of life's ocean. I thank God for my wife."

Such is the furnace out of which the pure gold comes. His determination was now fixed. The ministry became his joy and delight. He had been licensed to preach by the Baptist church in Nashville, of which Rev. R. B. C. Howell, D. D., was pastor, September 7, 1844. The conflict, of which we have spoken, came after that approval. Now he pursued his work as a teacher and gave himself also to theological studies under the direction of Dr. Howell, mingling with his teaching and studies an occasional supply of neighboring pulpits. Having completed his preparations, he spent parts of the years 1848–49 in different places in New York, as a supply and as a candidate, but being from the South, he was looked upon suspiciously, and the open door did not present itself, until June 24, 1849, when he received a call to become the pastor of the First Baptist Church in Lockport, N. Y., which he accepted. He was ordained over that church, August 22, 1849. The sermon was preached by Rev. V. R. Hotchkiss, D. D., now of Buffalo.[1] The charge was given by his brother-in-law, Rev. J. M. Haswell, D. D., now of Burmah, the right hand of fellowship by Rev. S. M. Stimson, and the prayer of ordination by Rev. Mr. Sawyer. He undertook this new labor amid grave difficulties. The former pastor of the church, Rev. Elon Galusha, for a long time a marked and influential man in the Baptist denomination, became a "Millerite," and drew off from the First Baptist Church a section composed of "fully one half of the membership," to

---

[1] His brother, Alanson P. Mason, D. D., was to preach the ordination sermon but was taken sick on the way, and was not able to be present.

which he was preaching when Mr. Mason assumed the pastoral office. The church was in a demoralized condition. It was divided, disheartened, and disposed to lean solidly upon the wisdom and influence of the new pastor. The church was found to be so weak, — a weakness resulting from differences of opinion and the lack of discipline, — that a *coup d'etat* in Baptist policy became necessary. The members of the church decided to disband, and a new church was formed and recognized, composed of more homogeneous elements. Mr. Mason became their pastor. He healed dissensions. He guided the affairs of the church with discretion. The divine blessing accompanied his labors. And when he resigned he left a thriving, vigorous church. One who was a prominent and intelligent actor in these scenes, referring to Mr. Mason's executive ability, says: "I have very distinct and abiding impressions of the trying circumstances through which we passed at Lockport. The dignified Christian spirit which he manifested under these trials, and the rare common sense with which he met and mastered them, impressed me with the fact that he was no ordinary man." The esteem which he had secured from other denominations as well as in his own, during his residence in Lockport, is so beautifully expressed by the following letter, addressed to him when leaving for his new field of labor in Cambridgeport, Mass., that we take pleasure in quoting it.

LOCKPORT, N. Y., *Feb.* 26, 1855.

Rev. S. R. MASON, —

DEAR BROTHER: The near approach of the time of your intended removal from our village, and your consequent withdrawal from the immediate and close intimacy which we have enjoyed with you as ministers of these churches, has prompted us, while reviewing and cherishing the memorials of our intercourse, to express to you in this deliberate way the great satisfaction we have had in your society, our high appreciation of your unvarying courtesy and friendship, our regret that we are to be deprived of your presence, your assistance, and your counsel, and our earnest desire that you and yours may be blessed in all your ways, and that you may be abundantly successful in your efforts to preach the gospel of Christ, and to make full proof of your ministry.

With the prayer that God may bless you in your work and bestow on you an abundant reward in heaven, we give you our parting salutatious and the right hand of fellowship, and subscribe ourselves, your brethren in the ministry,

    WILLIAM C. WISNER, *Pastor of Pres. Church.*
    H. L. DOX, *Pastor of Lutheran Church.*
    S. STILES, *Pastor of Methodist Episcopal Church.*
    E. W. KELLOGG, *Stated Supply, 2d Ward, Pres. Church.*
    EDWARD W. GILMAN, *Pastor of Congregational Church.*

He began his labors as pastor of the First Baptist Church in Cambridge, March 4, 1855. It was a large, intelligent, and influential body. He at once found himself associated with ministers of broad and refined culture. He measured himself with others, and determined to excel. How well he succeeded, let the body which grew and strengthened itself under his ministrations, let his brethren in the ministry who universally respected and loved him, let the denominational societies which sought his counsel and confided to him their most sacred interests, let the city of his adoption, which honored him by intrusting to him her choicest educational institutions, testify. We could easily fill pages with resolutions of esteem passed by various organizations, civil and religious, when death snatched him away, had we space. He was a man who could not be hid; a man whose very appearance expressed character, character which expressed power.

The sixteen years of his faithful service in Cambridge were brought to a sudden and mysterious close. As if God in his own way was making him ready for a higher service, his last sermons to his own people, August 13, 1871, were upon themes pertaining to the heavenly home to which he aspired. In the morning of that day he preached upon " the characteristics of the heavenly world," from Rev. xxi. 23 : " And the city had no need of the sun, neither of the moon, to shine in it : for the glory of God did lighten it; and the Lamb is the light thereof." In the afternoon he preached upon " the necessity of being right in character to secure life's highest good," from Luke xi. 35: " Take heed, therefore, that the light which is in thee be not darkness." The next Sabbath he spent with his friend Rev. Nelson J. Wheeler, at Newport, R. I., when the subjects of his discourses, both morning and afternoon, and the topic on which he spoke in the evening prayer-meeting, were a fitting summary of his public life-work. In the morning he preached from the familiar text, "Come unto me, all ye that labor and are heavy laden, and I will give you rest," enforcing clearly and emphatically the all-sufficiency of Christ for human salvation. In the afternoon he preached from the words, "It doth not yet appear what we shall be," drawing from the text the theme that "the future of the child of God is not revealed by his present," and showing that in his physical, intellectual, and moral nature, man's "highest possible conceptions must fall far below the reality." The way to eternal life and the bliss of eternal life, the sum and substance of all his preaching, were thus his last pulpit utterances. In the evening, at the close of the meeting, as was his custom, in a few well-chosen, terse sentences, he set forth the positiveness of God's Word. It is a revelation to be implicitly believed; not to be explained to the satisfaction man's vain curiosity or man's proud reason. He noticed Paul's answer to the jailer, "Believe on the Lord Jesus Christ and thou shalt be saved," and pressed upon the impenitent the positive command to believe on Christ, with the equally positive assurance of salvation as the result of implicit faith. Then with great solemnity charging his hearers to remember these words as his last counsel to them should they never hear his voice again on earth,— a fact the more remarkable as he was careful to avoid all hackneyed expressions, — he closed the meeting with these words, "The positiveness of the gospel." A fitting close to a spiritual ministry! It was a halo of celestial radiance encircling the setting sun! The next Sabbath he had entered upon the heavenly life, and was enjoying the results of a gracious positive revelation from God for the rescue of sinful man! He did not deem it so then; but an infinitely wise God had timed the occasion, the service, and the hour.

For the next Sabbath, he had arranged an exchange of pulpits with Rev. J. C. Foster of Beverly. Singularly, he seemed to have some premonition as to the result of that exchange. Several times during the week previous, he remarked to his wife that he did not want to go. He appeared worried about it, and when the parting came on Saturday evening, August 26th, he literally tore himself away from his family, repeating the expression, that he wished he had not agreed to go. It was, however, to be so. He left Boston for Beverly, at twenty minutes to eight, ten minutes after the regular time, and at the Revere station, the train, being behind time, was run into by the express train for Portland and Bangor, hurrying to death Dr. Mason and more than a score of others.

It is not for us to dwell upon the horrors of the scene, nor upon the grief of his family and people, when the news reached them that he whom they loved was no more. His body was found on the top of the locomotive, apparently not much bruised. His watch had not stopped. He was not recognized by any one present, but was identified by his name in his pocket-book. His remains were borne to his home the next Sabbath afternoon, and on the Thursday following, funeral services were held at his house and at his church, conducted by Revs. N. J. Wheeler of Newport, R. I., R. H. Neale, D. D., of Boston, J. G. Warren, D. D., of Newton, and by Professors H. Lincoln and A. Hovey of the Newton Theological Institution. His body was entombed in the cemetery of Mt. Auburn. During the services the city of Cambridge honored him with the emblems of mourning. In fact the sea of upturned faces in the church, the large body of clergymen of various denominations, and the representatives of many public institutions then present, the flags of the city at half-mast, the tolling of the city bells, all emphasized the language of the prophet, "All ye that are about him bemoan him, and all ye that knew his name say, How is the strong staff broken and the beautiful rod." On the next Sabbath, a tribute to his memory was given to the church and congregation which had so long enjoyed his ministry, by the writer of this sketch.

As writes a friend, " Untimely his death seems to us, but we know it was not. It was God's time. Whatever was the recklessness of man, and however criminal were the human agents in that disaster, and however just the public indignation toward them, the providence of God was over all, in all that scene of death and suffering. The servant of God is immortal until his work is done. It was the summons of his Master that called him home. It is affecting to know, that in his satchel was found after his death, a manuscript sermon on the text, "Thy will be done." He was intending to preach it the next day. The theme of his discourse was the duty of submission in all things to the will of God. May we not receive it as his farewell message to his family, to his church, to his friends everywhere?"

At his death he left a widow and seven children, for whom his people at once made generous provision. A great man had fallen in Israel. They loved him as such; and they affectionately availed themselves of the privilege of caring for those so dear to him who had so earnestly and unselfishly cared for them.

It is no easy task to delineate the characteristics of such a man as Dr. Mason was. By the foregoing sketch of his life, it will be seen that providential circumstances tended to beget in him self-reliance, independence of thought and action, and a hardihood of character, which, unless purified and modified by divine grace, would have made him as a man unlovely and unattractive. His whole nature would have been granitic. A fatherless boy, thrown upon his own resources at a period of life when he needed the tenderest and most careful culture, subsequently compelled to force his way through difficulties to secure an education and reach the goal of his ambition, we naturally expect him to become cold and unsympathetic. And yet, from the testimony of his sister, Mrs. Haswell, it appears that from his earliest childhood, while he was peculiarly shy and sensitive, his tenderness of heart was apparent to all. A bird's nest was in no danger from him. His choicest companions were his older sisters. "Healthy and active, and like most boys full of fun and mischief, he was not like some in delighting in cruel sports. He joined his sisters in their in-door amusements as heartily as they did him in out-door sports." "He was a dutiful son. Only once he attempted to resist his mother's will, after she became a widow, and then, as he related it himself years afterward, 'she brought him to with the rod.'" In his intercourse with his brothers, he had a habit which his later friends will recognize, of putting the query, when any bold assertion was made, "Well, how do you know?" While, however, neither in his early life, nor in the culture of the "schools," was there

b

much to give delicacy and finish to his character, a study of the elements of his power and success, leads us back to his lineal inheritance, and causes us to see that in the catholic yet uncompromising father and the self-distrusting yet conscientious mother, was that rare combination of strength and beauty, massiveness and tenderness, which made up the man.

This was not indeed the first impression, either in private or in public. It was as the " strong staff," the emblem of power, — power to support or power to crush, — that he was at first recognized on the street or in the pulpit. He seemed born as one to command. He seemed as one who loved the arena of strife, as one of those who snuffed the battle from afar, and felt himself equal to his foe. There was something imperial in his very bearing, in his crisp remark, in his bold assertion, in his tenacity for the precise statement of a principle, in his determined adherence to a position when once it had been taken. As the " beautiful rod," shooting out of the ground, with its buds clustering thickly upon it, welcoming the dew and the shower, rather than the thunder and the lightning, more sensitive to an east wind or an autumnal frost than to a cyclone or a tornado, none knew him, except those who experienced the wealth of his affections around the hearth-stone, the gentleness of his spirit in the sick-room or at the bed of death, and the few intimate friends to whom he sometimes opened his real nature and who were allowed to see him as he really was. An incident occurred when on a visit to his friend Rev. Mr. Wheeler, then residing in Skowhegan, Me., which illustrates this side of his character. " While walking along one of the streets," says Mr. W., " we met a little child who was crying. The neglected creature was anything but attractive in outward appearance. But the Doctor stopped and spoke some comforting words as we passed. We had not gone far, before the little one cried out ' Mother! Mother!' As quickly as though he had been its mother, he turned back, went to the child, took it by the hand, inquired out its home, and refused to leave it until its friends appeared. Then, as we continued our walk, he said, ' Ah! that word " Mother," when uttered by a child in trouble, touches a tender chord in my heart.' This may seem very simple when read, but it was most moving as witnessed." An item in the writer's own experience confirms him in the opinion, that this element of kindness and loveliness, so generally thought to be deficient, was genuine and active. Years ago, when he first settled in Cambridge, my own pastorate at Newton commencing about the same time, I hesitated to exchange pulpits with him, because I had heard that he was stern and morose and forbidding, a critic of the critics, a preacher not easily satisfied with the pulpit efforts of any one. Through the intercession of a common friend, there came a Sabbath when he stood in my place and I in his; and at the close of the services of the day, in conversation with my wife, it appeared that he was as afraid of me as I of him. And then I learned the fact, confirmed by many other proofs, that down deep in his soul was the tender shoot pressing its way up to the surface, to be exposed to zephyrs and rough winds and biting cold, exquisitely sensitive to the amenities of life and to Christian courtesies. Then I learned that the strong shepherd's staff, ready to beat off foes, and to defend friends, was held by a hand which trembled lest the blow might do even an imaginary injury. He often lamented that his lack of self-demonstration prevented his being appreciated in his true character. Really he was as catholic as the air we breathe. He was bold to defend or to rescue. He was often timid and shrinking lest he should crush what he would foster.

"In deeds and motives untold by the tongue,
By chisel uncarved, by poets unsung,
The Beautiful lives in the depths of the soul."

This genial element of his nature is still further illustrated by his deportment in his autumnal vacations. During the later years of his life, he was accustomed to spend them with his friend Mr. Wheeler, among the forests of Maine, or the lakes and mountains of northern New York. "He had a natural taste," writes Mr. W., "amounting to a passion, for life in the forests. When worn down with work, his letters used to express a longing for this favorite mode of recreation. And when autumn found him in the wilderness, he entered with the spirit of a boy into its varied scenes of hunting, fishing, boating, and sight-seeing. Everything interested him, even the unavoidable hardships of such a life. No one enjoyed more keenly every ludicrous incident that enlivened the passing days. His hearty laugh over them was contagious. Our evenings in camp were spent in recounting the incidents of the day, and rehearsing mirthful stories and witty sayings, when our rounds of merry laughter would wake the echoes from the neighboring cliffs. Our conversation would often take a more serious turn, and some theological question would be started or some topic of Christian experience would be discussed, when the Doctor was peculiarly happy, familiar, and suggestive. Never was he more instructive and interesting in his preaching than on his vacation Sabbaths with the groves for God's temple, and the sons of the forest for his auditory. They are Sabbaths never to be forgotten."

The same elements of character marked his piety. It could not be otherwise if they had distinguished the man, for the Christian is simply the unrenewed man set right. The old nature is started in a new and pure direction when it is " begotten again unto a lively hope by the resurrection of Jesus Christ from the dead." The spirit of God, the author of the new man, takes the man as he is, with his rough qualities and his amiable qualities, and moves him forward to the fullness of Christ. This new man is to become Godlike. He is to be filled with all the fullness of God; but this fullness, which in reality is nothing but purity of heart and life, technically called holiness, is simply the development of the new life given him, which takes under its supervision the ruling characteristics of the old life, modifying and subduing the hurtful and self-destructive. To be a Christian, is to possess an enlarged and divinely directed manhood. The ambition of the Christian is to attain the stature of a being in whom " mercy and truth have met together, righteousness and peace have kissed each other." Power and love, justice and benevolence, are the united elements in the being with whom he would enjoy perpetual companionship. A nature which would feel hypocrisy in himself and others, as sensitively as our Lord did that of the Pharisees; a nature which would respond as quickly to the look of need, as did our Lord to the diseased woman who touched the border of his garments; a nature which would incorporate into itself the Sermon on the

Mount and bathe itself in the sweet influences of our Lord's intercessory prayer; a nature which feared not man, but feared and loved God, because it was pervaded with and regulated by the Spirit of God, the great Helper of man; a nature strong to do and tender to feel; to do all good things and feel all pure things, — this is the ideal of the new man in Christ Jesus.

It was this ideal which Dr. Mason sought to make actual in his piety. From early life he had been the child of conflicts over religious questions. At one time we find him skeptical, almost a stiff doubter; at another a sincere inquirer and on the verge of belief. Now he throws off prayer; then he is earnest in his supplications. The crisis in New Haven, when he passed into the power of an endless life, and the crisis at Huntsville, when he was lifted from the depths of despair to the firm rock of his ministerial purpose, both present the antagonism of a stern will with an honest faith. And when faith won the victory, so strong was his conviction of sinfulness, so dominant seemed the old depraved heart, so crucifying was it at times to rule his spirit and possess his soul in patience, comparing the actual with the ideal, the language of Paul was never too strong for him, " Not as though I had already attained, either were already perfect; but I follow after, if that I may apprehend that for which also I am apprehended of Christ Jesus." While with bold Peter, he would say to himself, " Giving all diligence, add to your faith, valor; and to valor, knowledge; and to knowledge, temperance; and to temperance, patience; and to patience, godliness; and to godliness, brotherly-kindness; and to brotherly-kindness, charity," he craved also with the humble Paul, " the fruit of the Spirit, love, joy, peace, long-suffering, gentleness, goodness, faith, meekness, temperance, against which there is no law."

The manifestations of his piety strongly confirm us in the belief that such was his ideal of the Christian life. No one ever heard him pray who did not feel that he honored God, and walked with Him; that he stood in awe of Him; and yet approached lovingly near to Him. He never prayed in ruts nor by forms. He had a petition to present, and it was offered in the meekness and submissiveness of a child. The writer once heard him utter but three sentences in a public prayer, and yet it was far from flippancy or irrelevancy. It comprehended all that needed to be said. It bore us to the throne of all mercy, for the reception of all mercy. Nor did any one ever hear him preach who did not feel that the Scriptures were his ultimate appeal, that to them he brought every emotion of his soul as the crucible which should remove the dross and clarify the gold. God Himself, with whom he loved to dwell alone in his study and in the woods, and God's Word, comprehensive in its scope, yet minute in its requirements, massive in its structure, yet entering into the thoughts and intents of the heart; God the great God, and yet the incarnate God, his law and his gospel just like Himself, was his conception of a true life which he would attain himself, and urge upon others. Hence his zeal for integrity in Christian conduct. Hence his anathemas upon public sins. Hence his tenacity for the minuter matters of life, and the avoidance of even the shadow of unchristian influence; not to ride rough-shod over public opinion; not for the sake of eccentricity; not for the pleasure of having his own way; not to present to the world, a puritanic type of character in the offensive sense; but that through the strength and beauty of that God who works within us " both to will and to do," earth might resemble heaven, and man be holy and without blemish. The language of Job, with reference to his own noble purposes, expresses Dr. Mason's determination with reference to his Christian character; " Till I die, I will not remove mine integrity from me : my heart shall not reproach me so long as I live."

As was the man, so were his theological beliefs. Very few men whose theological training has not been secured in the schools ever systematize their religious convictions. Though the doctrines of Christianity may be cordially and confidently accepted by them, they generally lie in their minds as " disjecta membra," fragmentary truths, each a whole in itself. The result is, that they put forth each truth as the all of truth, push it to an extreme application, distort it, so that it loses much of its force as a divinely revealed truth. Their theology, if such it may be called, is a one-sided, inconsistent theology, totally unlike the mind of God who is so emphatically one. Their utterances are mere dogmatisms. They are heart-explosions. What is said on one doctrine is essentially denied or contradicted in the discussion of a kindred doctrine. Their preaching and their writings resemble conglomerate granite, solid it may be, but full of all kinds of pebbles and stones without beauty or order, rather than the homogeneous Scotch granite, whose effect upon the eye is uniform and impressive as a whole. Their theology is an emotional theology, or an imperial theology, or a didactic theology. It catches the ear, warms for the moment the heart, but will not bear the light of reason, nor the comparison of truth with truth. It can never build up " the church of the living God, the pillar and ground of the truth."

Dr. Mason never allowed his heart to run away with his reason. His mind, eminently constructive and self-poised, was ever searching for foundations, laying firmly the corner-stone, building out and up from that and from that alone. He spared neither toil nor time to learn the whole of a subject, look at it from all sides, weigh it in the scale of opposing theories or modifying truths, and consider it as presented and expounded by those who held opposite opinions. He indorsed no human authority. He copied no distinguished divine. He loved the clear, practical Andrew Fuller, and the theoretical, speculative, uncompromising Griffin; but he likewise appreciated the golden-mouthed Chrysostom and the imaginative Jeremy Taylor. He could learn something from the fierce, hirsute South, but he grew stouter under the sway of the princely Edwards. He repelled no wind of theological opinion, truthful or untruthful, yet standing firmly upon the revealed will of God, though, as we have seen, sometimes terribly shaken by its stern and sweeping requisitions, as all truth-searching minds are, he wrought out from it his own system of belief, solid as the hills, beautiful as the sculptured marble. So independent was he in his methods of investigation that he always believed that it was best for him that he never had received the discipline and teachings of any theological school. Unquestionably, self-dependence begat self-reliance, gave freshness to his pulpit utterances and an authoritative control over his people. But in almost any other mind, the tendency of such methods is to narrowness, positiveness, the attempt at impossibilities, especially in the practical application of the teachings of Christianity. He mined into the deep heart of God, prayerfully, carefully, searchingly mined, and out came the jewel worthy of his Master's crown. And how he gloried in showing it in its native brilliancy! How he delighted in bringing out a truth in its precise form, in its exact statement, reveling in it as a truth of God, putting it in varied lights, so that others might see it in its pure beauty, turning it about, side after side, and almost impatient because others did not see it just as it appeared to his own vision! How the sermons of this volume reveal his enthusiasm in exhibiting God's greatness in God's goodness, God's sovereignty and man's freedom, God's redemption for man's sinfulness, God's authority and man's obedience, God's promises with man's fidelity, God's incarnation and man's divine nature, God's throne in man's heaven, God's eternity and man's destiny! How those last sermons to his own people on heaven, and the stern fidelity requisite to reach it, his last remarks in his own prayer-meeting on unexpected death, and the sermon he intended to preach at Beverly on Christian submission, make a sort of summary of his theological opinions, so strong, yet so tender, the staff and the rod! Like the stars in their courses, " they all stand together ; not one faileth."

The same characteristics of power and fitness distinguished him as a preacher. With a theology angular, positive, precise in its phraseology, there was combined the richness of a ripe Christian experience, enabling him to give every man his portion of meat in due season. He was willing to work for the truth, but he longed to have others receive it just as he expounded it. He stripped off all disguises. He hated shams. He despised cant. He laid the heart bare to the quick, but he had a better remedy for healing it than false emotions and fanatical ecstasy. He was satisfied with the results he had reached by searching the Scriptures, and comparing them with his own spiritual life, and he was therefore firm, bold, earnest in his pulpit utterances. Hence he magnified his pulpit, and relied upon his pulpit as the chief power for good. He did not ignore pastoral work, but his pulpit was to him God's throne, from which, Sabbath after Sabbath, God through him expressed his will. He believed in his pulpit as the divinely appointed agency to guide and form society, according to the principles symbolized in the cross. He wanted God to dwell among men, and sincerely believed that if they would listen to God's word and practice it as thus enunciated, their highest weal would be secured. He expected and demanded that men should search for God in the sanctuary, rather than be sought after and taught in their homes. Perhaps he trusted to the power of his pulpit too much. But he deemed himself set apart as a preacher of the gospel and a defender of the gospel, and he would have men come to him, as they did to Moses, as the expounder of the law, rather than go out after them and constrain them to come to the house of God. He would have a magnetism in the pulpit, like that which Christ manifested in the synagogue of Nazareth when " the people were astonished at his doctrine : for his word was with power : " like that of Paul in Antioch of Pisidia, when the people besought him that " these words might be preached to them on the next Sabbath." The following note from Professor Edwards A. Park of Andover, shows by the impression which his pulpit efforts made even upon a stranger, how worthily he executed his purpose. " I spent a Sabbath," he says, at Cambridgeport, " and heard Dr. S. R. Mason preach in the year 1871. I shall not soon forget the impression made upon me by his services. I recognized in him at once a firm conscientiousness. He obviously spoke what he deemed himself bound to speak. His conscience made him bold. His sermon was like the voice of a trumpet. It was an instructive sermon, and all his services indeed were fitted to build up his church in sound doctrine. I was impressed by the solidity of his thoughts and words and ways. In these times of sensationalism it is refreshing to hear such a man. I inwardly resolved to hear him often."

Dr. Mason's sermons, however, were not merely strong and convincing. They were fitted into the needs of his people. Among numerous instances so well known to his people, two as spoken of by Mr. Wheeler will explain our meaning. " I remember," he writes, " his relating to me the occasion of his two best sermons. While visiting a mother, who had just been bereft of a little child, he was trying to console her with the thought of Christ's sympathy: that He not only felt for her, but also felt with her. Her reply was, ' How can He feel with me, when He never had a little child to lose?' This question suggested to him the sermon he preached the next Sabbath from the text. ' For we have not a high-priest who cannot be touched with the feeling of our infirmities.' At another time, after preaching a sermon on the severity of the Christian conflict, as he was leaving the house, he overheard an impenitent person saying, ' Well, if the Christian life is so hard and trying in its experience, I think I will not try it.' The text immediately flashed upon him, ' Take my yoke upon you and learn of me: for my yoke is easy and my burden is light. The next Sabbath he preached from it." The writer heard Dr. Mason but a few times, but judging from what he has heard, the one dominant characteristic of his preaching was its immediate, decided impressiveness. Everything was sacrificed for an impression which would be felt and remembered. His people easily understood what he meant, knew that the theme was logically and scripturally sustained, and felt that it was designed for them, then and there. Few congregations were ever so elaborately indoctrinated. His pulpit was a critical place for a novice. Many among his listeners knew that they could teach him the way of God more perfectly. Dr. Mason's style was clear, his argument compact and well illustrated, and his appeals true and clinching. He did not enter a labyrinth, which may lead everywhere and end nowhere, but he went first himself into the temple of God, into the holy place through the veil, into the most holy place, where, filling his golden censer with celestial fire and receiving the incense from the great high-priest, all aglow himself with the beauty and glory of the place, he came forth with an offering worthy of the acceptance of all. His ministry was a ministry to bring manhood into kinship with Godhead. His ministry was for babes, only as babes under his nurture might attain to the stature of the fullness of Christ.

To develop such, he had thoughts suited to all. Sometimes they were a nugget of gold in the form of a costly promise, and he heaved it out for his hearers to trade upon many days. Sometimes it was a boulder of quartz rock, as a huge prophecy; and he crushed it himself and taught others to become muscular by showing them how to crush out the choice ore. Sometimes he brought a little golddust, as a story or a parable, and put it into the hands of the child and told him how to make it pay in soul-wealth. And many times he brought the fine gold of a clarified doctrine, meeting the needs of all, and proving itself "profitable for instruction in righteousness." Whatever he brought was worth something. Myriad-sided was the gospel he proclaimed; equally so was it in its applications.

> "Simple, grave, sincere,
> In doctrine uncorrupt ; in language plain,
> And plain in manner; decent, solemn, chaste,
> And natural in gesture: much impressed
> Himself, as conscious of his awful charge,
> And anxious mainly that the flock he feeds
> May feel it too."

As a pastor Dr. Mason was a man of broad conceptions and noble aims. Gifted with unusual executive ability, he brought all his energies to bear upon the prime object of his public life, namely, to "watch for souls." He could give himself to the culture of one soul, search out the secret of its special needs, and put his individual stamp upon that one, as was evident from his power over young men when entering business, and more especially over those who were being educated for the ministry. His influence upon such persons possessed the power of a fascination. They felt him in every decision of life. They reverenced him as a father. He engraved his own religious convictions upon them, and stirred them to an enthusiastic consecration of their being to their high calling. He felt his responsibility in this direction and wielded his influence with a passion. To train a man, to impress upon him the idea of the greatness of manhood, was his chief ambition. He loved to take hold of a man whom he could guide and direct. This passion expressed itself, not only upon those of his own flock, but upon men wherever he found them. Says Mr. Wheeler, from whom we have quoted so frequently, "One thing that was noticeable in his forest tours was the interest he felt in the leading men of the settlements we visited. In these remote settlements, there is usually one man whose will is the law of the community. He interested himself especially in such persons, and endeavored to impress them with a sense of their responsibility, as the leaders of others. We once passed a Sabbath in a settlement situated thirty miles in the wilderness, and nearly sixty miles from any church. As usual, we preached during the day. It was near midnight before the Doctor appeared in his bed-room; and then he stated that he had been passing the evening with the landlord — the recognized leader of the settlement — and had tried to show him, not only his personal responsibility to God, but also his peculiar responsibility to those around him. And during a stay of several days, he became so deeply interested in this destitute community, that he offered to raise $200 or $300 annually towards the support of a suitable missionary among them." In all his movements for the spiritual thrift of his people, in their public enterprises, such as that of the erection of a new house of worship, and in the raising of funds for benevolent purposes, he laid his hand on men, exemplified what he sought by his personal sacrifice, and by a sort of magical influence carried out his designs. What the First Baptist Church of Cambridge is to-day, its noble position among the churches of the denomination, is due very largely to his personal power over its individual members, the wealthy and the strong.

Nor did he neglect others, less influential than these. His letters to his wife when she was absent from home, and he remained at work, are filled with sketches of the condition and wants, temporal and spiritual, of the poorer members of the church; in some instances almost a full biography; showing his perfect familiarity with their position, his thorough sympathy with them and his plans for their comfort and happiness. As an instance of his happy method of quenching jealousies among the less influential of his people, and as giving a true insight into his soul, we quote his own language addressed to his wife, in the freedom of private correspondence

We simply suppress names. He says, "I must give you an account of a good thing I got off on old Mr. ——. You know that they all think that I am as proud as Lucifer, and that I stand aloof from them (*i. e.*, the family). Well, I met the old man on the sidewalk, and shook hands with him. Said I, 'I have not seen you often since you came back.' 'Haven't you,' said he, 'I have seen you.' 'Where?' said I. 'On the street,' said he, 'a half a dozen times.' This was so said as to imply that I was unwilling to speak to him. 'Have you?' said I, 'then you have treated me very badly, to pass me by without speaking to me.' You ought to have seen his face. 'Do you think so?' said he. 'Yes,' I replied, 'I don't like to have my friends pass me in that way on the street.' 'Well now,' said he, 'I didn't know that. I thought you did.'"

But it was his church, as the body of Christ, to which he gave his strength. His ideal of a church of God was lofty and grand. He believed in her as the great missionary force for the weal of the world. Examination for admission to her membership was always searching and discriminating. The discipline of members, when necessary, was prompt, decisive, and kind. It was his day-dream and his night-dream, "Oh! that this people may be found walking in the truth and in love." He knew that much self-abnegation would be demanded from him and from them, to reach the realization of his conception. He felt his own deficiencies. He prayed over them and wept over them. But a church which is an emblem of that glorious church, "without spot or wrinkle, or any such thing," was a reality which so dazzled him and ravished him, he could not repress his longings that for once he might see on earth a type of the heavenly antitype. He knew that manly natures, which are sternest when great emergencies arise, are usually endowed with the gentlest affections, as the softest down is found upon the eagle's breast. He knew that "soft piety enters at an iron gate." And though he sometimes failed, and none felt the failure so keenly as he, yet as the leader and guide of his people, their teacher and brother, his endeavor was to 'feed his flock like a shepherd; to gather the lambs with his arm and carry them in his bosom." How well he executed his purpose, was manifest in the pride with which he ever spoke of his people, and in their pride in him as one whom they gloried to praise and follow. What complete control over them he possessed, may be shown by a little incident he related to a friend during the latter part of his ministry. He was an enthusiast for congregational singing. He had labored persistently, to secure good singing and effective singing as an inspiring part of public worship. At one time his organist did not seem to be of the same mind, and often perplexed him. On a given Sunday, when entering his pulpit, he found a young Congregationalist minister who had come there by mistake. The young man seemed embarrassed, and Dr. Mason kindly offered to exchange with him, and let him remain where he was. The offer was accepted. Dr. Mason had selected his hymns, and left them for the young man to use if he chose. He returned to his own church just as the people were singing the last hymn. As the organist played the tune previous to singing, he noticed that a common metre tune was played while he knew that he had selected a long metre hymn. He supposed, at first, that the young man had selected another hymn, but as the singing went on, he found that the tune did not fit the hymn, and that they were all confused. During the interval between the first and second verses, Dr. Mason walked up into the pulpit, and said, "Now, let us sing the Doxology, in Old Hundred." They sang it with a will. The organist was conquered.

Such was the resolute, ruling spirit of the man. Such is the power a pastor can wield over a people who love and reverence him. Dr. Mason deserved to be so regarded by his people. His labors in their behalf were untiring. His devotion to their highest interests was unselfish. To serve them, and to stimulate them to secure a broad, full, completed Christian life was his constant ambition. "Calais, when I die, will be found written on my heart," said Queen Mary on her dying bed, when mourning the results of the capture of that ill-fated city. Cambridge, so distinguished for its social, intellectual, and religious culture, and especially the First Baptist Church in

Cambridge was on the heart of Dr. Mason, when, "in the twinkling of an eye," he passed from the cares and conquests of earth to the rest and joys of heaven.

Dr. Mason was a sincere friend, an earnest, sympathetic Christian, a truth-searching theologian, an effective preacher, a wise and judicious pastor. To his family, he has bequeathed a life full of sunny memories. By his people, his name will always be honored. In his denomination, he will long be considered one of its choicest ornaments. By all who knew him he will be esteemed as a PRINCE IN ISRAEL.

The Rev. Dr. Neale of Boston, who labored side by side with Dr. Mason, during his pastorate at Cambridge, has furnished the writer with personal reminiscences so unique and genial, that they would be mangled by quotations from them. They are therefore appended.

DR. NEALE'S TRIBUTE.

It was my privilege to know Dr. Mason quite intimately from the time he became a pastor in this vicinity. He was in every respect a strong man, — strong in body, mind, and heart. His personal presence was commanding. His erect manly form, the forward bent of his head, his thoughtful, earnest look, gave you at once the impression that he was a man of more than ordinary power. His bearing at first, and when his countenance was in repose, seemed somewhat haughty and cold, but those of us who knew him, can never forget the simplicity of his spirit, the warmth of his friendship, the tenderness of his heart. As a husband, father, brother, friend, he was one of the kindest of men, genial among his ministering brethren, and ever accessible and affectionate to the people of his charge. On all occasions, however, he was dignified and courteous. It may be said of him, as of Dr. Sharp and the late Baron Stow, that he never said or did a foolish thing. Putting on no airs of saintship, it was yet natural with him to be serious, as conscious of the grave responsibilities that rested upon him as a minister of God.

Dr. Mason, though far from being morose or puritanic, was

yet strict in his morality. He avoided the very appearance of evil. The injunction of the Apostle, " Whatsoever things are true, whatsoever things are honest, whatsoever things are just, whatsoever things are pure, whatsoever things are lovely, whatsoever things are of good report, if there be any virtue, and if there be any praise, think on these things," was practically exemplified in the life and teachings of our departed brother. He would not sanction any infringement upon the sacredness of the Sabbath, and refused to preach to a company of soldiers who proposed to attend his church, unless they would promise not to ride in the Sunday cars. Dr. Mason was a very sincere man. He could be sportive, and relished a joke, and certainly was at times capable of the keenest sarcasm, but he was careful not to exaggerate, or allow anything to escape his lips that should unnecessarily hurt a brother's feelings. He always meant exactly what he said. He hated deception in every form. He was no fawning sycophant. He never by word or act sought the good opinion of persons whom he thought unworthy, and never appeared to be friendly unless he was so in reality.

Dr. Mason had a high sense of his official duties. He was confided in as a man of sound judgment, and accordingly placed in many positions of public trust, not only in his own denomination, but in the community where he dwelt. These he filled with scrupulous care. As a member of the School Board at Cambridge, as well as of the Executive Committee in Boston, he was conscientiously present at the meetings, and acquainted with all the questions that came before them, and felt himself individually responsible for whatever vote he gave. Our dear brother was emphatically strong in the grace that is in the Lord Jesus. His type of piety was characteristic. He made no mere show or pretense. His was no stereotyped experience, nor a second-hand faith. He came to the original fountain and thought for himself. His doctrinal sentiments were decidedly evangelical. He was evidently converted by the grace of God, into the great and glorious truths of the New Testament. They were written on his heart by the Holy Spirit, and grasped by his strong intellect as the undoubted teaching of inspiration.

All these things combined made him decidedly one of our ablest preachers. It was good to see and hear him in the pulpit; you were sure of being instructed. He understood the things whereof he affirmed, and never failed to bring forth beaten oil into the sanctuary. He believed, and therefore spoke. What, after all, gave the greatest impressiveness to his preaching was the unselfish and lofty motive by which he was obviously influenced. There was no effort at display, no attempt to be eloquent, or even profound. He thought not of himself or what the people might think of him. He aimed only to communicate the message intrusted to him, as an ambassador of Heaven. These are some of the things, deeply written on my memory and heart of the late Dr. Sumner R. Mason. He was a good man, and a good minister of the Lord Jesus, watching for souls as one that must give account.

The day after the death of Dr. Mason, the Hon. Henry S. Washburn composed the following tribute to his memory, which we are allowed to insert in this sketch: —

SUMNER R. MASON.

'Twas at a golden wedding feast,
  Just one brief waning moon ago,
I marked how lightly Time had touched,
  Thy manly form now laid so low.

Age leaned upon thy strong right arm,
  And children prattled by thy knee,
While crowned with benedictions came,
  Thy words of wisdom warm and free.

And moving thus among thy flock,
  In all thy manhood's port and pride,
I felt how greatly blessed were they
  Who shared the love of such a guide.

Oh, vanity of human trust!
  When cloudless seemed thy favored sky,
The gathering tempest hurled its blast,
  And all our hopes in ruin lie.

God shield the hearts which bear to-day
  The burden of so great a woe;
Where but to Thee, O Love divine!
  Can they for help and succor go?

Yet, while I mourn, my early friend,
  That thou hast passed away so soon,
'T were well, among thy gathered sheaves,
  In Autumn's golden afternoon, —

Thy work all finished and complete,
  To hear the Master bid thee come,
And from the heights of Zion shout,
  The reaper's pæan, *Harvest home!*

So, casting all our grief on Him
  Who ever doeth all things well,
We'll heap the turf upon thy breast,
  And breathe for thee our last farewell.

SERMONS.

SERMON I.

THE PERMANENCE OF THE WORD.

Is. xl. 8, end. — *The Word of our God shall stand forever.*

HERE, as in several other places in the Bible, the permanence of the "Word of God" is contrasted with the transitoriness of men upon the earth: "All flesh is grass, and all the goodliness thereof is as the flower of the field: the grass withereth, the flower fadeth: because the Spirit of the Lord bloweth upon it: surely the people is grass. The grass withereth, the flower fadeth: but the Word of our God shall stand forever."

The Apostle Peter refers to this, and kindred passages, when he says that the Word of God is that by the instrumentality of which the soul of man is regenerated; and that it is this that is preached unto men for their salvation by the preaching of the gospel. The Apostle thus identifies the Word of God of which the Prophet speaks, with that word which is extolled in the Psalms as converting and purifying and saving the soul; and with that of which our Saviour speaks when He prays, "Sanctify them through thy truth: thy Word is truth."

The "Word of God" of which the Psalmist and the Prophet wrote, was that portion of the Old Testament which had been given up to that time. The "Word of God" of which our Saviour spoke, was all of the Old Testament, and so much of the New as He had given to his disciples. The "Word of God" of which the Apostle Peter spoke, embraced yet more. It took in all that holy men had spoken by the Holy Ghost, not only in the Law and the Prophets, but in the New Testament also.

But the words of the prophet, though they had immediate reference to what had been already written in his day, were equally applicable to all that should be thereafter written by the inspiration of God. For it was as true of the Word of God that was yet to be written, that *it* should stand forever, as it was of that which had already been written. It was true of it all, that not one word of it should fail. It should stand forever, firm and unchanged. Each vanishing age, and each departing generation, should leave it as they found it. Each dawning age, and each coming generation, should find it as their predecessors left it.

To one who reflects on the transitoriness of man, and all that pertains to him, on the earth, — and who does not thus reflect at this period of the year? — and feels the sadness that such reflection is calculated to produce, there is relief and encouragement in this thought. Time will dissolve all human relationships, sweep away all human interests, and undermine all earthly human supports; but it is not in time, nor in eternity, to destroy the Word of God; nor to alienate man's inheritance in it; nor to undermine it as the foundation of his hopes, and the pledge of his immortality. This thought, brought home to the mind, makes of man something higher and nobler than flesh; makes him superior to all things earthly; lifts him out of the sphere of change and decay, and imparts to his own being a permanence and enduring worth, in comparison with which the material universe sinks into insignificance. The thought, brought home in humility and faith, enables one to say: "Though all flesh is grass, and all the goodliness thereof as the flower of the field: and as the grass it withereth, and as the flower it fadeth; yet because the Word of our God shall stand forever, and all my hopes, and all the interests of my immortality, are assured by it, therefore I myself shall stand with it."

Your attention is invited to some of the particulars that are involved in this general proposition: "The Word of our God shall stand forever."

1. In the first place, *every statement of fact* which the Word of God makes will remain, and be found to be a true state-

ment. The statement itself will never be modified nor annulled; and the thing declared will never be proved to be false. Each statement will, on the contrary, in the form in which it now stands, always convey a truth to the minds of men; and increase by so much their store of real knowledge. From the present moment, and onward to the end of time, and then during all the ages of eternity, God will stand by all that He has uttered, and maintain its verity against all that venture to call it in question; and in vindication of all that accept it and rest upon it as true. This much, at least, is asserted by the words of the prophet. Nothing less than this is involved in the general declaration: "The Word of our God abideth forever."

It follows, therefore, that the time will never come when it will be proved that the *narratives* of the Bible are only fables and myths. The past itself is, indeed, a guaranty for the future in regard to this matter. Not unfrequently, in the past, has this theory of myth and fable been set up against the narratives and historical statements of the Bible; and especially against those that must, if they are true, have been written by men supernaturally and divinely enlightened; and more especially against all that relate to the working of miracles. Beginning with the narrative of the creation, and following on down through all that is set forth as miraculous, and through most that is not common to both the Bible and profane history, the enemies of the revelation have, at one time or another, declared those portions of it to be mere inventions, and have brought all the resources of great learning and great abilities to the task of demonstrating their declaration to be true. Almost every department of literature and of science has been made to play its part in this grand enterprise. Almost every important discovery or theory in archæology, in the structure of the earth, and in the movements of the stars, has been paraded as a witness against the simple statements of revelation. For a time those who have thus paraded these things have exulted, and proclaimed themselves the victors in the great controversy of the world against the Bible; and for a time its timid friends have feared and trembled lest these boastings should turn out to be true. But in every instance, when the discovery that was put upon the stand as a witness to convict revelation of falsehood, has had any bearing whatever on the Bible, it has ended by confirming its truth. Egypt, hoary with an antiquity dating back far beyond the earliest historic periods of the world; Assyria, filled with the melancholy memorials of buried cities and forgotten nations; the earth's surface, and the vault of heaven, all have been invoked, and the response of each has been an unequivocal testimony against those who have called them forth. Like the evil spirit which turned upon the sons of Sceva the Jew, at Ephesus, when they attempted to exorcise it by the name of Jesus, these witnesses that have been invoked to testify against the Bible, have answered: " God we know, and his Word we know, but who are ye?" The Bible has remained unscathed. Its friends have been strengthened in their faith. Their confidence in it as the Word of God has become firmer and more intelligent and more sustaining. Its account of the creation, and of the beginning of human history, has become clearer and more satisfactory. All its histories, its miracles, and its revelations, have shown, in sharper outline and clearer impression, the seal of truth. It has become yet more manifest that the Bible is indeed the Word of God.

From the fact that we are considering, it follows, further, that not alone the *narratives of the past*, but, if we may so speak, *those of the future*, also, will never fail. They will all be found ultimately to answer as exactly to the things that are yet to be, as does the narrative of the past answer to the things that have been. All prophecy will be found in the end, as so much of it has been found already, to be *prewritten* history. All prophecies will yet be read as we now read those pertaining, *e. g.*, to the captivity of the Jews in Babylon, to the destruction of Jerusalem, and the coming of the Messiah. The day will come when men will thus look back on all that is foretold of the triumph of the gospel in the world, of the destruction of Antichrist, and of the Messiah's final coming, and the day of judgment. But the same spirit that prompts men to attempt to falsify the testimony of the Word of God respecting the past, prompts them to deny also its declarations regarding the future. Hence the class of men that do the one, always do the other. They who deny the Scriptural account of the creation of the world, e. g., sneer at the predicted ending of it. They who deride the account of the beginning of human history, have no patience with the prophecy of its termination. They who are sure that God never has wrought a miracle on the earth, and that He never can, are equally sure that He will never interfere with the present order of material things, nor interpose to fulfill the predictions of his Word regarding them. There are now, as there were in the days of the Apostles, "Scoffers, walking after their own lusts, and saying, Where is the promise of his coming? For since the fathers fell asleep, all things continue as they were from the beginning of the creation," and will continue without ending. But if it is true that "the Word of our God shall stand forever," then that which is written in that Word as prophecy will yet come fully to pass, and "the day of the Lord will come as a thief in the night; in the which the heavens shall pass away with a great noise, and the elements shall melt with fervent heat, the earth also, and the works that are therein shall be burned up;" and all that is preliminary to this in the prophetic record will have its fulfillment.

All that has in the past indicated the truth of Scriptural *history*, has gone so far also towards the support of faith in the *prophecies* of the Bible. Hence it is that there never was a time when the friends of revelation rested with more confidence in the certainty that prophecy will be fulfilled than they do this day. Never was there a time when they were manifesting their confidence with more firmness. This confidence lies indeed at the foundation, and is one of the main sources of support and inspiration in all the great missionary enterprises of our age, and in many of the great social and governmental reforms that are pushing the world towards its millennium. It is because Christians believe that the world is to be evangelized, in accordance with the predictions of the Word of God, that they engage so heartily in these enterprises, and go on in them from year to year with ever increasing earnestness, and more and more liberal devotion, notwithstanding the errors of rationalism and the cold-heartedness of multitudes who falsely bear the Christian name. It is true that they are moved in this matter by their loyalty to the commands of Christ, and by their love of righteousness, and their intense desire for the salvation of souls; but connected with all these, and supporting them, is the calm and settled conviction that the glorious day shall yet dawn on this world which is predicted by the Word of God, when the name of Jesus shall be known by every nation under heaven, and shall become the talisman of salvation to multitudes, from them all, that cannot be numbered. In other words, they believe that is to be which God has predicted; therefore they have energy and courage and hope, in labors and sacrifices, to bring it to pass.

2. In the second place, the general statement before us involves the permanency of all the *principles* which the Word of God sets forth as true. The time will never come when any principle which the Word of God enunciates will have a character different from that which is assumed for it, in its enunciation. That which is set forth as righteous will be found righteous; and that which is set forth as wrong will be found wrong; not only while the world shall stand, but so long as the throne of God endures. That which was a right moral principle for Adam, and Noah, and Abraham, and David, and Paul, and John, is a right moral principle for all men now, and will always remain so. Nothing can ever become intrinsically wrong for any man, which was intrinsically right for any one of these; and, on the other hand, nothing can become intrinsically right for any man, that was intrinsically wrong for any one of these.

Take, for example, the great fundamental principle of all human intercourse, as our Saviour announced it: "Whatsoever ye would that men should do to you, do ye even so to them." This, He says, was the principle of human intercourse laid down in the law, and insisted on by the prophets. It cannot change. It never was wrong to act upon it; it never was right to disregard it, in the dealings of men with men. It can never become a false principle of conduct. Through time and in eternity it will remain, and men will be righteous in their intercourse with each other just as they act upon it, and wicked just as they go contrary to it.

Take again the principle of repentance as governing the conduct of the wrong-doer. It never was right for a wrong-doer not to repent; it never will be right for him not to repent. On earth, in heaven, in hell, it is, and always will continue to be, wrong for him not to repent. He is under solemn obligations to repent. It is a principle inherent in his moral being, and required by the very nature of moral government. The Bible sets it forth in this light. Nothing will ever change its character. No modification of circumstances, no change of condition or state, will ever suspend its operation.

Take once more the principle of faith as the Bible sets it forth, making it the grand and indispensable condition of acceptable service and of intercourse with God. It was right for Adam to have faith in God, and wrong for him not to have it. It was absolutely essential to his serving God acceptably, and to his remaining in communion with Him. It has been the same with all men since his day; it is the same with all men now; it will remain the same with all men through time and in eternity. The principle can never change. It will always remain true, that, "without faith it is impossible to please God;" and, therefore, that "he that believeth not shall be damned; and he that believeth shall be saved."

Take once more the grand principle which the Bible enunciates in requiring all men to love God supremely. This requirement is based on the eternal fitness of things. God always has been, He is now, and He will forever remain, infinitely more worthy of love than any and all the creatures that are, or that ever will be made. However great in goodness and worthiness any creature is or can become, his goodness and worthiness are limited; and, when compared with God, they are infinitely below Him. It is impossible that this difference between God and creatures should ever be done away with. God will ever remain worthy of infinitely more love than creatures, and therefore the command to love Him supremely, which underlies all moral obligations, will never cease to be binding; never cease to be the fittest expression of the true relation of the creature to the Creator; never cease to be the governing principle in the conduct of all holy beings.

This fact of the permanence of moral principles, as they are taught by the Bible, has in it power to arouse, and to sustain in vigorous action, the best energies of the soul now; and to fill it with the sublimest anticipations for the future. It is our confidence in the permanence of right that supports us in right courses of life, and in labors for the promotion of righteous causes and ends, when everything else, without this, would give way, and our energies would become paralyzed. Because that which is inherently right will always be right, it is worth one's while to cling to it; and because that which is right must ultimately triumph in the government of a righteous God, that which is done for its promotion cannot be labor spent in vain.

There are times in the lives of most earnest-minded men, who desire their energies to be rightly directed, when they can find almost nothing else but this principle to cling to. They would be instantly overwhelmed with despair if they were to lose their hold upon it. Within, and without, wickedness seems to bear undisputed sway. All endeavors to subdue it, or to advance the cause of truth and righteousness, seem to be like water spilt upon the sand. They vanish away, and no fruit appears. The temptation comes upon them to give over the seemingly unequal and useless struggle, and to fall in with the current that sets in against goodness with a force as irresistible as that of the tide when it rolls backward to their source all the streams that are striving to gain the sea. They would yield to the temptation, and make shipwreck of all their hopes, and of all good enterprises, if they could not fall back on the eternal rightness of right, and on the consequent certainty of its ultimate triumph. Though all that is done for the right seems as feeble, and all that labor for it as helpless, as the strugglings of the streamlet to pursue its course to the sea against the might of the incoming tide, yet because they have learned that right remains as permanent in its character as the principle of gravity, and is ever pressing its way towards its goal, and as certain to reach it as are the waters of the rivers to reach the sea, they take heart, and nerve themselves anew for the struggle and the certain victory. No better illustration of this can be found than is furnished by the history of the cause of human rights against the cause of human slavery. Both in England and in this country, years of most earnest and self-sacrificing labors were expended, apparently in vain, before anything seemed to be accomplished. All the resources of powerful governments, of trade and commerce, of social respectability and social degradation, were combined, now in silent and dignified contempt, now in fierce madness that raged like a tempest, against the feeble endeavors of a few earnest and hopeful men, full of love for all that was good, but counted and treated as the offscouring of the earth. Personal violence, despoiling of goods, murder, every form of indignity, misrepresentation, and abuse became their portion; yet the huge iniquity against which they lifted their puny arms and feeble voices, gloated on its prey, and seemed to be entrenched in eternal security. They toiled on through years of darkness, with no star to light up their way but the star of truth; with no stimulant to their hope but a firm confidence in the permanence of right; and even sooner than they had dared to hope, they saw the foundations of the system begin to give way, and its walls to totter to their fall. Before they could fairly adjust themselves to the opening of the new era that they themselves had inaugurated, the whole superstructure gave way, like the defenses of Jericho before the hosts of Israel. Wilberforce, Clarkson, and a multitude of others — many gone to their reward, many others yet living — were seen not to have toiled in vain. Their confidence in right was not misplaced. Their hopes did not make them ashamed.

Take this as the precursor and promise of that which is to be in the contests of right with wrong, in all its forms on earth, and how grand and glorious the prospect! The millennium is sure!

Take the confidence in the permanence and the triumph of right which these men manifested, and its vindication by the silent but mighty intervention of a righteous God, as a type of that confidence which is justified regarding all good in the government of the Almighty, and what a prospect opens before us, beyond the boundaries of this world! The hour will come when it shall be seen that no good deed, no holy aspiration, no righteous purpose and endeavor, has been in vain. Each one has been a seed, which, though it seemed to die and come to nought, has been instinct with eternal life, and is yielding a rich harvest for an eternal reward.

It will be seen that the Word of the Lord has not returned to

Him void, but it has accomplished that which He has pleased, and prospered in the thing whereto He sent it. Nothing that it has revealed, as history past; nothing that it has foretold, as history to come; nothing that it has enunciated as principles of righteousness, — will cease to be true. All will endure, — revelations, as elements of real knowledge; principles, as of eternal worth and unchanging certainty.

In nothing, then, I remark in conclusion, can the Word of God be trusted in vain.

1. Its *promises* will never disappoint any hopes that are built upon them. They will all be fulfilled.

2. Its *threatenings* will never fail. A threatening is only a promise of evil. As every promise of good, so will every promise of evil have its exact fulfillment.

3. No *encouragement to goodness*, and no *discouragement* to *evil*, which the Bible holds out, will come to nought. To the end of time they will endure. Through eternity they will be real. Both alike rest on the assertions of the Almighty. All things else may fail. These cannot. "The Word of our God shall stand forever."

SERMON II.

THE ONCE DELIVERED FAITH.

JUDE 3. — *Ye should earnestly contend for the faith which was once delivered unto the saints.*

SAINTS is a common designation for believers in Christ. The two terms are interchangeable in the New Testament. To be a believer in Christ was to be a holy person; one separated from his sins and consecrated to God and his service. The invariable effect of true belief in Christ is to bring about this separation of the believer from his sins, and this consecration of his whole being to God. Hence the designation *saints* was strictly appropriate, and it remains appropriate, as a title for all true believers.

What Jude says in the verse before us, is, that it was needful, there was a necessity, that he should write to all such believers, and exhort them to contend earnestly for their faith. But if it was necessary for him to give this exhortation, it is, of course, necessary for them to give heed to it and obey it. And not only so; not only is it *necessary* for them to obey it; they are under solemn *obligation* to obey it. It is not a matter which they may do, or neglect to do at their pleasure. For an inspired exhortation is a divine command always. It takes the form of an exhortation because it is a fellow man who utters it. But because it comes directly from God, and is an expression of his will, it is, in its substance, a divine precept. It is invested therefore with all the force and authority of a divine command. It is binding on the conscience, and must be obeyed.

Let us then give our attention to this inspired exhortation, which is also a divine command, and consider what it involves: "Contend earnestly for the faith which was once delivered unto the saints."

In the first place there is something for believers to contend for. There is a Faith. That is, there is something to be received, and trusted to, and rested in, and acted on, as undeniable truth, and therefore a reality that can be contended for. For the word *Faith* has this meaning here, as it has also in other passages of the New Testament. It means that which has been *revealed* to faith, and which faith accepts and believes in. This includes, of course, all the truths of the gospel. All the doctrines, and revelations which God has been pleased to give us in his Word, and which men must accept, and have faith in, simply on God's authority, because God has spoken them,— these are the objects of faith. These then constitute *The Faith*. It is a system of revealed truth, by the hearty acceptance and belief of which men can be delivered from sin, and prepared for the Kingdom of God. A few other passages will make this plainer.

The word is used in this sense in the sixth chapter of the Acts of the Apostles, where Luke says, " The word of God increased, and a great company of the priests were obedient to the faith." That is, they were obedient to the gospel; to its truths, and its commands. Paul uses the word in this sense in the Epistle to the Galatians, when he says of the churches in Judæa, " But they had heard only, that he who persecuted us in times past now preacheth the faith which once he destroyed." That is, he preached the truths and doctrines of the religion of Jesus Christ. He uses it in the same sense again in the First Epistle to Timothy, when he says that " some professing science, falsely so called, have erred concerning the faith." That is, they had utterly mistaken and failed to apprehend and understand the truths of the gospel. They have not comprehended the gospel system. They are altogether in the dark regarding the gospel considered as an object of knowledge. A system of doctrines and facts revealed to be accepted on divine testimony, and on this testimony alone to be understood and believed. Again he says in this same epistle, " Now the Spirit speaketh expressly, that in the latter times some shall depart from the faith, giving heed to seducing spirits, and doctrines of devils." They would leave the gospel; abandon its doctrines; deny its revelations; disregard its precepts; and, in place of them, receive for truth the sayings of seducing spirits; and for doctrines the utterances of devils.

These passages show the meaning of the word before us. There are many others of a similar character, but there is no need of bringing them before you now. These all join with our text in asserting the fact, that there is a distinct and well known body of religious truth revealed in the New Testament. There is a well defined system of religious doctrines and facts. There are plainly uttered and inspired truths. These truths, these doctrines, these facts, are given by inspiration, delivered to the saints. God has spoken them. Because God has spoken them they are objects primarily for faith to deal with. God has delivered them, once for all, that they might be believed and acted on as certainties. In other words, they are not human speculations to amuse men and to be admired by them, which may be something, which may be nothing; which may be mere speculation and not realities; and, therefore, if a man contend for them he may be contending for a thing that has no existence. They are not the results of human reasoning, to be criticised, and confirmed as true, or condemned as false, according as they may strike the fancy of those who study them. They are not a system of moral and religious philosophy, elaborated by human thought, and human genius, to draw admirers and partisans; or to awaken rivalries and stimulate to the elaboration of opposing systems. They are none of these; but simply and purely, *a revelation*. Truths, not primarily to be reasoned about, but to be believed in; not to be speculated upon, but to be trusted and obeyed; not abstract and barren dogmas for the intellect to think about, but vital principles, and divine utterances, for the heart to love, and to be purified with; for the whole soul to cherish and to be saved by. They are solemn and substantial realities divinely declared, and to be accepted on the authority alone of this declaration.

God has not left the world to depend on itself alone for a knowledge of those things which men must know in order that they may obtain salvation; but which they are powerless to obtain by their own wisdom. He has come forth in plain speech, the speech of men themselves, and made these things known. He has revealed his own being, *i. e.*, and shown to men the relation which they sustain to Him. He has lifted the veil that hides the future from the unaided eye of man, and bidden him look beyond, and see a world of retribution; and of eternal consequences, following the present life. He has spoken to conscience by his law, and given certainty and definiteness to all those surmisings of guilt, and those vague but fearful apprehensions of rewards to ill deserving, which conscience, without the Word of God, always awakens in the soul. He has declared his unwillingness that men should be compelled to receive these rewards of sin : and He has demonstrated his desire that they should be saved. He has pointed out with clearness and fullness and precision the provision which he has made that they may not perish, but have eternal life. He has plainly declared to them the terms and conditions on which they may have remission of sins, and be restored to the divine favor, and made heirs of heaven. All this He has told them. He has made it fully known in the gospel. The doctrines, the facts, the threatenings, the commands, the promises, the prophecies and revelations, that reveal these things constitute a body or system of divine truth. They make known all that it is needful — in order to salvation — that we should know of God and his will; and of the way to eternal life. And this, as it stands before us in the Scriptures, but especially in the New Testament, is a system for faith. It is by faith alone that it can be appropriated ; by faith alone can it be known as truth. On this alone, as it is apprehended by faith, depend all our hopes and assurances both of the fact of a future state, and of the possibility and reality of happiness and bliss in that state. Hence this system is our Faith. It is the ultimate standard of faith in all questions as to what is truth, either in religion or in morals. It is the only ground of certainty, — the certainty of faith, — in respect to God, or his will, or his relations to men. Hence, again, it is the Faith. It is this system of truth, these truths of the gospel, for which, the sacred writer says, the saints should earnestly contend.

2. In the second place our text, in that it speaks of a *once delivered faith*, involves, that this system of truth and doctrines is *complete* in itself and sufficient for all time. It will always remain the only system for faith to receive and rest in and act upon. It will not be supplemented by additional revelations ; nor will it be set aside by new ones. It is a harmonious whole, with nothing wanting, and nothing superfluous. It is therefore THE FAITH, — the one system of faith, which, in

being *once* given, was given once for all. There was to be no repetition of its giving, and no recalling of it after it was given.

This is the meaning of that phrase which we so often overlook in quoting this passage, but which is full of significance, " Once delivered." The " Once delivered faith " are the writer's exact words. The writer of the Epistle to the Hebrews uses the same word to indicate the fullness and sufficiency of the sacrifice of Christ for the sins of the world ; and that the one offering was made at the same time, once for all men and once for all ages : " Nor yet that He should offer Himself *often*, as the High Priest entereth into the holy place *every year* with blood of others ; for then must He *often* have suffered since the foundation of the world ; but now *once* in the end of the world hath He appeared to put away sin by the sacrifice of Himself. And as it is appointed unto men *once* to die, but after this the judgment ; so Christ was *once* offered to bear the sins of many." This *once* was enough. There would therefore be no supplemental appearing of Christ to put away sin. So men die *once ;* it is appointed unto them to die once for all, — and once only. There is no return to life again ; and therefore no supplemental death. The one death is complete in itself, and it is forever.

Thus it is with the gospel. It has been delivered unto the saints once for all. As the expiation of Christ abides the one only, but all-sufficient expiation, never to be added to or taken from, so the truths of the gospel — its doctrines, its facts, its precepts, its terms of salvation, its promises, its threatenings — abide forever, the one only, but all-sufficient system of faith ; never to be added to, never to be taken from.

These two truths lie at the foundation of all controversies for the Faith. They must be assumed or established before any progress can be made. Until they are established all contention will be worse than useless. We shall only travel on a circle, or float at the mercy of whatever currents of influence may prevail around us. First of all we must have it settled in our mind that there is something to contend for, something real, something certain, something definite, something resting on an impregnable basis of truth. We must be sure that what we propose to contend for is not a fable, or fiction, or idle fancy.

Then in the second place we must have it settled that this reality, this certainty, is a whole. It is not a part merely to be supplemented, perhaps, by the very thing against which we contend. If the gospel is not a complete whole in itself, a system that cannot be added to nor taken from, then you can never know where you stand. If that which stands for a truth to-day may become no part of the system, and hence a falsehood to-morrow, then you may never be sure that when you contend for any part of the system you are not contending for a falsehood. And if any part which is to-day taken for a whole truth may to-morrow become only a half truth, by reason of some additional revelation, then you can never be certain that the very principle or alleged fact against which you are contending, is not that additional revelation that was to take away the wholeness from the truth for which you contend; and so by making it a half truth transforms it into a virtual untruth.

No; if we contend for the Faith, — a system of truth to be believed and acted upon, — let us be sure that we have such a system; and let us be sure that we know what it is, and why it should be believed and acted on. This is precisely what the Apostle Peter enjoins upon every believer's conscience when he says, "Sanctify the Lord God in your hearts; and be ready always to give an answer to every man that asketh you a reason of the hope that is in you." And that believers might do this, he, as well as the other sacred writers, has made provision that they may have these things always in remembrance; and give them proof that they have not followed cunningly devised fables; but that they have a sure word on which to rest, and for which to contend.

The two forms of unbelief to-day are, —

1. That which saps the foundations of all faith by casting discredit on the inspiration and authority of the Scriptures.

2. That which does the same by pretending to supplement the Scriptures.

SERMON III.
CONTENDING FOR THE ONCE DELIVERED FAITH.

JUDE 3.— *Ye should earnestly contend for the faith which was once delivered unto the saints.*

TO contend does not mean to quarrel. It does not mean to wrangle and dispute; nor to become angry and show temper; nor to be pugnacious and denunciatory. It does not mean any of these things. But a man may quarrel when he contends. His contention may consist wholly of wrangling and disputing. He may contend pugnaciously, and with the bitterest denunciations. And, on the contrary, he may, in some causes, contend most earnestly, and yet, the more earnestly he contends, the less of quarreling and wrangling will he do; the less of anger and enmity will he have; and the less of pugnacity and denunciation. It is by no means necessary, because a man contends, that he should be anybody's *enemy*, or indeed that he should have an enemy in the world. His antagonists may be his best friends; and even while he contends with them he may hold them in the highest esteem and love.

The word here used by the sacred writer was employed, not primarily to set forth quarreling, wrangling, and pugnacity, but the intense *efforts* which were made by those who took part in the races and public games. Those who contended in the races and games were compelled, if they accomplished anything, to put forth all their strength in intense and sustained effort to win the prizes. Those who entered the lists with them were their competitors and antagonists; but not by any means necessarily their enemies. So far from this they might be their best friends, their own brothers even.

But the word is also employed to describe the struggles of contending armies, and of real enemies, engaged in deadly conflict with each other. It is often employed in this manner.

But a moment's attention will show you that the idea of hostility and ill-feeling is not conveyed by the word itself, but by the connection in which it stands. It is the connection that suggests the enmity and fighting, if there is any. But the contention is all in the intensity and strenuousness of the efforts that are made, whatever may be their spirit or purpose. Hence you often say of a man that he contends earnestly, in some cause, or in the prosecution of some purpose, where you have no thought whatever of his being angry, or of his having enemies arrayed against him. The circumstances in which he contends, the spirit that animates him, and the purpose he has in view, determine whether his contention is a quarrel, or simply an earnest and determined endeavor to accomplish a desired result.

The contention to which the sacred writer here exhorts believers may be found in any class of circumstances; and therefore it may become, not only the strenuous putting forth of efforts, without the idea of conflict, but a contest with enemies, — a hand to hand fight, as it were, for victory. One who conscientiously, and with loyalty to Christ, contends for "the faith," may find it necessary to contend in both of these ways. The circumstances in which he is placed may compel him to fight valiantly for the truth, in direct opposition to those who are opposing it. He may be compelled thus to take the attitude of one battling face to face with foes, — foes to the truth, and foes to himself because he is a friend of the truth. He may have to meet them on their own ground, and with their own weapons; or, if not with their own weapons, yet with such weapons as will effectually parry their thrusts at the truth, and destroy their power to hinder it. The friends of the "Once delivered faith" have often been compelled, by fidelity to the truth, thus to meet its foes and contend for it in most serious and earnest conflict. But whatever may be the circumstances of the contention to which believers are here commanded, the fundamental elements of the contention are always the same; and the spirit in which it is to be carried on is always the same, namely, loyalty to the truth itself; and a warm and loving desire that men may be saved from all the consequences of disobedience by receiving the truth into their hearts, and acting on it in their conduct. If we look into the matter carefully we shall find, that earnestly contending for the faith involves three things, prominently; and these three things are separately enjoined throughout the Scriptures.

1. In the first place they who contend earnestly for the faith, *must earnestly, plainly, and fully declare the truths that constitute this faith,* — that is, the fundamental facts and principles and precepts of the gospel. Oftentimes the full, faithful, and earnest declaration of these constitute the whole burden of obedience to this divine command. Their very statement in this manner sometimes gives them such a triumph over ignorances and prejudices, that the gospel becomes at once enthroned in their place, and its enemies are transformed into friends. This is always the case where ignorance alone is the foe against which the truth has to contend. Then the simple announcement of the gospel is like the rising of the sun upon the face of the world. Darkness is dissipated by his coming; and all nature is flooded with his light. So, where the heart of a man is right, and he needs only to know the truth to fall in with it and obey it, it is enough that the truth is held up before his mind. He grasps it; is enlightened by it; and submits his whole soul and life to its influence.

But few are they who are thus ready for the gospel. Few are they who have not, at least, self-interest and prejudice acting as allies of their ignorance, and bracing them up in opposition to some portions of the divine word. This is true of vast numbers of the real disciples of Christ. There are influences working about them and upon them which hinder the claims of the gospel, its principles and its precepts, from gaining control of their minds. And then, outside the pale of discipleship, there are none who have not, in addition to prejudice and interest, positive disrelish and enmity to the truths of the gospel, as allies of their ignorance. They are "alienated from the life of God through the ignorance that is in them." Something more is necessary besides a simple declaration of the truth to bring either of these classes to receive and obey it. The darkness is shut up within them, and the simple announcement of the truths of the gospel will no more dissipate it than the rising of the sun on the outside of your house will fill with light a curtained and blinded room in that house. You must draw aside the curtains, and swing wide open the shutters, if you would have your room bathed in the light that is flooding all the world without. So some power must be brought to bear on prejudice, and pride, and interest in the mind of many a disciple of Christ; some power that shall subdue them within him, before he will open his soul to the truth on many a subject, although this truth is made to abound in plainest and fullest announcements to his intellect. And so the washing of regeneration must come in and carry away the enmity and carnality of every *unrenewed* man's soul before he will open his heart to that word of prophecy which is as a light shining in a dark place. Something more, I repeat it, than a simple announcement of the truth is needed in order to give it the victory over ignorance and error in such minds.

Nevertheless, it remains true that no small part of the work of those who are called to contend earnestly for the faith, consists in *declaring* the faith to just these two classes of minds. It must be iterated, and reiterated, until their intellects, at least, shall be instructed. This must always be the *first* step in advancing the faith among men. The truth must be faithfully and fully declared to them. Their intellects must be flooded with the knowledge of it as the preliminary step towards the reception of it by their hearts; even as the world without must be flooded by the light of the sun, before you can hope to welcome his brightness within, into your opened room. In order to this there must, of course, be constant and faithful assertions of the truth, in plain and unequivocal announcements, and in full and accurate statements. This must precede and accompany all other methods of contending for the faith.

Hence it was that preaching and teaching were made so prominent by our Saviour when He sent his disciples forth to their great work. "Go teach all nations," He said. "Go ye into all the world and preach the gospel to every creature." That is, Go and declare it; announce it; proclaim it. This command took the precedence of all others in the great commission. Hence it was that the Apostle Paul, in writing his final letter to Timothy, charged him in that most solemn manner, "Before God, and the Lord Jesus Christ, who shall judge the living and the dead, preach the Word:" announce it, proclaim it, declare it; "in season, out of season." And hence, too, this same Apostle, writing to the Corinthians declares that it pleased God by that which some men think to be foolishness, namely, preaching the gospel, to save them that believe. That contention for the faith which wins men to it, and saves them by it, must, therefore, consist largely in giving utterance to it in plain, full, and unambiguous speech. In season, and out of season, they must plainly declare it, who would earnestly contend for it.

2. Contending earnestly for the once delivered faith involves, again, an earnest and faithful *defense of it against opposing errors.* The gospel is aggressive. It must make inroads upon the ignorances and prejudices and superstitions of the world, and triumph over them. Aggression is both its spirit and its destiny. When John the Baptist said of Christ, "He must increase, but I must decrease," he spake primarily of Christ and himself as religious teachers; and what he said was not only a condensation of centuries of prophecy regarding the gospel, but a recognition of its inherent aggressiveness.

But ignorance and error and self-interest will not yield their ground without a struggle in any man's mind. They will always array their forces for battle, and resist the truth. Every community, even the most enlightened, and which knows the most of the gospel, cherishes in this manner a vast amount of error and false doctrine as real truth. Nay, it can hardly be doubted that every man in such a community, even of those who love the truth, and intend to conform their thinking and feeling and acting wholly to its claims, is in this manner under the influence of many a false sentiment and principle which he will discover some day or other, and be amazed to discover to be utterly opposed to the gospel of Christ. These false doctrines and sentiments and principles generally embody themselves into forms of direct antagonism to the teachings of the gospel; and nowadays entrench themselves in nominally Christian systems and societies. Thus embodied, they enter into open warfare against the truth. They assail it as false, and demand their own enthronement in men's minds and hearts in its stead. The enemies of the faith thus meet the simple announcements of those who are contending for the faith, and by denouncing them as false, devolve on those who have made the first announcement, the necessity of standing by what they have declared, and vindicating its truth and the consequent falseness of that which has denied it. Herein is the justification of every friend of the gospel for contending for its doctrines or principles or precepts in the way of controversy, and holding up opposing errors and false teachings before the eyes of men, as errors and false teachings. Every false doctrine or precept or principle that holds sway in the public mind, or in the mind of any individual, is to be met, first of all, by a plain announcement of the opposite truth. If the false doctrine or principle or precept gives way before this simple and non-controversial setting forth of the truth, it is well. But if it holds its place still, and still demands the allegiance of men's hearts, and the obedience of their lives, then no champion of the truth is faithful to his trust, nor to the souls of men, if he does not attack the error, expose its falseness, and do his utmost to destroy its hold upon the public, or the individual mind.

All this is to be done, of course, in the spirit of the gospel itself. The contest must not be a *personal* one. It must not be conducted for personal triumph or personal gains. It must be for the truth. It must be with a sincere desire to save men from the baleful effects of error, and bring them into the blessedness of the truth, by bringing them into obedience to Christ.

While, therefore, this kind of contention for the faith may often call for strong language; and awaken deep feeling; and prompt the utterance of bitter denunciation and keen invective, it can never be one of personal hatred and ill-will. It is impossible for it to be otherwise than earnest, positive, even intense, if carried on by one who loves the faith and appreciates the vastness of the issues involved in its acceptance or rejection. As he loves the truth he cannot but be deeply in earnest. And since love of the truth is hatred of error and falsehood, the expression of his earnestness will certainly take the form of positiveness, of severe condemnation, and utter rejection. As he loves the souls of men, and desires their salvation by the truth, he cannot but hold in abhorrence anything that imperils their salvation by exalting itself against that truth. Great plainness of speech, therefore, will inevitably characterize his defense of the truth against error. He will be pretty sure to call things by their right names, even though it may have the seeming of severity, and be very unpalatable to all such as are blinded by the error, and are taking it for truth. And if at any time he has to deal with those who show clearly that their defense of error, and resistance to the truth, is willful, and from bad motives, and with wrong and selfish ends in view, his words will doubtless become stinging and full of indignation. It will be hardly possible for him, however, to be justified in going, with his imperfect knowledge and his but partially sanctified heart, as far as the omniscient and holy Redeemer went in this direction. It will be rare indeed that any one who contends for the faith against its enemies can have any right to say to them, as the Saviour said to the Pharisees and Scribes: "*Hypocrites!* For ye shut up the kingdom of heaven against men; for ye neither go in yourselves, neither suffer ye them that are entering to go in. Woe unto you: for ye compass sea and land to make one proselyte, and when he is made, ye make him twofold more the child of hell than yourselves." "Ye fools and blind! ye make clean the outside of the cup and of the platter, but within they are full of extortion and excess. Ye serpents, ye generation of vipers! How can ye escape the damnation of hell!" It will rarely be becoming in any uninspired defender of the faith to go as far as an inspired apostle could sometimes safely go in personal rebuke and denunciation. Paul could say with holy indignation against one who was withstanding the Gospel, and endeavoring to turn men away from it, — "Oh full of all subtilty and all mischief, thou child of the devil, thou enemy of all righteousness, wilt thou not cease to pervert the right ways of the Lord?" But we are specially told that Paul was then "filled with the Holy Ghost," as an infallible spirit of inspiration; and it was not so much Paul that uttered these terrible words, as it was the Holy Ghost who was in him, and showing him the sorcerer's true character, and guiding him to deal righteously with that character.

These examples are given to show us that indignation against the willful enemies of truth and righteousness, and corrupt upholders of error and wickedness, may be a holy indignation; and that it is not wrong but right to denounce them. At the same time these examples are given us in the omniscient and holy Redeemer, and in his inspired Apostle when acting under a special and full possession by the Holy Spirit, that we might not presume, in our ignorance and sinfulness and uninspiration, to go at all beyond the bounds of the clearest knowledge and the purest charity. Within these limits, censure and rebuke of error, and condemnation of those who uphold it against the truth, are legitimate. Nay, they are required of the faithful disciple of Christ. He may not withhold them. Loyalty to his Master, and faithfulness to the souls of men, demand them at his hands.

3. One thing further is involved in earnestly contending for the Once Delivered Faith: *It must be lived up to.* A gospel proclaimed, and a gospel defended against false doctrines, can never be sustained before the world, nor made the aggressive power that it was intended to be, unless it be a gospel carried out in the conduct of those who contend for it. And I do not mean only what is commonly meant by this trite and almost commonplace remark, "it must be lived up to," or "carried out in the conduct." Ordinarily it means no more, when it has any definite meaning whatever, — for often it is used without any such meaning, — than that those who profess the religion of Christ should live good moral lives and keep up the forms of their religion. They must not shock the public mind by any glaringly inconsistent conduct against the commonly received maxims and customs of social morality, nor against those that pertain to a religious life. They must be honest in their dealings in business; truth telling, and, in a measure, courteous in their intercourse with society; fair-minded and kind-hearted in their domestic relations; good church-goers, and passable covenant-keepers. Beyond these conventionalities and decencies of a Christian civilization, the words which I have used seldom are supposed to extend. But as I use them now they mean vastly more than this. They mean the rigid adherence to the teachings of the gospel, and the fearless and consistent carrying out of these teachings in the life. They mean a constant abiding in its revelations as truths; in its commands as duties, and in its principles as the only sure guides in the formation of character and the ordering of the conduct. Nothing short of this is a living up to the gospel. As a matter of fact, as things are now ordered, in almost any nominally Christian community, one may live

what passes for a good moral life, and meet the popular demands of a Christian profession, and yet by his whole spirit, and much of his life, go flatly against many of the plainest commands of the New Testament; flatly against some of its fundamental principles, and flatly against its whole spirit. Indeed it has come about, in many such communities, that " standing by the gospel," living up to it, in many of its commands and principles, will surely bring upon him the charge of " narrowness ; " of " bigotry ; " of " one-sidedness ; " of being a " hobby rider ; " of " carrying things to extremes ; " of " running things into the ground ; " and a multitude of other similarly genteel phrases.

Your own thoughts will supply you with specific examples of these general statements; and I need not dwell very long on them. I need not call your attention very much to the absurdity and uselessness, for example, of contending earnestly in words for the Lord's Day as a Christian Sabbath, and then consulting one's own convenience and pleasure alone in the use he makes of this day. I need not dwell long on the fruitlessness of contending earnestly for the gospel that claims that " it is more blessed to give than to receive," and that makes it the glory of the disciple to be as his Lord, " who, though He was rich, for our sakes became poor, that we, through his poverty, might be made rich," if one shuts up the bowels of his compassion, is selfish, grasping, illiberal. I need not linger to tell you how absurd it makes one, and how it degrades the gospel and gives it over into the hands of its enemies, to contend earnestly in words for its teachings, — for example, regarding love to one's enemies, and forgiveness of those who have injured him ; and yet to seek for revenge and retaliation ; to hold grudges ; to cherish roots of bitterness ; and hardness and unfriendliness of heart towards an offender. Nor to act the hypocrite by pretending to believe one to be better than you know him to be, — need not trust a thief as though you believed him honest ; nor a liar as though you believed him truthful ; yet may be kind, courteous, etc. I need not take your time now to say much of the destructive influence of that earnest contending for the faith which, for example, commends its doctrines and revelations in general terms, and yet ignores them, or denies them, in particulars ; that, for further example, seeks the salvation of men, and yet finds nothing from which salvation is to deliver them; that calls on men to repent, and yet, by practical treatment, denies that their sins are such as to need repentance, denies that except they repent they must surely perish; that proclaims "ye must be born again," and yet, by levity and carelessness and utter lack of discrimination, in dealing with their souls, with their hopes, and their claims of discipleship with Christ, teaches them that "being born again is only an empty phrase, having nothing whatever to do with one's prospects for heaven and eternal life. I need not linger to say how absurd a man makes himself by professing to love a gospel which has saved his own soul from death, and without which those who are destitute of it can never be saved,—a gospel which the Lord Himself has commanded all his disciples to give to all the world,— and yet takes no interest in missions, and does nothing for their support. I need not stay long to rehearse the folly of contending earnestly for a gospel that demands implicit obedience to all Christ's words on the part of those who love Him and hope in his mercy, and yet in conduct, refusing to submit to those words; whether it be in adhering to great moral principles, or in obeying positive precepts.

May the Lord grant us all grace to contend earnestly for the once delivered faith by faithfully declaring it in all ways within our reach; by faithfully defending it against all the encroachments of error and falsehood; and then, to make all this effective, and to give the gospel power, to contend for it by standing faithfully up to it, and living it out before God and men.

SERMON IV.

THE OBEDIENT ABLE TO KNOW THE WILL OF GOD.

JOHN vii. 17. — *If any man will do his will, he shall know of the doctrine, whether it be of God, or whether I speak of myself.*

"THE doctrine" is that which is spoken of in the preceding verse. In the midst of one of the great Jewish festivals Jesus went into the temple and began to teach. Some of those who heard Him were greatly astonished at the knowledge of which He showed Himself possessed, and asked whence he could have acquired it; since He had never studied in the schools, nor been taught by any of their learned men. In response to this inquiry, Jesus answered, that what He taught was not the result of study, nor the fruit of human learning, but a divine revelation. For this is the meaning of his reply, "My doctrine is not mine, but his that sent me." It was of this doctrine that He then added, "If any man will do his will, he shall know of the doctrine, whether it be of God, or whether I speak of myself."

The word *will* has here an independent force. Our Lord did not use it as an auxiliary of the word *do*. Unless we remember this when we read the passage, we shall take *will do* to be simply the future of *do*, and quite miss our Saviour's meaning. *Will* is an independent word. It is, moreover, the principal word in the sentence, and expresses the main thought. What the verse asserts is, that if any one wills, desires, is disposed to do the will of God, he shall know regarding the teachings of Jesus, whether they are of God, or merely human assertions, reasonings, and speculations. There is no reference to outward and special acts of doing the will of God; but to the disposition of the mind in respect of doing that will. The general principle involved is, that if the mind is rightly disposed towards God, and wants to do his will, it will distinguish between that which is divine and that which is only human in religious teaching. The doctrine of the text, then, broadly stated, is, that one who is rightly disposed towards the will of God and wants to do it, will easily understand what the will of God is when He reveals it.

Let me invite your attention to a few reflections on these words of our Saviour thus explained.

1. In the first place, I remark that our Lord gives us here a test, not so much of his teachings as of our own characters.

As his words are sometimes, but wrongly, taken, they are made a test with which men may experiment on what Jesus taught; and so, by experimenting, come to a decision in their own minds regarding its character, whether it is divine, or only human; and regarding its claims, whether it is to be held worthy of acceptance and obedience, or to be rejected. But this was not his method of dealing with men. From first to last He bore Himself as one who spake by authority, and who was to be heard as an authority. His words were final. He did not submit the question, whether or not they were divine or true, to any human tribunal. The only question regarding his ministry that He ever submitted to the judgment of men, was a very different one from this, and had reference solely to his own character, and to the fact that He was a divine messenger. He often pointed to his works as proofs of these; and that He was, therefore, worthy of confidence as a teacher and revealer of religious truth. But this truth itself He did not submit to men for them to test; and, by testing, to decide whether or not it was divine or human, true or false.

In the nature of the case a divine revelation must rest primarily on the authority of him who makes it. His own character and claims to confidence must be sustained by evidence submitted to the judgment of those to whom he is sent; and this evidence must be such as will carry conviction to candid minds that he is a messenger from God. This evidence, whatever it is, they ought to consider and decide upon: it is their prerogative, as well as their duty, to do it. They are qualified to do it, if they have intelligence enough to make them accountable, and are candid. But when they come to the revelation itself, the case is very different. This pertains, of course, to matters of which they are ignorant; concerning which they need information, but which, for the most part, they could not, or would not, discover by the use of their own faculties. They have no fitness, therefore, to sit in judgment on it. On the contrary, they are fit only to be learners; and a divine revelation always regards them in just this light. It is God speaking to them that they may hear, and by hearing know truths of which they are ignorant, but which He wishes to communicate to them; not that they may put themselves in the attitude of experimenters, and judges, to discover and decide whether or not his words are truth.

Our Lord told his disciples plainly that some men would receive his doctrines, and that others would not receive them; and that in both cases their action would depend, not on experiment and the sifting of evidence marshaled for and against the divinity of his words, but on the state of their hearts towards God. If their hearts were rightly affected towards God they would receive his doctrines, otherwise they would reject them. Hence He said to the caviling Jews, "He that is of God heareth God's words. Ye therefore hear them not, because ye are not of God." "I know you, that ye have not the love of God in you. I am come in my Father's name and ye receive me not. If another shall come in his own name him ye will receive. How can ye believe, who receive honor one of another, and seek not the honor that cometh from God only?"

2. I remark, again, that the truth here declared by our Saviour is often brought out in other parts of the Scriptures. They everywhere teach that a correct apprehension of divine truth depends on the state of the heart, and not on the mere exercise of the intellect. They unequivocally declare that if there is unfriendliness towards God, and an aversion to doing his will, men will not comprehend what He reveals regarding Himself and his will, nor will they receive it. Thus the Apostle John says, in his First Epistle, "He that knoweth God heareth us; he that is not of God heareth not us. Hereby know we the spirit of truth and the spirit of error." The Apostle Paul, in his First Epistle to the Corinthians, says to believers, "Now we have received, not the spirit of the world, but the spirit which is of God, that we might know the things that are freely given to us of God. Which things also we speak, not in the words which man's wisdom teacheth, but which the Holy

Ghost teacheth, comparing spiritual things with spiritual. But the natural man receiveth not the things of the Spirit of God, for they are foolishness unto him: neither can he know them, because they are spiritually discerned. But he that is spiritual discerneth all things." The same idea precisely underlies the Apostle's exhortation to believers in the twelfth chapter of his Epistle to the Romans, " Be ye transformed by the renewal of your mind, that ye may learn by experience what is the will of God, what is good, well-pleasing, and perfect." To the same effect the Psalmist also says, " The secret of the Lord is with them that fear Him, and He will show them his covenant." And again, " Unto the upright there ariseth light in the darkness."

It is, therefore, the doctrine, not of our text alone, but of the whole Bible, that divine truth is a test of character. When men come in contact with it it reveals the state of their hearts towards God, and towards the doing of his will. It is as the writer of the Epistle to the Hebrews has said, " The Word of God is quick and powerful, and sharper than any two-edged sword, piercing even to the dividing asunder of soul and spirit, and of the joints and marrow, and is a discoverer of the thoughts and intents of the heart."

3. I remark, in the third place, that what our Saviour here declares regarding divine revelations is in perfect harmony with what we observe in the communication and comprehension of human thoughts. Any man who has thoughts to communicate is most readily and most freely understood by those who are friendly towards him, and earnestly desirous of receiving his instructions, and being governed by them. On the other hand, he is almost sure to be misapprehended, and to be, at the best, but partially understood by those who are ill-disposed towards him personally, and especially disinclined to yield to the requirements that he has a right to make of them. If you were away from home, and wished to have certain things attended to about your house and grounds, concerning which you had very peculiar, but very fond, notions, to which of your family would you communicate your wishes — to those of them who had never manifested any interest in your peculiar plans, nor any wish to comply with your will regarding them, but, on the contrary, had set themselves, as a rule, against

your wishes and authority; or to that one among them all who had always taken a deep and tender interest in your ideas and plans, because of his interest in and regard for you, and had always shown himself disposed to carry out your wishes, and to be obedient to your will in all things? You would say, "It will do no good to write to the others. They have no sympathy with my notions, and no disposition to do what I want them to. If I write to them, and require them to attend to these matters, they will get only a confused idea of what I want. Their indifference regarding my wishes, and hostility to my authority, will be sure to prevent their entering into the spirit of my plans, and understanding my purpose. I must write to that one who alone can understand me, because he alone has sufficient regard for me, and enough of the spirit of obedience to enter fully into my ideas, and know precisely what I want done, and how I want it done. He will be sure to understand my wishes in this matter, because of his honest and loving desire to carry out my wishes in all things.

Every thoughtful teacher understands this principle. He learns among his first experiences that the pupils who are well disposed towards him, and desirous of receiving instruction from him, are the ones who most readily catch his exact thought, whatever may be the subject on which he is speaking; while those pupils that are hostile to him, and have their wills constantly set against his authority, will receive almost no benefit from his instructions.

Which of your clerks, or those in your employ, do you depend on to interpret or to carry out your most cherished and most peculiar ideas? Is it not that one whose earnest and unselfish disposition to please you in all things has made him capable of anticipating many of your wishes; and has so thoroughly identified him with your peculiar methods of business and habits of thought, that a single word, a look, a mere hint will reveal more of your mind to him, than the fullest and most accurate statements could reveal to others. His thorough readiness to do your will, and his manly devotion to your interests, make him instantly master of your thought, when you speak to him of matters in which he has a responsibility to you.

I say that this is *in harmony* with what our Saviour teaches us regarding our comprehending divine revelations. The main principle in both cases is the same. The willing and obedient and sympathizing are able to understand; the unwilling, the disobedient, the unsympathizing, will either misapprehend altogether, or get but indistinct, partial, and confused ideas from those who are in authority over them, and speak to them from a superior intelligence for their instruction and government.

But the cases are not wholly parallel. There is vastly more in the inability of a sinner to understand the revelations of truth which God makes, than there is in the inability of an unfriendly and unsympathizing subject in human relationships to understand those with whom he is connected in these relationships. There is a fixedness of will against the law of God, in the mind of every impenitent sinner, and a deep-seated moral aversion to holiness, that blind the intellect and prevent the understanding, far beyond anything that happens in the relations of any one human being to another. Sin enlists the whole being against God. It arrays all the forces of the soul against his authority, by enthroning self in the heart in deadly hostility to his will and government. The whole being is thus brought into subjection to the single principle of opposition to the will of God. A fearful moral inability to know God and understand what He reveals is the inevitable result. In this respect the effect of sin on the powers of the soul is analogous to that which the violations of the laws of one's physical being bring on the powers of his body. The habitual drunkard and debauchee soon destroys these powers, and he becomes unable to do with them that for the doing of which they were given to him. In like manner sin against God destroys the powers of the soul, and makes it unable to do with them that for the doing of which God endowed it with them. It ceases, that is, to be able to apprehend divine truth and to know God. This is the reason why our Saviour declares so emphatically that a renewal of these faculties is necessary to a right apprehension of spiritual things. As the bodily powers of the drunkard and debauchee would have to be renewed before they could again rightly perform their functions, so must the moral and spiritual forces of the soul be renewed before they can perform their functions. Hence our Lord declares, " Except a man be born again he cannot see the kingdom of God." Unless this renewal of the soul takes place, that kingdom will remain forever hidden from his sight. The things of that kingdom are the very doctrines, revelations, of which our Lord is speaking in the text; and it was of these that the Apostle was writing in the words which we have already quoted: "The natural man receiveth not the things of the Spirit of God, for they are foolishness unto him; neither can he know them, because they are spiritually discerned."

Nothing, therefore, but that willing mind and obedient spirit which are wrought in the soul by the Holy Ghost, brings a sinner into a moral condition fitted to understand divine truth. Nothing else brings him into friendship with God, and into harmony with his will. This does bring him into this condition, and as soon as he is in it, enmity and rebellion are gone, and the permanent condition of the soul is one of submission and obedience and love. It desires to do God's will. It is steadily disposed to do it. It has therefore the very fitness of which the Saviour speaks, to understand divine things, and the ability to know of his doctrines.

In view of this declaration of our Saviour we see, —

1. That the failure to apprehend a divine revelation in the teachings of Christ is the proof, not of a superior intellect, but of a sinful heart. It has always been the fashion for those who denied the inspiration and authority of the teachings of Jesus, to assume an intellectual superiority to those who receive these teachings as divine. They claim that it is because they are more gifted, have a higher culture, and keener penetration, and more independence of thought, that they are skeptics and unbelievers, and do not see the divinity of Christian truth. But if Christ is true, their claim is utterly false. What they do is not the result of an intellect of superior powers to that of others, but of a heart of superior wickedness.

Of those who make this claim there are two classes. One class is composed of those who have some acquaintance with the teachings of Christ from actual study of them, and deny their claim because of an assumed superiority to Him in actual knowledge and grasp of thought. These, however, are few in all the world. Few indeed are they who have ever listened attentively to the words of Christ, and not been constrained to say, "Never man spake like this man." For the most part those who really study the teachings of Christ become conscious of his authority, and of the divinity of his words, and are humbled before Him. They are very few who can, in his presence, assume to be his superiors and sit in judgment on Him.

But these few have given the cue to a vast crowd who constitute the other class of nominal skeptics. It is from these few that the great mass of unbelievers who never gave an hour's serious thought to the words of Christ, have learned to count it a mark of superiority of mind to profess to regard the teachings of Jesus as, at least, only human, and certainly far from authoritative. Knowing almost nothing of what the doctrines of Christianity are, having only the most vague and indefinite idea of what Christ really said and did, they are wont to put on the seeming of great learning, and of great intellectual acumen, and claim that their learning and their acumen have made them skeptics. But few, however, are deceived by their claim! Most men see through the thin covering with which both classes seek to give their skepticism a respectable parentage. It is easily seen that vanity is in fact the stimulus that sustains the profession of skepticism; while it is clearly known to all who really understand what the doctrines of our Saviour are, that all the skepticism there is in either class, is the fruit of enmity to God, and a determined unwillingness to do his will.

2. The indispensable preparation for the right study of divine truth is a spirit wholly obedient to the divine will. Without this men may get at the letter that killeth, but never at the spirit of the divine word that maketh alive. No amount of intellectual study will do that which it belongs to an obedient heart to do. Great learning will not make one acquainted with a God whom he hates. An obedient spirit will bring one so into harmony and sympathy with God's will and thoughts that he is prepared to learn by study.

3. There is the best of reason for the first and great requirement of the gospel, namely, that men shall begin the work of seeking God by repentance for sin, and reconciliation with God. While they cherish sin, and remain at enmity with God, they will never rightly discern spiritual things. Their love of sin, and opposition to the will of God, unfit them to understand

God's character or word. Besides the deadening influence of sin itself on the faculties of the soul, there is all the influence of prejudice and self-will and aversion to the truth which are alone enough to shut up every avenue to the mind against the truth. Every religious teacher ought to be thoroughly impressed with this thought whenever he attempts to impart a knowledge of divine things to the impenitent, " Except they repent they must perish ! " Until they are *disposed* to do the will of God they will never know of the doctrine. Until they break off their sins by a repentance that hates them and sorrows over them, and turn unto the Lord with a faith that works by love to Him, they will never see the kingdom of God, or know the truth that is able to save their souls.

SERMON V.

GOD THE SAME IN THE OLD TESTAMENT AS HE IS IN THE NEW.

1 CORINTHIANS viii. 6. — *But to us there is but one God, the Father, of whom are all things, and we in Him: and one Lord Jesus Christ, by whom are all things, and we by Him.*

YOU who look at the text in a reference Bible will find in the margin "and we *for* Him," instead of "and we *in* Him." The meaning is that our existence, our whole being, is intended to be subservient to God's pleasure, and to fulfill the purpose He had in view in creating us. The same form of expression is found in the thirty-sixth verse of the eleventh chapter of Romans, "For of Him, and through Him, and *for* Him are all things." It occurs also in the sixteenth verse of the first chapter of the Epistle to the Colossians, "All things were created by Him, and *for* Him." It is from such passages as these that the great general truth is elicited which has been so admirably expressed by the Shorter Catechism in answering the question, "What is the chief end of man?"

The text, taken as a whole, is an emphatic statement of the unity of God and the relation of believers to Him the source of all things; and of the Lordship of Jesus Christ, and his relation to all created things in general, and to believers in particular: "For though there be that are called gods, whether in heaven or in earth (as there be gods many, and lords many), yet to us there is but one God, the Father, of whom are all things, and we *for* Him: and one Lord Jesus Christ, *by* whom are all things, and we *by* Him." The contrast is between the faith of Christ's disciples, on the one hand, and the notions that prevailed in the world around them, on the other. To these there are many objects, real or imaginary, which stand for gods; but to us there is but one God; and He is, first of all, in our apprehension of Him, our Father. Not the Father as the first person in the Trinity, but as God, the self-existent and Eternal One, who is indeed Father, — and who becomes Father in the thought of all who apprehend God as He is revealed by Jesus Christ, the brightness of God's glory, the express image of God's person. This one God, is, in the second place, the source of all things, to a Christian's apprehension. All created things had their origin in Him alone; and did not, as others thought, owe their beginning to chance, or to a multitude of divine originators. Then, in the third place, God, as the Christians apprehended Him, was the end and aim of all their being. Not only was their existence intended to be for the doing of God's will, and glorifying Him, but it was devoted to this, and consciously. They were conscious that they lived not for themselves, but for God.

But there was something more than this in the Christians' apprehension of God. Not only was God — the eternal and self-existent One — their Father, the source and fountain of all things, and the end of their whole being, but there was a personal revelation of this God; a revelation made to his creatures in the act of creation, and still maintained in the Lordship of all created things, and in the redemption of those who call him Lord with believing hearts. God, the invisible, the unapproachable, the incomprehensible, is the source and fountain of all created things. But the creating act was performed by Jesus Christ, the personal manifestation of God; and the rule and government of all created things are in the hands of this same Jesus Christ, the Supreme Lord; and all who call God their Father in truth, that is, all who are Christians indeed, have become the children of God in his absoluteness by the same Almighty agent by whom creation itself was accomplished. As in creation He brought all things forth into actual being from God as their source and fountain, so in redemption He brought grace and salvation and sonship from the same God as their source and fountain, and made them the portion of all who received Him. It is thus that Christians are by Jesus Christ. By Him as all created things are; by him in their sonship with God.

The doctrine of the text, therefore is, first that there is but one God in the apprehension of all true believers; and that He, as God, is the source of all created things; the Father of all who rightly know Him; and the end and aim of all their being; and secondly, that this God revealed Himself to the apprehension of men as Creator; and actually created the universe, in the person of Jesus Christ, who is sole Lord of the creation which came from his omnipotent hand; and also the Redeemer of such as are saved, and the author of their sonship with God. The latter clause of the text conveys, therefore, the same idea that is conveyed by the noted passage in the third verse of the first chapter of Hebrews: " The Son, by whom God made the worlds, is the brightness of God's glory, the express image of his person, and upholds all things by the word of his power." Such, the Apostle says in our text, are the ideas of God which are entertained by the believers in Jesus Christ, in opposition to all the notions of the heathen pertaining to their gods and their ruling deities.

It is not my purpose, in this sermon, to treat of all this grand lesson, but to take one small part of it, and dwell upon that with a special practical aim. The notion is very largely entertained, and very industriously circulated, and dwelt upon in certain quarters, that the character of God as it is revealed in the Old Testament, and the relation which He sustains to man, are very unlike his character and relations as they are revealed in the New Testament. This notion is so often asserted, and asserted so boldly by those who entertain it, that many minds become imbued with the idea that this must be true, notwithstanding they still hold, in theory and profession at least, that both the Old Testament and the New are alike a revelation of the one only living and true God. Our text involves a denial of this notion. The One God who created the world, as He is revealed in the Old Testament, is the One God whom the Christians find revealed and spoken of as the Creator in the New Testament. They are one and the same Being. The methods of manifestation are the same in both Testaments. The character ascribed to Him, and the relation which He sustains to the created universe, and to all those who know Him, are the same in the New Testament that they are in the Old. Believers whose light was derived wholly from the Old Testament, worshipped the same God, and saw in Him the same attributes, and the same relations to themselves and to the world, as do those who have received the fuller light of the New Testament.

Let me now call your attention to a few of the representations which the Scriptures give us of the character of God, and of his relations to men. These representations will cover the ground that is taken by those who entertain the notions to which we have referred, and will demonstrate that they are not well founded.

1. In the first place God is represented as a *Father*. He is so represented in both the Old Testament and the New; and both Testaments represent Him to be the Father of precisely the same class of men.

In regard to this truth two fundamentally false assertions are constantly made, and easily believed by those who are thoughtless, or who are ignorant as to what the Scriptures do really teach. In the first place it is asserted that the New Testament alone reveals the fatherhood of God, and in the second place, that the Old Testament does not teach it. Indeed it is often said that the revelation of this, and of what is claimed to be its necessary implication, the brotherhood of man, was the grand and only distinctive doctrine which Jesus Christ taught the world. But as a matter of fact Jesus Christ never taught any such general fatherhood of God as it is claimed that He taught, namely that He is in the highest sense the Father of all men; nor did He ever recognize any participation of all men, without distinction of moral character and of relations to himself, in such a brotherhood as is involved in such teaching. He never taught that God is the Father of man as man, nor does the New Testament anywhere teach it. The New Testament does teach that God is the Father, in a high and special sense, of all who are in Jesus Christ by a true and living faith. He is the Father of all who are born, not of the flesh, but of the Spirit. It does teach that all those who have been born again, and been delivered from their sins by redemption, are the children of God in a high and special sense, and that they are consequently brethren in a high and special sense; in a sense in which no other men are children of God, or brethren with those who are his children. This doctrine comes prominently before us throughout the New Testament. Beginning with the Sermon on the Mount, when Jesus called his disciples to Him and taught them to say, "Our Father who art in heaven;" with a peculiar and tender emphasis on "Our;"

and assured them that as his disciples they were counted children of God, and so tenderly cared for by Him, as their Father, that the very hairs of their head were all numbered; beginning thus, with the direct teaching of the Lord Himself, and going onward to the end of the New Testament, the doctrine that God is indeed the Father of all who are in his Son Jesus Christ, is one of the plainest and most precious that is revealed. But this limitation is everywhere apparent. Of all those who reject the Son of God, Jesus Christ solemnly declares that God is not their Father. So He said to the unbelieving Jews. This is the teaching of all New Testament writers. The doctrine of the whole New Testament conforms to that statement found in the first chapter of the Gospel of John: "To as many as received Him, to them gave He power to become the sons of God, even to them that believe on his name." Hence the Apostle Paul says to Christians, addressing them as such distinctively, "Ye all are the children of God, by faith in Jesus Christ."[1] And again, in his Epistle to the Romans, he says, "As many as are led by the Spirit of God, they are the sons of God;" they have received the spirit of adoption whereby they cry from their hearts, "Our Father;" and "The Spirit Himself beareth witness with their spirits that they are the children of God." In the Epistle to the Galatians he says that the grand object for which God sent his Son into this world was to redeem them that were under the law, that we might receive the adoption of sons. This is the doctrine of the New Testament: God is the Father of all the redeemed. All those who know Him, love Him, trust in Him, and obey Him, are his children. This truth is involved in regeneration, in adoption, in heirship.

But this is equally the doctrine of the Old Testament. It is as unequivocally taught in the Old Testament as it is in the New. Thus Moses, speaking to the Israelites distinctively as the redeemed people of God, says to them, in the sixth verse of the thirty-second chapter of Deuteronomy, "Do ye thus requite the Lord, O foolish people and unwise? Is He not thy Father that hath bought [or redeemed] thee?" In the verse preceding, speaking of the rejecters of God, Moses says, "They have corrupted themselves; their spot is not the spot of his

[1] Gal. iii. 26.

children; they are a perverse and crooked generation." In later times we find the same doctrine, and the same limitation of it, still recognized and appealed to as the well-established doctrine of the Old Testament. Thus the Prophet Isaiah appeals to God in the name of his peculiar people, when they had sunken into great distress and obscurity, "Look down from heaven, and behold from the habitation of thy holiness and of thy glory: where is thy zeal and thy strength, the sounding of thy bowels and of thy mercies toward me? are they restrained? Doubtless thou art our Father, though Abraham be ignorant of us, and Israel acknowledge us not; thou, O Lord, art our Father, our Redeemer; thy name is from everlasting."[1] The same appeal is made, and same relationship claimed again, in the following chapter. And this is everywhere the teaching of the Old Testament, that God sustains a peculiar relation to those whom He has redeemed, — a relation which He sustains to no other class of men, — and this relation is that of a Father to them; and their relation to Him is specially and emphatically that of children. The author of our text sums up, in another part of this same epistle, the exhortations of God to his people of old, and makes his great promise to them to be this: "And I will be a Father unto you, and ye shall be my sons and daughters, saith the Lord Almighty." Both the Old Testament and the New, therefore, alike teach the fatherhood of God; but, at the same time, they alike teach that this fatherhood in its high and peculiar sense — the only sense in which the Scriptures ascribe fatherhood to Him as a distinctive characteristic of his relation to men — is limited strictly to those whom He has saved from sin and made his people by redemption. They both alike teach the sonship of men with God, but at the same time they limit that sonship to those who receive the Son of God as their Lord and Redeemer, even to those who believe on his name.

2. In the second place, every essential attribute of God, as He is revealed in the New Testament, is clearly and unequivocally ascribed to Him in the Old Testament. He is not, as is so often asserted, a being of any different character in the one case from what He is in the other. He is no more a being of justice in the Old Testament than He is in the New. He is

[1] Isaiah lxiii. 15, 16.

no more a being of love in the New Testament than He is in the Old. He is a being of no more sternness and severity in his feelings and conduct towards the wicked in the Old Testament than He is in the New. He is endowed with no more mercy, with no more pity, with no more long-suffering, with no more desire for the good of men, with no greater unwillingness that they should perish, with no greater readiness to save the penitent and believing and obedient in the New Testament than He is in the Old.

Look at a few of the passages in which the New Testament sets forth the sterner qualities of the divine character, and show his hatred of sin, and his disposition to punish it, and you will be convinced. "The wrath of God is revealed from heaven against all ungodliness and unrighteousness of men." . . . . "God will render to every man according to his deeds, unto them that are contentious and do not obey the truth, but obey unrighteousness, indignation and wrath, tribulation and anguish upon every soul of man that doeth evil. . . . . For there is no respect of persons with God. For as many as have sinned without law shall also perish without law; and as many as have sinned in the law shall be judged by the law, in the day when God shall judge the secrets of men by Jesus Christ, according to my gospel." The Apostles all speak in this same strain. Nothing can be found in the Old Testament that exceeds the fearful severity of their language when they are speaking of the justice of God, and the effect of that justice on the impenitent and the rejecters of the gospel. Of all such the unvarying testimony of the Apostles is that they must sink before the severity of divine justice. They all declare of God, that vengeance — avenging justice — is his, and He will repay for transgression and sin. This quality of avenging justice, and its destructive power on the wicked, are nowhere in the Old Testament more pointedly declared.

Nor is the language of our Saviour less emphatic, nor less terrible, when He speaks of God's justice and of its effects on the wicked and the rejecters of the salvation which He offers them. Nay, there is no language in the whole compass of the Bible so terrible in the exhibition of God's severity as is that which was used by our Saviour Himself. There is a sadness and tenderness ever in his tones as He speaks of the punishment of the finally guilty; but oh, how fearfully plain and pungent and faithful his words are! The man who hears divine commandments and does not obey them, is like the foolish man who built his house on the sand, and all his hopes are swept away by a fearful destruction in the hour of trial. " The day is coming when the doers of evil shall come forth unto the resurrection of damnation," and these shall go away into everlasting punishment. In the final day He will say to the wicked, " Depart from me, ye cursed, into everlasting fire, prepared — not for men — not for men — but for the devil and his angels." Is there anything in the Old Testament that can surpass these terrific words of the Man of Sorrows and of Love? Is there anything that can compare with them? The God of the Jews never uttered sentences to them in all their history so full of awfulness in setting forth the severity of his justice towards those who will live in sin and reject his offers of mercy. The character of God is, therefore, no different as respects its justice and severity as it is revealed in the New Testament from what it is in the Old. There is no discrepancy in the two revelations. The New Testament as clearly reveals justice and severity as does the Old.

But on the other hand the Old Testament reveals, as clearly as does the New, the mercy and loving kindness and compassion and long suffering of God towards men. There is not the difference in these respects in the character of God as it is set forth in the two Testaments that is often asserted; and as, not unlikely, multitudes of otherwise well instructed Christians firmly believe. Let me reverse the process and give a few of the many passages in which the Old Testament declares the love and mercy and tenderness of God; and you will see that its language is not surpassed by anything in the New Testament in this direction. The New Testament has new phases of these qualities of the divine character; and shows them more fully in their direct bearing on the great work of human redemption through the death of the Son of God; but it does not reveal them any more clearly, nor any more emphatically, as the distinctive attributes of God.

You will not fail to call to mind that wonderful passage in the thirty-fourth chapter of Exodus, where God spake to Moses in the Mount: " And the Lord descended in the cloud, and stood with him there, and proclaimed the name of the Lord. And the Lord passed by before him, and proclaimed, The Lord, The Lord God, merciful and gracious, long suffering, and abundant in goodness and truth, keeping mercy for thousands, forgiving iniquity and transgression and sin." This at the very beginning of the national life of Israel; and it was this God who stood before the faith, and in whom rested the hope of every believing sinner who learned the character of God from the Old Testament. Prophets, Psalmists, and all who were commissioned to reveal the character of God to men, spoke in the same strain, and revealed the same merciful, long suffering, gracious, and forgiving God. Nothing can be more tender and touching than some of the passages written by the prophets when they were setting forth these features of the character of Jehovah. Isaiah especially dwells upon them with peculiar fondness: "Ho, every one that thirsteth," etc.; "Let the wicked forsake his way," etc. And even the sterner and more denunciatory Ezekiel often comes back to them, and insists with great earnestness on the fact that if men will perish it is from no lack of mercy and compassion in God, but only because they will persist in rebellion against him, and in trampling his mercy under their feet. It was through this prophet, you will remember, that Jehovah pleaded with Israel in those memorable words, "Cast away from you all your transgressions, whereby ye have transgressed; and make you a new heart and a new spirit: for why will ye die, O house of Israel? For I have no pleasure in the death of him that dieth, saith the Lord God." Again, xxxiii. 11: "Say unto them, As I live saith the Lord God, I have no pleasure in the death of the wicked; but that the wicked turn from his way and live." We need not multiply passages of this kind. They abound in every part of the Old Testament. And it was only saying what all who knew the teachings of the Old Testament knew, when the Psalmist declared in that crowning passage in the one hundred and third Psalm: "The Lord is merciful and gracious, slow to anger and plenteous in mercy. Like as a father pitieth his children, so the Lord pitieth them that fear him."

We repeat, there is nothing in the New Testament more clear, nothing more tender, nothing more emphatic on this point, than large portions of the Old Testament. They who read the words of Jesus of Nazareth, and of his disciples, in telling us what the character of God is, read simply repetitions and confirmations of the descriptions of that character as given in what Moses in the Law, and the Prophets and the Psalmists did write.

The God of Moses and Israel, and the God of all the holy men in the Old Dispensation, and the God of Apostles and all who worship God under the light of the New Dispensation, are one and the same; one and the same in the relation which He sustains to men in general, and to his people in particular; one and the same in all the elements of his character, and in all the attributes of his being. In the Old Testament and in the New, his strange work is judgment,—his fond work is mercy. When it must be—as often in Old Testament history, when wickedness became rampant and hopeless He visited in wrath; when it must be—and the circumstances demand it now, and at the final day—He will still visit with wrath.

Such is the character of God. Against such a God have we all sinned. To the mercy and compassion and forgiveness and sonship of such a God the gospel invites us to-day. From the just anger, and the long delayed wrath of such a God does the gospel to-day invite us with words of warning and loving entreaty.

God grant us hearts to refuse not Him that speaketh.

SERMON VI.

THE OLD TESTAMENT REVEALS SALVATION.

LUKE xvi. 29. — *Abraham said unto him, They have Moses and the Prophets; let them hear them.*

IT is common to speak of this portion of our Lord's teachings as "the *parable* of the rich man and Lazarus." It may be seriously questioned, however, whether it would not be more accurate to call it "the *narrative* of the rich man and Lazarus." There is no intimation that it is a parable. It has few, if any, of the characteristic marks of a parable. It has all the characteristics of a narrative. There is no intimation, either in the words themselves or in the circumstances in which they were spoken, or in their evident purpose, that our Lord was not giving an account of actual persons and scenes and transactions. So far as anything can be made out from the record itself, the rich man was a real person, who once lived in this world, and fared sumptuously every day; and, after a life of self-indulgence and worldliness, died, and was buried; and in hell lifted up his eyes, being in torments. And Lazarus, so far as we can make out the case from our Lord's own words, was another real person, who lived on this earth at the same time that the rich man did; and after a life of extreme poverty and great sufferings, died, and was carried to Paradise, — the "Abraham's bosom" of the Jews. And if we take our Lord's words just as they are recorded, — and we dare not take them otherwise, — the conversation, which He says took place between Abraham and the rich man, was a real conversation, and not one that our Lord invented. The sufferings of the rich man, and the happiness of Lazarus, were real sufferings and real happiness, and not invented sufferings and invented happiness. The flame that tormented the rich man was as real a flame as any that can touch and torment a disembodied spirit. The flame that can reach and burn a spirit after it is separated from the body is not a material flame, indeed, but a spiritual one; yet none the less real because spiritual, but it may be far more terrible than any material flame can be to the soul.

No one can say, therefore, that the words before us are not a part of genuine narrative. No one has a right to affirm that they are a part of a fictitious story.

But if it were granted that our Lord uttered this account of the rich man and Lazarus as a parable, yet the meaning and purpose of it were the same as though He had uttered it as a narrative. The truths conveyed, and the lessons taught, are precisely the same in either case. In either case our Lord teaches us that there is an indissoluble connection between the life that now is and that which is to come; and that the destiny of each man in the world to come is determined by the life he leads and the character he forms, in the life that now is. A worldly, self-indulgent, easy, self-pampering life *here* leads with unerring certainty to woe and torments and unavailing regrets in the world that is to come. This is the solemn truth, the grand lesson of the narrative, if it be a narrative. It is the solemn truth, the grand lesson of the parable, if it be a parable.

Bearing this truth and this lesson in mind, let us now give our attention to that portion of our Lord's words which we have read for our text: "Abraham said, They have Moses and the Prophets; let them hear them."

This was said as an answer to the rich man's request that Abraham would send Lazarus to testify to the rich man's five brothers, lest they also should come unto his place of torment. By testifying the rich man meant bearing witness to the fact that there is a hereafter; to the reality and fearfulness of the sufferings of the lost, and to the certainty that such a life as the rich man had lived would end in such torments as the rich man was now suffering. He vainly thought, just as multitudes now think, that all that his five worldly-minded, easy-living, self-pampering brothers needed to turn them from such a course of living, and set them earnestly upon the great work of repentance and holy living and preparing for heaven, was the testimony of one who should rise from the dead and speak to them.

But Abraham told him plainly that they already had all the

testimony that they needed; all that could be of any avail to them. The writings of Moses and the Prophets were enough. These contained the very testimony, and uttered the very truths that the rich man wanted Lazarus to go and declare. And not only so, but when the rich man urged the case and insisted, that if one should go to them from the dead they would repent, Abraham declared emphatically that if they heard not Moses and the Prophets, they would not be persuaded even though one rose from the dead and warned them.

By Moses and the Prophets are meant the Scriptures of the Old Testament. What Abraham declared was that these Scriptures clearly taught the great fact of a future state of existence; the great fact that that existence would be to every man an existence in happiness or in misery; and the great fact that this happiness and this misery depended wholly on the character and life that each man lived in this world. Such were the truths that Abraham announced to this lost soul; and these are the truths that are clearly involved in the words before us.

Our Saviour, by quoting, indorsed the language of Abraham. He showed that he accounted the reply of Abraham to the rich man just and sufficient. By this indorsement of Abraham's words He made them his own, and thus taught us a lesson of great importance regarding the Old Testament, namely, that the Old Testament contained all that was necessary in order to the salvation of those who would heed its teachings.

Let us look at a few of these teachings, and we shall see how fully they involve this truth.

1. In the first place, they teach the moral government of God over men, and, by teaching this, they set forth clearly the accountability of men to God. This is the meaning of moral government in its bearing on men, or any other moral agents. It means that they are responsible to God for their conduct and characters, and that God will hold them rigidly to this responsibility. It means, also, that God has so constituted men, and so ordained consequences of conduct and character, that men cannot but reap the fruit of their own doings, either as rewards or as punishments. Because a righteous God rules over men, *therefore* they will reap what they sow. They are

answerable to God for what they do, and He exacts the account through the operation of those very principles of retribution by which He has bound consequences to conduct, in the moral and spiritual world, as closely as He has bound effects to causes in the material world.

All this was plainly taught in the Old Testament. It is one of the most prominent of its doctrines. Every one of its readers became familiar with it, and had it constantly impressed upon his attention. He read again and again the sentiment which the Psalmist uttered in the words, " Thou renderest to every man according to his work ; " and which the Prophet uttered when he said, " Ah, Lord God, behold thou hast made the heaven and the earth, by thy great power and stretched-out arm, and there is nothing too hard for thee ; thou showest loving kindness unto thousands, and recompensest the iniquity of the fathers into the bosom of their children after them ; the Great, the Mighty God, the Lord of Hosts is his name, great in counsel and mighty in work ; for thine eyes are open upon all the ways of the sons of men ; to give every one according to his ways, and according to the fruit of his doings." Often must the rich man have heard, even in the midst of his life of feasting and self-indulgence, the words of the wise preacher, " Know thou, that for all these things God will bring thee into judgment. . . . . For God shall bring every work into judgment, with every secret thing, whether it be good, or whether it be evil."

By such language as this, — and it prevails all through the Old Testament, — those who read it were fully taught the moral government of God over men, and their accountability to Him. They were made, therefore, to know that their future destiny was placed in their own hands ; and that they could not escape the legitimate consequences of their conduct and method of life. They had light enough, if they would heed it, to guide them in choosing a right course of life ; and to persuade them, if mere knowledge would persuade them, to turn away from wrong courses. The fact of the moral government of God over men made the wretchedness of the future as certain to an evil doer, or a rejecter of God's authority, as it could be made by any testimony that could be given, even though one were sent from the dead to give it.

2. But, secondly, not only were the readers o. the Old Testament taught the moral government of God over men, and hence their accountability, and the certainty of reaping the consequences of their conduct either as rewards or as punishments, but they were assured of this by the plainest and most positive declarations that inspired men could utter. The matter was not left to inference. The inference from the fact of moral government was, indeed, so necessary that they would have been without excuse for not seeing it, and acting on it. But in this, as in almost everything else involving the well-being of men, God added line upon line, and precept upon precept; and made the way of life so plain that a wayfaring man, though a fool, need not miss it.

I know that it has often been asserted that the Old Testament did not reveal a future state, nor deal with any rewards and punishments, saving such as were temporal and material. But this assertion cannot be maintained. Every attentive reader of the Old Testament knows that it is not true. Those who lived under its light were taught the existence of a future state, and the dependence of its conditions on the life and conduct and character of the present. Look at the case as it stands. Even the earliest of all the Old Testament books contains a clear and confident assertion of such a state. Job comforted himself in view of this future, which would be one of vindication, for him, against the false charges of his enemies; and one of redemption from the sins of which he was really guilty. The latest and ripest scholarship is emphatic in declaring that Job's words " refer to an existence beyond the grave;" and that " the view which restricts his language to an *earthly hope* is opposed to the proper force of the words, to the connection of thought, and to the spirit and tenor of the whole book." " I know," said the afflicted patriarch, " that my Redeemer lives, and in after time will stand upon the earth; and after this my skin is destroyed, and without my flesh, shall I see God."[1] David, in like manner, looked forward into a future state to find his sweetest anticipations and fullest joys: " Thou wilt not leave my life in the grave, neither wilt thou suffer thy Holy One to see corruption. Thou wilt show me the path of life: in thy presence is fullness of joy: at thy

[1] Bible Union's translations and notes.

right hand there are pleasures for evermore." .... "As for me, I will behold thy face in righteousness: I shall be satisfied when I awake with thy likeness." Such was the language of faith and hope and joyous expectancy, as the friends of God and righteousness looked forward into the future. Their future was not one that was bounded by the grave, and came to its end there. It rather began there, and stretched away into the unending years of God's eternity. The language, too, is that of established belief. It indicates a settled habit of mind ; as though those who used it were accustomed to solace themselves with such hopes and anticipations, and to offset the ills of this life with thoughts and assurances of promised joys in the world to come. And this is just what the writer of the Epistle to the Hebrews says regarding those ancient worthies who lived and served God and were saved by the light of the Old Testament only : " They all died in faith, not having received the promises, but having seen them afar off, and were persuaded of them, and embraced them, and confessed that they were strangers and pilgrims on the earth. . . . . They looked for a city which hath foundations, whose Maker and Builder is God." Thus also our Saviour interpreted the Old Testament. Taking even the earliest of Moses' writings, he said that they taught the future life. " I am the God of Abraham," etc. God is not God of the dead, but of the living ; this silences the Sadducees. A future of bliss for the righteous was thus clearly taught by the Old Testament.

A future of misery for the wicked was as clearly taught. The passages that we have quoted, affirming a judgment to come, in which God will bring all deeds before Him for award, are, like the passages in which the righteous comfort themselves by thoughts and hopes of a future of happiness, the expression of settled and well-understood beliefs. The facts of judgment and retribution upon the whole of life were treated as items of a common and familiar faith. And then, to exclude the possibility of supposing that this judgment and retribution could have sole reference to the temporal consequences of conduct, we have, in the book of the Prophet Daniel, an announcement of the resurrection, and of eternal retribution, almost as clear as they were announced by our Saviour, and in almost the precise words : " The multitude of them that sleep in the dust of the earth shall awake, some to everlasting life, and some to shame and everlasting contempt." Our Saviour's own words were but little plainer, and a little fuller of detail: "The hour is coming, in the which all that are in the graves shall hear the voice of the Son of Man, and shall come forth; they that have done good, unto the resurrection of life; and they that have done evil, unto the resurrection of damnation."

When we read the announcements which the Old Testament makes of judgment and retribution upon every work of man, and upon every secret thing, whether it be good, or whether it be evil, we do not read them as those read them who lived in Old Testament times, unless we read them in the light of these clear assertions of a future of bliss for the righteous, and these announcements of judgment and retribution following a resurrection of all the dead. The rich man, and his five brothers, read all these revelations of a future of happiness or of misery in just this light. The resurrection and eternal life, or the everlasting shame and contempt, revealed by the Prophet Daniel, stood side by side with the "judgment," and the "rendering unto every man according to his deeds," of all the prophets, of the wise Preacher, and of the Psalmist.

If, therefore, those who had the Old Testament went down to death, they went down fully and faithfully warned and instructed. Moses and the Prophets had testified to them as plainly as one could have testified to them if he had been sent to them from the dead. They were warned, they were instructed, they were remonstrated with; they were invited and entreated to choose the way of life; and they had it plainly pointed out to them. God most solemnly assured them that "the soul that sinned, it should die;" and that, though hand joined in hand, sin should not go unpunished. If they went down to death they were without excuse. The way to have escaped it was clearly pointed out to them.

3. This brings me to say, thirdly, that the Old Testament plainly taught the way of a sinner's salvation. It did not teach it as fully as the New Testament teaches it; but it taught it plainly; and therefore was sufficient for the salvation of those who gave heed to it.

What we have been dwelling upon has had reference more to the clearly announced consequences of evil conduct, and of wrong methods of living, than to the possibility and way of salvation from evil consequences already incurred. Very much of the Old Testament, as well as of the New Testament, is taken up with declarations regarding the punishments and evil points of sin, to deter man from committing it. If revelation stopped here, there would be little hope or comfort in it for the sinner who has already ruined himself by transgression. There would then remain nothing for him but " a fearful looking for of judgment and fiery indignation." But the revelation of the Old Testament does not stop here. It both fully recognizes the wants of such a sinner and provides for them. It recognizes the fact that every human being is such a sinner, and yet recognizes the fact that there is hope for him. And this, notwithstanding its pointed and sweeping declarations regarding the fixedness of the law that binds consequences to conduct; the harvest to the sowing. It recognizes a provision of mercy in the divine government; and clearly teaches the fact that God can " be just and justify the guilty ; " though it does not fully show how this can be done. It remained for "the Lamb of God" to come and take away the sin of the world by the the offering of that blood which cleanseth from all sin ; and is " a propitiation for our sins ; and not for ours only, but for the sins of the whole world," before the method of divine forgiveness and mercy could be clearly understood. But that Lamb was typified ; that propitiating blood was foretold, and pointed to ; and in view of it the fullest invitations were given to sinners to return unto God ; and the fullest and most earnest assurances were made to them, that returning, they should find favor and be saved. " There is forgiveness with God that He may be feared," was the declaration of all the sacrifices of the Old Testament dispensation, and of large portions of Old Testament language. " Let the wicked forsake his way, and the unrighteous man his thoughts; and let him return unto the Lord, and He will have mercy upon him, and to our God for He will abundantly pardon," is the burden of all prophetic utterances, after they have charged home the guilt of sinners upon them, and warned them of the evils and punishments that are in store for them. " Repent, and turn yourselves from all your transgressions; so iniquity shall not be your ruin. Cast away from you all your transgressions, whereby ye have transgressed; and make you a new heart and a new spirit; for why will ye die, O house of Israel? For I have no pleasure in the death of him that dieth, saith the Lord God; wherefore turn yourselves, and live ye." This is the burden of all God's addresses to the guilty and ruined throughout the Old Testament.

Nothing further was needed, therefore, in the way of testimony regarding either the fact of a future world, or of the consequences of sin and false living, or of the possibility and way of salvation, to make the readers of the Old Testament understand their accountability, their exposure to the fearful consequences of sin in the world to come, or the necessity of repentance and a return to God in order to salvation. The consequences of sin, the reality of a future world, the dependence of the destiny of that world on the conduct and character of men in this world, and yet the possibility and way of salvation by the mercy and forgiveness of God, these were all revealed in the Old Testament. They were so plainly revealed that men could not fail to find them who would give heed to the words that revealed them. The revelation was therefore abundantly clear, and abundantly full, to have saved from death every soul that perished under their light. The revelation was so clear, and so full, that Dives need not, after death, have lifted up his eyes in hell, being in torments. He might have been carried by angels, as Lazarus was, to Abraham's bosom; and he would have been carried there had he given due heed to Moses and the Prophets. The revelation is so clear, and so full, that the rich man's five brothers had no need that one should go from the dead, and testify to them of sin, and of righteousness, and of future retribution. The testimony which they had was so full and so clear that no further testimony could have added to its strength.

But you and I, my hearers, have not only all this, but we have all of the New Testament besides. We have not only all that the rich man and his five brothers had, and having which they had no excuse for living false lives, and went down to death with all their blood on their own head; but we have the testimony of one who did rise from the dead.

They had the dawning of the day; we have the noon-day shining of the sun.

SERMON VII.

THE WORTH OF MAN.

Ps. viii. 4. — *What is man, that thou art mindful of him? and the son of man, that thou visitest him?*

THESE questions express amazement on the part of the Psalmist. He was considering the glory of God as it is manifested in the material creation, and exclaimed, " O Lord our Lord, how excellent is thy name in all the earth! who hast set thy glory above the heavens."

At this point his thoughts turned to the works of God among men. Here also his glory was revealed : " Out of the mouth of babes and sucklings hast thou ordained strength," or, as our Saviour rendered it, " hast thou perfected praise," " because of thine enemies, that thou mightest still the enemy and the avenger."

It was at this point that his amazement began. It was astonishing to him that this great and glorious God should make any account whatever of men, and condescend to heed either their praises or their evil dispositions toward Him. He therefore exclaimed, " When I consider the heavens the work of thy fingers, the moon and the stars which thou hast ordained; what is man that thou art mindful of him ? and the son of man, that thou visitest him ? "

It was true, and the Psalmist could not shut his eyes to the fact, that this great and glorious God did concern Himself with men ; that his mind was affected by their enmities and evil dispositions, and that He did take pleasure in their subjection to his will, and seek to honor Himself by the praises of even the weakest and obscurest of the race. He did, as a matter of fact, take cognizance of men in all the variety of their conditions, and was tenderly regardful of them and interested in them. This was a matter of wonder to the Psalmist whenever he looked at the grandeur and magnificence of the visible creation, and thought of the insignificance of man considered as a part of that creation.

This has been a standing wonder among men from that time till the present. Some of the most specious, if not the ablest arguments against the fact of a written revelation from God have been drawn from this very source; as have also those against the great central truth declared in this revelation — THE ATONEMENT. It has seemed to multitudes of men incredible that the Creator and Sustainer of worlds of such untold number, and such inconceivable magnitude as compared with the earth, should make choice of this inconsiderable globe, this mere speck in his creation, and its handful of inhabitants, a handful compared with the unnumbered millions of beings that are supposed to exist in other and grander worlds, for such momentous transactions. Many men have gone to the length of discarding the Scriptures, and counting the plan of salvation through the intervention of the Son of God an absurdity, simply on the ground that this earth is so insignificant a part of the material universe, and that its inhabitants are so few and worthy of so little supposed consideration compared with other created intelligences.

But the fact remains to us as it did to the Psalmist, that God is "mindful of man, and that He has visited him." To our minds the mission of the Son of God to this world is a great and unquestionable truth, and such a demonstration of the love and condescension of God as cannot be brought into doubt in the smallest measure by any of the discoveries of science, or by any of the inferences that can be drawn from these discoveries. This we know, of whatever else we are ignorant, and however strange it may seem to us when we think of it, — this we know, that God has in this manner manifested the deepest interest in the well-being of man, and the highest appreciation of his worth and importance among creatures. The history of the world abounds moreover with instances of his interposition in their behalf of sufficient number and magnitude to establish the fact of a constant oversight and interested government among men, and for their welfare; and the cross of Christ is a proof that will stand through eternity, and carry conviction to all who duly consider it, that God counts man to be of greater worth, and of more importance than all material things. He gave his only begotten Son, the Creator of the universe, for man's redemption. This gift is God's measure of man's worth. It shows that He counts him as much more important than the material universe, as the Creator of the material universe is more important than the universe itself.

Let us now give our attention to some things that we learn from the Scriptures on this subject. Why is it that God shows such great consideration for man? Why does He count him of so much importance, that He is even mindful of him, and has visited him with such love and condescension?

1. In the light of the Bible we know that it is not because of his body.

Man's body is important: it is of great worth: it honors God by the perfection and adaptation of its members. No one can contemplate it, thoughtfully and rightly, in its structure and uses, and not feel constrained to exclaim with David, "I will praise thee; for I am fearfully and wonderfully made." It was on man's body as a part of the creation that God looked and saw everything that He had made, and behold it was very good. Its capacities are immensely greater, its adaptations immensely more numerous, than are those of any other earthly bodies. The body of the highest creature below man is but a clumsy machine compared with his, though marvelous in its structure and its adaptations to the purposes for which it was made. But even man's body is, at best, only an instrument, and, in its present form, is intended only for temporary uses. Soon it is to be taken to pieces and resolved into the general mass of unorganized matter out of which it was formed. "Dust thou art, and unto dust shalt thou return," is the divine appointment for it; and in this appointment God has manifested his estimate of its value. It is of immense value because it has received so much of its Maker's care and skill in its structure; but its value is all subservient and temporary, and all destined to come to naught when it has been made use of to accomplish a specific end. Beyond this it has no worth as a body, and ceases to be. In the resurrection, even, it has no being or recognition as an organization like the present one of flesh and blood. The body of the resurrection will be a spiritual body. And even that body will be of value, not for itself alone, but, like the body of the present state, its worth will be subservient — useless in itself — of value only as the instrument of the soul.

2. Again, in the light of the Scriptures we know that the high estimate that God puts on man is not on account of his moral character or deeds. If there is any one thing more plainly revealed in the Scriptures than anything else, it is that the moral character of men, considered as men, is fearfully depraved, and their lives sinful. The race as a whole, and every individual member of it, is, in his unregenerate state, unholy, and morally unlovely in the sight of God. There is a *something* in him that taints all his moral acts, all the elements of his moral character, to such a degree that he cannot, in this condition, please God. For the plain assertion is, "They that are in the flesh cannot please Him."

When we look at the law of God and consider its claims, it is not difficult to discover what a part, at least, of this something is. The law of God is the expression of what a moral agent's character ought to be, and what ought to be his acts, and the habit and aim of his life. A perfect moral character, judged by this law, — and this is the law by which God judges, — a perfect moral character, one that God can take pleasure in, is a character that spontaneously, and without ceasing, prompts one to "love the Lord his God with all his heart, and with all his soul, and with all his strength, and with all his mind; and his neighbor as himself." And a perfect life is one that carries out, by spontaneous and uninterrupted choice, all the promptings of such a character in all the conduct and in all the relations which one sustains to God or men. Nothing short of this is moral perfection. Nothing short of this is obedience to God and conformity to his will. But coming short of this is positive disobedience and transgression of the divine law. A character that prompts anything short of this is depraved. It prompts acts of disobedience and disregard of God.

Any man with this character is therefore living in hostility to the will and government of God; and if the law of God requires only that which is right, and if moral goodness consists only in the carrying out of the spirit of this law, and if moral goodness of character consists alone in its conformity to this law in all its desires and motives and promptings, then of course moral goodness cannot be affirmed of any life that falls short of absolute and entire consecration to God's will; nor of any character that embodies any element of selfishness and transgression.

This was evidently the ground that our Saviour took with the man who "came running and kneeling to Him, and asked him, Good Master, what shall I do that I may inherit eternal life?" "And Jesus said unto him, Why callest thou me good? there is none good but one — God." This young man was, and had been from his youth, a pattern of amiability and fair dealing with all his fellow-men. He solemnly declared that he had from his earliest years kept faithfully each of the commandments that the Saviour repeated to him, "Do not commit adultery; do not kill; do not steal; do not bear false witness; defraud not; honor thy father and mother." Our Lord did not question that the young man was sincere in this declaration, nor did He deny its truth. On the contrary, it is evident from the verse that follows it that He admitted that the young man was sincere in his declaration, and that the declaration was true, judged by the common standard of moral action; for it is immediately added, "Then Jesus, beholding him, loved him." There was much to love in such a life and character. No one who was right-minded could help loving it.

But, at the same time, our Saviour did not take back what he had just said, "There is none good but one — God;" but, on the contrary, he went on to say, in all tenderness and fidelity, "One thing thou lackest." There was one fatal hinderance to his having the favor and approval of God on his character and life, notwithstanding there was that in him which God Himself loved. One thing thou lackest in order to the possession or enjoyment of eternal life. One thing, therefore, stood between him and the favor of God. What that thing was is plainly enough indicated in the direction that follows, "Go thy way; sell whatsoever thou hast and give to the poor, and thou shalt have treasure in heaven; and come, take up the cross, and follow me." This tore off the covering from the young man's heart; for it is added: "And he was sad at that saying, and went away grieved; for he had great possessions." All his fancied goodness was earthly, and not heavenly; and all was subservient to a supreme regard for his worldly interests.

These held sway in his soul, and were the object of his strongest love and intensest devotion. He did not love God "with all his heart, and soul, and mind;" but he loved these interests, and lived for them, and therefore lived in constant rejection of God, in the constant setting at naught of his authority, in the constant transgression of his law, and in the constant indulgence of sin. Was not his moral character deformed and unlovely then? Was it not depraved? Was not his life such that God must be displeased with it?

But if this was the character and life of one so eminent in what is called goodness, and if in him they were so offensive to God that they stood between the young man and eternal life, then it cannot certainly be the character and life of men generally, the vast majority of whom are so immeasurably inferior to this young man in what passes for moral goodness; it cannot be the moral character and life of men, I say, that moves God to think so highly of them, and to count them so valuable.

3. But, thirdly, we learn from the Bible that it is for what men are in themselves, in their mental and spiritual being, that He estimates their value at so high a price.

That it is for that which they are in themselves, as distinguished from their moral character and deeds, is evident, first, because all his manifestations of regard for them have been made towards them while they were possessing a character that was offensive to Him while thus living in sin against Him. "For God commendeth his love towards us in that, while we were yet sinners, Christ died for us." And, secondly, because it was for men as they were, in spite of the unloveliness and depravity of their moral characters and lives, and to save them from this unloveliness and depravity, that God gave the life of his only begotten Son as the price of their redemption; for "we were redeemed, not by silver and gold, but by the precious blood of Christ."

This distinction between what men are in their own natures, and what they are in moral character, is too often lost sight of by us, and we are led into much confusion by losing sight of it. But the sacred writers never overlooked it. They always looked at man — when they spoke of him as the object of God's love and high estimation — as something distinct from his character; and they looked on his character as something good or bad pertaining to man in his essential being, and determining his destiny. Hence they always look on man himself as the creation of God. His essential being is that which God pronounced good at the beginning, and which He has ever counted the most valuable thing on earth. But man's moral character they look upon as something not of God's creating, but of man's own making. They therefore look on the former, or man himself, — his essential being, — as that which was worthy of God's love, and which He did so love that He gave his only begotten Son to save it from the ruin into which sin had plunged it. The latter, man's moral character, they look upon as that on account of which God is angry with him every day that it remains unchanged; which holds him in ruin; and which, unless it is changed, will make his ruin eternal. In the former they see that which the Son of God took upon Himself, and in which He now appears as our Intercessor in heaven. In the latter they see that from which He sought, by taking their nature on Himself, to deliver them, and, by securing for them another character, to make them fit, themselves also, to appear and forever dwell in heaven.

When the Psalmist asked the questions before us, he was thinking of man as he is in himself, in his essential being, in some measure at least, for he immediately adds, "For thou hast made him a little lower than the angels, and hast crowned him with glory and honor. Thou madest him to have dominion over the works of thy hands." He recognized the true dignity of man as a creation of God. He declared his great elevation and his importance by reason of the inherent and essential elements of being with which God had endowed him. The moral degradation into which he had fallen in his alienation from God, his devotion to sin, the guilt and ruin he had brought on himself by his transgression of the law of God and departure from Him, — all this the Psalmist often confessed, as all who are guided by the Scriptures, or by careful observation of men in the light of the Scriptures, must confess; but he did not forget, and we have no right to forget, that man himself, in the faculties of his soul, the essential elements of his being, remains unchanged. Could he be changed in these he would not be man, but would become something else. It is with man in this respect as it is with the fallen angels. In themselves, in their essential being, they are the same that they were in heaven. They are endowed with the same faculties that made them capable of a heavenly service. If you deprive them of these faculties they cease to be the beings they were, and become something else. But their moral character was changed by their sin. This was no longer what it had been, but it became something else — something very different. In the essential elements of their being they remain the same. Angelic nature in them is still good, as the creation of God; and its capabilities in them are the same that they are in the angels that have kept their first estate. But the moral character that was righteous in the sight of God, and that made them fit for heavenly service and companionship — this exists in them no longer. In their moral character there is not one trace of resemblance with that which they once had, nor with that which holy angels now possess. In moral character they are an offense to God, and by it made worthy of the severest visitation of his wrath.

It is the same with man. In the essential elements of his being, he is just what he was when he was first formed in Adam, and had his home in the garden of Eden. But the moral character which man had in Adam, and which made him fit for that garden and for communion with a holy God, is gone, and in its place is a character that is displeasing to God, and deserving of his wrath in punishment.

It is man himself, therefore, irrespective of any present character, man in his inherent capabilities, man having a being such that, with a holy character, he is a fit companion of the angels in heaven, man with such a nature that the Son of God chose to take it upon Himself, not only to accomplish the great work of human redemption, but to bear it and to appear in it through the ages in heaven; man with such a being as, with a holy character, fits him to be a child of God and a joint heir with Jesus Christ in the inheritance of God; it is man thus considered whom God esteems so highly, and counts so valuable. It is man thus considered of whom God is ever mindful, and whom He visits in his condescension.

We see in the light of this subject, —

1. What is meant by human depravity. Not human faculties, but human character is wrong. The elements of man's

being are still what God made them. Human character is sinful. Its depravity is such that no word but *total* adequately expresses the true state of the case.

This distinction must always be kept in mind if we would form just judgments of men. If we count the essential elements of their souls, — their souls considered as a creature of God, — depraved and worthless, we shall despair of them utterly, and never have any faith in them.

But what is more, if we confound their essential being with the moral character superinduced on that being, we shall have little or no stimulus to seek their salvation. The distinction becomes vital at this point. We must recognize the inherent worth of the soul underneath all its depravity, and in spite of it, or we shall never become workers together with God in seeking to save it. We do not seek the salvation of beasts, because we do not see this inherent value in them. The true worker with God in the gospel, commends his love for the lost in seeking them in their sin.

2. We, see secondly, what is meant by the regeneration or renewal of the soul ; and the absolute necessity of its renewal in order that it should have the favor of God and dwell in heaven. The regeneration or renewal of the soul is the renovation of its moral character. Regeneration pertains solely to the moral character, and not at all directly to the substance of the soul. Its spirit or temper is changed, not its faculties. Its capacity to love, *e. g.*, remains unchanged by regeneration, but the object of its love becomes different, and so the character or moral quality of its love itself is different. Its capacity for obedience to the behests of a higher power remains unchanged ; but the authority to which obedience is given becomes different ; and the character of the obedience rendered is therefore different. The love of the soul must go out and rest in God or it can never please Him. The obedience of the soul must recognize and honor the authority of God or it will forever remain in rebellion against Him, and call forth his displeasure and deserve punishment.

3. We see in the light of this subject how full of hope the gospel is for sinners. Its grand announcement is that God so loved the world, etc. He loved a world in its ruin and guilt. What He loved He was not willing to let perish. It

was that which was in ruin and under guilt that He wished to save. Hence his name, *Jesus*, because He saves his people from their sins. His people, their very selves, not from the essential elements of their being, but from the sins that had brought this being into ruin. It is therefore only that which is ruining you that God asks you to give up by repentance. If He can see you separated from *this*, his love for you will draw you into his presence, and fill you with his peace and cover you with his glory. It is that you may be saved from this, that you are commanded to come to Jesus Christ. You cannot deliver yourself. He alone can deliver you. " To as many as received Him, to them gave He power to become the sons of God, even to them that believed on his name."

SERMON VIII.

SIN NECESSARY IN A MORAL SYSTEM.

―――◆―――

MATT. xviii. 7.—*It must needs be that offenses come: but woe to that man by whom the offense cometh.*

THERE is no darker problem, nor one that is a severer trial to faith, than the existence of moral evil in the government of a holy and almighty God. How it came; for what reason it was permitted; why it is suffered to continue; are questions to which no thoughtful mind is a stranger, and at which the faith of but few intelligent believers has not, at times, been staggered.

In the words of the text, our Lord recognizes the prevalence of moral evil in the world, and enunciates a great and important fact pertaining to it; a fact which, though it does not answer all of the mind's merely speculative inquiries, yet throws light upon some of them and furnishes an important aid to its faith. He declares, that even in the government of a holy and almighty God, there is a stern necessity that there should be sin, as his words are recorded by Luke: " It is impossible but that offenses should come "; as his words are recorded by Matthew: " It must needs be that they come." That is, as we understand his words, carrying them back to the great principle that underlies them and gives them their greatest significance, sin is necessarily involved in a moral system; it was impossible, in the nature of things, that it should not be committed. Thus much at least is revealed by the word of our Saviour; and though it does not enable us, as we have said, to know all the reasons why evil is permitted, yet it is much that we hear the voice of divine authority assert that it was impossible but that it should come; and it is a relief to faith to be assured by One in whom it trusts that there was a necessity that it should come.

Nor are we altogether in the dark regarding the reasons of this impossibility. We cannot sound them to their lowest depths, but there is light thrown upon them from two sources suggested by the text, and to these I first invite your attention.

1. In the first place, we see in the character of moral agency itself why moral evil must be possible in a moral government, and in this possibility perhaps a necessity for it, or at least an impossibility that it should not be. It is impossible that a moral agent should not be able to sin. For a moral agent, be it remembered, is one who has, and he is a moral agent only as he has, the ability to do either right or wrong, in any given case. He is one who acts voluntarily in all his accountable conduct; always choosing freely, either to do or not to do, the act that lies before his mind as one that is possible to him. The act, be it right or wrong, of which his mind conceives as thus possible, he freely chooses, or as freely refuses to commit. If he commits it, it is only because he chooses to commit it; if he does not commit it, it is only because he chooses not to commit it. Without this power and freedom of choice there could be no moral agency, no accountability. And without beings endowed with this power and freedom there could be no moral government. God would then be only a physical ruler; and creatures would be only machines, or, like animals, merely irresponsible agents, without moral character or dignity or worthiness. Every right act, therefore, of a moral agent, involves an opposite wrong act as possible, and that might have been done in its stead; and the power to do right involves necessarily the power to do the opposite wrong.

Such is moral agency. It is constituted by the possession of the ability to do wrong, not less than the ability to do right; and no power can be brought to bear upon the former to destroy it, and make sin impossible, that would not destroy also the latter, and make holiness impossible; nor can we conceive of the possibility of an agent being created with the latter without also the former.

When, therefore, the creation of moral agents was determined upon, it was with this possibility in view, and involved. They must be created with this possibility, or not created at all; and if a moral system was to be inaugurated in the universe, it must be with the fearful liability wrought into its existence, that its subjects might, if they should so choose, use all the powers with which they should be endowed for righteous and holy uses and most glorious ends, for sinful and unholy uses and most ignominious ends.

Such a system would necessarily be one of motives. Motives would be the power by which alone such beings could be governed. The moment they were controlled by other influences than those coming from motives, and leaving the mind free to yield to them or to resist them, that moment the government of them would become something higher or lower than moral government; and they would become, to that extent, not agents acting, but objects acted upon. The great and controlling power of moral government must be in its motives. The strength of such a government would, therefore, depend upon the amount of motive power that it could bring to bear upon the minds of its subjects to influence them to do right. Its weakness, if it had any, would be in the fact that motives to wrong-doing would avail, in some instances, to induce the committing of sin. The only way of removing this weakness would be, not the making of moral agents unable to yield to them or feel their power, for this would destroy their character, but multiplying the number and increasing the power of motives to right action.

At this point we come in sight, I think, of what may constitute the necessity of which our Saviour speaks; or the impossibility mentioned in his words as recorded by Matthew. The necessity may be in this: that the number and power of motives to holiness must be increased by an exhibition of the consequences of sin. But for this exhibition, rightly and timely made, the whole moral universe might be seduced into rebellion, and work thus its entire ruin. It certainly could not but strengthen the power of all motives to holiness, and weaken that of all motives to sin, to have the fearful consequences of sin fully exhibited to the view. Let its legitimate fruit be clearly seen and seen as certain, and it is shorn of much of its power to allure.

Besides, there is much in the *consequences* of sin clearly seen, to open the eyes of those who look upon them to its real character. They will judge of the tree by the fruit that it bears, and their judgment will be more accurate and trustworthy than it could be without such a sight. When the holy angels saw those who had transgressed and fallen, hurled from heaven and consigned in hopelessness and misery to the great prison house of the universe in the world of woe, by their sin, and this as its legitimate consequence and deserved punishment, its true character could not but be far better understood than it had been before. Its heinousness and malignity would be more clearly apprehended. So also when the unfallen inhabitants of heaven as well as those who have been saved, look down upon the unfolding of sin into its consequences in this world, or from this world in hell, the same result can but follow. And when they saw the crowning act of sin in this world, that which revealed its whole character, showing, in the murder of the Son of God, that its only stopping place, if it could have full sway, would be in the dethronement of God and the destruction of everything that is holy and lovely in the universe, then, as never before, they must have understood its nature and been filled with holy detestation of it. Then all its motives must have become weakened, and its power to draw them from their allegiance to God forever broken.

It may also have been impossible for moral beings to have obtained the fullest knowledge of the character of God, and so to have felt the fullest power of motives for allegiance to Him, unless they had been permitted to see Him in his relations to sinners, and in his dealings with them. His attributes would be more clearly seen and better understood by such a sight than they could be without it. His justice as a fact, and as to its nature, would be more vividly imprinted upon their minds, and more fully understood by them after they had seen it thus displayed, — and certainly his mercy and love would be seen in a new light, when they came to look upon Him in the gift of his only begotten Son, delivered up for sinners that they might be saved, and then looked upon a just God, just still, but showing mercy, and forgiving them and adopting them as his children and making them heirs of eternal glory, through the merits, intercession, and atonement of the Redeemer. Every exhibition of the love and compassion and mercy of God that was made consistently with his justice, and without infringing upon his holiness, would be a clearer revelation of Himself, and thus an augmenting of motives to love and trust Him.

But in order to this exhibition, there must needs be sinners toward whom it could be made. Pardoning mercy and compassion and grace cannot be shown except to the guilty. If, therefore, the full force of motives derived from the character of God were to have sway over holy minds, and lend their influence toward strengthening and making secure the interests of the moral universe, it was impossible but that offenses should come. Sin was, in this respect and to this extent, necessary. Malignant as it is in its character, fearful as it is in its fruits, and without excuse as is its commission on the part of any moral agent, yet in dealing with it, in checking its sway, and undoing its consequences, through the atonement of Christ, God has so revealed the glories of his character, and so multiplied and strengthened the motives to holiness, that not only his government over moral beings has been made more secure, but those very beings, all that are holy, are lifted into the sphere of permanent and unendangered allegiance to their God. Motives for them to commit sin have been so weakened and destroyed that they have ceased to be felt, while motives to holiness have been so multiplied and increased in strength, that they never can lose their sway. Thus "where sin abounded grace did much more abound." This was the view of the Apostle Paul. And to those who would pervert the truth thus developed, and say that in so teaching he said, "Let us do evil that good may come," his only but all-sufficient reply was, "their damnation is just." They cannot, without deep and damning guilt, make this use of the doctrine.

2. The second source of light to which I invited your attention, respecting the necessity that there should be sin in the world, is found in the fact itself, that sin exists in the world. If it had not been necessary, the character of God is a guaranty that it would never have been permitted. If it had been possible, consistently with the perfection of a moral system, and the best interest of the universe, for Him to have prevented it, his character makes it certain that He would have prevented it. He has no pleasure in sin. It is the abominable thing that He hates. It is always, and in all circumstances, and everywhere, offensive to Him. "He is of purer eyes than to behold evil, and cannot look on iniquity." For "the righteous Lord loveth righteousness; his countenance

doth behold the upright." "As I live, saith the Lord God, I have no pleasure in the death of him that dieth, but that he turn and live." He not only, *i. e.*, has no pleasure in sin, but He has none in its legitimate and necessary result, the death of the sinner. Sin itself, and its consequences, are all odious to Him. But for *a must needs be*, therefore, sin could never have found a place in any of his creatures.

This introduces us to the second clause of our text: "Woe unto him through whom they come." From this clause we learn two great lessons, each of them serving to check and refute the objection which we have already noticed to the doctrine of the first clause. The spirit of the passage, as an answer to this objection is, Let no one take refuge in the doctrine of the impossibility but that sin should be, and be encouraged himself to become a sinner; for "*Woe unto him through whom the offense cometh.*" For, —

1. There is nothing in this or in any circumstances of a wrong-doer that can lessen his responsibility or take away the guilt of his wrong-doing. If he commits sin it is because he chooses to do it. He desires to sin more than he does to do right, and he follows the prompting of this desire against the dictates of his conscience, and often against both his conscience and his judgment. The very fact that the sinner's conscience condemns him for wrong-doing puts it beyond question that he was without excuse for doing it, and makes it certain that he was fully responsible in the doing of it, and that he is guilty. No man's conscience condemns him for a thing for which he does not know himself to have been responsible; nor for that for which he does not know himself to have been guilty. His conscience would cease at once to condemn if he could know that another was the responsible author of his sin, or even if he could look upon himself as other than the free and voluntary agent of its commission. If he could come to count God the author, or in any sense the doer of his evil deeds, conscience would become silent. He would not be, nor would he apprehend himself to be guilty.

2. The other great lesson which we learn from the second clause of our text is, that the fruit of wrong-doing is evil and only evil to him who commits it. He cannot but eat that fruit. No consequences for good which God will bring out

of his sin, will lessen in the least his punishment. He meant it for evil, and as he meant it so shall it be to him.

This is the teaching of all the Scriptures: " Whatsoever a man soweth that shall he also reap." " Though hand join in hand, the wicked shall not be unpunished." " Behold ye have sinned against the Lord: and be sure your sin will find you out." " Though a sinner do evil a hundred times, and his days be prolonged, yet surely I know that it shall be well with them that fear God, which fear before Him: but it shall not be well with the wicked."

It is true that because sentence against an evil work is not executed speedily, therefore the heart of the sons of men is fully set in them to do evil. But delay to punish is not remission of penalty. The long suffering and patience of God, with sinners, is not forgetfulness of their sins, or a ceasing to hold them in abhorrence. The laws of his government are often left, in mercy, to work slowly; but they are never repealed, never suspended.

SERMON IX.

THE IMPUTATION OF ADAM'S SIN.[1]

ROMANS v. 18, part.—*By the offense of one, judgment came upon all men to condemnation.*

THE Association of last year saw fit — in my absence, and without my consent — to assign to me " The Doctrine of the Imputation of Adam's Sin," as the subject of a sermon to be preached on this occasion. Imputation to whom, the minutes do not state. I have taken it for granted, however, that the meaning was, *to Adam's posterity*.

Inasmuch, also, as the subject was referred to me for a sermon, it is to be presumed that the Association desired a Scriptural, rather than a metaphysical or historical discussion of it.

The doctrine which I am thus to treat I find plainly taught in the words which I have read to you as my text: " By the offense of one, judgment came upon all men to condemnation." This, if I understand the subject, is the exact, as it is the Scriptural statement of the doctrine in question. Sentence of condemnation came upon all men by the offense of one. All men were, by the appointment of God, made subject to the penalty of this one man's one offense. In other words, when Adam sinned, he, by that sin, brought upon all his posterity the doom with which he himself was threatened, and which he himself suffered as a penal consequence of his transgression.

This is the doctrine of the imputation of Adam's sin to his posterity. To judicially subject a child to the punishment, or penal consequences, of his father's sin, is to impute the father's sin to his child. The sin is so set to the child's account that he is made liable to the penalty, and is therefore judicially counted and treated a sinner because of his father's sin. Thus, also,

[1] Prepared and preached for the Boston North Baptist Association, by appointment, as the second in a series of doctrinal sermons, September, 1858.

when the posterity of Adam are, by the appointment of God, subjected to the penal consequences of the sin by which he fell away from holiness. This sin is so set to their account that they are judicially counted and treated as sinners because of it.

Before we proceed to the direct Scriptural argument by which we shall attempt to show that this doctrine is true, let me call your attention to the fact that the principle — that is, the subjecting of certain individuals to the consequences, even the penal consequences of another's acts — has ever pervaded both the natural and providential government of God over this world. No law of nature — that is, no appointment of God in nature — is more clearly established than that by which the physical condition, and oftentimes the moral condition, of a child is determined by some act of his parent in which he had no direct participation. Whole families are not unfrequently made to eat the bitter fruit of a parent's misdeeds which were committed perhaps long before one of the family was born. Sometimes by one deed of guilty license, sometimes by a course of conduct that has been in violation of the laws of his physical system, a parent has brought upon himself and entailed upon his posterity a diseased constitution, that is to them an inalienable inheritance of misery. The glow of health never mantles in beauty over the face of his children, nor can they ever know the thrill of ecstasy with which pure health inspires and elevates and nerves to energy and action the soul that dwells with it in the same body. The father has sinned, and the children inherit the curse. The poison which was taken into the root has spread itself through all the branches of the tree.

The same is true also respecting the moral health of families. Guilty unfaithfulness on the part of parents in the training and education of their children, brings forth its bitter fruit in moral disease and death in the children's history.

If we turn to the Scriptures we find that they again and again declare that this principle is that upon which God has acted in his providential dealings with men. He Himself often placed his treatment of individuals and families and nations on this very ground. He inflicted punishments or bestowed blessings on them because of the action of others. The curse of Ham was, by special providential appointment, made to rest upon his children, and they became servants of servants to their brethren. God assured Abraham that even Sodom should be spared its fearful visitation for the sake of ten righteous persons if they could be found in it. All Israel fell under the displeasure of God, and his anger was kindled against them at Ai, because of Achan's sin. He "took of the accursed thing," and all the people were in consequence counted and treated as transgressors. Eli sinned against God by parental unfaithfulness. His sons in consequence made themselves vile, and the punishment of Eli's sin fell upon all his posterity. "I will judge *his house* forever," said God, "for the iniquity which he knoweth." "There shall not be an old man in thine house forever; and all the increase of thine house shall die in the flower of their age." David sinned in numbering the people of Israel and Judah. By that sin he brought the pestilence upon seventy thousand men and laid them low in death.

Look also at the scene which filled the prophet's eye when he "saw beforehand the sufferings of Christ and the glory that should follow." More than seven hundred years of the future was opened to his vision, and he beheld at that distance, One despised and rejected of men; a man of sorrows, and acquainted with grief. He had done no violence, neither was any deceit in his mouth. Yet it pleased the Lord to bruise Him: He put Him to grief. He was taken from prison and from judgment, and brought as a lamb to the slaughter. He was stricken, smitten of God, and afflicted. Why? Because the Lord laid on Him the iniquity of us all. Therefore "He was wounded for our transgressions, He was bruised for our iniquities; the chastisement of our peace was upon Him; and with his stripes we are healed."

The *principle* here announced — the subjecting of some to the consequences, even the penal consequences of another's conduct — is therefore not unknown, but, on the contrary, it pervades, and ever has pervaded, all the natural and providential government of God over this world.

From this preliminary and general view let us come directly to the doctrine of our text, "The imputation of Adam's sin to his posterity." Let the explanation of the doctrine which we have given be borne in mind continually as we proceed: namely, that we mean by the imputation of Adam's sin to his posterity, their subjection, by the righteous appointment of God, to the penalty of his sin. He stood as the constituted representative of all his descendants. He acted for them; and the whole race had its probation in him. If he should pass the probation and come forth righteous, he would secure a righteous inheritance for all his children. If he should fail in the probation and come forth a sinner, all the race should be counted as having sinned in him, and a judgment of condemnation should rest upon them. His sin should be counted their sin, and his punishment should be visited upon them also.

Perhaps this principle may be made more clear by a simple illustration. An absolute monarch, suppose, has in his gift an office and its accompanying honors, which he determines to make hereditary. He calls a serf or a peasant into his presence, and formally invests him with the office and its honors, and makes them hereditary in the peasant and the family that shall be born of him. He imposes, however, one condition, upon faithful compliance with which all shall depend. If he keep the condition for a certain time then the honor is legally the inheritance of his family. If he fail in the condition, the inheritance is forever forfeited, both for himself and all his family to the latest generation. If now the peasant is faithful in his probation, he is faithful for those whom he thus represents. If he fails in his probation, he fails for them. The penalty of his sin is judicially inflicted on them.

1. That this doctrine is true is evident, first, from the fact that the Word of God explicitly declares it. It would be difficult, if not impossible, to state the doctrine more plainly than it is stated by our text and several passages in its immediate connection. Look at a few of these passages: Ver. 12: "By one man sin entered into the world and death by sin; and so death passed upon all men, for that all have sinned." Ver. 15: "Through the offense of [the] one [the] many are dead." Ver. 16: "The judgment was by one to condemnation," *i. e.*, "By one offense was the sentence of condemnation." Ver. 17: "By one man's offense death reigned by one." Ver. 19: "By one man's disobedience many were made [constituted] sinners." Our text: "By the offense of one, judgment came upon all men to condemnation" [sentence of condemnation].

It should be borne in mind that all these passages are used

by the Apostle as parallel to, but in contrast with others in which he sets forth the doctrine of the imputed righteousness of Christ to believers. This is the doctrine which he had been stating and which he is now illustrating.

In the last verse of the fourth chapter he had taken up the very thought which is expressed in the language of Isaiah, which we a few moments ago quoted, and declared that "Christ was delivered up to death for our offenses;" and in the fifth chapter he goes on enlarging upon the thought and repeating it in new forms and with new emphasis; saying that Christ died for us; that we are justified by his blood; and that we are reconciled to God by the death of his Son. Then, by way of further illustration and enlargement, he lays hold of what he regarded, and what was held among the Jews to be an admitted and clearly taught truth respecting the headship and representative character of Adam in his probation, and respecting the participation of the race in the penalty of his sin. Laying hold of this truth, he makes it throw light upon the great truth he was enforcing; showing that as by one man's disobedience the many were made sinners, so by the obedience of one, many — even all who receive the gift of righteousness — shall be made righteous. In other words, Paul here in these passages illustrates and magnifies the doctrine of justification of believers by the obedience of Christ, by contrasting it with the admitted and understood doctrine of the condemnation of the race by the disobedience of Adam. The common doctrine of that day, and for centuries afterward, among those who held to the teaching of the Scriptures, regarding the effect of Adam's first, i. e., his representative sin, was this, — using the language which is common in Jewish writings, — "Adam was a head to all the children of men; when he sinned, all the world sinned, and his sin we bear; through Adam's eating of the fruit of the tree, all the inhabitants of the earth became subject to the penalty of death."[1] Paul, in the passages before us, takes up these common sentiments which were supposed to be clearly taught in the first chapters of Genesis, and by asserting them in his character of an inspired Apostle, has fixed upon them the stamp of divine indorsement and authority. So closely does he view the paral-

[1] Quoted by Gill on Rom. v. 12. See also *Prin. Theo. Ess.* 1st Series.

lel in the statement of the two doctrines, that if one is set aside both must be. If Adam's sin is not passed over to his posterity, then the righteousness of Christ is not reckoned to believers, who are Christ's seed as the race is the seed of Adam. But if Christ's righteousness does not answer the claims of the law on believers, so that by that righteousness put to their account they may be treated as just or justified; then if they are justified at all it must be by their own personal and inherent righteousness; and the whole scheme of redemption is a nullity, and Christ died in vain so far as all the purposes of an atonement are concerned. But it is by the obedience of Christ that the believing sinner is counted righteous; and therefore it is by the disobedience of Adam that his race are counted sinners. This is the very point of the comparison and the contrast; and in this one particular it is that Adam is here said to be the figure or type of Him that was to come.

Let these passages speak their own language, and there is no mistaking their meaning. It is not till men feel themselves called upon by some theory, or by an unauthorized sense of responsibility to defend the character of God, or shield it from the plain statements of his own word, that passages so clear in themselves become perplexing and obscure.

Ever since the days of Pelagius volumes upon volumes have been written in the exercise of this mistaken care for God's character, or for other reasons, on these passages, with the hope of softening down their rugged plainness. But there they stand as rugged and as plain as ever; like a huge mountain of granite that rears its head to heaven in testimony of some fearful convulsion and upheaving of the earth. The winds, and rain and snows, and thunder and lightning have for centuries spent their fury upon it, in vain. It still stands, and still testifies. So these texts will continue to say and reiterate the saying that, " By the offense of one, judgment came upon all men to condemnation; that through the offense of the one, the many are dead." No criticisms, nor critical emendations; no apologetic explanations for the Apostle; no rhetoric; no mistaken and unauthorized tenderness for the character of God; nor sentimental tenderness for the character of man; no processes of " explaining away," will lessen one iota the stern plainness by which they assert the great and solemn truth that sentence of condemnation has passed upon all men because of the one great sin by which Adam, and the race in him, were plunged into ruin. Our view of the meaning of these passages is confirmed by what we advance as a second argument.

2. The truth of our doctrine is proved by the fact that the Scriptures uniformly represent all the descendants of Adam as being born into the penalty with which he himself was threatened, and which he suffered for his first or representative sin.

The penalty with which Adam was threatened was *death*. "In the day that thou eatest thereof," said Jehovah to him, "*thou shalt surely die.*" In the very day that Adam eat of the forbidden fruit, he died. Lust conceived in him and brought forth sin; and his sin, when it was finished, brought forth death. That which fell upon him, *on that day* as the penalty of his sin, was *death*. He *existed* on earth for seven hundred years after he sinned, but if we receive the Word of God as true, he existed *a dead man*, unless and until he was regenerated by the Spirit of God. Let it be remembered that the dissolution of the body was not once mentioned or recognized in all this transaction as being death. Death, the penalty of his sin, was something wholly independent of bodily existence.

What then is death, we are compelled to inquire, when it is, according to the Word of God, the portion of a man yet in the full enjoyment of bodily existence? The Scriptures furnish an unequivocal answer. "He that heareth my word, and believeth on Him that sent me," says our Saviour, "hath everlasting life, and shall not come into condemnation; but is passed from death unto life." Faith is the instrumentality by which a sinner passes from death unto life. But faith is that by which the grace of God removes a sinner from under condemnation, displeasure, and wrath, and brings him into the favor of God and the enjoyment of pardon. For "He that believeth on the Son of God is not condemned, but he that believeth not is condemned already, and he shall not see life, but the wrath of God abideth on him." To be condemned of God, then, as a sinner, and to be under his displeasure, is to be dead.

Again, the Scriptures declare, "We know that we have passed from death unto life, because we love the brethren. He that loveth not his brother abideth in death." But in another passage we are told that " Every one that loveth is born of God." To be born of God, then, is " to pass from death unto life." An unregenerate man is a dead man. He has no love to God. This is death.

This was Adam's condition the moment he sinned. He was under condemnation, he was under displeasure. The favor of God was lost. He had no love to God remaining. His heart was wicked. He had chosen himself before God, and God abandoned him to himself. And thus he existed *a dead man*, unless — again we say — and until he was regenerated by the Spirit of God, and brought out from condemnation into justification and pardon and favor, by faith in Him who was promised as a Deliverer.

That death, then, which rests upon a man though he exists and moves, and acts and sins, and suffers and enjoys, is composed, according to the Scriptures, of these two elements: entire estrangement and alienation of heart from God on the one hand, and on the other abandonment of God, the loss of his favor. God rejects him, condemns him, and is displeased with him. This is death; and this was Adam's condition the day he sinned. This was his penalty for that one sin.

Now what we say is, that the Scriptures uniformly represent all the descendants of Adam as being *born* into this penalty. The penalty is upon them before they have committed actual personal sin. To be of Adam born is to be under the displeasure and abandonment of God.

" That which is born of the flesh is flesh," says our Lord. And, adds the Apostle, " they that are in the flesh cannot please God." To be " of Adam born " is to be in the flesh. To be of Adam born, therefore, is to be under displeasure of God.

Again, Paul, writing to the Christian Ephesians, and placing himself on the same level with them, says, " We were *by nature* the children of wrath, even as others."

By natural descent from Adam, then, we are abandoned of God and condemned. It would be impossible to state in clearer or stronger language the fact that men are born into penalty. By their very nature they are inheritors of wrath, and are therefore dead as Adam was the day that he sinned. Sin took his life away and left him with nothing but a carnal existence. His nature was from that moment carnal and not spiritual. This nature he sent down to all his offspring; and with the nature the curse that was resting upon it. To be born in this nature is to be a sinner; because none but sinners can be children of wrath. But whence comes this wrath? Why this condemnation? The nature was never on probation, so far as the Scriptures instruct us, but in Adam. For whose sin, then, but his does this curse rest upon this nature and upon all who partake in it?

Now, in the light of this passage we are prepared to look again at the language of those passages which we have already quoted; and we shall see that they derive new force in their direct statement of the doctrine of imputation. In the twelfth verse of the fifth of Romans, Paul says, "By one man sin entered into the world, and death by sin; and so death passed upon all men, *for that* [or *because*] *all have sinned*. "How have all sinned that they should be under death? Actually and personally? Death is on them before they can do this; they are children of wrath by nature. Are they not then counted as sinners, and is not the sin of the great head of humanity imputed to them?

Again, in the nineteenth, verse Paul says, "By the one man's disobedience the many were made sinners." How made sinners? By imitation? By following his example? They are treated as sinners before they can imitate. They are children of wrath by nature. Did they not then stand, representatively, by the appointment of God, in Adam, and when he, the federal head sinned, were not all his descendants, by this sin, made sinners?

The whole gospel scheme is based upon this fact, that men are born into death, or, which is the same thing, into penalty. "Except a man be born again he cannot see the kingdom of God." Regeneration is a birth out of nature into grace; out of carnality, and so out of the curse that rests on the carnal nature, into spirituality; out of death into life. It is a translation from darkness to light, from the kingdom of Satan, or from among the enemies of God into the kingdom of his dear Son. It is being created anew in Christ Jesus unto good works; it is, in fine, passing from death unto life. Regeneration is thus the undoing of Adam's work on his posterity.

It removes original sin. This is the central truth of the gospel system, and it is all based on the truth that men are born into death (*i. e.*, penalty). Hence it is that Paul says of Christ, that if He died for all, then were all dead. He came to a race already lost, already in death, and Himself died, *i. e.*, came under condemnation and felt all the horrors of abandonment of God. He thus died, that as many as should receive the gift of righteousness in Him, might have life, and have it more abundantly. Not only life from the death into which the one man's sin had plunged them, but from the death into which their own personal and actual transgression had plunged them still deeper. Therefore, "if by one man's offense death reigned by one; much more they which receive abundance of grace, and of the gift of righteousness, shall reign in life by one, Jesus Christ." He was thus made sin for us, "that we might be made the righteousness of God in Him."

By the commission of Jesus Christ I am authorized, my hearers, to hold out to you to-day, for your acceptance, this perfect righteousness, that it may take the place before God, and in the eye of his law, of all your sinfulness, and all your personal guilt. By the deeds of the law there shall no flesh be justified in the sight of God. Remaining under law all must remain sinners. But the righteousness of God is by faith in Jesus Christ unto all, and upon all them that believe. Your participation in the ruin of Adam was without your personal consent. It was so by the righteous appointment of God; but your participation in the righteousness of Christ is, by the same righteous Judge, made dependent on your consent, even the consent of faith. Though you are yet children of wrath, both by nature and by personal transgression, if you are not justified in and by the righteousness of Christ, still, God is not willing you should perish. His mercy yearns over you; He has demonstrated it by proofs that even you cannot question. For He so loved the world, this same alienated and cursed and corrupted world, that He gave his only begotten Son, that whosoever believeth in Him might not perish but have everlasting life.

SERMON X.

THE LAW OF PROVIDENCE TOWARDS THE WRATH OF MEN.

PSALM lxxvi. 10.—*Surely the wrath of man shall praise thee: the remainder of wrath shalt thou restrain.*

IF the Bible teaches any one doctrine more explicitly than another, it is the doctrine that asserts the direct special superintendence of God in all the affairs of this world. It does not attempt to unfold to the view of men all the methods of this superintendence, nor to explain to human comprehension all the immediate purposes for which it is exercised, nor the particular reasons by which it is governed. The fact alone is clearly and fully asserted, and everywhere recognized. Indeed the very existence of the Bible, *as the Revelation of God*, is a standing confession and illustration of the doctrine. All its statements of the relations of God to men, and of men to God, are repetitions of it. Every promise it makes to the good, the penitent, and the believing, and every threatening it utters against the impenitent and rebellious, and every claim it makes upon the hearts and services of men, and every charge of unfaithfulness and unworthiness it urges against them, rests upon this doctrine as its foundation, and is pervaded by its admission.

The doctrine of a special and direct providence is the doctrine emphatically of the Bible. It is also, and no less, the doctrine of the human soul. It pervades it and governs it. In all times, among all classes of men, barbarous or civilized, the fundamental idea of a divine direct superintendence has held its sway; and they have not failed in some way to give it scope and manifestation. In idolatrous rites, in prayers, in oaths even, and in superstitious observances, men bear testimony always to the inborn conviction of the presence around and above them of an interested Power upon whose pleasure their destinies are more or less suspended. God has not left Himself without a witness in the hearts of men more than in his Word. The spontaneous prompting of the heart is, as it is also the assertion of the Bible, " His kingdom ruleth over all." In the silent, mysterious, mighty, and minute processes of nature, and in the lives of men, both in the prosperity and adversity of a common and unmarked history, and in the more striking and momentous events of a checkered and uncommon career, whether of individuals or of nations, both the Bible and the human soul recognize and confess without reserve the direct agency of an overruling Power. Men may partially obliterate this sentiment for a time from their hearts, by a cherished and philosophizing skepticism ; or they may deprive it momentarily of an active and direct influence by the indulgence of unholy passions, but the history of the world and the experience of individuals show that the sentiment cannot be wholly eradicated from the soul. One vivid flash of heaven's lightning, or one angry utterance of its terrible thunder, is oftentimes enough of itself to dissipate the most obdurate skepticism and to disarm passion of all its deadening power. The approach of death, by the sudden casualty that compels its instant realization, or by the tempest, or by wasting disease, is almost always sure to reinstate in its control over the mind the thought and the belief of an immediately ruling Providence. The same potent influence is also oftentimes exerted by an hour of serious meditation, when, for the moment, the heart is compelled by some mysterious spell to be honest with itself; and also by those sudden, solemn, unwelcome reflections, by which the realities of a fleeting, but accountable life, and of an approaching judgment, and eternity, rush in upon the soul, and, like the incoming of a mighty wave of thought, carry away all the barriers it had raised for its security against seriousness and concern.

As in the case of individuals, so is it with communities and nations. The sentiment that bears testimony to an overruling God may seemingly die away from the public mind, and lose its power over the public conscience. But it will not remain dormant. Sooner or later it will awaken and assert its sway. The judgments of God in great public calamities ; sudden and pressing dangers to the national safety ; the barbarities of unrestrained brutality, when passion has unrebuked license in public men, and an unscrupulous selfishness is enthroned at the head of affairs in the persons of weak and wicked rulers; the approach of invading foes, or the development of wide-spread and powerful domestic conspiracies, — these and dangers like these, which show how little help is in man, are each enough to arouse and quicken into lively activity the national sentiment of an interested overruling Providence by driving men to that Providence for protection and deliverance. The world's history abounds with demonstrations of this. In this respect it is true, as it is written by the prophet Isaiah, "When the judgments of God are in the earth the inhabitants of the world will learn righteousness." It is enough that when men begin to feel the quicksands of all merely human foundations moving from under their feet, they instinctively grasp after the support of an uncreated hand. And this grasping is the soul's confession of an ever active and observant providence of God. There is no other refuge into which it can flee. The spontaneous cry of the national as of the individual's heart is, when the pressing necessity of overwhelming danger is upon it, "There is no help but in God. The arm almighty, that rules over all, must rule for our safety or we are ruined."

This was the confession of the people of God as it was uttered by the Psalmist in the words of our text. They looked back upon the dangers that had just threatened to overwhelm them, — probably the invasion by the hosts of Assyria, under Sennacherib, — and in view of it, and of their wonderful deliverance, when " God arose to judgment to save all the meek of the earth ;" the language of their hearts was that of inspired truth : " Surely the wrath of man shall praise thee : the *remainder* of wrath shalt thou restrain." In this divine utterance, prompted by the Spirit of God, his people gave expression to both the doctrine of a direct and special providence of God in all the affairs of men, and also *to the law of that providence* in cases like that under consideration. They declared the method of God's providence over the unholy passions of men when they are aroused and directed against a righteous cause or those engaged in maintaining it. The law of God's providence in such cases, as it is here declared, is to permit wicked and violent men to proceed just so far in their wrathful work as will be to his own glory, and then to curb their passions and put them under the strong hand of Providential restraint. But inasmuch as the wrath of man, as here spoken of, has its manifestation only in wicked plans, purposes, and measures ; and as the praise or glory of God is really promoted only by the triumph of truth and righteousness, under his government, the teaching of the text, — that is, the lesson to be learned from this statement of the law of Providence towards the wickedness of violence and passion, — is, that wickedness, planned and perpetrated against a righteous cause, is, under the government of God, made to advance that cause.

Whatever mystery may hang over the problem of the existence of evil in the government of a holy and almighty God, the fact of its existence none question. None question but the history of this world exhibits a protracted and yet unended contest between good and evil. Sin has risen up to oppose holiness ; error often has triumphed over truth ; injustice has often hurled justice from its throne, and ruled in its stead ; right and equity have often been trodden under foot by tyranny and oppression ; brute force directed by wicked hands has come in conflict with moral and intellectual strength and felled it to the earth with savage ferocity. Inalienable and God-given liberty, both civil and religious, has been bound in the fetters of despotism ; and the cry of enslaved millions has gone up from our world into the ears of a righteous God, calling in tones of despairing agony for avenging justice. Crime and cruelty have not only prevailed and disfigured the fairest portions of earth, but they have been patronized and protected by the depositaries of power, and apologized for and defended by the voices and the pens of such as have held high places of influence and respectability.

It has always been so. Wickedness has been a power against goodness. The servants and agents of wickedness have always been arrayed against the cause and the supporters of righteousness. Whenever men have espoused this cause and avowed their allegiance to God in it, wicked men and devils have been arrayed in opposition.

But in the face of all this the teaching of God's Word, as found in our text, is that He will overrule all this wickedness to his own glory, and that wicked opposition itself to the cause that is righteous, shall be made to further the interests of that cause. This we have seen was the declared law of God's providence over the wrathful wickedness of men. Wickedness planned and perpetrated, advances the cause it aims to destroy.

Is the inquiry made, How is this done? By what means does God in his providence turn the wrath of men to his own praise by making their wickedness serve the cause of truth? The answer is given us only in part. The word of God and the history of his dealings with men furnish some particulars in reply. They answer, —

1. That wickedness planned and perpetrated against a righteous cause is made to advance that cause by sometimes calling down directly the avenging judgments of God upon the wicked perpetrators, and thus removing them from the work of opposition and giving the awful sanction of God's manifest interference to the righteous cause.

Recorded instances are not wanting in the history of men when God has thus interposed for a righteous cause and its people. The king of Egypt, at the time of Israel's deliverance from their bondage in that land, has the immortality of a Scriptural execration for his acts of cruelty and wickedness against the rights of God's people, and the cause they were chosen to uphold. Again and again did the avenging judgments of the Almighty fall directly upon him for his wickedness; and when he pressed his proud tyranny to the last limit of divine forbearance, God arose in his majesty and swept him from the earth. God's people were delivered. The cause of righteousness was triumphant. The Lord was magnified in the eyes of both friends and enemies. The haughty and idolatrous Egyptians were taught effectually, that Jehovah was God, and the people of Israel were brought to fear Him and trust in his word and power.

Another noted instance of a direct avenging judgment upon wrathful wickedness, and in furtherance of the righteous cause it sets itself to oppose, is the one to which the Psalm that contains our text is thought to have special reference. The hosts of Assyria came upon Jerusalem and with taunting words against Jehovah demanded its surrender. But the king of Israel sought the interposition of the Almighty: " Lord, bow down thine ear and hear," he prayed; " Open, Lord, thine eyes and see : and hear the words of Sennacherib, which hath sent Rabshakeh to reproach the living God. O Lord, our God, I beseech thee save thou us out of his hand, that all the kingdoms of the earth may know that thou art the Lord God, even thou only." In answer to that prayer God said to the king of Assyria by Isaiah the Prophet, " Because thy rage against me, and thy tumult is come up into mine ears, therefore I will put my hook in thy nose, and my bridle in thy lips, and I will turn thee back, by the way by which thou camest. For I will defend this city to save it, for mine own sake and for my servant David's sake." The fulfillment is briefly told. " It came to pass that night that the angel of the Lord went out, and smote in the camp of the Assyrians a hundred fourscore and five thousand : and when they arose in the morning behold they were all dead corpses."

> " Like the leaves of the forest when summer is green,
> That host with their banners at sunset were seen :
> Like the leaves of the forest when autumn hath blown,
> That host on the morrow lay withered and strown."

In the language of Archbishop Leighton, the hook that God put in Sennacherib's nostrils to pull him back again, was more remarkable than the fetters would have been if he had tied him at home and hindered his march with his army.

The history of the Jews abounds with examples of this kind of interposition against the wickedness of his enemies and the enemies of his people. And it is in their history, if anywhere, we must find the *declared* examples, for it is only in *their* history God has chosen to declare the *directness* of his agency in the affairs of men. The history of the Jews is especially intended to set forth and illustrate the principles of God's government on earth for the support of truth. It is as it were a miniature model, exposing to the view of men the operations of the providence of God on a scale and under circumstances they can comprehend. And all these instances of special interposition in avenging judgments are but illustrations of the general law of Providence which we are considering. He bids us see in these examples his interest in the cause of justice and of right, and his active favor towards it which cannot in other cases be so manifest to our view. For these manifest interpositions are not the usual methods of God's dealing. Ordinarily avenging justice is long delayed. He usually permits men to presume very far upon his forbearance before He rises for strict judgment. He is not willing that any, even the most violent of his enemies, should perish. He waits long that He may be gracious. But from the examples of Scripture we have no right to affirm that He does not, even now, sometimes, according to these examples, visit by sudden and direct avenging judgments the opposers of his will.

Yet this is not, we say, the usual method of his providence. He usually works out a vindication for down-trodden truth and righteousness through the ordinary operation of known and recognized intermediate agencies. Hence we remark, —

2. That the history of God's dealings with men shows us that great wickedness perpetrated against a righteous cause is sometimes made to further it, by God in his providence giving up the planners and perpetrators to be swayed by their passions rather than by prudence. He leaves them to take counsel of their desires rather than of their wisdom. Thus they bring their own cause into bad repute, expose its baseness, and turn the favor of men from it to that which they oppose.

Passion is always blind, and always suicidal. Its aim is gratification, without regard to consequences. But mere selfish gratification blindly pursued, and unchecked by the restraints of reason, is self-consuming. The drunkard, e. g., as soon as the voice of wisdom is drowned by the din of his passion for strong drink, becomes a hopeless prey to this passion. It puts no bounds to itself and has none but gratification, and this, thus blindly pursued, inflames the passion yet more and more till the wretched victim is consumed by its maddening and wasting violence. Thus, too, the passion of avarice, when once it has transformed the man on whom it fastens into a miser, ever urges him on to its gratification, but snatches the very food from his mouth, and the clothes from his body, by which his life would be sustained.

Only give passion its sway without the restraint of wisdom, and soon, like an engine given up to the power that propels it, and left without the regulating hand of the engineer, it rushes madly upon its own ruin. Judas thus took counsel of his desires rather than of his wisdom. Behold the madness to which they drove him. Julian, the apostate, after his career of desperate folly striving against the Almighty, was compelled to honor God and give his influence for the cause he had vainly endeavored to destroy, — " O Galilean, thou hast conquered! " The Jews, when their city was besieged by the Roman general Titus, took counsel only of their desires and unauthorized hopes of miraculous deliverance as in ancient times. Their desires counseled only suicidal madness. So clearly recognized was this principle of the divine administration, that even the heathen marked it, and embodied it in a proverb that has come down to our own times, that " whom the gods intend to destroy they first make mad." Unholy desires overriding and trampling down the judgment and the reason, make this madness. God withdraws the gracious restraints of his hand, and blind passion has its maniac sway. This is the case of every sinner, who, by continued impenitency, rejects the claims of God. The command goes forth from the throne of mercy itself, " Let him alone, he is joined to his idols." No condition of one in this world so fearful. To be given up of God to the idols of his heart, to hasten on to his own destruction under their blind guidance; to be pressed forward to ruin by their urgency — wretched state! The avenging judgment of God already fallen upon the obdurate sinner, who, in the providence of God, becomes his own destroyer!

3. But there is yet a third and perhaps more common way in which great wickedness is, in the providence of God, made to further the righteous cause it aims to destroy. God permits the perpetrators of it so far to succeed in their wickedness that it recoils with reactive violence upon themselves, by arousing a spirit of just opposition and provoking a severe retaliation.

As passion is suicidal, so wickedness is ever reactive. Indeed this reactive characteristic is what gives to wicked passion its suicidal power. It turns its violence back upon him who commits it. In these cases,

> " We still have judgment here; that we but teach
> Bloody instructions, which, being taught, return
> To plague the inventor: this even-handed justice
> Commends the ingredients of our poisoned chalice
> To our own lips."

All wickedness committed against others, especially the just and those sustaining a righteous cause, is injustice. It is the assumption of an unauthorized and unlawful control over the person and right of its victims. But the soul of man is so constituted that it cannot but resent flagrant injustice. It cannot brook it. Sooner or later such injustice will rouse opposition, not only in the heart of the personally injured, but in the hearts of all observers, who are not themselves the injurers either by direct participation in the wickedness, or indirectly by sharing in the gains of the wrong-doing. The injured and the innocent will be moved to indignation, and ultimately to open, determined, and perhaps offensive as well as defensive opposition. God has wisely placed this rein of restraint on the neck of human power, and given to injured humanity the heart to draw that rein down when a just resentment is provoked. The oppressed may long endure the cruel weight that despotism puts upon them, but all experience shows that the elements of reaction will in time be called forth, and there is no vengeance like that of the long injured and oppressed under the hand of unholy power. Who has not heard and read verifications of this truth in instances falling out almost daily in social life, and often in civil? The feeble and timid arm of woman, how often has it been nerved by the burning thought of her injured innocence, her tarnished honor, and her betrayed confidence, to wield with daring and fatal energy the weapons of of death against her betrayer! How often has the throb of manly resentment animated the heart of a slave on whose brow God had set his own signet of freedom, to strike the master, who held him in unholy bonds, dead at his feet! Nor are the instances rare in which a whole community of such slaves have thus vindicated their title to manhood in attempts to tear off the iron grasp of a cruel task-master from their necks. It was the increasing tyranny, and the heavier and heavier burdens laid upon the bondmen in Egypt, that made them at length ready to free themselves at the bidding of God from their enslavers, and become the instruments of their enslavers' ruin. Haman, Mordecai, Jews. It was the same principle at work upon the Commons of England that at last, in 1649, cost Charles the First his life, and exacted such fearful vengeance of the English nobility. In the same principle, likewise, did our own civil freedom and independent national existence have their beginning. Grasping too much, and enforcing her claims with wicked hands, England lost her colonies and her revenues, and was driven to the humiliation of treating with despised dependents as victorious equals. The measures of tyranny were permitted to go so far, and to become so far successful, that they recoiled with increased force upon itself; and thus advanced, with a rapidity we can poorly estimate, the great and holy cause of freedom and righteousness against which it had been arrayed.

Inference. 1. This being the law of providential control of the wickedness of men in all the past, we infer that the friends of any righteous cause have no reason to despair of its success. God does not change. The laws of his providence do not change. In Him is no variableness, neither shadow of turning. He is the same yesterday and to-day and forever. As in the past, so now the law of his providence falls upon and controls in every deed of violence, in every scheme of unholiness, and in every wicked purpose conceived or executed. The cause of righteousness against which the wrath of man is aimed may now, as in former times, seem checked — seem destroyed — crushed out of being; but the law of providence towards the wrath of man, as illustrated in the past, and asserted in God's Word, shows us that it will yet rise and advance, furthered on, even, by the means which had seemed to destroy it. The cause of human freedom, *e. g.*, may be often crushed down. It is the instinctive prompting of the power that opposes it to put forth all its energies to hinder and destroy it. The hand that can lay the iron yoke of slavery upon the neck of man and of woman and bind it there, can also, and will, deal iron blows against him who would remove that yoke and bid the oppressed go free. But its blows will nevertheless be often paralyzed by the interposition of a God who loves righteousness; sometimes it will expend its violence in vain in the blindness of its own passion; and at length, if it continue, it must rouse in banded and desperate hostility the multitudes upon whom its blighting influence directly and indirectly fall. The past few years have given us instances of each of these methods of Divine Providence in dealing against this stupendous wickedness. The slave trade was at a favorable providence-chosen moment suppressed by being put in the rank of piracy, and outlawed by almost the whole civilized world. This is the avenging interposition of Providence in behalf of freedom. The enactment of the Fugitive Slave Law, and the removal of the Missouri Compromise restriction, it does not require great discernment to see, were the acts of men given up to the counsel of their desires, rather than their discretion. What effect has been produced upon every freeman's mind by every instance of the execution of the Fugitive Slave Law? Has not his hatred of slavery been intensified? Has not every slave who has been hunted down on free soil added hundreds to the ranks of committed and active advocates for liberty? The policy that devised and urged that law to its enactment, and gloried in its execution, is revealed to have been strangely, suicidally unwise for its own ends. I need not point out the many evidences we have had, and are having, of the same demented policy that devised and pressed through with such indecent haste the Kansas-Nebraska act. It was designed to open still greater areas to slavery; but freedom will, under the very act itself, snatch them from the grasp of slavery. The wrath of man bent on human oppression, and the civil and religious degradation of millions yet unborn, is in fair prospect of turning to the praise of God in the triumph of the cause of freedom, and of civil, social, and religious elevation. The acts following this, — acts of lawlessness which the barbarous tribes of the wilderness or of the desert would blush to confess as their own; acts of wanton insolence and robbery; acts of treachery, and of systematized anarchy, — these on the free people of a free territory, and then on unprotected and unoffending individuals at the seat of government, acts of lawless violence — and on a senator who dared speak the promptings of a true and noble soul, on him fell the blows of the assassin. And all because the wrathful wickedness of the slave power was rebuked. These indicate the last step to which God permits the wrath of man to go in an unholy cause. It may commit other acts of the same kind. More of its fury may be necessary to sufficiently rouse and fuse the minds of freemen for harmonious and determined action. It has required already thirty years or more of incessant toil, under just such displays, to bring out and sustain a sentiment and a purpose that now begin to give signs of promise. And the law of Providence still operates. The very wickedness against which this law is arrayed has been doing the work that Providence has ordered it to accomplish, and never can the evil become so enormous or defiant that this law cannot reach and govern it: " The wrath of man shall praise thee, and the remainder of wrath shalt thou restrain."

2. It behooves each one to see to it that he is on the side of God and righteousness. He can be so fully only by reconciliation with God — forgiveness through Christ. Otherwise, indulging enmity towards Him, our very enmity must be turned against ourselves, in vindication of Him against whom we are arrayed. All are under bondage of sin, Christ offers us freedom in eternal deliverance ; and whom the Son makes free, is free indeed. The terms are simple, the conditions easy : " Let the wicked forsake his way, and the unrighteous man his thoughts ; and let him return unto the Lord, and He will have mercy upon him, and to our God, for He will abundantly pardon."

SERMON XI.

THE DUTY OF SINNERS TO MAKE THEM A NEW HEART.

EZEKIEL xviii. 31. — *Cast away from you all your transgressions, whereby ye have transgressed; and make you a new heart and a new spirit: for why will ye die, O house of Israel?*

THIS was the command of God to men who were living in sin; yet complaining of the evils which their sins were bringing upon them. They charged these evils as an injustice upon God. "The way of the Lord is not equal," they said. God answers, "Are not my ways equal? Are not your ways unequal?" He charges this home upon them, and shows them that the evils of which they complain are the fruit, not of his injustice, but of their own sins, and of nothing else. If they will break off from these, the tree that bore the evil fruit shall disappear, and they shall have good for evil. Hence He declares, "When the wicked turneth away from his wickedness that he hath committed, and doeth that which is lawful and right, he shall save his soul alive. Because he considereth, and turneth away from all his transgressions that he hath committed he shall surely live, he shall not die." The command of the text is issued with this statement in view: "Cast away from you all your transgressions, whereby ye have transgressed, and make you a new heart and a new spirit: for why will ye die, O house of Israel?" They were thus enjoined to cease doing that which must bring death in its train, and so to turn their hearts away from it as to remain free from its further commission.

God was here dealing with the house of Israel, not simply as Israelites, but as *sinners*. This is clear from the fact that in pointing out to them the cause of their ruin, and showing them their duty, He takes them back to those fundamental principles of moral character and conduct which are common to all moral beings. The command which He utters is based upon these fundamental principles. It is therefore as applicable to all transgressions of the law of God as it was to the house of Israel, and is the measure of the duty which all sinners owe to God and their own souls.

This is the light in which the context compels us to regard the command before us: It is the measure of a sinner's duty. It sets his duty before him in three particulars, by heeding which he will secure both perfection of character and eternal life.

First, the words before us make it plain that it is the duty of sinners to break off from and forsake the commission of all sin: "Cast away from you all your transgressions whereby ye have transgressed."

The fact that this is commanded by the Almighty both reveals and enforces it as an immediate duty. We must admit that his command runs parallel with duty, and measures it in the matter commanded, or we must deny that He has authority to issue the command. If we admit the moral perfection of the divine character and his authority over moral beings, then obedience to every divine command is the solemn and immediate duty of every one to whom the command comes.

Besides, that the command which we are considering is the measure of a sinner's duty, and binds him to cease at once from the commission of all sin, both our own consciences and the Word of God fully proclaim. Every conscience intuitively decides that the wrong-doer ought at once to stop doing wrong. It is a contradiction to every man's moral sense, and an obliteration of the very idea of conscience, to say that it is right for a wrong-doer to continue to do wrong, — no matter what the wrong may be that he is committing. But if it is not right for a wrong-doer to *continue* to do wrong, then it is his duty to *cease* from doing it. It cannot but be his duty to do that which he ought to do, and certainly he ought to do right, and not wrong.

Now this is just what the text commands, in opposition to the theory and practice of every impenitent sinner who justifies himself one moment in his impenitence. The Almighty says to him, " Cast away from you all your transgressions, whereby ye have transgressed." Transgression is sin ; and all sin, whatever it may be, is wrong-doing. To cast away transgression is, therefore, to cast away wrong-doing, — to break off and cease from its commission. In other words, to cast away transgression is to stop doing wrong.

The Bible here joins with and gives new power to conscience and common sense. It is a fundamental element in all its moral teachings that nothing can justify any wrong-doer, whatever his wrong may be, in continuing in it a single moment. Its unvarying and universal command to sinners of every grade is, " Put away from you the evil of your doings from before mine eyes, cease to do evil, learn to do well." " Let the wicked forsake his way, and the unrighteous man his thoughts." " Break off your sins by righteousness, and return unto the Lord."

The gospel lays the obligation still more open, and makes the duty still more plain. By its first great command the duty of repentance is made peremptory and immediate. But an essential element of repentance, that without which there is no repentance in any given instance, is ceasing to do the wrong repented of. This ceasing from doing wrong is as necessary a part of repentance as was the turning of his face homeward, and forsaking the service of the heathen swine-herd, a part of the prodigal son's return to his father's house. When, therefore God, by the gospel, commands all men everywhere to repent, He demonstrates it to be their duty to cease from sin, — to stop doing anything that is wrong.

Conscience and common sense are thus everywhere sustained by the Bible in insisting upon it that it is the duty of sinners to sin no more. In whatever their sin consists they are without excuse for continuing in it for one moment. There is no plea upon which they can justify themselves, unless they can show that wrong is right, and that to do wrong is to do right.

2. Another fact established by the words before us is, that it is the duty of sinners to cease to love that which is wrong, and to love that which is right. In other words it is their duty to cease from the indulgence of unholy affections, and to exercise those affections that are holy. This is established by the second part of the command, " Make you a new heart."

The word "heart," when it is used of the soul, commonly

indicates the affections. A man's heart, in such cases, is his affections; or more properly speaking, the seat of his affections. It is that capability of a moral being by which he loves and hates moral objects. It is, therefore, the centre of his spiritual being, the source of his moral life, and that which gives character to all his moral acts. This what our Saviour teaches when he says, "Out of the heart proceed evil thoughts, murders, adulteries, fornications, thefts, false witnesses, blasphemies." Jeremiah refers to the same central and controlling agency of the heart when he says, "It is deceitful above all things and desperately wicked." Solomon teaches the same truth when he says, "Keep thy heart with all diligence, for out of it are the issues of life."

It is to the moral nature what the physical heart is to the body. It sends to the remotest extremities of it, and to every particle of its substance, that which is to be its life or death, its health or disease. In the one case, as in the other, whether in the spiritual or the physical nature, if the energies which the heart sends out are healthful all is well; if they are poisonous all is ill. That is, if the blood with which the physical heart animates and sustains the body is what it ought to be, the body will have life and health; if it is not what it ought to be, there will be disease, suffering, and death. So if the love with which the spiritual heart animates and sustains the spiritual being is right, such as it ought to be, there will be spiritual health and life; but if it is not what it ought to be, there will be spiritual disease and death.

As the physical heart ought to send out only that which is right and healthful, so ought also the spiritual heart. But there is as much difference in the ought of the one and of the other as there is in their natures. The one is physical, the other is moral. The ought of the one is a physical necessity, that of the other is a moral obligation. The ought in the one case implies no responsibility, necessarily, on the part of the one spoken of. In the other case the ought charges the entire responsibility upon him. Though a man ought to have good blood circulated through his body by his heart, he is not necessarily blameworthy if his blood is altogether bad. But when we say of him that the love or hatred which he indulges towards moral good and evil, or towards anything, when his love or hate is a moral act, ought to be right and not wrong, we understand, and our consciences and judgments will not allow us to understand anything else, but that if it is not right he is guilty. It ought to be right, for it is his duty to love that which is morally good, and to exercise that love which it is right for him to have ; and he is blameworthy if he does not : and it is his duty to hate that which is morally wrong, and he is guilty if he does not. For example, if a man hates truth and justice and fair dealing, he does wrong. He is guilty. It is his duty to love these, and to hate falsehood and injustice and wrong dealing ; and you cannot divest yourselves of the conviction that the whole responsibility of his love or hatred in this matter is upon himself. You cannot but consider him worthy of censure and condemnation if he loves that which it is wrong for him to love, or hates that which he ought to love.

And you are not alone in this judgment. The whole world judges as you do. The whole system of human jurisprudence, and the laws, whether written or prescriptive, that govern in all social and business and civil relations, are based upon this great and universally recognized principle, that a man ought to love right and hate wrong, and that he is guilty, and ought to be treated as guilty, if he does not. The whole world will say that if a man hates righteousness he does wrong. They will say that he ought to love it, and that he is a wicked man and is blameworthy if he does not. In all their intercourse with each other, men act on this principle, and no plea ever justifies any sane man if he loves not that which is right.

Now this, as we understand it, is the ground upon which the command before us rests for its authority over the sinner's conscience. When he is commanded to make him a new heart, if he understands the meaning of the words, his conscience binds him to obedience as a solemn and immediate duty. The Almighty deals with him in perfect harmony with the dictates of his moral sense, and just as he himself deals with those over whom it is his province to exercise moral government. The command, "Make you a new heart," which God lays upon him, is the same that he would lay upon one under his authority when he directed him to cease to love that which is wrong and begin to love that which is right. A change of heart consists in this very thing. A new heart is one that loves right and hates wrong, whereas the old heart loved wrong and hated right. Herein is the necessity for the commanded change. The sinner is doing what he ought not to do, loving wrong and hating righteousness, and he is commanded by Jehovah to do it no more, but do at once what he ought to do, — love that which it is right for him to love, and hate that which he ought to hate.

I find nothing else commanded in the words before us. God was remonstrating with sinners because of their wrong-doing, and nothing else. He justified Himself against their complaints that his ways were wrong, by showing them that his ways were, on the contrary, all right, and theirs wrong. Then He expostulates with them and warns them not to continue in ways that must end in their utter ruin.

The command by which He does this, though in three parts, is all one, and all included in the first member of it: "Cast away from you all your transgressions whereby ye have transgressed." This one clause covers the whole ground, in fact. But lest the minds of those addressed should linger upon the outward acts only of transgression, and not follow the command down into the depths of the soul, the other clause is added, necessarily carrying the mind inward, and requiring it to look upon the transgressions of the heart as well as those of the life. The wrong-doing of both is alike a transgression; that of the latter, indeed, only the development and manifestation of that of the former. So that a sinner cannot put away all his transgressions unless he puts away those of his heart, as well as those of outward conduct. The same reasoning, therefore, by which the obligation of the first command is shown, shows also that of the second. The fact that a wrong state and exercise of the heart are transgressions settles the whole question. A man has no right to transgress with his heart any more than he has to transgress with his head or his hands. Until, therefore, it can be right for a man to do wrong it will be his duty to cease indulging wrong affections and have those that are right. But to cease from having and indulging wrong affections and to have and indulge those that are right is to have a new heart. So far, then, as a sinner does his duty in ceasing from wrong-doing with his heart, and doing right with it, so far he obeys the command before us, and makes him a new heart. This is the same thing that we asserted as one of the lessons of our text, that it is the duty of sinners to cease to love wrong, and to love right.

3. It will not be necessary for us to dwell on the third particular of this command, "Make you a new spirit." If we read the context carefully we shall see that the new spirit required of the sinners here addressed, — and the same is required of all sinners, — is, that they have and be influenced by a right temper of mind instead of a wrong one. The house of Israel were querulous, fault-finding, peevish, and fretful, throwing the blame of their ills, like a peevish and unreasonable child, off from themselves upon God. They were self-excusing and proud. The thing required of them was that they should condemn themselves wherein they were guilty, and be humble in view of their wickedness. In other words, to bring the whole matter to a single point, they were required to be honest and honorable and manly. Their spirit was a dishonest and an unmanly one. All their querulousness and fault-finding and self-excusing and censure of the Almighty, were simple dishonesty. They knew they were in the wrong, but were not willing to confess it. The new spirit God demanded of them was a spirit of honesty and honorableness, instead of that under which they were acting.

The moral sense of every man pronounces in favor of this requirement. No man has a right — and all men feel this to be true — to be dishonest, or to let this evil temper or spirit have sway in his mind. We are brought thus to the same position and proof to which the other clauses of the one command have led us, that because it is the duty of every man to cease to do wrong and to do right, and because it is wrong for him to be governed by a wrong spirit or temper, therefore it is his duty, the duty of every sinner, to cease to have and exercise such a spirit, and to have and exercise one that is honest and true and becoming.

The applicability of this clause of the command to all sinners is manifest the moment that we look at the reasons they give for remaining in sin. There is ever a falsehood at the bottom of them. There is a want of honest dealing with God and their own souls. In one form or another they almost invariably attempt to shift off the responsibility of their guilt from themselves to God, as did the house of Israel. They are querulous, self-excusing, proud, and self-willed, whereas they ought to be self-condemning, humble, and submissive. But to say they ought to be of this temper is to say that it is their duty to be.

Thus we find the divine command before us is, like all other such commands, the measure of the duty of those to whom it is addressed. God commands nothing of sinners that they ought not to do. It is their duty to cease to do wrong and to do right in all circumstances and on all occasions. It is their duty to love righteousness and hate iniquity, whatever the righteousness or the iniquity may be. A man is wicked just to the extent that he loves wickedness. It is the duty of sinners to have and exercise a right spirit in their dealings with all, with themselves, with their fellow men, and with God. They have no right to have, and to be governed by, a wrong spirit. It is their duty, therefore, to cast away from them all their transgressions whereby they have transgressed; and to make them a new heart and a new spirit. God commands them to do it. It is their duty to obey.

1. In the light of this subject we see the awful guilt of impenitence. "God commandeth all men everywhere to repent." To remain impenitent is to disobey this command. And to disobey this command is to determine not to cast away transgressions, not to cease from wrong-doing, but to cling to it, and practice it, though the Almighty commands the contrary.

With what justness did our Lord say to sinners, "Except ye repent, ye shall all likewise perish."

2. We see also the folly and ruinousness of refusing to believe in the Lord Jesus Christ. It is a faithful saying and worthy of all acceptation, that He came into the world to save sinners. If left to themselves they will perish. For, with all their responsibilities on them, and with all the capabilities necessary to make them responsible, they are yet lost, so lost that He only can deliver them. They will continue to love sin, and to commit it, and to have and exercise a wrong and deceitful spirit, unless the Lord Jesus Christ has mercy upon them and saves them, even from their own selves. He only can deliver them from the guilt of ruining their own souls eternally.

The very thing the Saviour came into the world to do was to save sinners from perpetrating their own ruin. He did not come to help them save themselves; by supplementing their powers with grace, — He came to save them. He is able to save to the uttermost, — that is, to the full extent of their need, all that come unto God by Him; and this He will do.

There is thus no help for you but in the grace and mercy of our Lord and Saviour Jesus Christ.

From a higher level than that occupied by the prophet when he wrote our text; a level as much higher as the gospel is higher than the Mosiac law; as much higher as the fulfillment is higher than the type and the promise; as much higher as the blossom and the fruit are in advance of the germ and the bud, I call upon you in the name of Christ to turn at once to Him for mercy. I have his own authority for it that you cannot come to Him in vain. To as many as come, his word is pledged that He will give them power " to become the sons of God." That which, in your own strength, you never will do, — " make you a new heart and a new spirit," — this will be done by his grace for every one who looks for it to the Lord who is exalted a Prince and a Saviour to give repentance and remission of sins. " He that believeth on the Son hath everlasting life; but he that believeth not on the Son shall not see life, but the wrath of God abideth in him."

SERMON XII.

THE SINNER'S INABILITY TO COME TO CHRIST.

John vi. 44. — *No man can come to me, except the Father who hath sent me draw him.*

THIS was said to cavilers. Frivolous and fretful men had heard the discourse of Jesus, regarding his true character, and the great purpose of his mission to this world; and their response to his solemn and momentous words was the querulous and peevish remark, "Is not this Jesus the son of Joseph, whose father and mother we know? How is it then that He saith, I came down from heaven?" As though this had anything to do with the matter in hand, or affected, in the least, the truths that He was uttering, or lessened their importance! Jesus had said, "I am the bread of life; he that cometh to me shall never hunger; and he that believeth on me shall never thirst." He had set this truth forth the day before by a most lively and impressive figure in the miraculous feeding of five thousand persons with "five barley loaves and two small fishes," and had thus, as by other miracles, and by the whole tenor of his life and teachings, rendered it impossible for any candid and serious mind to receive his words with levity or captiousness. Whatever his parentage, or his earthly connections and history, these things were infinitely more than enough to outweigh them all, and put them beyond consideration in estimating the value of his words. They who could think of them, at such a moment, and bring them forward as invalidating his testimony regarding himself, showed themselves irreclaimable triflers and hopelessly insensible to all the appeals that the truth could make to their reasons or their consciences.

Our Saviour's reply to these men was a severe rebuke; and yet it seems deeply tinged with sadness. Looking upon their stupidity and self-conceit, He beheld them both guilty and helpless. They were too thoroughly wedded to folly, and too much in love with themselves, to give any encouragement to hope that they would ever become wise or humble enough to learn the truth, or be willing to seek for it where alone it could be found, in the Son of God. Hence He said to them, "Murmur not among yourselves. No man can come to me, except the Father who hath sent me draw him. Every man that hath heard, and hath learned of the Father, cometh unto me." All who have not thus heard and learned of the Father are too much filled with self-conceit, too little regardful of the truth, too unconcerned about the great interests of their souls, to have any disposition either to heed the lessons of wisdom which the Saviour teaches, or to come to Him for salvation. They cannot come to Him while they continue to cherish self-conceit, and pride, and trifling, and captiousness, and love of sin.

Let us give heed to these sad and too little regarded words of our Lord: "No man can come to me except the Father who hath sent me draw him."

1. I remark, in the first place, that this declaration is in perfect harmony with what the Scriptures throughout teach regarding the helplessness of men who are in sin; and regarding the efficient cause of their salvation, if they are ever saved. Without lessening in the least the guilt of human sinfulness, but, on the contrary, greatly enhancing it, the Scriptures represent all men as finding so much pleasure in sin, and as loving it so well, and being so desperately devoted to it, that they are in absolute hopelessness unless gracious influences come upon them, causing them to taste somewhat of the bitterness of the cup that sin puts to their lips, turning their love into hatred of it and winning their devotion to holiness in its stead. The gist of their teachings on this subject is contained in those noted words of the Apostle Paul, so full of meaning, reaching so far down into the secret recesses of the soul, and revealing so clearly the active cause, and the fearful responsibility, of sinful preferences and conduct. "The carnal mind is enmity against God; for it is not subject to the law of God, neither indeed can be. So, then, they that are in the flesh cannot please God." "The natural man receiveth not the things of

the Spirit of God: for they are foolishness unto him; neither can he know them, because they are spiritually discerned." Our Saviour's words to Nicodemus are of the same import: " Verily, verily, I say unto thee, except a man be born again, he cannot see the kingdom of God."

This is the condition of men who are under the dominion of sin. While they are under this dominion, and give themselves up to its sway in their hearts and over their lives, they cannot understand and feel the force of divine truth, nor be conformed in life to its requirements. While they are cherishing sin, and giving themselves up to the indulgence of it, they cannot desire to be delivered from it; nor can they come to Christ, either for salvation or discipleship and service.

Not only so, they not only cannot come to Christ while they are in such a state of mind, but they will always remain in this state of mind unless God delivers them from it by the power of his grace. If men are ever saved from sin it is by the gracious interposition of God in their behalf. They are graciously drawn to the Saviour by the Father who sent Him. This is the uniform teaching of the Scriptures regarding the moving and efficient cause of a sinner's salvation. There is no other such cause but the influence of God's grace turning him from sin, and drawing him to Jesus Christ as a Saviour. Until God sends down this influence and sheds it upon the sinner's heart by the Holy Spirit, he remains in love with sin, and averse to holiness. He does not want the salvation that is offered to him in Jesus Christ, and he will make no effort to secure it.

A few passages of the Scriptures touching this point will indicate with sufficient distinctness their general drift, and show their entire harmony with the words of the Saviour that are in our text: " Except the Father who sent me draw him." " As many as received Him," so says the evangelist John, " to them gave He power to become the sons of God, even to them that believe on his name: who were born, not of blood, nor of the will of the flesh, nor of the will of man, but of God." The Apostle James says of the Father: " Of his own will begat He us, with the word of truth." The Apostle Paul, writing to the Ephesians says: " You hath He made alive, who were dead in trespasses and sins. For by grace are ye saved through faith; and that not of yourselves: it is the gift of God: not of works, lest any man should boast. For we are his workmanship, created in Christ Jesus unto good works." And to Titus he writes: "Not by works of righteousness which we have done, but according to his mercy He saved us, by the washing of regeneration, and renewing of the Holy Ghost, which He shed on us abundantly through Jesus Christ our Saviour."

It is not necessary to quote further passages of this description. The Bible abounds with them, and all its teachings respecting the elements of a sinner's salvation, and the manner and causes by which he is saved, positively declare, or distinctly imply the same things. Salvation is gracious: Jesus Christ is the author, as well as the finisher of each believer's faith; if men are left to themselves, and not convinced of sin, and renewed by the Holy Spirit, they remain in impenitency and unbelief.

Hence it is that we find that the Apostles and all inspired preachers of the gospel went to their work hoping for success in winning men to Christ, and saving them from sin, only through the special intervention of God in bestowing the convicting and converting influences of the Holy Spirit on those to whom they preached. Their spirit of dependence on God was always like that which Paul manifested when he rebuked the Corinthians for their partisan and man-worshipping spirit in making, some, one minister of Christ; and some, another, their spiritual head; and ascribing to him the saving efficacy that followed his preaching. "Who then is Paul, and who Apollos, but ministers by whom ye believed, even as the Lord gave to every man? I have planted, Apollos watered; but God gave the increase;" and like that which he showed when he wrote to Timothy respecting those for whom he was laboring: "If God peradventure will give them repentance, to the acknowledging of the truth; and they may recover themselves out of the snare of the devil, who are taken captive by him at his will."

Hence, also, it was that they went forth to their work with much and earnest prayer; and earnestly seeking to secure the prayers of other Christians in their behalf. Their writings show clearly that they had no hope in any other instrumentality, if the instrumentality of prayer were not employed. They never forgot the lesson that the Lord taught them when

He directed them to "remain in Jerusalem until they were endued with power from on high;" and then, in answer to their united and continued supplications, poured out his Spirit upon them, and upon those who heard them on the day of Pentecost. From that hour onward their own prayers went up without ceasing to God for his blessing upon their labors, and their constant exhortation to other believers was, " Brethren, pray for us that the word of the Lord may have free course and be glorified." Their own prayers, and their earnest entreaties for the prayers of their brethren were the same confession, in another form, that Paul made to the Corinthians, that nothing they could say or do would bring any man to repentance, and the acknowledging of the truth, if God should withhold the gracious influence of his Spirit. They were the expression of a solemn conviction that never left them, nor became faint and uncertain in their minds, that Jesus Christ was exalted a Prince and a Saviour, to give repentance, as well as remission of sins ; and that nothing but his grace could open any sinner's heart to receive the truth.

2. I remark again that the experiences of converted men, as they are given in the Scriptures, are in harmony with these words of our Saviour. They all acknowledge a depth and desperateness of sinfulness that made them powerless without divine grace ; and ascribe their recovery to holiness — their coming to God and salvation — to the fact that God drew them and made them "willing in the day of his power." God saw them in their guilt and helplessness; He had thoughts of mercy toward them ; He came to their deliverance ; He renewed them by his Spirit ; He delivered them from the power of darkness, and translated them into the kingdom of his dear Son.

The Psalms especially, and the Epistles, abound with the expressions of such experiences. Both Psalmists and Apostles are constantly looking back to a period of guilty helplessness, when they were without God and without hope, and finding in their deliverance from that fearful state, cause for overflowing gratitude and never-ceasing thanksgiving. Look at a few of these expressions : David says of God, " He brought me up also out of a horrible pit, out of the miry clay, and set my feet upon a rock and established my goings. And He hath put a new song in my mouth, even praise unto our God." "He sent from above, He took me, He drew me out of many waters. He delivered me from my strong enemy, and from them which hated me: for they were too strong for me." "Thou hast delivered my soul from death."

The Apostle Paul, referring to his own conversion in particular, says: "God, who commanded the light to shine out of darkness, hath shined in our hearts, to give the light of the knowledge of the glory of God in the face of Jesus Christ." This was the method of his salvation. Up to that time he was, he intimates, in the same condition as those whom he mentions in the verse but one before this, "In whom the god of this world hath blinded the minds of them who believe not, lest the light of the glorious gospel of Christ should shine unto them." For, as he says in another place, "We were by nature the children of wrath even as others — among whom we all had our conversation in times past in the lusts of our flesh, fulfilling the desires of the flesh, and of the mind." Contrasting his present with his past, when he was writing to the Corinthians he exclaimed, "By the grace of God I am what I am; and his grace which was bestowed upon me was not in vain." And with the same contrast in his mind he says to the Galatians, "It pleased God, who called me by his grace, to reveal his Son in me."

With the mind that he had when he started for Damascus he could not know the Son of God, nor come to Him for light and salvation. But God called him by his grace. God arrested him in his career of guilt. God drew him to Jesus Christ, and revealed to him the glory and excellency of his Son.

The other writers of the New Testament express themselves in the same strain. There is no need to quote their words further. Every one traces all his salvation back to the mercy of God in coming to his deliverance when he was guilty and helpless and ruined; and drawing him by the gracious influence of his Spirit to the Redeemer, not only for salvation but to learn of Him, to receive Him as the manifestation of God, and to serve Him with the willing consecration of an all-absorbing love.

Nor, we may remark in passing, has Christian experience

changed. It is the same still. Where there is a Christian experience there is a past of wretchedness and guilt and helplessness. The mind looks back to it, as the Psalmist did to the horrible pit and the miry clay from which none but God could deliver him; and, as the Apostles did, to the time when they were dead in trespasses and sin, and none could bring them to life but God; to the time when they were in darkness, blinded by the god of this world, and none but God could shine into their hearts to give the light of the glory of God in the face of Jesus Christ. They are conscious of a contrast between their present and their past which was not wrought by the will of the flesh, nor by the will of man, but by God Himself. As they think of this contrast they are constrained to say as Paul said when he looked at it, "By the grace of God I am what I am."

Watts has gathered up and put into words, in some of his richest hymns, the emotions and sentiments which all believers at once recognize as their own. Looking back to the ruin to which he was hastening he exclaims:—

> "Lord! I adore thy matchless grace,
> Which warned me of that dark abyss,
> *Which drew me* from those treacherous seas,
> And bade me seek superior bliss."

Looking at his present state among the saved, and a guest at the festal board of his Lord, he cries:—

> "Why was I made to hear thy voice,
> And enter while there's room,
> When thousands make a wretched choice,
> And rather starve than come?

> "'Twas the same love that spread the feast,
> That sweetly drew me in;
> Else I had still refused to taste,
> And perished in my sin."

3. I remark again that the words of our Saviour which we are considering, are in harmony with the observation and experience of men in other things besides those that are religious, and that pertain immediately to the salvation of the soul. They observe daily in others, and experience it in themselves, that a man in one state of mind cannot do the things to the doing of which another state of mind is absolutely essential.

A man that is angry with another, e. g., and cherishing a desire and purpose to injure him, cannot, at the same time, love him, and be seeking to do him good. A child that is disobedient in heart towards his parents, and wholly given up to seeking his own pleasure regardless of them, and of their will, cannot at the same time be an obedient and dutiful child. A man that is thoroughly dishonest and giving himself up to unscrupulous dealing in all his transactions with men, cannot, with such a disposition, be honest, and love and earnestly desire to practice fair-dealing. No man is stumbled, or finds anything out of the common line of men's thoughts, in the words of the Apostle Peter, when, speaking of grossly sensual and licentious men, he says, "Spots they are, and blemishes, sporting themselves with their own deceivings while they feast with you: having eyes full of adultery, and that cannot cease from sin."

In all these cases we recognize a guilty inability. The angry and revengeful man must cease from anger and revengefulness, before he can treat his enemy rightly. The disobedient and undutiful child must come out of a disobedient and undutiful frame of mind or he cannot treat his parents as he is required to treat them. The dishonest man and cheat cannot be honest and true while he is governed by the principles that now control his life. The sensualist and adulterer cannot cease from sin so long as his sensualism has dominion over him.

Nor do we, in any of these cases, find any alleviation of guilt, or any lessening of responsibleness, in this inability. On the contrary, the greater the inability the greater the guilt, and the more fearful the responsibility. We do not think of excusing them on account of their inability; but we condemn them with greater severity the greater their inability becomes. The severest and most denunciatory of all our censure of men is that which we feel, and which we cannot help but feel, towards him who has so long and so wholly abandoned himself to dishonest practices, and to the sinful indulgence of his passions, that duplicity and cheating and sensuality have become, as we say, a part of his very being. Our whole moral nature loathes him. We can no more count him guiltless and irresponsible, than we can approve of wrong as wrong, and honestly pronounce that to be right which we know to be wrong.

But how is it with men in their relations with God? What

is his own testimony regarding them? "Their heart," He says, "is deceitful above all things, and desperately wicked." That is, they themselves, as God sees them, are thus deceitful and wicked. For we must guard against a not uncommon mistake of laying off upon our hearts what belongs to our very selves. If a man's heart is deceitful and wicked, it is he himself, as God sees him, that is deceitful and wicked.

Again, Paul, speaking for God, and by the inspiration of the Holy Spirit, says, "We have proved, both Jews and Gentiles, that they are all under sin; as it is written, There is none righteous, no, not one: there is none that understandeth, there is none that seeketh after God."

This is the state of a sinner's mind towards God. His heart is turned away from God and holiness. The spirit of disobedience to God is in his heart, and his whole life is animated with either a fixed hostility to God's authority, or a senseless disregard of it and of his requirements, that shows that God is not in all his thoughts, and that the doing of God's will is no part of his concern.

Can he come to Christ in this state of mind? Coming to Christ is not an act of the body, but of the soul. For this to come to Christ there must be mental and spiritual exercises. There must be sorrow for sin, and desire for holiness. There must be a casting out of the spirit of disobedience to God and disregard for Him, and in its place there must be the spirit that desires to obey and to please Him. The spirit of self-serving and self-trusting, that puts him who indulges it above the requirements of God, above his authority, above his all-sufficiency, must be taken away, and humility and faith must take its place. For faith is the act itself of coming to Christ; and faith is trusting God instead of self; it is resting in his sufficiency rather than in the sufficiency of self. It is the abandoning of all reliance on self and on sin for help and happiness, and resting only in Christ for them.

But does a sinner ever come into this state without the convincing and converting influences of God's Spirit? Does he ever break off his sins by righteousness and turn to the Saviour unless he is moved thereto by the grace of God? On the contrary, does he not remain unconcerned in his sins till the Spirit reproves him of them? Does he not love his sins and abide in them, until God gives him a new heart? or, lest we should deceive ourselves with words, until God graciously brings him to be willing to stop being and doing wrong, and causes him to desire to be and to do right?

If, then, men are so evilly disposed that they will always reject God, and always rebel against Him, unless a power above them comes down and saves them from themselves by turning their hearts away from that to which they ought not to be devoted — to which they have no right to be devoted, and influencing them to do that which they ought to do, and which it is wrong for them not to do, — is there anything strange, anything that lessens the responsibility and guilt of sin and impenitence and unbelief, when our Saviour says, "No man can come to me except the Father who hath sent me draw him?" The *cannot* is of the same nature as that which we are continually recognizing in the ordinary relations of life. It is the cannot of an evil disposition that is not willing to do right, and therefore one which can never palliate guilt, nor take away responsibility. It is a cannot that waits upon and finds all its strength in *I will not!* It is a cannot, therefore, for which we ourselves are wholly responsible and alone guilty; and at the same time it is one that nothing but the regenerating influence of the Spirit of God ever removes. It is not the cannot of one who wants to come to Christ, but of one who does not want to come to Him. The not wanting to come to Him is the guilty thing that God's grace must remove, or the sinner is lost. The cannot of our text does not apply, I repeat, to any one who wants to come to Christ. If one wants to come to Him he is already drawn by the Father. If he wants to come to Christ it is his privilege now to accept as true, and as intended for him, the words of the glorified Redeemer in his last verbal message to men: "The Spirit and the Bride say, Come. And let him that heareth say, Come. And let him that is athirst come. And whosoever will, let him take the water of life freely."

SERMON XIII.

CHRIST IN THE OLD TESTAMENT.

LUKE xxiv. 27, 44.—*And beginning at Moses and all the Prophets, He expounded unto them in all the Scripture, the things concerning Himself. And He said unto them, These are the words which I spake unto you while I was yet with you, that all things must be fulfilled, which were written in the law of Moses, and in the Prophets, and in the Psalms, concerning me.*

THE Evangelist John tells us that there were many things in the life of Jesus which were not written. Many of his words were spoken for those only who heard them. Others were spoken not to be recorded in the precise form in which He uttered them, but to reappear in the writings of the Apostles in general precepts, or in the light of a fuller doctrinal development after his death. We have no reason to believe that the Evangelists have recorded all the instances in which He spoke the words that are alluded to in the text. There is no doubt that He often taught his disciples the great and fundamental truth that the predictions of the Old Testament regarding the Messiah were to have their fulfillment in his death and resurrection. A few of these instances are given in the gospel narratives; and they are so plain and unmistakable that we wonder how their minds could have remained so darkened on the subject; and how they could have been so unprepared for those great events when they occurred. His language appears to us to be too full and too definite not to have been clearly understood: "Then He took the twelve and said unto them, Behold, we go up to Jerusalem, and all things that are written by the prophets concerning the Son of Man shall be accomplished. For He shall be delivered unto the Gentiles, and shall be mocked and spitefully entreated, and spitted on: and they shall scourge Him and put Him to death: and the third day he shall rise again." This is very plain, and is a specimen of his method of dealing with his disciples during the latter part of his ministry, "while He was yet with them." And yet they did not understand what He meant. For it is added in the next verse, "And they understood none of these things: and this saying was hid from them, neither knew they the things which were spoken." Their difficulty was that they had formed, and they were cherishing certain false ideas regarding the character and work of the promised Messiah, and these hid from their minds the truth which their Lord declared to them. And it was not until after his resurrection that these false ideas could be dislodged. The disciples clung to the notion that the Messiah Himself was to abide with them forever. They knew that an atoning sacrifice was to be made for the sins of men; but they would not receive the thought that the Messiah Himself was not only to offer, but to be that sacrifice. It was to compel them to receive this single truth that He did what the Evangelist relates a few verses further on: "Then opened He their understanding that they might understand the Scriptures, and said unto them, Thus it is written, and thus it behooved the Christ to suffer, and to rise from the dead the third day; and that repentance and remission of sins should be preached in his name among all nations, beginning at Jerusalem."

It was never absent from our Saviour's mind that his coming, his life-work, and his death and resurrection were all in exact accordance with the predictions of the Old Testament Scriptures. From first to last He plainly regarded Himself, and his work for sinners, as the great central thought of the Old Testament. It was all written with distinct reference to Him; and each part of it, if read without Him in mind as its great fulfillment, would be, if not meaningless, yet shorn of its divine dignity and its real importance.

In that walk with the two disciples, as they went to the village of Emmaus, Jesus did for them what He did for the twelve after the two had returned to them with the glad tidings that He was indeed risen from the dead, and that He had appeared to them and talked with them. "Beginning at Moses, and all the Prophets, He expounded unto them in all the Scriptures the things concerning Himself." It was in this manner, in part at least, that "He opened their understanding, that they might understand the Scriptures."

The threefold division of the Scriptures which is here made

was the common one in the time of our Saviour. The "Law of Moses" included the whole of the Pentateuch, or the "Five Books of Moses," as they are now commonly designated. The "Prophets" comprised the Book of Joshua, Judges, Kings, Chronicles, and all the Prophets except the Book of Daniel. The Psalms, the Book of Daniel, and such of the sacred writings as were not included under the two preceding heads, — "the Law" and "the Prophets," — formed the third class, and were called the "Holy Writings" by way of special eminence. When, therefore, our Saviour uttered the words of our text, He affirmed that all the Scriptures, every division of them, contained predictions regarding Himself and his work; and what He did for the disciples when He began from Moses, and from all the Prophets, and expounded unto them in all the Scriptures the things concerning Himself, was to take up each division of the sacred writings and show what in each one was written concerning Him and unfold its true meaning, and point out its fulfillment in Himself. He took them back to the Garden of Eden, and quoted to them the words which were spoken in the ears of the fallen pair; and which brought the first faint gleams of the far-distant morning into the darkness that had settled down upon the world through their transgression. Then as never before the disciples were made to apprehend the deep spiritual meaning, and the far-reaching import of those words: "I will put enmity between thee and the woman, and between thy seed and her seed; he shall bruise thy head and thou shalt bruise his heel." Then as never before they began to understand something of the greatness of the promise made to Abraham, and something of the purpose of his calling, and of the founding of the Jewish nation. The littleness of thought in which they had been educated, and which made the Jewish nation, and everything Jewish to their minds, an end in itself, began to be displaced; and the largeness of God's purpose, that took in the whole world and all time, began to dawn upon their minds, when Jesus quoted to them the words of Jehovah to Abraham, "In thee shall all the families of the earth be blessed," and showed them that the only real and true fulfillment of these words was in Himself, and in what He had done for the world in making atonement for its sins and becoming its Intercessor. Then, as never before, they were enabled to know the purpose of God in that wonderful series of interventions by which the descendants of Abraham, in the tribe of Judah, had been kept distinct from all other people, and their nationality preserved to them through so many hundred years — even after the ten revolted tribes had forever disappeared — in spite of so many influences outside of themselves, and in spite of so many suicidal acts on their own part, calculated to destroy it. All became clear and consistent when the Lord quoted and unfolded the meaning of that wonderful prediction of the patriarch Jacob in giving his dying blessing to his sons: " To Judah he said, The sceptre shall not depart from Judah, nor a law-giver from between his feet, until Shiloh come; and unto him shall the gathering of the people be."

All these passages, and we know not how many more, were brought before the minds of the disciples, from the first book of the Old Testament, and they were made to see how many were the things that were written concerning Himself, even in the dawning of time, and in the earliest of all writings.

In like manner, passage after passage was quoted to them from the other books of Moses, and from the Prophets, and from the Psalms, until they were enabled to see the whole history of Jesus of Nazareth, from his miraculous conception to his crucifixion and resurrection, all clearly delineated in the books that had been written for hundreds and thousands of years before this history passed from the divine purpose into actual realization. Thus He showed them the meaning of the strange words of the prophet Isaiah, written more than seven hundred years before; and their yet stranger fulfillment in his own miraculous origin: " Behold a virgin shall conceive, and bear a son, and shall call his name Immanuel!" Thus, too, he made them understand, what they had never clearly comprehended before, the blessing which the prophet Micah pronounced upon the little and hitherto insignificant village of Bethlehem. The prophet looked down through many centuries, and saw the stable and the manger which furnished shelter and a resting-place for the new-born Messiah and his mother in Bethlehem, when " there was no room for them at the inn." Then the prophets wrote, " And thou Bethlehem Ephrata, though thou be little among the thousands of Judah, yet out of thee shall He come forth unto me that is to be ruler in Israel; whose goings forth have been from of old, from everlasting."

And thus He went on through all the Scriptures, till the disciples clearly saw how utterly erroneous had been all their previous notions regarding the life and character of the Christ; notions that they, in common with all the Jewish people, had imbibed from the false teachings of their learned men, who had perverted the divine word by their false interpretations, and covered its plain utterances out of sight by their own fanciful speculations and baseless assertions. Then, for the first time, the disciples saw the fitness of their Lord's method of life, — his humility, and unostentatious devotion to his lowly work, and its harmony with the predictions of the prophet when he wrote of Him as " a man of sorrows, and acquainted with grief ; as despised and rejected of men ; appearing to them as a root out of dry ground, having no form nor comeliness ; so that when they saw Him, there was no beauty that they should desire Him." Then for the first time they began to apprehend the true meaning of those dark passages, both in the Psalms and in the Prophets, which would not bend to the prevalent theories of a grand and ever-triumphant Messiah, coming forth and abiding in all the pomp and prosperity of an all-conquering hero. As our Saviour read to them the twenty-second Psalm, beginning, " My God, my God, why hast thou forsaken me," and containing such words as these, " All they that see me, laugh me to scorn ; they shoot out the lip, they shake the head, saying, He trusted on the Lord that he would deliver him : let him deliver him, seeing he delighted in him. . . . . For dogs have compassed me ; the assembly of the wicked have inclosed me ; they pierced my hands and my feet. I may tell all my bones : they look and stare upon me. They part my garments among them, and cast lots upon my vesture." As He read this, and then turned over to the sixty-ninth Psalm and read, " Reproach hath broken my heart, and I am full of heaviness : and I looked for some to take pity, but there was none ; and for comforters, but I found none. They gave me also gall for my meat ; and in my thirst they gave me vinegar to drink ; " as the Lord read these startling passages to his rapt disciples, and made them understand that they all pointed to Him, and that they had all been fulfilled in Him, how vividly the scenes in the garden of Gethsemane, and on Calvary came back again into their minds; and in what new and glowing light they began to think again of those scenes, and to comprehend their awful meaning! Those scenes were now no longer mere chances that had befallen their Master. They were no longer mere incidents in his life; incidents which they had sadly thought might have been avoided if their Master would only have been governed by their wishes, and come forth with his omnipotence, and in vengeance, against his enemies and persecutors. These scenes were no longer mere incidents in the life of their Lord, but they now became, to the minds of the disciples, consistent and necessary parts of one great and inseparable whole; portions of the divine plan that had stood written for ages on the pages of inspiration, and had now come out in exact accordance with that plan, and in fulfillment of the eternal purpose of God.

And then when their Lord came to the fifty-third chapter of the prophecies of Isaiah, and read those most wonderful of all prophetic words, " Surely He hath borne our griefs, and carried our sorrows; yet we did esteem Him stricken, smitten of God, and afflicted. But He was wounded for our transgressions, He was bruised for our iniquities: the chastisement of our peace was upon Him; and with his stripes we are healed. All we like sheep have gone astray; we have turned every one to his own way; and the Lord hath laid on Him the iniquity of us all..... He is brought as a lamb to the slaughter, and as a sheep before her shearers is dumb, so He opened not his mouth..... Yet it pleased the Lord to bruise Him; He hath put Him to grief: when thou shalt make his soul an offering for sin, He shall see his seed, He shall prolong his days, and the pleasure of the Lord shall prosper in his hand." When our Lord read these words to his disciples, and made them understand that these also all had their fulfillment in Himself, and that they gave the true meaning and purpose of his sufferings and death, then, for the first time they apprehended the doctrine of an atoning Messiah, and saw clearly that, " thus it was written, and thus it behooved the Christ to suffer, and to rise from the dead the third day." To such of them as had been the disciples of John the Baptist, a new and glorious light spread over those once strange words of their former master, as he looked upon

Jesus and said, "Behold the Lamb of God that taketh away the sin of the world!" They now began to comprehend the true import of those words of John the Baptist, and to know something of the manner in which their Lord fulfilled them. With this comprehension came also the germs of new thoughts regarding the meaning of all that sacrificial system that God had ordained, and under which they had been brought up and educated. These germs of thought were not then fully matured; it took years to mature them fully. But the disciples began then to apprehend what Paul so fully unfolded afterwards in the Epistle to the Hebrews, that all the sacrifices and rites of that dispensation were but types and prophecies of the great sacrifice which Isaiah so clearly foresaw and foretold, and which had now been accomplished under their own eyes in the crucifixion of their now risen Lord.

It is not unlikely that while our Lord was thus "opening the understanding of his disciples, and expounding unto them in all the Scriptures the things concerning Himself," He brought before their minds some of those wonderful passages in the Old Testament that were written by the prophets, who beheld not only the sufferings of the Christ, but also the glory that should follow those sufferings in a reward of eternal greatness and majesty to Himself, and in the salvation and eternal blessedness of a multitude that no man can number from all the nations and kindreds of the earth. If He did so, then He told them the true meaning of those words in the ninth chapter of Isaiah, which have no meaning, and can never be satisfactorily interpreted, saving as they are understood as referring to the Messiah, and as fulfilled in Jesus of Nazareth: "For unto us a child is born, unto us a Son is given; and the government shall be upon his shoulder; and his name shall be called Wonderful, Counselor, The Mighty God, The everlasting Father, The Prince of Peace. Of the increase of his government and peace there shall be no end, upon the throne of David, and upon his kingdom, to order it, and to establish it with judgment and with justice from henceforth even forever." When the disciples heard this, and learned that it was all said of their crucified but risen Lord, they began to comprehend something of the significance of his resurrection, and to have some faint glimpses of the glory and dominion to which it was the fitting prelude. It was a preparation for them to hear those grand words from their Lord which constituted his final commission to them, and to all who should come after them in the ministerial office : "And Jesus came and spake unto them, saying, All power is given unto me in heaven and in earth ; Go ye therefore, and teach all nations, baptizing them in the name of the Father, and of the Son, and of the Holy Ghost; teaching them to observe all things whatsoever I have commanded you : and, lo, I am with you alway, even unto the end of the world." It was a preparation also for their hearing those words so full of judicial majesty and authority, which are given, some of them by Luke, and some of them by Mark : "Repentance and remission of sins must be preached and in my name among all nations : Go ye into all the world and preach the gospel to every creature. He that believeth and is baptized shall be saved ; but he that believeth not shall be damned."

Such are a few of the many things that were written in the "Law of Moses," and in the "Prophets," and in the "Psalms," concerning the promised and predicted Christ; and· which Jesus of Nazareth appropriated to Himself, and declared that they had their fulfillment in Him alone. These were some of the passages which He quoted and opened to the minds of his disciples when He "expounded unto them in all the Scriptures the things concerning Himself." They embrace all the great salient points of sacred history, and unfold and interpret the purpose and intention of God in ordering and watching over that history, from its first dawning in the garden of Eden, through all the vicissitudes of the descendants of Abraham, and down to the fullness of time predicted for the coming of the Promised Seed who should bruise the serpent's head and redeem a fallen world, and open to the ruined race a way to eternal life.

In view of this summary of the teachings of the Old Testament and their fulfillment in the life and death and resurrection and character of Jesus of Nazareth, and in view of the interpretation which He himself put upon them, his mission, his words, and his religion, become matters of the gravest and most solemn moment. His mission becomes the fulfillment of an eternal purpose. It was the coming forth of Him who was from the days of eternity. He is no mere man. He is the eternal God become flesh. His mission is the central thought in all divine plans for this world, the great event for which all other events were arranged, to which all preceding events looked forward, and for which they were a preparation; to which all succeeding events look back, and are its interpretation, — the steps of its progress towards final triumph and glory.

His words become the words of the infinite God; and they are clothed with all divine majesty and authority. They are pure truth; the revelations of the divine will; and of the divine purpose yet awaiting fulfillment towards this world, and towards the men of this world in the world that is to come.

His religion becomes the one and only religion of God among men. It is that by which alone all who have pleased God, and been saved from his wrath, and from the punishment due to their sins have governed their lives, which they have cherished in their hearts, and to which they have conformed their characters. It becomes the only religion by which men can now serve God and be accepted by Him. Its precepts are full of authority, and must be obeyed. Its rites are of God, and no man may set them aside, or tamper with them. Its spirit is the spirit of heaven; and no man can hope for heaven saving as he cherishes it in his own soul. Its sacrifice is the only sacrifice for sin, the only atonement. Its Intercessor is the only advocate and mediator of sinful men with a holy God.

This review of the teachings of the Old Testament regarding the Christ, and this fulfillment of them in Jesus of Nazareth, intensifies, therefore, every claim of the gospel, and augments immeasurably the responsibility of those to whom the gospel is preached. Every sentence is an urging of that pregnant question of the Apostle to the Hebrews, " How shall we escape if we neglect so great salvation ? " Every sentence confirms those words of Peter to the Jewish Sanhedrim, " Neither is there salvation in any other; for there is none other name under heaven given among men, whereby we must be saved." Every sentence enlarges and gives a broader meaning to that encouraging declaration of the author of the Epistle to the Hebrews : " This man, because He continueth ever, hath an unchangeable priesthood. Wherefore he is able also to save them to the uttermost that come unto God by Him, seeing He ever liveth to make intercession for them."

Let us thank God that we have a religion that comes to us from eternity, and is not the product of human fancy ; that we have a Saviour whom the eternal God provided from eternity, one only and all-sufficient Saviour, whom all the Scriptures of the Old Testament foretold, whom all the Scriptures of the New Testament declare; that we have a revelation that comes from the counsels of eternity, full of all needed truth, always consistent with itself, always satisfying to the understandings and consciences of the sincere, always bearing with itself the authority of God, and standing as the pledge of his deep and abiding interest in men, and of his eternal faithfulness in his dealings with them.

SERMON XIV.

CHRIST THE OBJECT OF WORSHIP.

MATT. xi. 28. — *Come unto me all ye that labor and are heavy laden, and I will give you rest.*

IT is a matter of the first importance, in considering and applying this passage of Scripture, to inquire whether the invitation and promise which it contains, were intended for all ages and all classes of men, or whether they were limited to the time and circumstances in which they were uttered. Does our Lord invite the laboring and heavy laden now to come to Him, and at all times, or was the invitation to have force only while He was bodily present with them?

If the latter view of the passage be the true one, then its invitation and promise were not intended for us, nor for our times. They were the words of a mere man calling the needy to him, and promising them aid and relief while he was bodily among them.

But if the former view be the true one, then it is the privilege of the needy and suffering now to go directly to Christ for succor and relief, not less than it was the privilege of those who lived when He was in the flesh. He is a very present help in trouble, no less for us than He was for those who looked upon his person and heard these precious words as they fell from his own lips; and Christ Himself, in his own person, is the Being to whom we may, to whom we ought to betake ourselves for help in time of need; on whom our souls may repose and find support; and with whom we may commune directly by prayer and thanksgiving and supplication.

Do the Scriptures justify this understanding and application of the passage before us? In other words, is it right and proper for the needy and suffering to come directly to Jesus Christ for succor, and to call upon Him directly for comfort and support in their trials and necessities? Is it right to regard Him and to approach Him as One who, in Himself, hears and answers the prayers of men?

Let me direct your attention to two or three proofs from the Scriptures that this view of the text is the true one. And I do it, my hearers, with the earnest desire that you may be brought to listen to the invitation, and believe in the promise, and experience the blessedness and satisfaction and rest of soul which come from direct personal communion with our ascended and ruling Lord.

1. The Scriptures gives us the example of the Apostles and early Christians in favor of thus communing with the Redeemer. They were accustomed to come directly to Him in their worship, and to call directly upon Him in times of sorrow and of need. They always pointed inquirers who asked how they might be saved, directly to Jesus Christ. They directed them to Him alone, and commanded them to trust in Him. They used no other name. They encouraged no hope of salvation from any other Being. This is a very significant fact.

When they were dealing with such inquirers, they did not use the name of God. Reason: "No man hath seen God at any time. The only begotten Son hath revealed Him." They did not use the name of the Father. Reason: "No man cometh unto the Father but by me. He that hath seen me hath seen the Father."

Moreover, a fair interpretation of most of the passages in the Acts, and in the Epistles, in which the Apostles called upon "the Lord" in their worship and prayers, shows that they almost always, if not always, were looking directly to the Redeemer when they used this word. To their minds, "the Lord" was the Redeemer Himself. It was the Lord Jesus Christ with whom they communed in their worship, and whom they addressed in their petitions to the throne of grace.

In the seventh chapter of the Acts of the Apostles, for example, the sacred historian informs us that at the close of the trial of Stephen, he saw the glory of God, and Jesus standing on the right hand of God; that is, in the place of power and dominion. Stephen thus told his persecutors; but they refused to hear him further, and hurried him away to the place of execution. "And there they stoned Stephen," it is written, "calling upon God, and saying, Lord Jesus receive my spirit.

And he kneeled down and cried with a loud voice, Lord lay not this sin to their charge. And when he had said this, he fell asleep."

Now, did Stephen die an idolater? Did he spend his last breath in prayer to a mere man, or to a being of his own imagination? You cannot be made to believe that this was the death scene of an idol-worshipper. But if he was not an idolater giving to a creature the honor that belongs to God only, but was a true worshipper of the one only living and true God, as he must have been if he was, as the inspired penman declares, a man full of the Holy Ghost, then by his example, we know assuredly that it is right and proper, the duty and privilege, indeed, of the suffering and needy, to call upon Christ for help now, and at all times to make Him the object of their worship and their prayers, and the refuge of their souls.

The account of the conversion of the Apostle Paul shows that what Stephen did in the hour of his great extremity, the disciples were accustomed to do on all occasions. If you will look at the narrative, you will see that throughout it is the Lord with whom both Saul and Ananias have to do; and that there may be no doubt who the Lord is, He makes Himself known, at the outset, in a manner not to be misunderstood. For, when Saul, overcome by the light that suddenly shined upon him from heaven, fell to the earth and heard a voice saying to him, "Saul, Saul, why persecutest thou me?" He asked, "Who art thou, Lord?" The Lord said, "I am Jesus, whom thou persecutest." And when Ananias went to lay his hands on the stricken man, he said, "Brother Saul, the Lord, even Jesus that appeared unto thee in the way as thou camest, hath sent me that thou mightest receive thy sight, and be filled with the Holy Ghost. And now why tarriest thou? Arise and be baptized, and wash away thy sins, calling on the name of the Lord."

The first word that Paul received in the gospel was thus spoken to him directly by the Lord Jesus Christ; and the first Christian act which He performed was calling thus on Jesus Christ in solemn religious worship. As he began, so he continued to the end of his course, calling upon the name of the Lord.

Thus, when he was in trouble because of that thorn in his

flesh, which he says was the messenger of Satan to buffet him lest he should be exalted above measure, then he says, " I besought the Lord thrice that it might depart from me. And He said unto me, My grace is sufficient for thee; for my strength is made perfect in weakness." "Most gladly," therefore, exclaims the adoring Apostle, " will I rather glory in my infirmities that the power of Christ may rest upon me." He leaves us in no uncertainty who the Lord is, to whom he made his supplication. It was none other than He who said to the weary and heavy laden, "Come unto me," and his words were as much for Paul, years after the glorification of the Redeemer, as they were for the tired and troubled who surrounded Him in the days of his humiliation.

The last petition that he ever penned, so far as what he wrote has come down to us, was uttered to Christ. He was writing to Timothy and closed his letter with these words, " The Lord Jesus Christ be with thy spirit."

Shall we fear to tread where Paul walked? Was Paul, the great Apostle, the chosen teacher of the Church of Christ, was he a mistaken and an idolatrous zealot? He was an inspired Apostle, and a worshipper of the true God. Jesus was to him the manifestation of this God. As such he bowed before Him in worship and praise; as such he called upon his name and lived.

But if Paul was a worshipper of the true God, then it is our privilege also, as it was his, — and our duty too, — to make his Lord our Lord, and to come, as he did, directly to our Redeemer for help in every time of need, and continually to maintain an intimate and soul-refreshing communion with Him. For us, as for Paul, the name of Jesus is the only name whereby we can be saved. It is for us the name that is above every name, and to which we may and must bow in humble adoration, and in grateful dependence. His words, " Come unto me all ye that labor and are heavy laden," extend to us and are a part of our priceless heritage in Him.

2. The Scriptures ascribe to Christ the attributes which make Him the hearer and answerer of prayer.

The first and most obvious attribute necessary to such a Being is omnipresence. He whom men — all men in all places, and at all times — may worship, and to whom they may address their prayers and be heard and answered. He must at all times be in all places. There must be no place which his presence does not fill. Wherever a creature can be, there especially must He be. Otherwise He could not there be worshipped. There the worshipper and suppliant would find that his ear was heavy that it could not hear.

This is the attribute upon which every one who prays places his first reliance. "*God* is here," says the needy and suffering soul: "*God is here*, therefore I may call upon Him and He can succor me." That which makes God a hearer of prayer to you when you enter your closet, is, first of all, that God is there. It is because God is in your home that He is to your mind the hearer of prayer at your family altar. And He is the hearer of prayer to us to-day in this sanctuary, first of all because He is here; also, as He is in every sanctuary on earth. He will be the hearer of prayer to you to-morrow when you go again into the scenes of the world, and mingle in its affairs, because there is no mart of business so crowded, no place of trial and temptation, or of sin or of holy service, so secluded that He is not there. He is the hearer of prayer to the dwellers or the wanderers in the remotest regions, on every mountain, in every valley, in every city, on every island, because the universe furnishes no place whither you may go from his Spirit, or whither you may flee from his presence. On the ocean also as on the land, He is the hearer of prayer, first of all, because, "if you take the wings of the morning, and dwell in the uttermost parts of the sea, there He is; and there his hand may lead you, and his right hand hold you." His way is in the sea, and his path in the great waters.

Such must be the attribute of the Being who can be called, in any proper sense, the hearer of prayer; and such must be the attribute of Him who can say to all the sons of want and sorrow, — and his words not be a pretense and a mockery, — "Come unto me and I will give you rest." Such, therefore, must be the attribute of Jesus Christ if his words have any application to us. If He be not omnipresent we do but delude ourselves when we suppose that we have anything to do with these words; and we are only tantalizing and deceiving the suffering and the afflicted when we direct them to Jesus as their Saviour and Comforter, in whom they may find rest for their weary souls.

But we are not left to argument and inference in this matter; this attribute is ascribed to our Saviour by the inspired Word. He Himself claimed it, his own words place the fact beyond question. Look, for example, at the thirteenth verse of the third chapter of John, " No man," said He in his conversation with Nicodemus, " hath ascended up to heaven, but He that came down from heaven, even the Son of Man who is in heaven." He was then upon the earth, in the land of Judæa; yet He was then also in heaven. Consider the peculiar character of this language, and you will not fail to see that nothing short of the possession of omniscience would justify it.

On another occasion, you remember, He said to his disciples, addressing them as his Church on the earth, and laying down the rule for the discipline of his churches in all ages, and giving to that discipline the promise of his own sanction, and the approval and confirmation of heaven : " For where two or three are gathered together in my name, there am I in the midst of them." There is no place excepted. He who was really in heaven when He was at the same time visibly and bodily and as really present upon the earth, is now no less, and no less really, on the earth, though He is visibly and bodily present in heaven. Wherever two or three can come together in his name, He is with them. He is in every sanctuary of earth today. In every land where He has disciples that have met to call upon Him, He is with them. He is in the churches of Asia, in those of Africa, in those of America, in those of Europe, and of the isles of the sea. He is with us.

Again, when He gave his disciples the great commission, sending them forth to preach the gospel in all the world, teaching all nations, and baptizing them in the name of the Father, and of the Son, and of the Holy Ghost, He gave them this glorious and all-sufficient promise : " Lo, I am with you alway, even unto the end of the world."

Language could not be more explicit. There is no place into which a disciple of Christ can go, but Christ is there with him. Because He was both in heaven and on earth at the same moment; and because He is, at all times, everywhere, therefore is his presence pledged to every disciple wherever he may be, or wherever he may go, in the work of the gospel. Because of his omnipresence, and only because of this, Christ could say, — and it would have been cruel and blasphemous trifling for Him to have said it but for this, — " Lo, I am with you alway." Go where you may, I am there. You are not alone. You shall never be alone. Fear nothing, therefore, in the carrying out of my commission; I, who have healed the sick, and raised the dead, and fed hungry thousands, in your sight, and laid my authority upon the winds, and my commands upon the waves, in your presence, and in your behalf, I am with you. Not, " I will go with you." This would imply that He was not present, except as He went with them. But I *am* with you. Let Peter go eastward to Babylon, and Paul westward to Rome, and let the other disciples be scattered abroad, never so widely, preaching the Word; still Peter in Babylon, and Paul in Rome, and each disciple, even to the remotest corner of the world, would find his Lord with him at all times, — a present help in all emergencies. And so He said, " Where two or three are gathered together in my name, there am I." Not there will I be. Let them not be afraid to assemble in his name, even in the presence of his enemies; for their Lord is there. Let them not shrink from doing his whole will, and carrying out all his instructions, for He is present to behold, to reward, to protect, to chasten, and, if need be, to punish, — " Lo, I am here in the midst of you!"

These words of comfort and hope are enough. They leave us no room to doubt the reality and efficacy of our Lord's presence with his people at all times and in all places. He is not limited. He is omnipresent. There is no mockery, then, in his words; no trifling; but solemn and tender earnestness, and sustaining truth. And they remain in full force for us, and for his disciples in all ages. They are, like Himself, the same yesterday and to-day and forever. The invitation and promise which they contain are our own; and we can claim them and rest in them without fear or misgiving. We can plead them before Him in personal prayer for ourselves, and we can commend them to the needy and suffering and afflicted at all times, as intended for them, and sure of fulfillment to them. Because He is omnipresent, He can say, and there is meaning and power in his words, when He says, " Come unto me all ye that labor and are heavy laden, and I will give you rest."

2. But omnipresence alone would not be enough. He who can succor the needy and the suffering as widely as this invitation and promise reach, and be to them all that this invitation and promise encourage them to hope for, must have omnipotence also, as well as omnipresence. He must be all powerful, as well as everywhere present. The fainting heart could never trust Him fully if He were less than almighty. Let there be any limit to his power to save and to succor, and He would cease to be a hearer and answerer of prayer. Limit his power, and his arm is shortened that it cannot save. The really and consciously needy soul craves the support and protection of Absolute Almightiness. Nothing short of an apprehension of this can impart to such a soul a sense of security. This attribute must then belong to our Saviour, if his words are to have any vital meaning, and any sustaining and rest-giving power upon our minds.

Is this, then, one of our Saviour's attributes? His history while He was in the flesh gives us many indications of its possession by Him. All material things then yielded to his power. He had only to speak, and it was done; to command, and the purpose of his will stood fast. All the elements were under his control. Diseases of both body and mind ceased to be when He laid his hand upon them. Death loosened his grasp, and his hand fell powerless from his victims, as often as the Son of Man asserted his will against him.

But our faith in the almightiness of Christ does not rest on this alone. Alone this might not be sufficient to sustain our faith. But this proof is supported and confirmed by the most explicit statement of the divine Word. When He sent forth his disciples to their great work, his words to them were, "All power is given unto me in heaven and in earth." He said this as an encouragement to undertake the seemingly hopeless enterprise which he was committing to them. Go forth, and fear not, He said, for I who bid you go am almighty. I, who am almighty, will be with you to the end of the world. I hold in my own hand, and will wield for your protection, and for the success of your great undertaking, all the resources of omnipotence.

It is in harmony with this, and an acceptance of it as true, when Paul says, in the third chapter of his Epistle to the

Philippians, that Christ shall, at his appearing, change our vile body, that it may be fashioned like unto his glorious body, according to the working whereby He is able even to subdue all things unto Himself."

Nothing is too hard for Him! All the forces of nature, all the powers of heaven and of hell. All things in heaven, in the earth, in all the worlds with which unmeasured space is studded, — principalities, powers, angelic hosts, and demoniac hordes, all things, He is able to subdue unto Himself. It is no wonder, therefore, that in the first chapter of Revelation He is distinctly named "The Almighty:" "I am Alpha and Omega, the beginning and the ending, saith the Lord, which is, and which was, and which is to come, the Almighty."

Have you any fear, my hearer, to commit yourself directly unto the keeping of Him who is almighty? You might well have fears to do so, if there were nothing but the fact of his almightiness to encourage you. This very attribute might then be your ruin. You would fall before it, and be crushed into ruin. But when this is possessed by Him who gave his life for us, and who uttered the gracious words of our text, and his truth stands pledged to fulfill to you his promise, then you need have no fear. With such a support you cannot fail of present help in every time of need. You cannot but be safe in dealing directly with Him in all your necessities, and communing with Him in all your prayers.

3. We are confirmed yet more in this view of our privilege to deal directly with our Redeemer, in our acts of worship, and in our supplications for aid, when we find that not only omnipresence and almightiness, but the government of the universe is in his hands; and that He himself actually reigns supreme over all created things. He holds the sceptre of universal dominion. Wherever his omnipresence is, there is also his almighty power, upholding, guiding, governing. All things yield to his will. Not an angel lives in heaven that does not execute the Redeemer's mandate. Not a lost spirit in the world of woe, but confesses his sway. All things in all worlds are his subjects. He rules over them and does his pleasure among them.

Are we treading on forbidden ground here? Do we state more than the Word of God has again and again asserted? Is it not distinctly said of Him, that He "upholds all things by the word of his power?" that "by Him all things consist?" that He is "head over all things to the Church?" and, as we just now quoted, that "all power in heaven and in earth is given unto his hands?"

My hearers, are you ready to admit all this? You are, if you are ready to behold in the Redeemer all the attributes and prerogatives which the Scriptures ascribe to Him. If you take the Bible for your guide, you are ready now to behold in the hand of Christ the sceptre of all dominion.

He rules in nature. It is He "who hath gathered the winds in his fists; who hath bound the waters in a garment; who hath established all the ends of the earth." There is no department of the government of nature which He does not administer.

He rules in providence. The issues of life and death are in his hands. He holds the destiny of every creature. It is He who will decide and pronounce upon that destiny in the day of judgment. For it is the judgment-seat of Christ before which we must all stand, that each may receive the awards of this life in eternal retribution. He rules, too, in your daily life, believing hearer; and it is He who is causing all things to work together for good to them that love Him. It is He who causes the wrath of man to praise Him, and the remainder of wrath He will restrain." He it is who is overturning and overturning among the nations of the earth, and preparing the way for His final and glorious appearing.

Let us not delay, then, to join with the ten thousand times ten thousand and thousands of thousands of angels and living beings who are to-day in heaven, saying with a loud voice, "Worthy is the Lamb that was slain to receive power, and riches, and wisdom, and strength, and honor, and glory, and blessing."

It is the will of the Father that we should do all this. For the Father loveth the Son, and hath given all things into his hands. The Father judgeth no man; but hath committed all judgment, or rule, unto the Son; that all men should honor the Son, even as they honor the Father.

Can you fear to come to such a Being? Can you fear to come to Him when He invites and promises as He does in these words that are before us? Are you afraid of idolatry in so doing?

Not until you make Him something higher than God can you commit idolatry in your dealings with Him. But you may so deal with the Blessed Redeemer as to commit something worse, if possible, than idolatry. For you may fail to give Him the honor which belongs to Him. You may set Him lower in your esteem than you do God. You may divest Him, in your thoughts, of all his prayer-hearing attributes. You may deny his omnipresence. You may question his omnipotence. You may, in your imagination, wrest from his hand the sceptre of universal government. All this you may do; but you cannot exalt Jesus too high; nor honor Him too much, nor trust Him too confidingly, nor serve Him too faithfully. Not until you have placed Him, on all these things, above God, need you fear. Not until, in all these things, you have exalted Him into the throne and place of God, ought you to cease to fear.

"Kiss the Son," then, my hearer; "kiss the Son, lest He be angry, and ye perish from the way when his wrath is kindled but a little. Blessed are all they that put their trust in Him."

SERMON XV.
CHRIST THE OBJECT OF WORSHIP.

MATT. xi. 28. — *Come unto me all ye that labor and are heavy laden, and I will give you rest.*

IT is not the mission of the gospel to threaten and denounce men. On the contrary its messages are invitations and promises to the needy and suffering. It never forgets, indeed, that men are condemned; that they have broken the law of a holy God, and trampled ruthlessly upon his authority; and that they are therefore deeply and inexcusably guilty and hopelessly lost. The gospel everywhere assumes all this to be true, and insists upon it as being the real and universal condition of men. But it does this not as its primary work, but only for the purpose and in the way of offering the guilty pardoning mercy, and saving them from death. The very soul of the gospel is embodied in those hope-giving words of our Saviour: "God sent not his Son into the world to condemn the world, but that the world through Him might be saved." The world is condemned, but the gospel brings to it the offer of pardon. It is lost, but the gospel brings to it the offer and makes known to it the provisions and the condition of salvation. But for condemnation there would be no need of pardon, and the offer of it would be useless and foolish. But for the lost condition of men, as a race of sinners, the offer of salvation to them, and the announcement of the provisions for it, and the conditions of securing it, would be vain and unpardonable trifling.

It is, then, only because men need salvation that the gospel offers it to them; and only because they need pardon that the gospel tells them of redemption through the blood of Christ, even the forgiveness of sins. It is because these necessities of the human race are permanent, remaining from age to age, and because they are never superseded by any condition or circumstances into which they can be brought, that the gospel remains in force and of vital importance to men, and will remain so until the end of time. All its invitations and promises are the heritage, therefore, of every age, and of all classes of the human family. As none are, or ever will be, exempt from the wretchedness and fearful liabilities which rendered the gospel a necessity when it was given, so it will never cease to be adapted to their wants and all-sufficient for their salvation. As with the gospel, so with Him who speaks to men in it, He remains to them "the same yesterday and to-day and forever." His words of promise have as direct a bearing upon men of one age as they have upon those of another. They are meant for all ages alike; and Christ who speaks them is as able and as sacredly pledged to make them good to all who accept them now, as He was in the days of his sojourn in the flesh.

As we recently endeavored to show, this is the true light in which to regard the words of our text, if they have any meaning whatever for us, or if we have any right to consider them as addressed to us, or intended for our acceptance.

I did not then finish my argument in favor of such an understanding and use of the passage. We then looked at only two, out of five or six proofs that the words before us are as much our inheritance in Christ as they were the inheritance of those who heard them from his own lips; and that it is as much our privilege to accept this ever precious invitation and promise, by coming directly to the Redeemer in prayer and in communion of soul, as it was the privilege of those who saw his bodily presence. Nay, our privilege is greater in this respect than theirs was. They had not learned to rise, in their conceptions of the Son of God, above his merely bodily presence; but we have been taught to recognize and depend upon his spiritual omnipresence, and therefore we are never limited by time or place or circumstances. Wherever we are, there our Lord and Saviour Jesus Christ is, and we can approach Him with boldness in acceptance of his gracious invitation, and confidently depend upon an immediate fulfillment of his soul-sustaining promise.

The two arguments in favor of such an immediate coming to Christ in prayer, and such direct communing of soul with Him were, first, the fact that the early disciples and inspired

Apostles were accustomed thus to act. They prayed directly to Jesus Christ, and communed with Him. The Lord upon whom they called was none other than the Lord Jesus Christ. The second argument was found in the fact that the Scriptures fully and unequivocally ascribe to Jesus Christ every attribute necessary to constitute Him the object of worship, and the hearer and answerer of prayer. They ascribe to Him omnipresence, and omnipotence, and the supreme government of the universe.

He who has these is certainly able to hear and answer our prayer. He, certainly, can commune with our souls, and refresh them by his grace. He, certainly, can ever make good the words which He has left on record for our hope and support. It is our right to come to Him as to one whose arm is never shortened that it cannot save, nor his ear heavy that it cannot hear. Nay, more, not only is it our right and privilege to come directly to Him thus; it is our duty. He who has all power in heaven and in earth, whose is the government of the universe, demands our homage and our trust. If our worship be not the worship of God known only in Him and through Him, our worship is idolatry. It is not God indeed, but an image of our own creation, that we then worship. The invitation and the promise of our text can be heeded only by pleading them directly with Christ; they can be answered by none but Him. It is a mistake to suppose that it is optional with us to recognize God in Jesus Christ or not, and optional whether or not we honor Him as God. It is the will of the Father that all men should honor the Son even as they honor the Father; and they only see or know the Father, who see and know Him in the Son.

3. In further proof of such an understanding and use of the gracious words before us, I call your attention, thirdly, to the fact that the Scriptures ascribe to Christ all the acts by which Deity has ever been manifested to men.

It is this feature of the Scriptures which gives permanent force and vitality to the invitation and promise of our text. They make Christ, our Redeemer, to be that Being in whom are truly found all the prerogatives, and by whom alone have been done and are done those acts, which are fundamental in all scripturally formed ideas of God. Every act which the mind can fix upon as having manifested God, or as now manifesting Him, is the act of our Lord and Saviour Jesus Christ.

Let us look at this matter a little closely. Creation is the first and most palpable manifestation of God. As we open our eyes and look upon the world in which we are, and upon the worlds that are above us, we spontaneously and necessarily connect them in our minds with a Creator. Some Being has made all these worlds. This is the inevitable verdict of every man's reason, if it gives any verdict at all, when he looks upon the works of creation. Nor is this the only idea in his mind on this point when he thus judges. It is supplemented, and inseparably connected with this other idea, namely, whoever the Being is that made all created things, He is God.

This idea lies at the foundation of all ideas of a Supreme Being, or true God. If you cease to ascribe to Him the works of creation, he ceases, in your mind, to be the Supreme Being, or true God. Take away creative power, and you have taken away the essential and necessary attribute of Deity. Transfer the act of creation from God to another, and you have transferred the prerogative of Deity from Him. But you cannot make this transfer. For whenever you think of this power, and this act, the Being with whom you associate them is God. He is manifested in them and by them. He has made Himself known by them.

This is the teaching of the Bible, as it is also the experience of our own minds. Paul assures us, in the first chapter of Romans, for example, " that which may be known of God is manifest to men; for God hath showed it unto them. For the invisible things of Him from the creation of the world are clearly seen, being understood by the things that are made, even his eternal power and godhead."

The Psalmist teaches us the same lesson. " The heavens declare the glory of God; and the firmament showeth his handy-work." To be possessed of human powers of thought, and of reasoning, and to look abroad upon the works of creation, with those powers in exercise, is to behold the existence and the work of a Being whom the mind names Supreme and God.

> "Behold the lofty sky
> Declares its Maker, God;
> And all his starry works on high
> Proclaim his power abroad."

This fact, that we must recognize the being of God in the Creator of the world, is assumed throughout the Scriptures. They take it for granted that we cannot separate creatorship from Deity. To be Creator is to be God; and to be God is to have been the Creator. Hence in the very opening sentence of the Bible the great fact is declared, which all men, who have not first silenced their reason by sophistry, are prepared to receive and credit, and it is declared as though, in truth, men could not deny or question it. "In the beginning God created the heaven and the earth." The sacred writer makes this declaration at the outset, that he may lift the minds of his readers above all thoughts of the idols and gods of the heathen world, and connect the Being of whom he is going to write with an act to which no idol god ever laid claim. Jehovah, unlike Baal or Jupiter, or any other false god, was Creator. In creation He made his first, and out of redemption, the most unmistakable and most glorious manifestation of Himself to intelligent beings.

This thought is at the foundation of every act of truly divine worship. If you pay homage to a being who is not Creator of the world, and all things in it, and so of yourself, then you fall short of divine worship and become an idolater.

Inseparably connected with this is another idea which is also at the foundation of every prayer that ever goes up from a burdened soul to God. The maker of all things, in whom we first behold God made manifest, is also the upholder of the worlds He has made. This is the continuance of his first manifestation, that which He made in creation. No prayer could ascend to any Being, no call could be made on Him for help in time of need, if the needy did not behold in the Being to whom he would make his appeal, the ruler and governor of the elements and circumstances by which He is surrounded. You could not ask your daily bread from one whom you did not think able to give it. You could not ask for protection in times of danger, nor deliverance from distress, from one in whom you did not behold power to protect and deliver. Your every prayer to a deliverer presupposes rulership in Him as the ground of his power to deliver. How else could He hear and answer prayer? If He has not absolute dominion over you, and all that pertains to your welfare, why ask Him to do that which, without such dominion, He would be utterly unable to perform?

Such are the fundamental ideas of God in the mind of every true worshipper. In and by these two things especially has God manifested Himself to men. In and by them He continues the manifestation. To be Creator, Upholder, and Ruler is to be the Being to whom if to any, the needy and suffering may come, and with whom they may commune in prayer. He is the Being to whom they may betake themselves for refuge and help in every time of need, and against every opposing or oppressing ill, if the way of approach to Him be not utterly closed. If it be, then indeed there is no being to whom the afflicted soul can betake itself in its extremity. Then there is none who can help; none who can deliver; none in whom the soul can indeed recognize a helper.

Now what we affirm is that the Scriptures clearly and unequivocally ascribe these acts by which Deity is primarily manifested to men, and in which we find the prerogatives of that Being to whom alone we can betake ourselves for divine help, these acts the Scriptures unhesitatingly ascribe to Him who uttered the invitation and promise contained in our text.

First, nothing, indeed, is more clearly revealed by the Scriptures than that Christ Himself is the Maker and the Upholder of all things; that He is, in fact, the same being of whom Moses wrote in the first chapter of Genesis: "In the beginning God created the heaven and the earth." For example, after ages of tampering with the sacred text, and of ingenious criticism, of most unnatural transpositions and transformations of the words of the Holy Ghost contained in the first chapter of the Gospel by John, they still continue boldly and unshrinkingly to put all the glory of creation upon Christ, even as Moses put it upon Jehovah. "In the beginning was the Word, and the Word was with God, and the Word was God. All things were made by Him, and without Him was not anything made that was made." He having been made flesh, was in the world, and the world was made by Him, though the world knew Him not. Language could not be more explicit. The writer has so arranged his words, and so plainly put his thought into them, that his meaning cannot be mistaken. "The Word that was in the beginning with God, and was God, and that was made flesh and dwelt among men." He, John declares, was the Supreme Creator. But he and Moses wrote under the inspiration of the same infallible Spirit who searches all things, even the deep things of God. They were both writing, therefore, of the same Being; Moses of God revealed in creation alone; John of God become man, and revealed in the flesh.

Again, Paul writing to the Colossians takes up the same truth, and urges it home upon his readers with all the earnestness of his ardent and comprehensive mind: "By Him were all things created that are in heaven, and that are in earth, visible and invisible, whether they be thrones, or dominions, or principalities, or powers. All things were created by Him and for Him: and He is before all things, and by Him all things consist."

The author of the Epistle to the Hebrews takes up the same strain and presses it home upon the minds, not of those who had been heathen, but of those who had been taught from their infancy to know the Creator, and nominally, at least, to worship Him under his true name: "God hath in these last days spoken unto us by his Son, whom He hath appointed heir of all things, by whom also He made the worlds, who being the brightness of his glory and the express image of his person, and upholding all things by the word of his power, when He had by Himself purged our sins sat down on the right hand of the Majesty on high." Still further on the writer says of God, — God in his invisible unrevealed Deity, — that He said to the Son, " Thou Lord, in the beginning hast laid the foundation of the earth, and the heavens are the works of thine hands."

Need we multiply quotations? Are not these enough to settle the point beyond a doubt? According to the Scriptures, then, the true and only manifestations of God to men have been made in and by the person of the eternal Son. The incomprehensible and the inconceivable God dwelling in the light which no man can approach unto; whom no man hath seen, or can see; of whom, in his absolute and essential deity, men can form no conception, — He is manifested to men in the person of the Son. Without the manifestation of Himself by the act of creation and of the continuance of creation, nothing could be known of Him. All that is known of Him, is known in and by the person of the Lord Jesus Christ. He alone is God manifest. He is the image of the invisible God. Thus the whole tenor of revelation is a reiteration and confirmation and elucidation of our Saviour's words in the verse preceding our text, and from which the text receives its permanent and saving power: "No man knoweth the Father but the Son and he to whomsoever the Son will reveal Him." It was upon this foundation that He planted Himself when He said with such tenderness, such majesty, and such authority, and with sweeping universality: "Come unto me all ye that labor and are heavy laden, and I will give you rest."

Many men are fond of talking of God as their Father, and of professing their faith in the Father who are, nevertheless, unwilling to give to Jesus Christ the honor to which He is exalted by the Scriptures, namely, of being the Creator and Upholder of the universe, and the only manifestation of God to men. Leaving to Christ, it may be, everything but the acts and attributes by which God manifests Himself to us, they take these, namely, creation and upholding, from Him, and putting them — in their minds — upon some other being who has no existence, saving in their own imaginations, they name this being — this figment of their fancy — this unreal nothing — their Father, and worship it as their God.

But the Father, according to the Scriptures, is not in his own proper personality the Creator, or the Upholder of the world. The Father of whom the Bible speaks is not known in his distinct personality by any such manifestation. It is only in the personality of the Son that God is thus revealed; and the Father — the representative of absolute, incomprehensible, and inconceivable deity — is known to us only as the Son reveals Him. He tells us of Him; and calls Him Father; but beyond this we cannot go. Our thoughts at once become lost when we attempt to go one step beyond our Saviour's person and works and words. We find ourselves in a shoreless sea which has neither surface nor soundings. Our lines of thought cannot measure it, nor our powers of comprehension conceive it. We are overwhelmed with deep, awful, impenetrable mystery. We hear a voice exclaiming, "Canst thou by searching find out God? Canst thou find out the Almighty unto perfection? It is as high as heaven; what canst thou do? deeper than hell: what canst thou know?"

We are compelled to fall back then simply on the manifestation of God made in creating and upholding, and there rest. But here we find only Christ, our blessed Saviour. It was by Him that all things were created. By Him alone do they subsist. He tells us of the Father. By faith we receive his word; but beyond that word we cannot take a single step. He tells us of the Holy Spirit. If we attempt to conceive of Him out of the very words by which Christ reveals Him, again we are lost. All is vagueness, and perplexing speculation.

Thus, my hearers, we are shut up to the Lord Jesus Christ as the only Being in whom we can behold God. He only is God manifest. He is the image of the invisible God.

4. Here we find another argument in support of our interpretation and application of the words before us. The privilege of the weary and heavy laden to come directly to Christ in prayer, and to commune with Him as the God and hope of their souls, is confirmed by the fact that the Scriptures direct us to look upon and to consider Christ as God revealed. It is not necessary, after what has been already said, to multiply passages in support of this assertion. Two or three will be enough. In the first chapter of the Gospel of John we are told by the Evangelist that " The Word (that was God, and that made all things) was made flesh and dwelt among us, and we beheld his glory, the glory as of the only begotten of the Father, full of grace and truth." Matthew tells us that this becoming flesh and dwelling among men, was in fulfillment of the words of the Prophet Isaiah: " Behold, a virgin shall be with child, and shall bring forth a son, and they shall call his name Emmanuel, which being interpreted is, God with us." Hence John says again, " No man hath seen God"—God in his simple and uncreated essence—the only begotten Son, who is in the bosom of the Father, He hath declared or revealed Him. He has made Him to be known. In harmony with all this are those words of the Lord Himself which are recorded in the fourteenth chapter of John, and which are so clear that they cannot be misunderstood: " I am the way, the truth, and the life: no man cometh unto the Father but by me. If ye had known me ye should have known my Father also: and from henceforth ye know Him and have seen Him. Philip saith unto Him, Lord, show us the Father, and it sufficeth us. Jesus

saith unto him, Have I been so long time with you, and yet hast thou not known me, Philip? He that hath seen me, hath seen the Father; and how sayest thou then, Show us the Father? Believest thou not that I am in the Father, and the Father in me? Believe me that I am in the Father, and the Father in me."

In the light of these passages we can easily understand the words of the prophet Isaiah, as he looked down through the intervening ages and saw the day of the Messiah, and behold his glory and rejoiced in it. He saw Him who should swallow up death in victory, and wipe away all tears from the eyes of his people, and take away their rebuke from off all the earth. Then he exclaimed as though he felt himself actually carried forward to those glorious days, and living in the times of the Redeemer, the incarnated Jehovah, whose coming had been the hope of all the godly in all ages and the burden of prophecy, he exclaimed, "So this is our God; we have waited for Him, and He will save us: this is Jehovah; we have waited for Him, we will be glad and rejoice in his salvation."

5. The remaining arguments to which I wish to call your attention, need but a moment's consideration. They grow out of what has been already said, and are only the authorized recognitions on earth and in heaven of the truth we have advanced.

The fifth argument for the understanding which we have of our text, and for the application which we wish to make of it, is found in the fact that the Scriptures plainly and repeatedly call our Redeemer God, and call upon all intelligent beings to worship Him as such. It is natural, and to be expected that they should do this. Indeed they could not but do it, if we have rightly interpreted their teachings. The first chapter of the Epistle to the Hebrews, for example, is full of this style of address. "Unto the Son He saith, thy throne, O God, is for ever and ever. Let all the angels of God worship Him." In the first Epistle of Paul to Timothy we find this language, so exactly in harmony with the general teaching of the Scriptures on the subject, that all critical difficulties which some find in the passage vanish away from our minds. " God was manifested in the flesh, justified in the Spirit, seen of angels, preached unto the gentiles, believed on in the world, received up into glory." "The Word was God," says John in his Gospel; and in his first Epistle he says, with the unshrinking boldness of one taught of the Spirit, "We are in Him that is true, even in his Son Jesus Christ. This is the true God and eternal life."[1]

No wonder, then, that Paul, when he was speaking of the honor that had been vouchsafed to the Israelites, to whom pertained the adoption, and the glory, and the covenants, and the giving of the law, and the service of God, and the promises; whose are the fathers, and of whom, as concerning the flesh, Christ came; no wonder that he should boldly declare of Him, that "He is over all, God blessed forever!" No wonder that Thomas should cry out when he saw the Lord as He was, "My Lord and my God!"

6. This is the honor which our Redeemer has upon the earth. He is not less honored in heaven. This is the sixth argument for the application that we make of our text. The Bible plainly represents Christ to be the Being on whom the eyes of the heavenly inhabitants are fixed in adoration, and before whom they bow in holy worship: "And I beheld, and I heard the voice of many angels round about the throne, and the living beings, and the elders; and the number of them was ten thousand times ten thousand, and thousands of thousands, saying with a loud voice, Worthy is the Lamb that was slain to receive power, and riches, and wisdom, and strength, and honor, and glory, and blessing. And every creature which is in heaven and on the earth and under the earth, and such as are in the sea, and all that are in them heard I saying: Blessing and honor, and glory, and power, be unto Him that sitteth upon the throne, and unto the Lamb for ever and ever. And the four living beings said, Amen. And the four and twenty elders fell down and worshipped Him that liveth for ever and ever."

Are not the invitation and promise of our text permanent then? and is it not filled with living force and with hope for us, my hearers? It was He who is the same yesterday and to-day and forever, who spake them then; it is He who speaks them now. They cannot, therefore, but abide in power, even as He himself abides. To whom can we go, if not to Him? To whom can the needy and suffering betake themselves for refuge

[1] I am not unaware of the criticisms on this and the following passage.

and relief, if not to God, in that person in whom, and by whom alone He has been pleased to make Himself known? It was He who spake through the Prophet, " Look unto me, be ye saved, all the ends of the earth."

It is He who says to-day, " Come unto me all ye that labor and are heavy laden, and I will give you rest; and him that cometh to me I will in no wise cast out."

SERMON XVI.

ONLY THE NAME OF JESUS SAVING.

Acts iv. 12.—*Neither is there salvation in any other: for there is none other name under heaven given among men, whereby we must be saved.*

PETER had just healed the lame man who was laid daily at the Beautiful Gate of the temple to ask alms of those who were going up to worship. The miracle drew around Peter, and John who was with him on this occasion, a great multitude eager not only to look upon the man who had been so suddenly and miraculously cured of a life-long lameness, but to see the men who could wield such miraculous power. The Apostles, as they were always wont to do, promptly turned the minds of the people away from themselves as the supposed authors of the miracle to its real author; and then began to preach Christ and his gospel to them.

But "as they were speaking to the people, the priests and the rulers of the temple, and the Sadducees, came upon them, being grieved that they taught the people, and preached through Jesus the resurrection from the dead." They arrested them, therefore, and cast them into prison.

The next day they were brought before the Sanhedrim and interrogated, not touching the matter for which they had been arrested and imprisoned, but regarding the noted miracle which they had wrought. " By what power, or by what name have ye done this?" they asked. Peter answered promptly and plainly that the lame man was healed by the name of Jesus Christ of Nazareth. Then, going forward to the true character of Jesus, he declared as promptly and as plainly that this Jesus was the Messiah, and that there could be no salvation but by Him; that his name alone was the one which they and all other men must call upon if they would escape impending ruin.

It is manifest, therefore, that the salvation of which Peter spake was not simply the healing of bodily ailments, like the restoring to soundness of limb the man who had been lame from his birth. This salvation was one of the evidences of the truth that Peter and John were preaching, and it was pointed to by them simply to confirm the assertion which they made respecting Jesus of Nazareth, that He was the Christ. The salvation of which Peter spake was that salvation which, according to the Law and the Prophets, the Messiah had come into this world to accomplish — salvation from the wrath of God and from the dominion and penalty of sin. The salvation of which Peter spake was, therefore, the salvation which is set forth in those precious words of our Lord Himself: " God so loved the world that He gave his only begotten Son, that whosoever believeth in Him should not perish, but have everlasting life." To this salvation the mind of Peter went as soon as he began to speak of Jesus as the fulfillment of prophecy; to this salvation he carried forward the minds of those to whom he was speaking: " Be it known unto you all, and to all the people of Israel, that by the name of Jesus Christ of Nazareth, whom ye crucified, whom God raised from the dead, even by Him doth this man stand here before you whole. And this," he added, instantly advancing to the great truth that was uppermost in his mind, and which he was commissioned to preach to all men, namely, the Messiahship of Jesus, " this is the stone which was set at naught by you builders, which, in fulfillment of prophecy, has become the head of the corner."

The accused assumes the place of accuser. Becoming apparently unmindful of the fact that he is a prisoner at the bar of the supreme court of his nation, and looking now on the members of the Sanhedrim, not as his judges, but as guilty and ruined sinners, he charges their guilt home on their consciences with the severity of unshrinking faithfulness: You, even you, are the murderers of the Messiah. His crucifixion was your work. His blood is upon your garments. The avenger of innocent blood, the blood of the Holy One, the hope and consolation of Israel, is upon your track. Their case was desperate. They were ruined.

But Peter, true to the spirit and office of a minister of the gospel, does not stop here. In the same sentence in which he charges their terrible guilt upon their consciences, and reveals to them their ruin, he announces the possibility of pardon and salvation. They may yet be saved. There is hope for them, — but only in that same man whom they have so contemptuously rejected, and so foully murdered, — but whom God had raised from the dead, and in doing so had vindicated Him and his claims against all their hatred and contempt. By this very man, in whose name the lame man had been cured, by Him they may be saved from their guilt and ruin. But they can be saved by no other.

Such is the salvation of which Peter spake to the Sanhedrim when he said, "Neither is there salvation in any other: for there is none other name under heaven given among men, whereby we must be saved."

It is to the latter clause of this verse to which your attention is particularly invited: "There is none other name under heaven given among men, whereby we must be saved." The name is Jesus Christ. There is no other being on whom sinners may call for salvation — and their call be answered. The Apostle's words are clear and explicit. They are all-comprehensive and all-exclusive. They apply to all classes of sinners, and cover all time. They reach back from the moment when Peter was giving them utterance to the first sinner to whom salvation was ever offered in this world; and they stretch forward and take in the last human sinner to whom salvation will ever be given. There has been from the first, and to the last there will be, "none other name under heaven given among men whereby we must be saved."

The word *name*, as you are well aware, means the *being* that bears it. It includes his personality, his power, his prerogatives; and to say that the name of Jesus Christ of Nazareth is the only one whereby men must be saved, is to say that Jesus Christ of Nazareth is the only person who acts as the Saviour of sinners; that his is the only power that can reach a sinner in his wretchedness and ruin and deliver him, and that it is the prerogative of Jesus of Nazareth alone to save. No created being, not even the Archangel can save sinners; the Father and the Holy Spirit will not in their own name save them. They have committed the business of salvation into the hands of the only begotten Son, and they will never trench on his prerogatives.

Such is the ground covered by our text. It is a single assertion; an assertion made by divine authority and by divine inspiration. Nothing can make it stronger: it is already, and just as it stands, the voice of the Almighty. It needs no proof, it is a divine revelation. It is also in perfect harmony with all else that has been revealed on the subject by the Word of God.

Let us then accept the declaration and give our thoughts to a few of the lessons which it necessarily involves.

1. Sinners cannot be saved by preaching to them the name of God. God is not the specific name that the gospel gives to the Saviour of sinners. It speaks of this Saviour as indeed God. It says distinctly that He is God, and that in Him dwells all the fullness of the Godhead. It is unequivocal and outspoken upon this point. It leaves us in no doubt about it. But yet God is not his specific name, nor the name by which He is to be preached, nor the name by which He is to be called on for salvation.

The reason for this is plain. God is a general term, and is in general use by all classes of men to designate that conception of their minds, whatever it may be, which they have of a Supreme Being, whom they count an object of worship. All men have such an object of worship, and apply to it this name, in one form or another. It is the most general and comprehensive of all designations for objects of religious worship. It is absolutely universal in this respect. If, therefore, the name of God were preached to men for their salvation, every one's mind would go at once to that object which he was accustomed to count worthy of divine homage. He would suppose that this was the Being intended. His mind would therefore stop with this Being, and rest in it. There would be no advance in his thoughts, or his knowledge, and no turning away from that which bore the name indeed of a real Being, but was, in fact, only a creation of his own fancy, or the work of his own hands. If he were directed to cry to God, and to call on the name of God for salvation he would call upon and cry only to the idol of his own conceiving or fashioning. He would cry in vain, therefore, — and for the same reason that the prophets of Baal cried in vain " from morning even until noon, saying, O Baal, hear us ! But there was no voice, nor any that answered."

As a matter of fact men have never lost the sentiment or notion of God from their minds. The fundamental idea of a Being to be worshipped, who has authority over men and is, to a greater or less extent, the arbiter of their destiny, has always remained with them. But the true conception of the Being and character of God has dropped out of their thoughts. This they have lost. " As they did not like to retain God in their knowledge, God gave them over to a reprobate mind, and they changed the truth of God into a lie, and worshipped and served the creature rather than the Creator." The consequence has been that the vague sentiment of God which has remained with them as a part of their very being, has gone forth blindly, like the instinctive clutchings of a drowning man, and laid hold of such objects as a sinful heart and a perverted imagination have chosen, and has deified these and fallen down and worshipped them as gods. In this manner, and from this cause the world has been filled with idols of untold number, and of infinite variety of character, and to each has been given the name of God. Athens, we are told, had thirty thousand of them. Ancient Egypt was as full of gods as of quadrupeds. Africa, ancient and modern, has as many gods as there are reptiles in its overteeming rivers and swamps and forests. A beastly fetichism has converted not only its reptiles but its wood and stone into gods.

The consequence of this condition of things is that in a godless world yet crowded full of gods, the name God, of itself, determines nothing. To the thoughtful and earnest mind the question will come home, as often as the name of God is preached to it. Who is God? What is God? To which of the countless beings and objects that bear this name does it truly belong? Does it belong to any? Is it not the name of that which men conceive to be, but which is not?

This question of who is God, was the precise point in controversy, you remember, between Elijah and the prophets of Baal on the occasion to which we just alluded. This appears more clearly when we read the passage with the specific name Jehovah, in place of the general term, Lord. Baal's prophets claimed that Baal was God, and they had seduced a large part of the nation to believe and practice as they taught. Elijah, on the contrary, clung to the old belief that Jehovah and not

Baal, nor any other being, real or imaginary, was God; and his exhortation to the backslidden and hestitating people was, "If Jehovah be God, follow him; but if Baal, then follow him." Hence his prayer in the presence of this people was, "O Jehovah, hear me, that this people may know that thou art God." And when the fire came down, in answer to his prayer, "and consumed the burnt sacrifice, and the wood, and the stones, and the dust, and licked up the water that was in the trench," the people acknowledged that the contest between Elijah and the prophets of Baal was fairly decided in favor of the God of Elijah. "They fell on their faces, and said, Jehovah is God, Jehovah is God." All vagueness and indefiniteness of thought were banished from their minds, and He who had revealed Himself to their fathers, to Abraham, and Isaac, and Jacob, and to Moses, under the name of Jehovah, and who had so often and so signally manifested Himself in all their history as God indeed, besides whom there was no other, became a definite, distinct, clearly apprehended Being to their thoughts. If they had followed up this momentary conviction, and become the true worshippers and servants of Jehovah, their ruin might have been averted. The name of Jehovah would have become their tower of strength, and wrought out for them a national and a personal salvation.

This leads me to remark that, in perfect harmony with the assertion of the Apostle in our text, the Scriptures of the New Testament uniformly represent that Jesus Christ is the only personal manifestation of God under the new dispensation as Jehovah was under the old, — the only manifestation, that is, on which men can look and get a distinct conception of Him as a Being, a Person. They testify with one voice that no man hath seen God — in his absolute essence — at any time. The only begotten Son who is in the bosom of the Father, He hath made Him known. God, in his absolute essence, is He of whom the Apostle Paul says that "He dwells in light which no man can approach unto; whom no man hath seen, nor can see;" but who had been revealed to men in the person of the only begotten Son. It was He who made the worlds, and manifested God in creation. It is He who governs the universe and manifests God in providence. It is He who has power on earth to forgive sins, and uses that power in saving the guilty and condemned from death, and manifests God in redemption. He is thus to the apprehension of men God the Creator, Ruler, Redeemer. There is no manifestation of God that has not been made by Him, and in his person. To the patriarchs and prophets He was Jehovah; to the Apostles and to us He is Jesus. His name is specific. It designates a distinct and clearly manifested Being, — a Being of well defined character and of definite acts. Our minds can look upon Him, can commune with Him, can rest in Him, and depend upon Him. His being and character are not lost in a vague generalness, nor do they withdraw themselves into dim and shadowy unrealness; but they stand out clear, manifest, unmistakable. They who come to Him for salvation are able to say, each one of them, with the definiteness and positiveness of the great Apostle, " I know whom I have believed."

The experiment has often been tried, of preaching the name of God to men for their salvation; and, as often as tried, has proved an entire failure. You remember the incident in the history of the Moravian missionaries among the Greenlanders: Long and patiently did they preach God to them, — God the Creator; God the Ruler; God the All-wise, the All-knowing, and the Almighty, — but never lifted their dark and vacant minds out of the vagueness of the general designation to which they had always been accustomed, by pointing them to the person in whom alone the being and character of God are made known. As a last and desperate resort they began to preach Jesus Christ to them. The effect was instantaneous. The Holy Spirit, whose office it is to convince men of sin because they believe not on Him, and to reveal to the minds of men the things of Christ, took the preaching of that sacred name and made it the power of God to their salvation. Their dull and dreamy notion of God was quickened into vigorous life, and being directed to God made manifest, it awakened their whole moral nature to activity and intense earnestness. They then began to know who God was. They saw what He was. They apprehended his character. They felt the greatness of his love and were subdued before it into penitence, and inspired with faith and loving obedience. From that hour the mission to Greenland was no longer a failure. The name of Jesus wrought mightily, and the salvation of great numbers attested its virtue and its power.

It has always been so in Christian missions. No other name but that of Jesus has ever won the heathen from their idols to the worship of the only living and true God. All other names have left them still in darkness and death. And it is the same wherever salvation is preached, not alone among the heathen but in the most Christianized communities. Preach to men in general terms of God, and they go on in death, and in devotion to some form of worldliness. Preach Jesus to them, let them see God in Him, and let them know by seeing Him who God is, what He is, what his heart is towards them in all their wretchedness and guilt, — do this and we soon find that we are using that instrumentality by which the Holy Spirit is ever wont to bring sinners to seek after and obtain salvation. When men preach Jesus Christ, preach Him faithfully, preach Him crucified, preach Him Lord, it becomes manifest the world over and in all time, that his name was rightly chosen by the angel, when he said, " Thou shalt call his name Jesus, for He shall save his people from their sins."

2. Another inference from the words which we are considering is, that sinners cannot be saved by preaching to them the name of the Father.

This is a favorite substitute with many for the name of Jesus Christ. If their ministry were interrogated it would testify that they had determined, not as did Paul, to know nothing among the people, save Jesus Christ, and Him crucified; but the Father, and Him, not as revealed in the Gospels, but as their imaginations painted Him, and as they, in common with the philosophers of the heathen world, can conceive of Him without any aid from a special divine revelation. And thus it has happened that a new gospel is to-day widely preached; a gospel that proclaims salvation in the assumed fatherhood of God, instead of salvation in Christ crucified.

But there are two very obvious reasons, if we take the Bible for our guide, why sinners cannot be saved by this preaching. In the first place, it is false. God is not the Father of men in the high and peculiar sense of that term, until they have already been saved. Until then they are not the children of God. Until then they do not belong to the family of God, but are by nature "children of wrath." This is the uniform testimony of the New Testament. Until sinners have been saved through the mercy of Christ, from condemnation and death, they are strangers and enemies, without God and without hope in the world. God commendeth his love toward us in that while we were yet enemies Christ died for us. After salvation comes adoption. After reconciliation and pardon as rebels and enemies to the government of God, comes the investiture with sonship. Hence our Lord said to those who rejected Him, " If God were your Father, ye would love me." " Ye are of your father the devil."

To preach to men not yet saved by Jesus Christ, that God is their Father, is therefore both to contradict the words of Christ, and to put one's self in direct antagonism to the whole tenor of Scriptural teaching regarding the character of the impenitent and unbelieving, and their relations to God. The work of salvation must be wrought for them and in them before they can truthfully call God their Father. In order to sonship with God they must first be born of God. By the new birth alone does the sinner become a child of God. " That which is born of the flesh is flesh."

This great salvation none can secure for sinners but He who has been exalted a Prince and a Saviour, to give repentance and remission of sins. To Him alone must men be commended, to Him alone they must go for the salvation by which they become the children of God, and God becomes their Father.

Another reason why men cannot be saved by preaching to them the name of the Father is, that they do not know the Father, and they cannot know Him until He is revealed to them by the Son. As He only has manifested God to the intellect of the world, so He only makes the Father known to the sinful soul. This is his own explicit declaration : " No man knoweth the Father but the Son, and he to whomsoever the Son will reveal Him." " No man cometh unto the Father but by me." " He that hath seen me, hath seen the Father."

That Being, therefore, to whom men give the name of the Father, before they have been savingly enlightened by Jesus Christ, and have come to the Father by Him, and seen the Father in Him, is not the Father. It is not God. It is a creation of men's fancy ; and is as much an idol as anything that ever received the homage of ancient Roman and Greek, or of modern Brahmin or Buddhist.

He, therefore, who sees the Father, sees Him first of all in Christ Jesus. If one sees not the Father in Him, one sees Him not at all. Christ is the gift of the Father's love. In Christ alone is the manifestation of the Father's heart towards men. Through Christ alone does the Father's voice reach the ears of men. For Christ is the Word of God. He, therefore, who has the heart of a son towards God, is moved to love as a child by first beholding the love of God as a father in the giving of his only-begotten Son. He who truly sees God as his Father, sees the Father's heart in that of Jesus Christ. He who truly hears himself called a child of God, hears the glad sound first in the mercy of the Lord Jesus Christ. He who has the spirit of adoption, and cries from the heart, " Abba, Father," as he looks to the throne of a holy God and righteous lawgiver, has that spirit, and cries thus to God, because he has been pardoned as a penitent sinner by Him who alone has power on earth to forgive sins, and has been clothed by Him with the robe, and endowed with the prerogatives of sonship. " To as many as received Him, to them gave He power to become the sons of God, even to them that believe on his name."

This is the position which the Scriptures assign to Jesus Christ. He is the only Saviour of sinners. His is the only name on which they can call and find salvation. He only makes God known to men as the Father; He alone brings them into such relations to God that He becomes their Father and they his children.

The Apostle Paul was looking upon Jesus Christ in just this light when he commended Him so highly to the Philippians, and declared that his name had become higher than that of any other being, and that to which all creatures should sooner or later render homage : " Let this mind be in you which was in Christ Jesus : who being in the form of God, thought it not robbery to be equal with God ; but made Himself of no reputation, and took upon Him the form of a servant, and was made in the likeness of men ; and being found in fashion as a man, He humbled Himself, and became obedient unto death, even the death of the cross. Wherefore God also hath highly exalted Him (after He had humbled Himself) and given Him a name which is above every name ; that at the name of Jesus every knee should bow of beings in heaven, and beings in earth, and beings under the earth; and that every tongue should confess that Jesus Christ is Lord, to the glory of God the Father."

It was not the language of mistaken zeal, therefore, that Doddridge used when he wrote those tender and earnest words,—

> "Jesus, I love thy charming name;
> 'Tis music to mine ear;
> Fain would I sound it out so loud
> That earth and heaven might hear."

Nor was it the enthusiasm and exultation of an idolater that moved Duncan when he wrote that majestic hymn, beginning,—

> "All hail the power of Jesus' name!
> Let angels prostrate fall:
> Bring forth the royal diadem,
> And crown Him Lord of all."

Nor was it the fondness of a mistaken faith doomed to sad disappointment that inspired Watts to write so devoutly,—

> "People and realms of every tongue
> Dwell on his love with sweetest song:
> And infant voices shall proclaim
> Their early blessings on his *name*.
>
> "Let every creature rise and bring
> Peculiar honors to our king:
> Angels descend with songs again,
> And earth repeat the loud Amen!"

All these writers, and all who exalt the name of Jesus, making it the watchword of hope to a ruined world, the talisman of salvation to the lost, the eternal joy of the saved, are moving within the limits of Scriptural example and command. They are as one with the Father and the Holy Spirit; as one with all the holy angels; as one with all inspired men; as one with all the ransomed in heaven.

3. The third inference from the words before us therefore, is, that they who turn away from Jesus Christ and refuse the salvation that He offers them, must be lost.

There is no other being in the universe on whom they can call for salvation, and be answered. There is no other Saviour known in heaven. God has provided no other salvation for lost men but that which Christ offers them. The Holy Ghost reveals no other Saviour to those whom He convinces of sin.

Let me urge this thought on your serious attention, my dying hearers. You are shut up to the grace and mercy of this one Being, Jesus Christ, if you would live. Your sins can never be forgiven unless Jesus Christ becomes your propitiation. You can never become a child of God, never an heir of heaven, unless Jesus Christ shall make you one. There is salvation in no other: "for there is none other name under heaven given among men whereby we must be saved."

This is the reason why He himself says to you, "He that believeth on the Son hath everlasting life, but he that believeth not the Son shall not see life, but the wrath of God abideth on him." This is the reason why He commissioned his disciples to preach to every creature, declaring in his name and by his authority, "He that believeth and is baptized shall be saved; but he that believeth not shall be damned."

It is with this commission that this young servant of Christ comes to you now to take the pastoral oversight of this people. He is Christ's messenger to you. His one work is to proclaim salvation to you in Christ's name and perfect you in that salvation.[1]

[1] Preached at the ordination of Walter W. Hammond, as pastor of Pierrepont Street Church, Brooklyn, N. Y., Thursday evening, September 10, 1868.

SERMON XVII.

HOW JESUS SPAKE.

JOHN vii. 46. — *Never man spake like this man.*

GREAT multitudes were now flocking to Jesus and attending upon his ministry. As they heard his instructions, saw his miracles, and felt the influence of his presence, they began to be convinced that He was the Christ, and they were declaring their convictions aloud.

The Pharisees and chief priests became alarmed at this movement among the people, and sent officers to arrest Him and bring Him before the Sanhedrim. But when they came where He was and heard Him speaking to the crowds about Him they could not execute their commission. There was a something in his person and bearing that struck them with awe. His words fell upon their ears with a strange and mysterious power. They were helpless before Him, though they had come armed with all the authority of the highest court of the nation.

They returned without Him, therefore, to the Pharisees and chief priests; and, to the inquiry, "Why have ye not brought Him?" their reply was, "Never man spake like this man." They gave no explanation: they offered no excuse. They had felt the restraining power of the Lord's presence, and yielded to the subduing influence of his words. They probably did not understand clearly why they had returned without accomplishing the object for which they had been sent; and it was impossible, doubtless, for them to give a satisfactory reason for their strange conduct.

Other passages in the Gospels bring to light this same awe-inspiring and subduing power of the Lord's presence and words. It is said, for example, by Luke, that those who heard his discourses, "were astonished at his doctrine, for his word was with power." Again, on a memorable occasion when He had put the Sadducees to silence in their attempts to confound Him, and had so replied to the quibbling interrogatories of the Pharisees that they were silenced also; from that day forth, says the Evangelist, no man durst ask Him any more questions. They were unable to withstand the power of his words, and they feared again to provoke that power against themselves.

A still more marked example, resembling the one before us, is that given by the Evangelist John, — when the hour of our Lord's final sufferings was near. Again officers were sent out to arrest Him and bring Him before the Sanhedrim. He saw them coming, and "went forth to meet them; and said unto them, Whom seek ye? They answered Him, Jesus of Nazareth. Jesus said unto them, I am he. As soon then as He had said unto them, I am he, they went backward and fell to the ground."

You will call to mind also that interesting scene described by the Evangelist Luke, when the parents of Jesus found Him in the temple, when He was but twelve years old, "sitting in the midst of the doctors, both hearing them, and asking them questions. And all that heard Him were astonished at his understanding and answers."

There was ever this mysterious power in the presence of Jesus, and this majesty in his speech. Men could never trifle with Him, nor treat his words with levity. Nor has this influence left his words as they have come down to our own times. The experience of the officers of the Jewish Sanhedrim has been repeated in every age, and among all people who have heard or read the words of Jesus in the Gospel. They reach, and move the hearts of men, and arouse their consciences. They compel solemn and earnest thought in view of the responsibilities of human life. They awaken awe and reverence in view of the certainty of a coming judgment, and the realities of eternity. Few, indeed, are they who in any age have read the words of Jesus with careful attention, that have not, at one time or another found themselves uttering the same words that the officers used in their reply to the question of the Sanhedrim. There are thousands now, in all parts of the world, that daily close the New Testament, if not with the exclamation, certainly with the vivid conviction, "Never man spake like this man." There is a something in his words, something in the way in which He speaks, that distinguishes Him from all other religious teachers, and gives what He says a power that is found in no other writings.

Let us give our attention for a few minutes to the style of our Saviour's address, the manner in which He spake. Wherein, so far as we can discover, was his manner of speaking unlike that of other great teachers?

1. The first thing that we notice is the air of authority with which the words of Jesus are spoken. They seem to be the utterances of one who was conscious, not only of a right, but of a divine commission, to speak; and who regarded those whom He addressed as under obligation to heed whatever He taught, and to obey all that He commanded. It is the same whatever the subject of which He treats. If He speaks as a revealer of hidden truth, making known the deep mysteries of the divine nature, and of human destiny, He speaks as one whose prerogative it is to reveal hidden things, and to require men to give attention to them. If He utters words of counsel and consolation to the ignorant and afflicted, He does it as one who knows that his counsel is more than advice; that it is binding on the consciences of those to whom He gives it; that His consolations are more than the expression of sympathy, that they bring those to whom He ministers under obligation to receive them, and be comforted. If He opens his mouth to pronounce censure and rebuke, it is as one whose censure is a divine condemnation, and whose rebuke is the admonition and warning of heaven.

It is the same whatever the circumstances in which He is placed. Though a lad of but twelve years, He sits among the doctors in the temple as one who has a right to be there; and not only answers their questions, as one having authority to teach the teachers of the nation, but asks them questions also as one whose prerogative it is to sit in judgment on them, and hold them to an account for the manner in which they discharge their office, and for the matter that enters into their instructions. And, though He is a dutiful son, living in loving and filial subjection to his parents, yet there is the tone of deferential authority, and of conscious lordship, held in obedient submission to his mother, when He responds to her amazed inquiry, "Son, why hast thou thus dealt with us? Behold thy father and I have sought thee sorrowing." There is no disrespect, but there is authority in submission, when He replies: "How is it that ye sought me? Wist ye not that I must be about my Father's business?"

When one of the first men of the nation came to Him and patronizingly confessed the conviction of the principal religious teachers that He was one commissioned of God, Jesus, so far from seeming flattered by such attentions, and receiving the patronage as something for which He ought humbly to acknowledge his indebtedness, responds in such a manner as reveals to Nicodemus, and makes him keenly realize that he is dealing with one who cannot be looked down upon, but must be looked up to. He cannot be patronized. He is rather one who has patronage to bestow, and from whom men may receive it too and not lose their manhood and self-respect. To Nicodemus' confession, "Rabbi, we know that thou art a teacher come from God: for no man can do these miracles that thou doest, except God be with him," Jesus responds with the air of a superior invested with authority over the rulers themselves: "Verily, verily, I say unto thee, except a man be born again he cannot see the kingdom of God." There is scarcely anything in all the Scriptures, not even the giving of the Law that was promulgated amid thunderings and lightnings, and the manifestation of the divine presence on Sinai, that is more imperial in its tone than these solemn words of the young and despised Nazarene to the Jewish ruler. He never abated this authoritative tone in his dealings with the leading men of the nation, and the members of the Sanhedrim. He always spoke to them as one having authority to judge them, to teach them, to warn and rebuke them for their sins, and to offer pardon and salvation to them on his own conditions. Even when He had permitted Himself to come unto their hands, and was arraigned before them as a blasphemer, and then handed over to Pilate for punishment, as a malefactor, his bearing is still that of a king. Whether we look at his calm and dignified silence, as He submits Himself without a murmur or complaint to their brutal indignities, or to the few and pithy replies He makes to the direct questions of those who have Him in their power, both his silence and his words are alike the expression of an unruffled consciousness of superiority and of Lordship. The same is true of all that He uttered while He was hanging on the cross. He still spake as a prince, and his words were with power. Look at the two last sentences that fell from his lips: "When Jesus saw his mother, and the disciple standing by whom He loved, He saith unto his mother, Woman, behold thy son. Then said He to the disciple, Behold thy mother. And from that hour that disciple took her unto his own home." His words were spoken in infinite love and tenderness, but they were spoken to be obeyed. Both the mother and the disciple so received them, and yielded the obedience of devoted love and profound reverence. The last sentence of all bears the same impress of sovereignty: "It is finished." He is conscious of his mission and of its purpose; and as his work comes before Him in review He passes sentence upon it for Himself. With unfaltering confidence He pronounces his work "finished." They are the words of one who feels that He has the right to judge and pronounce for Himself upon his own mission; and authority to declare the purpose of his mission accomplished.

Thus it is that the whole bearing of Jesus, from the first to the last of his earthly history, makes an impression on the reader similar to that which was made on the people who heard his Sermon on the Mount. The Evangelist says that it came to pass that "when Jesus had ended these sayings, the people were astonished at his doctrine; for He taught them as one having authority, and not as the scribes." The tone and manner of his words amid the tempest on the sea run through all that He spoke among men: "He rose and rebuked the wind, and said unto the sea, Peace; be still. And the wind ceased, and there was a great calm. And the disciples feared exceedingly, and said one to another, What manner of man is this, that even the wind and the sea obey him!"

It was not an air of authority put on, — the state and dignity of a prince assumed; but it was the spirit of authority dwelling in Him as a part of his own being, and going forth from Him, as the rays of light and heat go forth from the sun, and making itself felt in silent might and majesty. It is this influence that makes itself felt now wherever his word goes, and is slowly but surely bringing the public opinion of the world into harmony with his morality, and enthroning his religion in the understandings and hearts of mankind. It is this power that is coveted and pretended to by all false religions from Buddhism to the Papacy and a godless High-churchism, but which they cannot obtain or wield. Their assumptions of it become — to all save the darkest minded, and the most hopelessly enslaved vassals of superstition and ignorance — most ludicrous and bombastic absurdities. The very words, which, on the lips of Jesus, are fitting and never excite in any intelligent and candid mind the sense of incongruity, become solemn mockery or ridiculous pretentiousness when uttered by pope or bishop or priest.

This spirit of authority with which the words of Jesus are instinct when uttered by Himself, or in his name, and especially when brought home to the heart and conscience by the Holy Ghost, is that which gives power and effectiveness to the truth in the conviction of sin, and in imparting to the penitent a sense of pardon and an assurance of acceptance with God. It is because Christ's words are words of divine authority that they bow the stubborn and rebellious heart of the sinner, and force him to cry for mercy; and it is because they are words of authority that that same heart, believing in the promise of pardon made to faith, receives the promise and goes from the mercy-seat having peace with God through our Lord Jesus Christ, rejoicing in hope of eternal life.

In the tone of calm, dignified, self-evidencing authority that is in the words of Jesus, it is true that "never man spake like this man."

2. Another characteristic of our Saviour's manner of speaking is found in the quiet, unostentatious claim which He evidently makes to perfect knowledge of every matter of which He treats.

He never speculates, nor theorizes; He never guesses or balances probabilities; He does not even argue and reason upon the subjects of which He speaks. He always speaks as one who knows; and there is that in his bearing that begets, in those who hear, an assurance that He does know everything whereof He affirms. Whether He speaks of the secret thoughts of men's hearts, or of the hitherto unrevealed purposes of God,

He speaks in calm, clear, unfaltering tones, with the ease and naturalness and unsuspecting assurance of one who is familiar with these thoughts and purposes, and knows that there is no possibility of his being in error. "Behold an Israelite indeed, in whom there is no guile," said He as He saw Nathanael approaching Him. Nathanael felt at once that Jesus knew him. He was astonished at the fact, but he could not question it. His response was, therefore, "Whence knowest thou me?" Jesus answered and said unto him, "Before that Philip called thee, when thou wast under the fig tree, I saw thee." This was enough for the true-hearted and guileless Nathanael. There was something in the words of Jesus which assured him that there was a divine knowledge in them. His heart, therefore, went out spontaneously to Him, and he made an immediate confession of Him as the Messiah: "Rabbi, thou art the Son of God; thou art the king of Israel!" And thus, onward to the end of his ministry, his bearing among those who were with Him and heard his words, convinced them that "He needed not that any should testify of man: for He knew what was in man." Those who came under the influence of his presence and teachings could appreciate the saying of the woman of Samaria: "Come, see a man that told me all things that ever I did."

It was the same when He spoke of God. There was no uncertainty in his tones. In all He said of God there was that which seemed to repeat the words that He had said to Nicodemus: "We speak that we do know, and testify that we have seen." And a candid reading of his words now will, and yet always does carry conviction to the mind of the reader, that the only begotten Son who is in the bosom of the Father hath declared Him.

Not only God and man, but time and eternity, are naked and open to his view; and He treats of them with the same calm confidence with which He speaks of the most familiar objects of his daily life. The relations of men to each other and to God, and the great principles that enter into these relations, and determine their duties and responsibilities, these are all treated in the same manner. He knows; he therefore asserts, but does not speculate.

It is this characteristic of our Saviour's teachings that gives them such an air of positiveness. He declares that things are, and that things are not. He announces unhesitatingly that things will be, and that things will not be. He affirms, without any attempt at proof, — his own words carrying conviction, because they are stamped with the impress of knowledge, — that certain things ought to be, and ought to be done, and that certain other things ought not to be, and ought not to be done. He commands and forbids with an air of absolute certainty that what He commands is right, and what He forbids is wrong; and the same seal of knowledge carries conviction to those who hear Him, that He is right when He commands and when He forbids. In fine, there never appears to be the shadow of distrust or uncertainty in his language, as though it was possible for Him to be mistaken.

Yet his positiveness is not that of dogmatism and self-conceit. It is the farthest possible from that of ignorance and narrow-mindedness, or of scanty and superficial knowledge. There is, therefore, nothing arrogant about it; nothing that is offensive; nothing that seems unnatural, and out of harmony with that gentleness and love and tenderness, and nice appreciation of fitness, which always gives such a charm to his character and presence.

With men generally, the most positive characters are those whose range of thought is most narrow. Those who are most positive in their general bearing and speech are those who know the least concerning the things of which they are most ready to speak. Enlarge their range of thought and they will become more humble. Add to their knowledge, and they will manifest far less certainty that they are always and in all things right, and competent to sit in judgment on any matter that may come before them. The wisest men are certain of but few things. They have arrived at a *knowledge* of these, and they treat of them with modest assurance. They trust in them confidently, and cautiously extend their inferences from them till they come to judgments, more or less satisfactory, regarding other things, as the things they know cast on these other things a clearer or more obscure light. With them there is positiveness as far as there is knowledge; and as their positiveness is manifestly the fruit of knowledge, it is not offensive to others. Men do not disrelish it, nor shrink from it, and condemn it in their hearts, as a thing unseemly.

This is the character of our Saviour's positiveness. It is that of one conscious of an absolute and perfect knowledge of everything concerning which He speaks. He asserts it because He knows it. Those who listen to Him are impressed with the conviction that what He says He knows. This is the reason why there is nothing dogmatical in his bearing, and why those who hear Him speak are not only not offended with his positiveness, but are won by, and rest in it, with a sense of perfect security.

It is this tone of positiveness that gives the words of Jesus such power over the hearts of men whose minds cannot be satisfied with uncertainties. Such men yearn for something sure to rest their faith upon. They cannot accept mere reasonings. They feel that there is the possibility of error in the most specious and logical of arguments. They cannot accept mere inference from premises that seem to be well established. If the premises are right, there may be nevertheless an error in the inference. They must have the *dicta* of absolute knowledge. They cannot be satisfied with anything short of the positive assertion of one who knows and cannot be mistaken.

This is in fact the condition of mind of every earnest inquirer after the will of God, and the way of salvation. He is beyond the point where mere argument is needed. He has been speculating and reasoning, it may be, on the great questions that pertain to his relations to God and eternity, and has amused himself and others by his speculations. But now all this is vain and trifling. He is in earnest now to lay hold on eternal life. He has now come to realize that he is in need of mercy and pardon; and he must know the terms on which they can be obtained. He cannot be satisfied now with anything short of absolute and positive declaration from the fountain of authority itself. He wants to be commanded, that he may obey. He craves assertion, that he may believe. His whole soul demands distinct and positive declarations and promises that he may trust and be at peace.

It is just suited to the necessities of the soul, then, that the religion that saves it is a religion of faith. It must go out of itself, and rest in God. It cannot trust in any of its own processess of thought, nor in any of the conclusions to which these processes may lead it. It must go out of all these and find rest in simple, childlike confidence in what God has said.

This is the whole philosophy of faith, and of salvation by faith. It is an impossibility that the soul should feel secure resting in anything but the word of divine authority and of divine knowledge.

The philosophy of rationalism is exactly the opposite of this. It cannot endure authority. It cannot put up with positiveness. It must evermore float on the current of its own speculations, and amuse itself with its own vagaries. But it can never find peace. It can never be assured. The religion of rationalism can never appropriate the language of Paul, " I know whom I have believed, and am persuaded that He is able to keep that which I have committed to Him."

The philosophy of churchism is based on this principle of authority and of positiveness; but it traces authority to a false source. It bids the soul trust, not in the word of Christ, not in his authority and knowledge, but in the dictum of a self-constituted priesthood, and in the ceremonies of a pretentious human organization arrogating to itself solely the name of Christ's Church. It speaks in the name of Christ and claims for its ceremonies and appointments Christ's authority. But the power of real authority is wanting. To the earnest soul, seeking for life, all the appliance of churchism, or, what is the same thing, ritualism, are a sham and a cheat. After it has gone through with them all, it still cries out for something that can give it peace with God. And it is not until it can hear the voice that stilled the tempest and raised the dead, speaking in revelation and commanding it what to do, that it can find rest. There is authority and knowledge in his words when such a soul hears them, and therefore it can take them and feel secure. When it hears them it is satisfied, and says, with a meaning unknown to the officers of the Sanhedrim, " Never man spake like this man."

SERMON XVIII.
THE RESURRECTION OF JESUS CHRIST THE GROUND OF HOPE.

1 PETER i. 3. — *Blessed be the God and Father of our Lord Jesus Christ, who, according to his abundant mercy, hath begotten us again into a lively hope by the resurrection of Jesus Christ from the dead.*

A LIVELY hope is a living hope. The Apostle's word is the same that is used by the sacred writers when they speak of God as the " living " God, to distinguish Him from the lifeless idols of the heathen. The hope into which a believer is begotten is called a living hope, because it is full of activity and power, like the living God; and is not dormant and inoperative, like the dead divinities of idolaters. It is a hope moved also and sustained by intelligence and thought and knowledge. It therefore imparts life and energy and purpose to the whole soul that indulges it. But the hopes imparted to men by the fables and false religions of the world were vague, indefinite, ignorant, thoughtless; and hence, for the most part, they were utterly powerless to influence the life, or shape the character of those who indulged them.

Nothing could be more gloomy and desolate than was the condition of the world in its hopes — rather, its hopelessness — respecting a future life when our Saviour came among men. Their minds were full of speculation; but full also of doubt and uncertainty. They were the prey of indefinite yearnings and fearful apprehensions. But there was no knowledge, no certainty, no assurance, no well-defined expectations. All was dark and unsatisfying, powerless to awaken and sustain hope, or to give elevation and purpose to thought and life. The grave was the only thing in the future of which they were sure. All beyond was dark and repellant to their imagination; to their knowledge it was blank uncertainty.

This was the dismal state of all those to whom the gospel of Christ came. They had no certain hold on a life beyond the present. There was nothing in the world's experience, or speculations and reasonings, that gave or could give any assurance of a life after death. But the gospel came to men, not only asserting such a life, but demonstrating its existence. It asserted it not as the surmise or the conclusion of a philosopher, but as the revelation of one who had showed Himself worthy to be believed as a messenger come from God. Then, by an amount of evidence that could not be set aside, and so simple, so clear, so satisfactory that candor and intelligence could not question its truthfulness, it proved that this same messenger, after He had been murdered by his enemies, had risen from the dead, and, in his own person, become an example of that living again after death which He had revealed as the destiny of all men. Like the return of Columbus from the western continent, He had declared his belief of its existence. On his return he could say, "I have seen it," and men could say it is there, for here is a man who has been there.

But this is only the lower immortality, — that of which the world dreamed and speculated, — not that which the gospel revealed to men as an object of desire. This immortality of mere existence, the gospel declared, might be an object that men ought to dread rather than covet. The true immortality consists not in the fact of an existence after death, nor in the eternal duration of this existence, but in its character. Men might exist after death, and their existence be one of misery. This the gospel declared would be the lot of all final enemies of God and holiness. The existence after death is true immortality only as it is an existence in bliss and in the favor of God.

The first kind of immortality — the highest that was conceived of by the world — was only existence in death, just as the life of an unregenerate sinner now is life in death. He is dead in trespasses and sins, though in the lower sense of life he lives. The immortality which Christ announced, and which He brought to light, and which the gospel sets before us as an object of desire, and commands us to make earnest endeavors to attain it, is an eternally holy and blissful condition of the soul raised to life out of its death in trespasses and sins, and confirmed forever in the favor and love of God in heaven.

Such a blissful condition of the soul is its immortality. Nothing else is true immortality in the New Testament sense of the term; as nothing is left in the true sense of the term but the union of the soul with God and his love and favor.

It is to a hope of this immortality that the Apostle says believers are begotten again by the resurrection of Jesus Christ from the dead. The lower immortality is never held up to men as an object of hope. The higher sense is always involved wherever the sacred writers speak of immortality. The verse following our text shows that this was what Peter had in mind as the object of the believer's hope: " Blessed be the God and Father of our Lord Jesus Christ, who, according to his abundant mercy, hath begotten us again unto a living hope by the resurrection of Jesus Christ from the dead, unto an inheritance incorruptible and undefiled, and that fadeth not away, reserved in heaven for you." The second clause is explanatory of the first. The hope to which those to whom he was writing had been begotten again by the resurrection of Jesus Christ from the dead, reaches forward to this pure and incorruptible inheritance in heaven. They are begotten to it again, as to something they once had, but which they had lost. They had it, as did all men, in the unfallen state of the race; but in the fall all was lost. To a hope of this lost inheritance the believer is begotten again by the resurrection of Jesus Christ from the dead.

Let us look at the connection of thought here announced. What is the connection between the resurrection of Jesus Christ and the existence of this hope in his disciples?

1. The resurrection of Jesus Christ is a perfect demonstration that all which Christ claimed for his mission was true; and a demonstration of the efficacy of his work to secure salvation for sinners. Christ claimed to have come to this world on a mission from God. God sent Him as his messenger. He claimed also that He came into this world to make the salvation of sinners possible. He pointed to his death and said, that, in dying He should become a ransom for sinners, and that through the shedding of his blood remission of sins would be secured for the penitent. These were the claims that Jesus Christ made while He was among men in the flesh. His character and **works gave** abundant evidence that his claims were true. No

man could look at his character, and reconcile that character with the supposition either that Jesus Christ was mistaken in his view of his own mission, or that He was an impostor. But there were multitudes of men then living, as there are multitudes of men living now, whose moral feelings were too low, and their moral perceptions too dull, to see and appreciate the harmony and glory of Christ's character. They were, therefore, to some extent at least, insensible to the impression which that character ought to make on all minds, and which it does make on all pure and elevated minds. For them, and also to some extent for all others, the miracles of Christ were necessary as proofs of his divine mission. They came in as proofs. Christ claimed that they were proofs. The leading minds, as well as the common minds of the nation acknowledged that they were proofs that Jesus of Nazareth was a teacher come from God.

But He was put to death. This fact threw much of the past of his history into doubt and uncertainty to the minds of those who, up to this point, had been well assured regarding Him. They had, many of them, taken Him for the promised Messiah. Their conviction that He was the Messiah was as firm as their conviction that He came from God. Indeed, the two were blended together, and upheld each other. If one was false they knew not what to make of the other. If He was not the Messiah, then not only were they in the dark regarding his true character, but his own claim that He was the Messiah was false. What then could they think of his claim to be a divine messenger? The divinity of his mission and the efficacy of his work as the Saviour of sinners, were indissolubly united. Something more was needed than even his character and miracles, to set the minds of his disciples at rest, after his death. These had been all-sufficient up to the moment of the crucifixion. From that moment they were obscured. The force of their testimony remained. This could not be invalidated. But something was needed that should connect them with the new scene into which the death of Jesus had brought the disciples; something that should connect the past and the present which had been secured by the crucifixion. In other words, his death had ended all the testimony of his life and character, which, but for his death, would have been all that their minds required. But now there was needed a testimony that should remove the cloud that death had brought over the testimony already given, and in removing that cloud should so supplement what had been given before, that no room should be left for doubt. This testimony was given by the resurrection of Jesus Christ from the dead. When his disciples knew that He had risen, then all the past was assured to them anew, and the testimony to the divinity of their Master's mission was carried through the grave, linking the life that was before death with a life after death, and leaving nothing more to be desired, so strong, so cumulative, so clear, that nothing could ever shake their confidence in it.

The same testimony which was made thus perfect and satisfactory regarding the divinity of his mission, established also the fact that the work which He claimed to do for the salvation of sinners was done effectually. His death was penal. It was endured, so He claimed, and so the gospel fully asserts, in behalf of sinners. In dying He bore their sins, and suffered their penalty. In this way alone could their sins be forgiven, and they be restored to the favor of God. His death became, therefore, in the light of his own teachings, as it was made by all the Scriptures, the great central fact in his mission. By his death He was to do the one great work of that mission. If his death was of the character that He claimed for it, then it was a satisfaction to divine justice for the sins of men, a propitiation, an expiation. If it was not of this character, then all their hopes were gone. He was not "the Lamb of God that taketh away the sin of the world," and they had looked to Him in vain. He was not the propitiation for our sins, nor for the sins of the whole world, and they had hoped in Him in vain.

As, therefore, the teachings of Christ needed the testimony of his miracles to demonstrate that they were divine ; so did his death need a great and unanswerable testimony to demonstrate that it was an expiation for sin. The resurrection of Jesus Christ from the dead was this testimony. It was so counted by his disciples, and it is so claimed by all the writers of the New Testament. It was God's unequivocal acknowledgment and assertion of the efficacy of the death of Christ as a propitiation for human guilt. By raising Him from the dead, God not only indorsed as true every word that Jesus of Nazareth taught, and every claim that He had made for Himself and his mission, but He proclaimed in tones that cannot be misunderstood nor denied, that the death of Jesus Christ removed every barrier that stood in the way of the forgiveness of sin, and the salvation and eternal life of the penitent sinner.

It was thus that He begot believers in Jesus Christ again unto a living hope — even to a hope of an inheritance incorruptible and undefiled, and that fadeth not away, reserved for them in heaven.

The Apostles always, therefore, exalted the resurrection of Christ and made it very prominent in their ministry. They preached " Christ crucified " as the real and only ground of a sinner's hope ; but they proclaimed the resurrection of Christ as the great and unanswerable demonstration that his death was a sure and all-sufficient ground of hope. The great argument was, and it remains the great argument of the gospel still, that because Jesus Christ rose from the dead, therefore his death was a satisfaction to divine justice for those in whose behalf He died. It was the expiation for their sins. In his death He was accepted of God as their ransom ; and deliverance from the penalty of their sins, and their full forgiveness through his blood, was made possible for them. His resurrection was the divine and unmistakable announcement of this acceptance.

2. The resurrection of Jesus Christ from the dead begets and sustains hope in the minds of believers because it is a satisfying proof to them that He is exalted to headship over them and to universal dominion in their behalf.

The resurrection of Jesus Christ was not simply a confirmation of the past in his teachings and claims, and of the efficacy of the work that He had already accomplished ; it was a pledge also of the future. It was a divine assurance that the claims which Christ had made for Himself and his kingdom in the future would prove to be true; and that He would be, and would do, all that He had foretold, and all that the great end for which He died required in order to its full accomplishment. Because it was a resurrection from such a death, it was the entering on the work of carrying out the purpose of that death. In this purpose was the exaltation of Jesus Christ to supreme dominion that He might rule, head over all things to his Church.

But if Christ was thus exalted, how could those who believed in Him fail of a living hope in Him regarding their own salvation? If He had died to redeem them, and now reigned supreme over all things for the especial purpose of completing the object of his death, how could they be despondent? They could not but hope. The resurrection of Jesus Christ was the divine assurance to their minds that He would by reigning for them bring every one of them off conquerors over every enemy, and give them an inheritance among the sanctified. Thus Paul reasons: "If we believe that Jesus died and rose again, even so also those which sleep in Jesus will God bring with Him." Hence he declares: "If thou shalt confess with thy mouth the Lord Jesus, and shalt believe in thy heart that God raised Him from the dead, thou shalt be saved."

This introduces us to a third thought, one intimately connected with this yet distinct from it.

3. The resurrection of Jesus Christ from the dead begets and sustains hope in the minds of believers because it is a satisfactory assurance of his immortality, and of the immortality of all who are in Him. That He rose from the dead was a proof, as we have seen, of the divinity of his mission, and of the efficacy of his death in making possible the salvation of penitent sinners; it was a proof also of his immortality, — of his immortality in both the lower and higher sense of the word. It showed Him superior to death, in its physical sense, because He rose from physical death in direct confirmation of his own words that He had power to lay down his life, and that He had power to take it again. It showed that He had entered into life in the higher sense, the life of the soul, to remain in it forever; because it was the clear declaration of God that his death had met and discharged the full penalty of the sin that He bore for his people, and under the weight of which He had sunk. When God raised Him from this death, which was suffered when He cried, "My God, my God, why hast thou forsaken me?" it was God's testimony that Christ had exhausted all the power of sin, and that He could never again be brought under its power. His immortality was assured to his people, therefore, by his resurrection. But it was for his people — for all those who believe in Him — that He submitted to death. It was the penalty of their sins He suffered. They

stood in Him before the law. They satisfied the law in Him. They rose in Him. They stood before the bar of divine justice and were accepted in Him. His death was their death, his resurrection was their resurrection. He took them into Himself and triumphed for them. His triumph was their triumph. His immortality is therefore their immortality. This is his own representation of the case: "Because I live ye shall live also."

No disciple who has learned his true relation to his Lord, and the real character of his Lord's death, can, therefore, fail of a living hope if he will consider rightly the power of his Lord's resurrection.

SERMON XIX.
NO CONDEMNATION TO BELIEVERS.

ROMANS viii. 1. — *There is therefore now no condemnation to them that are in Christ Jesus, who walk not after the flesh, but after the Spirit.*

THIS is a conclusion from the argument which the Apostle had been urging in the preceding chapters. His great aim was to show that " the gospel of Christ is the power of God unto salvation to every one that believeth;" and that therefore " a man is justified by faith without the deeds of the law." In Christ Jesus every believer has died to the law. He has so answered its penal claims that Christ has become the end or fulfillment of the law for righteousness to him. The necessary conclusion is, " There is therefore now no condemnation to them that are in Christ Jesus." I invite your attention to some of the reasons upon which this conclusion rests. To open the way for the better understanding of these reasons, I will make two negative remarks showing what are not reasons why there is no condemnation to them that are in Christ Jesus.

1. It is not because they do not sin. Christians do sin. None feel this more keenly than they do themselves. In all their being they are thoroughly conscious of it; and every one of them will admit most fully and unhesitatingly that the Scriptures are true in reference to himself at least, when they declare, " If we say we have no sin, we deceive ourselves and the truth is not in us." So far was the Apostle from making the conclusion found in our text rest upon such a basis, that, on the contrary, it was put in its present place as a special support and comfort to such as are most painfully conscious of sin; not only of sin in their outward acts, but of sin dwelling within them, and constantly making its presence and its power felt to their apprehension. The latter part of the

seventh chapter is a graphic description of this painful consciousness in the very persons in whose favor he draws the conclusion with which he begins the eighth chapter. In the seventh chapter he gives his own experience as to sinfulness and sinning. But he does not give it as an apostolic experience, nor as one peculiar to himself. He gives it as the common experience of true believers. He writes for them all, and his words are, and have ever been, the spontaneous utterances of all Christian souls, when he says, " What I would, that do I not; but what I hate, that do I." " For to will is present with me, but how to perform that which is good I find not. For the good that I would, I do not: but the evil which I would not, that I do." " I find then a law in my members, that when I would do good, evil is present with me. For I delight in the law of God after the inward man: but I see another law in my members warring against the law of my mind, and bringing me into captivity to the law of sin which is in my members. Oh wretched man that I am! who shall deliver me from the body of this death? I thank God, through Jesus Christ our Lord. So then, with the mind I myself serve the law of God; but with the flesh the law of sin." Immediately upon uttering this the Apostle brings in the declaration of our text. With a "*therefore*" that takes in this very experience, while it goes back to the beginning and includes all his argument, he assures all those who are tried with indwelling and outworking sin, as he himself was, " There is *now*, — even while we have this painful consciousness, and while we are engaged in this, at times, almost hopeless struggle, — there is now no condemnation to us who are in Christ Jesus, who — being in Him, and because we are in Him — walk not after the flesh but after the Spirit." For this, I remark in passing, is the exact force of the last clause of our text. It is thrown in, not as one of the conditions upon which exemption from condemnation is secure, but to indicate an unvarying characteristic of all who are in Christ Jesus. It is as true of all such, that they walk not after the flesh but after the Spirit, as it is that they are not under condemnation.[1]

The experience of Paul is reflected in that of all the Old and New Testament saints who have spoken to us on this subject.

[1] The best authorities reject this last clause as an interpolation. Yet it is true and Scriptural.

At the time when the Psalmist David showed the greatest faith in God, saying, " In thee, O Lord, do I hope : forsake me not O Lord : O my God be not far from me: make haste to help me, O Lord, my salvation,"— when thus expressing his piety, and his faith, he cries out, "There is no rest in my bones, because of my sin. For mine iniquities are gone over my head : as a heavy burden they are too heavy for me." This painful consciousness of sin eating like a canker into his soul, and poisoning the atmosphere he breathed, comes out frequently through the Psalms. It is especially prominent too in the Prophets. It pervades the writings of all the Apostles. No; it is not because those in Christ Jesus are sinless that there is no condemnation to them. If sinlessness be the ground of exemption, then none of the sacred writers can be counted among the saved.

2. It is not because God does not abhor and condemn the sin that is in them, and committed by them, as much as He does the sins of others, that there is no condemnation to them that are in Christ Jesus.

Sin itself is displeasing to God, whoever the sinner may be. In whomsoever found, it is "that abominable thing that God hates." There is sometimes cherished a sentiment directly opposite to this ; namely, that sin is a matter of small moment in the estimation of the Almighty, when it is found in one of his own children, as compared with what it is when found in others. Not unfrequently the very fact that true believers are exempt for condemnation, and that God does not visit their sin with avenging punishment, but pardons them for the sake of the Redeemer, is so stated, or the statement itself, though truly and scripturally made, is so misapprehended, or perverted, that this sentiment seems to be taught. Persons who preach faithfully the exact doctrine of the text, are thus, oftentimes, said to preach that the sins of believers are not as offensive in the sight of God as the sins of unbelievers are. But the dealings of God with his people have always taught a different lesson. " His wrath is revealed from heaven against all ungodliness, and unrighteousness of men," whether in believers or others. "He is of purer eyes than to behold evil ; and cannot look on iniquity." Besides He has never spared his children when they have clung to their sin ; but has visited them with the rod of his anger. How often did He explain to his people of old the reasons for their sufferings, when they came into trouble, by pointing them to the fact, that their sins had separated them from Him. And in the New Testament the same determination is apparent to have no fellowship with believers in their sins. "Remember from whence thou art fallen," said the Redeemer to the church at Ephesus, "and repent and do the first works, or else I will come unto thee quickly and will remove thy candlestick out of his place, except thou repent." This He said to them, notwithstanding that He had first commended them for their "works and labor and patience, and their intolerance of them which were evil;" and that they had borne, and had patience, and for his name's sake had labored, and had not fainted. It was the same with the other churches in Asia, however much there was in any of them to be commended by the Lord, yet wherever any sin was found unrepented of, his anger burned towards it. It was the sin of the Laodiceans that called from Him that most withering rebuke which showed so clearly his utter abhorrence of sin when it is cherished by his people. If it was still clung to He would spurn them from Him as a nauseous draught is cast from the mouth. No; sin in the people of God is not less hateful in his sight than is sin in others. Nay; is it not more offensive? The nearer perfect anything is, the more glaring and offensive a blemish, — oath from a lady as compared with one from a man. Sin itself is abhorrent to his whole being, and his whole being, as his throne, is in deadly and eternal hostility to it. If He cannot separate his people from their sins, He will separate them from Himself. Because He is holy He must do this. If He could connive at sin He Himself would become unholy.

But there is no condemnation to them that are in Christ Jesus, because —

1. He, in his own person, has so answered for all their sins that a full and unreserved pardon has been vouchsafed to them for his sake. This has taken them out from under condemnation. Christ Himself has so suffered and obeyed in their stead, that out of respect to what He has done they have been released from all the condemnation that their transgressions of the law of God had brought upon them.

This truth is set forth very strongly by the inspired writers.

They do not, indeed, encourage the idea which some men have attempted to support from their language, that believers were so in Christ that they absolutely and literally were punished in Him; and in his death suffered literally all the penalty of their sins. This view of salvation destroys the possibility of pardon. If you have literally and absolutely suffered the entire penalty of your sins, because of your oneness with Christ, then you need no pardon. Deliverance from all the penalty of sin is your right, and you can claim it at the bar of infinite justice. There is then no grace in the matter of your salvation. Salvation is by the law itself. But though the sacred writers do not teach such a sentiment, yet their language carries the idea that Christ, in his obedience and suffering, is the substitute of his people, so far, that out of respect to what He has done and suffered, the grace of God can reach every one of them in pardon, and in the renewing and sanctifying influences of the Holy Spirit. The language which they use in conveying this idea is so strong and so emphatic that we cannot overstate the Scriptural doctrine of the substitution of Christ, — that is, his suffering in his people's stead, — if we leave any room whatever for pardon and grace to reach them. If we stop short of making the sufferings and obedience of Christ so literally those of his people that all distinction between Him and them is lost sight of, and they have therefore a claim in their own right on the justice of God, because of what He has done, or rather, what they can do in Him, — if we stop short of this, and leave any room whatever for all of our salvation to be of grace and through pardon, — then we cannot, I say, press the idea of substitution too far. "He bore our sins." "He was made a curse for us." "The Lord hath laid on Him the iniquities of us all." "With his stripes we are healed." "The chastisement of our peace was upon Him." "Brethren, ye are become dead to the law by the body of Christ." "He who has no sin was made sin for us that we might be made the righteousness of God in Him." And, not to multiply passages further, "Christ hath become the end of the law for righteousness to every one that believeth."

These are strong words. There is no holding back in them. They teach unhesitatingly and unequivocally that Christ was in his sufferings the substitute of his people; and that He so answered for their sins that they are, on account of his sufferings, delivered from all punishment. But these passages must never be separated from others that define the nature of the salvation which He wrought out for his people. It is true "we have redemption through his blood," but that redemption consists in "the forgiveness of sins;" and if in forgiveness, then not in our having so suffered in our substitute that we have created for ourselves a claim on infinite justice to be delivered from the penalty of our sins. It is true that "the blood of Jesus Christ the Son of God cleanseth from all sin;" but it is only so far as to leave it true that "if we confess our sins, God is faithful and just to forgive us our sins," and thus in conjunction with forgiveness, "to cleanse us from all iniquity."

There is very little danger, however, I apprehend, of our pressing the fact of substitution too far. Our danger lies mostly in the opposite direction. We too often come so far short of apprehending the great truth that Christ died for our sins, that we have no foundation left to stand upon when we feel ourselves to be sinking under the burden of our guilt. We are, in other words, more in danger of attempting a legal salvation by ourselves than of carrying the idea of substitution so far as to make salvation legal in Christ.

2. There is no condemnation to them that are in Christ Jesus, because He is a continual substitute for them. As they were first delivered from condemnation because He so suffered in their behalf that pardon could reach them, so He is now so far their surety and substitute before the bar of God that his interposition saves them from coming again under condemnation.

This idea, too, is boldly and unequivocally set forth and dwelt upon by the sacred writers. They teach us that the moment we come to be in Christ, by the exercise of a living faith in Him, we come into a new relation to God. We are then no longer under the law, — as a condemning power, — but under grace. Christ remains what He then became, "the end of the law for righteousness" to us. We become so far his that He counts us his own body. He, as the head and representative of all, ever lives to make intercession for us. And if any of us sin He is our advocate with the Father. Believers stand, therefore, not in the relation of those amenable to the law and bound to answer its penal claims in their own persons, but as amenable directly to Christ, whose they have become by the purchase of his blood. He Himself answers for them to the divine law. By their faith they have committed to Him all their responsibilities to the law, as a condemning power. This is the meaning of all those passages that speak of his "making intercession for us" — his being "our advocate" — of our being "in Him" — and his being "our life."

This is what Paul teaches us in that memorable passage in the eighth of Romans, where he asks, "What shall we then say to these things? If God be for us, who can be against us? He that spared not his own Son but delivered Him up for us all, how shall He not with Him also freely give us all things? Who shall lay anything to the charge of God's elect? It is God that justifieth. Who is he that condemneth? It is Christ that died, yea rather that is risen again, who is even at the right hand of God, who also maketh intercession for us."

The fact that believers are in Christ, or that they are believers, implies that they are continual penitents, and that they are sincere lovers of holiness, and that they cannot be in love with sin. For "if any man be in Christ he is a new creature;" his heart has been changed, and remains changed. The new creation of God in Christ Jesus is " unto good works ; " and those who are new-created will never fail to aim at the doing of them. They that are in Christ Jesus are dead to sin, and therefore they cannot live any longer therein. This state of mind is as abiding in them as is the intercession of Christ in their behalf for their outward salvation. It is therefore always as proper — so far as pertains to their characters and dispositions — to continue them in a state of justification as it was to bring them into it at first. God does not, by keeping them in this state, encourage those who cherish sin in their hearts, and are enemies of his law. The presence in the soul of love to sin, and enmity to holiness, shows that there is no faith in the Redeemer in that soul ; and if no faith in Him, then there is no union with Him, and the soul is not in Him ; it is therefore yet under condemnation. But because the soul that is in Christ is in a state of allegiance to God, and cannot love sin, but must and will ever delight in holiness, and in the law of God, therefore there is a fitness that, if any of them sin, they should have an eternal advocate with the Father; and that He should continually answer in his own person all the claims of the law against them as transgressors. Thus it is true of them every moment, even when they most keenly feel the power of their sins, that there is now no condemnation to them that are in Christ Jesus. He has become, and now is, the end — the fulfillment — of the law for righteousness to them. And it is their privilege, when they become conscious of sin, to betake themselves at once, and with full assurance of faith, to the advocacy and the saving favor of the Lord Jesus Christ. They are not in the relation of criminals awaiting the infliction of penalty, but in the relation of children who have offended their father, indeed; and He may chasten them on account of it; but He will not put them among those whose hearts are at enmity with Him, and who have not become his servants in Christ Jesus. In the light of this subject we see —

1. The error of supposing that God does not receive a sinner into his favor until the sinner can feel that he is perfectly holy. This is a common error with very many who have been awakened to a sense of their sin and danger, and are asking what they shall do to be saved. This is the reason why they strive to obtain the favor of God by reforms of known sin, and by desperate resolutions. They are going about thus to establish their own righteousness as a ground of acceptance with God, and rejecting the righteousness which He has provided. He calls them to faith in One who has borne their sins for them, and not to self-righteousness. He calls them to avail themselves, by faith in the Redeemer, of the provisions of salvation which He has made in that Redeemer, and not to the vain attempt of answering the claims of a violated law by their own weak doings or trivial sufferings. He calls them to fall into the hands of the Redeemer as sinners, to be pardoned for his sake, and not to the hopeless task of making expiation in their own persons.

2. The error of supposing that God counts his people his enemies, and puts them again under condemnation, and makes them liable to penalty, when they fall into sin.

This is the first error extended to greater lengths, and rests on the same notion that a sinner's own righteousness is the ground of his acceptance with God, and that, therefore, one who has sinned must first atone for his sin by his own righteousness, before he can be restored to the favor of God. On the contrary, whenever a Christian is conscious of sin, and feels his soul burdened because of it, his privilege is to fly at once to the intercession of Christ, and to take refuge in his advocacy.

Hence it is that our Saviour, in teaching his disciples how to pray, directs them to say, not "Thou just and holy Ruler of men," but "Our Father." This designation governs all that follows. Hence when we say, "Forgive us our trespasses," the petition is not to God simply as a lawgiver and executor, and it is not to be offered in the spirit of one under condemnation, and appointed to suffer the avenging penalty of a righteous law, but it is to be offered in the spirit of a child, that has erred from the right way, while yet his heart has remained true to his father's person and government. And the forgiveness which is granted in answer to that prayer is not the forgiveness of a mere lawgiver, but of a tender father.

3. There is no such thing as punishment ever inflicted on one who is in Christ Jesus. Punishment, in the strict sense of the term punishment, is the infliction of penalty for violated law. This none who are in Christ Jesus ever suffer. They are pardoned.

"As many as I love I rebuke and chasten," says the Saviour; but He never visits them with penalty; He has become the end of the law, etc.; and if the law is fulfilled for them, then no punishment. They are thus not under law, but under grace.

SERMON XX.

THE TRIAL OF FAITH.

1 Peter i. 6, 7. — *Now for a season, if need be, ye are in heaviness through manifold temptations: that the trial of your faith, being much more precious than of gold that perisheth, though it be tried with fire, might be found unto praise and honor and glory at the appearing of Jesus Christ.*

LET us consider the manner in which faith is tried. According to the words before us, it is by " temptations: " " Ye are in heaviness through manifold temptations, that the trial of your faith may be found unto praise and honor and glory at the appearing of Jesus Christ."

There is some ambiguity in the use of the words " temptation " and " trial." " Temptation " really means " trial," though there is something of evil intent implied in the former that is not implied in the latter. To " tempt " a man is to " try " him. If, for example, you offer a man a bribe to tempt him to be dishonest, you try his honesty. If you offer a total abstinence man liquor to tempt him to violate his pledge, you put his principles upon trial.

The word that exactly expresses the idea of the Apostle is " proof." The word " temptations " indicates the trials to which those whom he was addressing were exposed; and the word " trial " points out the favorable result of this exposure; the proof of genuineness which the trials furnish; and the making of that which was proved more pure if there was in it any mixture of evil. For illustration, if the man to whom a bribe is offered to tempt his honesty, firmly refuses to receive it, then the temptation or trial of his honesty has proved it to be real and not assumed; and if there was any element of selfishness that was weakening this trait of his character, the trial that has proved it has purified his honesty and made it stronger. If the total abstinence man refuses the offer that tempts or tries his principles, the trial proves his principles to be what he professes them to be, and by calling them into vigorous and decided action against their opposites, has made them stronger and purer.

Anything, therefore, that tries or tests that which we call our faith is a "temptation." And if that which we call our faith endures the trial, and is not overcome by it, the trial proves it to be faith indeed,—and by bringing it into exercise, strengthens and purifies it.

It is this proof of our faith which the Apostle says is "much more precious than that of gold that perisheth, though it be proved with fire;" and it is this proved faith that will "be found unto praise and honor and glory at the appearing of Jesus Christ."

The purpose, then, for which God permits his people to come into trials or temptations, is, according to the text, to prove that which they take to be their faith, that it may be seen whether or not it is genuine; and at the same time, if it is genuine, to separate from it every impurity by which it is alloyed.

The reasons why faith is selected as the grace to be especially tried, are doubtless to be found first in the fact that it is the characteristic and most observable grace of the Christian character and then that faith is the central point of Christian character. Every other element is involved in that alone, so that by the terms of salvation, which the gospel proposes to men, everything is made to hinge on the possession and exercise of this single grace. Hence, in the phraseology of the New Testament, to be a Christian is to be a believer; or to be "in the faith." If one has faith in the Son of God, he belongs to Christ, and is numbered among his people. If he has not faith in the Son of God, he is not a Christian, and he has no inheritance among them that are. He is known and classified by this trait alone. If, therefore, a man's faith is tried, his whole character is tried. If his faith endures the trial, and so is proved by it, his whole character is proved, and his whole character will "be found unto praise and honor and glory at the appearing of Jesus Christ." To a believer every temptation or trial is, in some measure, a testing and a proving of his faith. This will be evident if we reflect for a moment on what it is that makes anything a trial to a Christian's mind.

1. In the first place, things are trials to us because they are contrary to our desires. If things are in accordance with our desires they are not trials. They become trials only by being contrary to us, and thwarting the purposes of our hearts. The providences of God, his dealings with us and ours, or with those towards whom our feelings are enlisted, are not in themselves alone considered pleasing to us. God does not deal with us in such a way as we should if we were left wholly to our own desires with Him, and hence we feel tried and are afflicted.

This element enters into every trial of a Christian's mind, from the least to the greatest. In many trials it is not so prominent to our apprehension as other elements, simply because it is overshadowed by these, but in by far the greater number of our trials this simple crossing of our desires is the element of trial. It reaches no higher. The thing that God has seen fit to order or permit in our circumstances or condition or relations or interests, is something different from what we, if left to our own selves, should have chosen.

Now notice how such a matter goes at once to a Christian's faith and puts it to the test, and, if it is genuine, calls it into vigorous exercise. His faith is trust in God, By his faith he has confided all his interests into the hands of Christ; nothing is kept back. According to his belief Christ is not only interested in all that pertains to him, — for this is Christ's teaching,— but is infinitely well-disposed towards him and sure to do for him, and by him, that which is for his highest good. This is the view that faith takes of the Lord, and of his dealings with those who trust Him.

But that which is a trial to us by crossing our desires tempts us to call the goodness of God into question; just as a little child distrusts the goodness and love of a parent when the parent crosses his wishes. We cannot understand how the goodness of God can be consistent with such thwarting of our desires, and checking of our pleasures. If our doubt and questioning were put into language in naked form, without any evasive palliation in the statement, it would be "Can God be good in thus crossing my wishes, and thwarting the purposes of my heart?" There is thus inaugurated a contest between trust and distrust within the soul. The question to be decided is, whether God or self shall have dominion over the desires.

Shall we walk by sight, still holding to our own preconceived views of what is best in our circumstances; or, shall we abandon these things as not best because God has not chosen them, and walk by faith, taking as best that which God has ordered, simply and solely because He has ordered it? Faith will do the latter. If it is strong and healthful it will do it promptly and cheerfully; if it is weak, it will do it, but not without a severe struggle and great pain. It is the mark of one who has passed beyond the childhood of faith into the fullness of the stature of a man in Christ Jesus, to say in sincerity, "Though He slay me, yet will I trust Him," and heartily accept the inspired assertion that "all things work together for good to them that love God." The novice, who is yet a babe in Christ, must take many lessons in the school of Christian experience, and exercise himself in many a struggle against unbelief, and against self-conceit, before he will bring all the events and circumstances of his life to the judgment of faith rather than of his own reason; to the supremacy of his Lord rather than to his own cherished self-sufficiency. The temptations to which he is exposed, the trials he is called upon to endure, teach him these lessons and give him this invigorating and purifying exercise. This was the peculiar element in the temptation of our Saviour, when Satan said, "Command these stones to be made bread." This is the element of trial in all those temptations, which you have to complain of in the condition in which Providence has cast your lot in life — (poor, — humble circumstances, — not great and commanding abilities, — feeble constitution, — the ten thousand annoying things connected with your lot which none but yourself can fully know, — reverses, etc., etc.).

2. Again, things are trials to us because they are contrary to what we deem wisest. God does not conform his dealings with us, nor with the world in which we live, to the dictates of our wisdom. Those events and those orderings of Providence which fall in with our own judgments, and which our own reasons pronounce wise, do not tempt us to question the wisdom of God. They do not try our faith in Him. To trust the wisdom of God then, is hardly trust at all. Certainly it is not the trust of faith. Faith always endures as seeing Him who is invisible, though it does not see Him. It is therefore a trusting

of God in the dark. It relies upon his wisdom both after the wisdom of his ways ceases to be seen by our reason, and when they appear to our own reason to be unwise.

But when his ways clash with the dictates of our reason, or even when they pass into regions where our reason cannot follow them, then the trial begins. The question is at once started in our minds, which of the two, our way or God's way, is to be counted better, irrespective of anything in it that touches directly our own wishes or fancied interests. When the ways of God seem to our reason to be unwise, — not the best that could have been chosen, nor the best adapted to secure the end proposed, then if we should give full and uncolored expression to our thoughts, we should find that just so far as there is a want or weakness of faith in us, there would be a declaration that God's ways are foolish and unbecoming, while those which we should have adopted, if the choice had been left with us, would have been patterns for the infinite Himself to adopt and follow out. "The foolishness of man thus perverteth his way: and his heart fretteth against the Lord."

All unbelief has in it this exaltation of its own wisdom above God's. It is the very nature of unbelief to make the wisdom of God foolishness whenever that wisdom is not in accordance with its own. When our first mother tasted the forbidden fruit she brought herself to the fatal deed by a series of artful reasonings against the wisdom of God, and in favor of her own: "She saw the tree that it was good for food." This was its first recommendation. Could it be wise or well that God had forbidden so good a thing to be eaten? Then, still looking, it became " pleasant to her eyes." Oh, why should it be forbidden. Certainly it is better that a thing so inviting should be enjoyed. Reason itself shows that an object appealing so strongly to my desires was intended for them, and ought not to be denied to them. Then, and more than all the rest, " it was a tree to be desired to make one wise!" This completed the argument. By this time the wisdom of God had fallen very low in her estimation: her own had risen very high. She therefore hesitated no longer. God's wisdom was set aside and her own preferred in its place. Her faith was tried and it failed.

Some such process of argumentation is often resorted to by

us, when his ways do not commend themselves to our wisdom. We sometimes yield to the trial, and follow for a season in the way of our own judgments. At other times we hesitate and struggle against the temptation, and, in the end, come off victors, becoming willing to count our own wisdom folly, and to walk in the ways of God and to trust in them, even when they seem to lead towards failure and disappointment. Abraham thus walked when he went with Isaac to the mount of sacrifice. When his faith had carried him above the conflict which began between his own desires towards Isaac and what God had commanded, and he had enough of confidence left in the Almighty to believe that He would in some way make his promise regarding Isaac good, then every step of the way God led him was one that would tempt him to question the wisdom of God in the means He had chosen toward the accomplishment of the end. Every step was one that compelled Abraham to deny his own wisdom and trust in that of God, though he had nothing but the character of God to rest upon, — nothing whatever in his present doings.

But after the struggle was ended, and his faith had triumphed over all the temptations that Abraham had found to let go his confidence, then his faith was proved. It was found to be genuine, and the power of unbelief was permanently lessened in his soul. This element must have entered largely into the trials of mind endured by the disciples after the crucifixion of our Lord.

Who of us has not been through similar experience, if we are the disciples of Christ? Similar, I mean, so far as the exercises of our minds are concerned, and the principles that were involved. There is hardly a distinctive doctrine of the gospel, e. g., or a dark and mysterious Providence which has not thus tried our faith and brought us distinctly to the issue whether we will condemn as folly the wisdom of God or our own.

This was the essence of that temptation of our Redeemer when Satan brought Him to Jerusalem and set Him on a pinacle of the temple, and said unto Him, "If thou be the Son of God cast thyself down from hence: for it is written He shall give his angels charge over thee, to keep thee, and in their hands they shall bear thee up, lest at any time thou dash thy foot against a stone." Human wisdom had long before dictated that the Messiah should manifest Himself in some scene of sudden and wonderful splendor to the people, and claim their homage. To have complied with the suggestion of the adversary would have met the demands of this wisdom. God had, however, appointed a way in all respects opposed to this — a way of deep and long continued humiliation, — and faith in God would abide in this way against the wisdom of the wisest men of the world.

3. Again, things are trials to us because they are contrary to our views of what is right. If a thing is contrary to our wishes, and against the dictates of our wisdom, yet if it is seen to be right, this goes very far towards the removal of the other elements of trial. We more easily learn then to question and deny our own wisdom, and to bring our wishes into harmony with the thing that is thus seen. But if the ways of God clash with our views of right and justice, then we are tried indeed. There is no trial to a righteous soul like this.

But God has chosen, and still chooses, sometimes to manifest Himself in this manner to his children. Rather let us say that oftentimes his ways, in our imperfect apprehension of them, are contrary to our sense of right. The history of this world abounds with such manifestations. The relations which men sustain to God, by virtue of their being members of the human family, rest under this dark cloud. Some of the grandest and sweetest doctrines of the gospel rest under it, to the view of multitudes of even Christian minds. Starting with the doctrine of divine sovereignty, and sweeping down through all its implications from election, foreordination, gracious salvation, and eternal retribution, there is not a single step of revelation that does not serve as a severe trial to all thoughtful minds, until they have ceased to live upon the food of babes in Christ, and fed long upon the strong meat of eternal truth. So, too, starting with the first recorded providence of God towards our fallen race, in their expulsion from Paradise, and coming down the track of his providential dealings to the present hour, there is no period that does not exhibit the ways of God with his creatures under this cloud. How can this be in the government of a righteous God ? is the mild and timid expression of a sterner and more daring thought that is lurking in the mind, and which, fully expressed, would be, "The way of the Lord is not equal;

his judgments are not right." Things of this kind enter largely into and form much of the web of human history. Wars, oppressions, tyrannies, the innocent made the prey of the guilty, the innocent suffering with the guilty, and on account of their misdeeds, falsehood triumphing over truth, vice over virtue, cruelty over mercy, the strong over the weak, the wicked, and they that are banded together for evil against righteousness, over the good and them that contend in a righteous cause.

Now look again and see how directly all these things go to try our faith. Faith in a righteous God is the very thing that is appealed to. All that class of trials to which we have alluded throw us at once into the necessity of deciding whether God is or is not to be trusted as righteous! To one who believes in Christ none of these things are independent of Him. For his own word is unequivocal that all power in heaven and in earth is in his hands. We cannot hide ourselves in any of those atheistic sentiments that exclude God from human affairs, and say that He is not ruling in them, and working out his highest purposes by them. We are compelled to admit his power and his purpose into all these dark things; and then to make our choice whether still to confide in Him as righteous and faithful, or to turn from Him.

Here begins the struggle of faith. This is the hardest work of all it is ever required to do. To rest quiet, and maintain our trust, when God seems to uphold at least, if He does not do wrong! Oh, it is hard to believe in the righteousness of God when we can see nothing but apparent unrighteousness in his ways.

But if there is faith it will rise up to the demand made upon it, and this test will search us through and through to find faith if it is in us. It may not rise up to the demand at once; but ultimately it will. For "this is the victory that overcometh the world, even your faith." Before the contest with unbelief is ended, faith will say with triumph in its tones: "Be still and know that Jehovah is God." It will rebuke the dark suggestions of unbelief with the inquiry, Who art thou that repliest against God? Shall not the Judge of all the earth do right? It will plead the cause of God with a self-denying humility, that honors God above itself, saying, His ways, it is true, are in the deep waters where I cannot trace them; they are in the thick clouds, and I cannot behold them. He hideth Himself, so that I cannot find Him. "Clouds and darkness are round about Him," yet I know that "righteousness and judgment are the habitation of his throne." My feeble powers cannot comprehend the Infinite One; my line cannot fathom the depths of his wisdom, nor measure the greatness of his purposes. I cannot even indicate his ways for Him. He is his own interpreter, and He will make them plain.

As it appears to my mind, the temptation of our Redeemer was of this kind, in a measure at least, when the tempter "showed Him all the kingdoms of the world, and the glory of them; and said unto Him, All these things will I give thee, if thou wilt fall down and worship me." Our Lord was in humiliation, deep and distressing: He was oppressed with the most pinching poverty: He was in disgrace and contempt. Yet He was conscious, in Himself, that honor, and glory, and riches, and power, and dominion, belonged to Him. In the providence of God, and by his ordering, He was kept out of his inheritance. Could this be right? Was it just that He should thus remain an outcast and an underling in his own dominions? Would it not be better and would He not be justified, to take his rights in the way that seemed open now for Him to secure them, rather than longer wait the slow and perhaps uncertain unfoldings and interpositions of the Father, who seemed to have hidden his face, and abandoned his Son to the miseries of his condition? The same trial seems to have come upon Him again, in another form, when that cry of bitter agony was wrung from Him on the cross, "My God, my God, why hast thou forsaken me?" To some extent in the garden when He cried, "Let this cup pass from me." It was faith rising against the temptation when He added, "Nevertheless, not my will but thine be done." Very many of the trials of the people of God are of this character. Even the providence of God seems to be enlisted on the side of wrong and injustice. Nothing but a faith that rises above all that is seen and temporal, into the purer regions of the unseen and eternal, and rests itself in a God whom it cannot see, will give us the victory in such circumstances. There must be a falling back upon the Word of God, and upon the great principles of his government, so far as his government has wrought itself out to our comprehension and history. The grounds upon which we stand, and the ends which we seek to attain, will be, and ought to be, more carefully scrutinized, that we may the more fully assure ourselves that they are indeed right; and then there must be the patient waiting, the calm and heroic endurance, the faithful and earnest and persistent endeavors, that are inspired by an unshaken confidence in the rightness of right, and in its certain triumph because God the Omnipotent is righteous.

When our faith has been brought up to this high standard, but not before, it gives us the complete victory over the world. It is then proved. It is found to be a faith that will make God God, that will put Him on the throne, over the heart, over the understanding, over the will, over all the desires and purposes of the soul, and over all the interests of creation. Thus it is shown to be, and has become, a faith that will introduce no discord into heaven, but will forever join its glorified millions in ascribing " blessing, and glory, and wisdom, and thanksgiving, and honor, and power, and might unto God for ever and ever." It is such a faith, and it is proved to be such, that it will keep him who exercises it in perfect peace and perfect obedience. It is thus found unto praise and honor and glory. God approves it; He puts honors upon it; crowns it with the glory of heaven.

SERMON XXI.
THE SERVICE OF CHRIST NOT HARD.

MATT. xi. 30. — *My yoke is easy and my burden is light.*

THIS language is addressed to such as are under a yoke that is not easy, and are carrying a burden that is not light. In the service of another than Christ their souls have become weary, and the exactions of their servitude are harder than they can bear. Christ says to such, Enter my service, become my followers, choose me as your master and teacher, submit to my authority, do my will. This, the yoke of my service, is easy; this, the burden of my requirements, is light.

Such, as we understand them, are the *yoke* and the *burden* of Christ. They are his service, and the duties which that service demands. To take his yoke upon us, as He here urges us to do, is to submit to his authority and consent to be governed by his will as his servants and followers. To bear his burden is to do and to suffer whatever He may require of us in this relationship of servants and followers.

The doctrine of our text then is that Christ's service is not a hard one. He is not a hard master. He does not make hard demands, nor lay heavy burdens upon them that serve Him. "His yoke is easy and his burden is light."

1. The terms *easy* and *light* are comparative. Our Saviour evidently puts his service and its duties in contrast with any and every service with its requirements, under which any whom He addressed might be laboring and heavy laden.

To the formalist, toiling in the bondage of Pharisaic traditions and staggering under its burden of ceremonies and unreasonable exactions; "tithing his mint, anise, and cummin," observing times and seasons with superstitious anxiety; guarding with painful carefulness his person and his possessions from the touch of legal uncleanness; groaning under the "yoke which neither his fathers nor himself was able to bear;" to him our Lord said, in the words before us, "in comparison with this yoke and these burdens my yoke is easy and my burden is light. Leave your bondage; lay down your crushing burdens. Take my service upon you, yield to my requirements, and you shall find them easy and light, and they shall be rest to your soul."

There was the stern legalist painfully endeavoring to establish his own righteousness before God by a vigorous compliance, as he supposed, with the demands of the law, — not knowing that " to condemn is all the law can do," for by it is the knowledge of sin, but not justification with God, — and to him laboring under so stern and exacting a master as is the law to a sinner, and sinking under so heavy a burden as his accumulated transgressions had laid upon him, the Saviour proclaims, Compared with this, my yoke is easy and my burden is light. I ask no such slavish toil, no such cheerless labor. I bind upon my people no such crushing burdens.

To the devotee of the world who is seeking in its varied forms of business or of pleasure the substantialness and the reality which his soul longs for, but fails to find; who is wearied with the fruitless chase, and sinking down in sadness under the burden of a realization of the world's vanity; who is heartsick with a consciousness that every object he has grasped or can grasp is but a gilded toy, when laid in the balance of the soul, or ashes when offered to its cravings; who is indeed burdened with the full and pressing conviction of the hollowness of the world and all its pretensions, — to him who is thus world-weary and heavy laden, Christ says in tones that would win him away from his bondage and fruitless toils, Compared with these, my yoke is easy and my burden is light. The very emptiness of all you now possess is a wearisome burden to your soul; the reality of what you find with me is less, far less heavy, nay it is lightness itself, since it rather bears up the soul than asks to be borne up by it.

And to him who has come to feel the guilt of his sins, and to tremble under the burden of the wrath which that guilt has brought upon him; who has found that the way of the transgressor is hard, and yet realizes that the galling yoke of sin is bound upon him, and feels himself unable to break it from his neck, — to him especially Christ speaks. He presses upon his attention the comparison between what he now is toiling under and that to which He himself invites him. Compared with the yoke of sin my yoke is easy, He says. Compared with the burden of your sins, their guilt and misery, my burden is light.

2. But though there is this clearly implied comparison in our Saviour's language, yet his words convey an absolute sense to the mind.

The service of Christ is not a hard service considered in itself alone, without comparison with any other service. The duties which He requires of his followers are, in themselves, not burdensome. They do not weary the soul, nor waste its life. On the contrary, the more the soul yields to his requirements the stronger does it become and the more vigorous. The more completely those who submit to Him enter into the service of Christ, the more do they "renew their strength. They mount up with wings as eagles; they run and are not weary; and they walk and are not faint."

1. I remark, first, that the service of Christ is not hard, because all its requirements are right, reasonable, and proper. He demands nothing unreasonable. He exacts nothing of any man that both his judgment and conscience do not unhesitatingly pronounce to be suitable. He asks nothing unjust.

Test his requirements, my hearers. Search his Word and you will find not one demand made of a servant of Christ, which your conscience and judgment do not at once approve. His first and great command, that which embraces in itself all others, is this, "Thou shalt love the Lord thy God with all thy heart, and with all thy soul, and with all thy mind." Is it not right that you should thus love God? Is He not worthy of such love? Is it more than simple justice for you thus to love Him? But out of this command proceeds every duty that an accountable being can possibly owe to his God. Every duty is included in it. If, therefore, the command itself is right, every duty that it calls upon you to render to God is right. There can be no wrong in that which is all right.

The second command which is indeed involved in the first is, "Thou shalt love thy neighbor as thyself." Is this wrong? Will your conscience, my hearers, condemn such love and say that it is not right? Do you sin in thus loving your fellow-man — your neighbor?

This requirement is also reasonable. Any object should be loved according to its worth. Your neighbor is in the sight of God as valuable as yourself. His soul is as precious. He may have sunk far below you in outward degradation and in overt guilt. His character may be vastly below yours in purity and honor, and this degradation you cannot take pleasure in, nor are you required to. But the man himself as the creature of God, and heir with you to a common inheritance, is as high in the scale of worth, and therefore worthy of as much love as you yourself are. If you then put him beneath your own self in your love you act unreasonably. You are unjust to him. For in your heart and in the presence of your conscience you cannot say but he is as the creature of God worthy of as much love as yourself. And when God demands that you exercise this love toward Him, his requirement is not unreasonable or unjust. He requires only that you love a thing according to its worth. And the sense in which He would have his command understood by us He has made too plain to be misunderstood. He has made it plain in the parable of the good Samaritan. Does not your conscience approve of such love to one's neighbor? Was ever one so depraved as to disapprove it? He has made it plain by his own example. While we were yet sinners He commended his love toward us in that then Christ died for us. He so loved the world when it was in guilt and degradation that He gave his only begotten Son, that whosoever believeth in Him might not perish but have everlasting life. While we are yet enemies and guilty, and plunged deep in misery, He sends his Spirit and calls us to repentance, and is long suffering that He may lead all to salvation. This is the love of God. It is love to us as his creatures, and as moral and accountable agents. It is not love of complacence nor love of our sin. If God so loved us, we ought also to love one another. It is right that we should.

But as the command to love God supremely embraces every duty toward God, so does this command to love our neighbor as ourselves embrace every duty God demands of us toward men. The command put into another form with practical specification is, " All things whatsoever ye would that men should do to you, do ye even so to them." This embraces every act of a man's life that is to affect others.

Never yet was a conscience so blinded or so seared, or so enfeebled and perverted but it would unhesitatingly pronounce every distinguishing requirement of the gospel to be right. Never yet was there a judgment so warped but it would pronounce every one of them just, and in the highest degree proper and reasonable.

But no requirement which is right and proper and just can be hard.

The service of Christ, therefore, is not a hard service, because its requirements are all right and proper. They are such as He ought to make of us, and such as every moral being ought at once and without ceasing to comply with.

2. The service of Christ is not hard, because in every demand it makes upon us, it seeks to promote our own highest interests.

The Word of God everywhere recognizes our own interests and happiness as connected with our duties. God is not willing you should be damned — you ought not to be willing. Under the law, the word of God is, " Obey, I beseech thee, the voice of the Lord, so it shall be well unto thee, and thy soul shall live." Under the gospel, the word of God always urges repentance, and always does it with the powerful motive, " Thou shalt live." The voice of the gospel is, " Believe on the Lord Jesus Christ, and thou shalt be saved." It was the gospel, therefore, which cried in the language of the prophet Ezekiel, " Turn ye, turn ye," and urged this as the reason, " for why will ye die?" and in that of Isaiah, " Let the wicked forsake his way, and the unrighteous man his thoughts, and let him return unto the Lord, and He will have mercy upon him; and to our God, for He will abundantly pardon."

This is the tenor of all the requirements of Christ's service. They seek the glory of God in the highest good of those who yield to them. Whatever He puts upon us to do, as his followers, He puts distinctly before us the promotion of our own best interest in the doing of it. Though He has undoubted right to our perfect obedience, regardless of any results that may accrue to us; and though obedience, implicit and entire, is our duty, whatever the consequences may be, and regardless of them, yet, as a matter of fact, He has never thus separated duty and interest, obedience and reward. " Whosoever shall give to drink unto one of these little ones, a cup of cold water only, in the name of a disciple, Verily I say unto you, he shall in no wise lose his reward."

That service can never be called hard, certainly, in which its subjects are thus dealt with. No servant is treated with severity who is never required to do an act, to discharge a duty, to forego an enjoyment, which his own best interests do not also require of him.

It is this feature of the service of Christ which makes it one of cheerfulness and hope. Hope is always an anchor to the soul. Hope shines in upon every step of the pathway that obedience marks out. There is ever before him who walks in it the recompense of reward. There is awaiting him, the Saviour's cheering words, "Well done, good and faithful servant, enter into the joy of thy Lord." However great the labor, however severe the effort to be put forth, either in doing or submitting to the will of Christ, hope shines down upon him who toils and him who suffers. Hope sweetens toils that else might be exhausting, and lightens burdens that otherwise would be crushing. Hope reaches forward and upward, and brings strength and support from heaven. It was when Paul cast his eye forward to the end of his course and thought of the rest of heaven in which all the mighty interests of his soul were centred, — it was then that he looked upon all the toils and sacrifices and sufferings which the service of Christ demanded of him, and exclaimed, "None of these things move me; neither count I my life dear unto myself, so that I might finish my course with joy, and the ministry which I have received of the Lord Jesus, to testify the gospel of the grace of God." There was no hardness, no severity, in the service of Christ, as Paul was then meeting all of its most urgent claims.

And again, when the providence of God led him as an Apostle and a Christian into deep waters, and the trials of a disciple and faithful follower of Jesus were pressing in upon him, and afflictions multiplied upon him in quick succession,— it was then that hope lifted up the burden from his soul that he should not be crushed beneath it, and made it easy, when otherwise it would have been too much for him to bear. "Our light affliction," said he, looking to the recompense of reward, the highest good which was working out for him in and by his trials, — " Our light affliction, which is but for a moment, worketh for us a far more exceeding and eternal weight of glory ; while we look not at the things which are seen, but at the things which are not seen."

At that moment the Apostle would have responded to the language of our text, and would have exclaimed from the fullness of his soul, " His yoke is easy and his burden is light." Though it was deep darkness all around him, yet because he was a servant of Christ, it was all light within him. The light of heaven which hope brought down to him from Christ the Promiser, dispelled the darkness from his soul.

After this, when Paul came to the final act of his earthly service to Christ, to honor him in a martyr's death, it was the same thing, — his highest good, connected with all his submission to the will of his master, — it was this that came in to lift the yoke from his neck and make it easy ; the burden from his shoulders to make it light. How calm, how peaceful is his whole aspect, when he says, with the martyr's suffering before him and in full view : " I am now ready to be offered, and the time of my departure is at hand. I have fought a good fight, I have finished my course. I have kept the faith ; henceforth there is laid up for me a crown of righteousness which the Lord, the righteous judge, shall give me at that day." The martyr's crown took away the sting of the martyr's sufferings. Every word breathes a most earnest and loving indorsement of his Saviour's language, " My yoke is easy and my burden is light."

What the service of Christ was to Paul, that it is to every one of his faithful followers. It has its reward full and glorious for each. Hope makes it a present reality and a future inheritance ; and there can be no hardness in the service that leads to such a reward. Indeed, the gospel, which is — in slightly another sense — the yoke of Christ, is nothing more than hope itself, shining in upon the otherwise unalleviated wretchedness and despair of sinners ; and the service to which it calls them is to flee from the cruel tyranny of sin that has so long held them ; to throw off its burden, which has so long crushed them ; and to escape from the wrath of God, and find refuge in his favor.

Such a service is not a hard one. There is no cruelty in it, but only goodness and mercy.

3. The service of Christ is not a hard service, because it is

a service of love. "The love of Christ constraineth us," is the language of every true disciple's heart, and his experience is, "We love Him because He first loved us."

But no labor of love is burdensome. Every yoke that love puts upon the neck, and to which love bows the neck, is easy to him who bears it. No burden that love imposes, and which love receives and cherishes, is heavy. Love makes all burdens light, and all tasks easy. Nothing is hard to love. Jacob served seven years for Rachel; and they seemed unto him but a few days, for the love he had to her. So we serve Christ a whole life-time in trials. Hence it is that every follower of Christ says from his soul, I delight in the law of God, after the inward man; and he often exclaims with the Psalmist: "Oh, how love I thy law; it is my meditation all the day." A service of love is not a hard service. There is no cringing servility in it. In servility there is fear, but perfect love casteth out fear, and a perfect service to Christ is a service of perfect love. Love to Christ now and forever, on earth and in heaven, will say: "His yoke is easy and his burden is light."

> "Love is the golden chain that binds
> The happy souls above;
> And he's an heir of heaven that finds
> His bosom glow with love."

The question that Christ puts to every inquiring sinner is, Believest thou me? But to the real believer, his inquiry is, as it was to Peter, "Lovest thou me?" Faith works by love, and ever brings into exercise that love which makes all works easy.

But the objection arises in your minds, — perhaps it has followed us at each step of our progress in this discourse, — Do not the Scriptures represent the way to eternal life as difficult? Do they not make the gate to the way straight, and all the way narrow? And is it not an entrance into this gate and a walking in this way which the Saviour demands of us? All this is true. It is true that the gaining of eternal life is a difficult matter for one who has sinned. The Scriptures do always so represent it. And I cannot see that the admission conflicts with what has been said.

1. It is hard for a sinner to repent. He clings to his sins. He does not like to give them up. The habit of sinning is like bars of iron that he cannot break. No sinner did ever yet, if we rightly understand the subject, find it easy to begin to re-

pent of his sins and forsake them. They have clung to him and made it difficult for him to turn to God. Yet he must repent or he cannot be saved. If he repent not he will perish.

But what is the difficulty here? Is it the work of repentance itself to which Christ is calling the sinner? Is it the exercising of repentance which is so difficult? No. It is the sinner's vigorous opposition to the claim of Christ. In this opposition of his own heart is all the hardness. The yoke of Christ is not yet on the neck; but the yoke of sin is, and this it is that is so galling. Christ calls you, sinner, to repent of your sins, and to forsake them. But this you are unwilling to do. Your conscience and your reason urge you to obey the call of Christ. But your will rebels. Then, you have not yet taken the yoke of Christ upon you. Submission to his authority, and yielding to his demands, and this only, is the taking upon you of his yoke. Only yield, — only let repentance for your wickedness take possession of your soul, as He requires, then the hardness is all gone. Every true penitent rejoices in his repentance. He is glad in his sorrow. He smiles through his tears. "The wormwood and the gall" are found in the resistance of the soul to the claims of Christ, while conscience is smarting under the keen accusings of the law. Cease to contend with Christ, and begin to serve Him, then the heavy burden rolls off, and the light one takes its place.

2. Christ demands that you shall believe in Him; and you must believe or you cannot have eternal life. But it is hard for the sinner to begin to believe. It is hard for him to forsake all his own righteousness, and to rest alone on the worthiness of Christ. It is humbling to his pride; it is crucifying himself.

It is hard for him, also, conscious as he is of guilt and unworthiness, to trust the faithfulness of the Redeemer. He fears to commit the vast interests of his soul into the Saviour's hands, and fall into his outstretched arms of mercy. Oh, it is hard for him to begin to do it. He feels as though he were required to step off from a lofty precipice, with nothing to support him but empty air. But God's Spirit comes to his help, and he thus exclaims: —

> "Why was I made to hear thy voice,
> And enter while there's room,
> When thousands make a wretched choice,
> And rather starve than come?

"'Twas the same love that spread the feast,
That sweetly forced me in;
Else I had still refused to taste,
And perished in my sin."

The gracious interposition of God in his behalf, removes this hardness, which his own unbelief puts in the way of his soul's salvation. But this unbelief, this refusing to believe, is not serving Christ. This is standing out against Christ's commands, and not obedience to Him. Every moment you remain in unbelief, my dying hearer, you remain in sin. Your unbelief is rebellion. You have not, therefore, the yoke of Christ upon you. It is not his burden which is pressing you down, and crushing your soul beneath its awful weight. But when the heart believes, — when it implicitly trusts and rests itself like a weary child on the arms of Almighty love and truth, — oh, then it is not hard!

3. And finally. It is generally made a hard task to walk in the path of obedience to Christ and persevere in it to the end of life. It demands constant watchfulness, — constant self-denial, — cutting off every right hand that offends, and plucking out every right eye that brings sin and ruin to the soul.

These things are hard to the natural man. They are trying to the flesh. But consider, though Christ demands self-denial, He does not demand that we should so set our hearts on things contrary to his will, and to our own interests, as to make self-denial, in its severe aspects, necessary. Nor does He ask us to cling to these things. The severity and the hardness of this, and of all else that makes up the life of a Christian, is in the struggle which self maintains against Christ, refusing to submit to Him and serve Him. Here is the only hardness of self-denial, — the only severity. But this, you perceive, is not serving Christ, but rebelling against Him. It is not doing his will, but resisting it. It is not submitting to his authority, but opposing it. It is not taking his yoke upon you, but rejecting it. It is not bearing his burden, but casting it off.

Let the heart fully receive Christ's law, let the will fully submit, yield a cordial and free and entire obedience of the soul to the Lord, then the struggle ceases; then peace smiles upon all within; the spirit rests in love and confidence on its Redeemer and Saviour. The yoke then is easy and the burden is light.

SERMON XXII.

CHRIST'S SYMPATHY WITH HIS PEOPLE.

Heb. iv. 15. — *We have not an High-priest which cannot be touched with the feeling of our infirmities: but was in all points tempted like as we are, yet without sin.*

IN the verse preceding this it is said, " We have a great High-priest, that is passed into the heavens, Jesus the Son of God." Of this High-priest it is here written that He is not one " which cannot be touched with the feeling of our infirmities, but was in all points tempted like as we are, yet without sin."

Though He is " the Son of God " and has " passed into the heavens," yet He can feel for his people in this world in all their weaknesses and temptations and sufferings. More than this, He not only feels for them but He feels with them. He enters into their sorrows as one who has felt what they feel, and is intensely interested in them personally as the objects of his special love and favor. This is the main thought of the text : " He is touched with the feeling of our infirmities." It is evident from what immediately follows, that the word *infirmities* has reference not only to weaknesses themselves, but to all the ills and trials and afflictions to which human weakness makes us subject. Mental and bodily sufferings ; the allurements and disappointments of the world ; the temptations of the great adversary, all are included, and all are felt by the great High-priest when his people feel them.

The doctrine of the text is that Christ sympathizes with his people in all their trials. He feels for them and with them.

" How can He do this ? " once asked a deeply afflicted father and mother. " How can Christ sympathize with us ? How can He enter into our feelings and know our grief ? " These parents were in very great distress on account of the loss of an only son, in the morning of his childhood. The words we have read to you for our text were quoted to them with the hope that, as they were Christians, they would be influenced to betake themselves with more earnestness and faith to their great High-priest for his sympathy and support in their heavy trial. These questions were their only response when the words before us were quoted to them. It was found to be necessary to open more fully to their minds the qualifications of " Jesus the Son of God," to be the High-priest of his people, and to show them that their limitation of his fitness was unauthorized and contrary to the truth. The three following answers were given to their inquiry, " How can Christ sympathize with us?"

1. He is omniscient. He knows all your circumstances, even to the most minute particulars. He knows every thought of your minds, and every emotion of your hearts. He reads them all far more clearly than it is possible for you to describe them. He sees every tear you shed, hears every sigh you heave. He goes with you when you go to the grave of your child " to weep there," and comes back with you when you return to your desolated home to weep yet more bitterly there. When you look upon the vacant little seat, the unoccupied bed, the unused playthings, and the unnumbered silent remembrancers of his face and form and presence, Christ is with you beholding too. He sees each thing you look upon, and knows all its history, and is acquainted with every feeling it awakens in your breasts. Your sorrows are among the " all things" which are declared — in immediate connection with the words quoted — to be " naked and opened unto the eyes of Him with whom we have to do. For there is no creature that is not manifest in his sight."

The omniscience of Christ is an essential element in his fitness to be our great High-priest, as it is of his fitness to be our Saviour and King. But for this He could not be either the Priest or Saviour or King which the soul craves when it becomes conscious of its wants. If Christ does not know me entirely, and all that pertains to me, then I cannot yield all my powers and my person to Him in faith and obedience as my King. I must then look for my king to one whose eye surveys a wider field, whose hand is laid with intelligent control on all within me and about me. So, too, if Christ is less than omniscient I cannot trust in Him as an all-sufficient Saviour. He must know all things to be a satisfying Saviour to a soul that has been awakened to a sense of its lost condition. If He knows less than all things, then He may not know the full extent of my ruin; and He may fail to provide the deliverance which my salvation calls for. And if He is less than omniscient, how can I come in faith to Him as my High-priest able to have compassion upon me, to the full extent of the infirmities by which I am encompassed?

But Christ is burdened with no such limitation in his great offices. "All power," He says to us, "is given unto me in heaven and in earth." Power to know all things is included. "In Him dwelleth also," so an Apostle assures us, "all the fullness of the godhead." No attribute of deity is wanting to Him; nor is any one attribute stinted in his possession. All are in Him in unlimited fullness. It is our privilege, therefore, to come to Him as one having in Himself all the fullness of knowledge. We may take the Evangelist's words in their farthest reach, when he says of our High-priest: "He knows what is in man;" and we must receive it as something more than the exaggeration of hyperbole when Peter exclaims, " Lord, thou knowest all things; thou knowest that I love thee."

We have not, therefore, a High-priest who cannot be touched with a feeling of our infirmities, because we have not one who does not know our infirmities and all our wants and trials; nor one who does not know all our circumstances and relations, and all the events, great and small, in our history.

"Those watchful eyes that never sleep,
Survey the world around."

He is omniscient. This removes the barrier which is raised up against us in all our endeavors to sympathize with those who are in trials which we ourselves have never felt. We can know another's sorrows only as we have experienced similar sorrows in our own history. We may feel for others who are suffering under afflictions of which we have no personal experience, — we may feel for them deeply, — but they will always know, and we ourselves shall know, that we do not in the truest sense feel with them. We cannot reach the hand of sympathy down to the depths of their grief. We cannot ourselves go down to where they are. There is a something that consciously separates us from them. That something is our ignorance. We cannot sympathize with them in the full sense of the term, because our own experience has not made us acquainted with their peculiar griefs. We do not know what they are. Nothing but experience can make us fit to sympathize. Let us once taste of the same sorrow, and learn in our own selves its bitterness, then the barrier is gone which separated us from them, and they and we become conscious that we now feel with them. But this knowledge of human sufferings enters into the omniscience of our High-priest. He knows them because He knows all things. He is ignorant of nothing. He knows intimately all that we are and all that we feel.

> "His wisdom is a boundless deep,
> Where all our thoughts are drowned."

All things are naked and opened unto the eyes of Him with whom we have to do.

2. Another answer given to the inquiry made by those sorrowing parents was, that Christ can sympathize with us in our trials because He himself drank the cup of human suffering to its dregs. He can feel for men, because He himself is a man. He can sympathize with men in their griefs and sorrows because He himself "was a man of sorrows and acquainted with grief."

It is not likely that the fact that our Lord is omniscient would have great weight with one in distress and needing divine sympathy, if the knowledge of this fact was not connected with the knowledge that He himself had suffered as a man, and tasted of human sorrow so as to know it, not alone by a divine omniscience but by sad personal experience. It is the remembrance of this truth that gives the others its power over our minds. There was something peculiar in the sufferings of Christ. His life on earth was such that each one who knows what that life was, is assured that no sorrows of any class of men are greater than those that He suffered. He was spotlessly holy in a world reeking with the foulest sins and most fearful rebellion against God. All his years were passed in the midst of scenes which were in harrowing discord to Him. The wickedness of men, their utter godlessness, their odious selfishness, all were a constant and heavy trial to his pure spirit. In addition to this He had all the common infirmities of humanity. He had its passions which must be curbed and controlled. He had its appetites which must be held in subjection, and through which He could be tempted. He had his human friendships to be broken in upon by the rude hand of death, or to be turned to enmities perhaps by the tongue of detraction and deceit and slander. He was a child, and suffered the trials of childhood. He was also a youth, and as such passed through the experiences peculiar to that period of life. He was a man, and bore on his shoulders all the responsibilities of manhood, and felt in Himself the full pressure of its realities. And who can say that his nights of solitary watching and wrestling prayer upon the mountains, — his incessant toils by day, — his heavy sorrows, — his deep poverty, — his loneliness in a world crowded with a generation that had no sympathy with Him, even as the young have no sympathy with the peculiar trials of the aged, — who will say that all these did not do for Him what many years have done for those who have grown old? Did He not, in the few years of his manhood, have an experience that carried Him through more than the ordinary experience of manhood down to the limits of extreme old age?

But there were trials, sorrows, agonies into which our Highpriest was plunged, which do not belong to the lot of ordinary men in this world, and which place Him far beyond all others in the depth and extent of sufferings. If you will remember the temptation to which He was subjected in the wilderness, — his agony and bloody sweat in Gethsemane, — the indignities and insults of his mock trial, — the crown of thorns, — the bearing of his cross to Calvary amid the jeers and taunts and cruel blows of the brutal soldiery and populace, — the crucifixion with all its horrors, — if you will remember these you will not doubt in your heart that your great High-priest drank far more deeply into the cup of human sorrows than any of us. Now add once more to all these ingredients of his sufferings that bearing of our sins by which He made atonement for us, and the picture of "a man of sorrows and acquainted with grief" will be complete. There is something very significant and touching in the language of the sacred writers respecting these sufferings of the Redeemer. They convey the thought that in bearing our sins He suffered not only their penalty but their consequences in Himself. He stood in the place of the guilty of every class and condition, — in the place of each of us, Christian hearers, — and bore in his own person what our sins had

14

brought down and all that they would else have brought down upon us. Listen to a few divine declarations of this great fundamental truth, the main-spring of all our hopes of salvation: " He was wounded for our transgressions, He was bruised for our iniquities, the chastisement of our peace was upon Him, and with his stripes we are healed." " Surely He hath borne our griefs and carried our sorrows." " Him who knew no sin God hath made to be sin for us, that we might be made the righteousness of God in Him." He experienced the sinner's doom that the sinner might enjoy the reward of his righteousness. His own words carry our minds still deeper into that awful abyss of mysterious suffering into which He was plunged when He " put away sin by the sacrifice of Himself." At the opening of that fearful scene that none but angels, perhaps, witnessed in the garden, He said to the three trusted disciples whom He had chosen to watch with Him in his agony, " My soul is exceeding sorrowful, even unto death." This was the extreme of suffering. It could go no farther. It was the sorrow of death! There was no deep beyond this. He had reached the lowest point to which humanity could descend. In this sorrow — sorrow unto death — He remained until the cry was wrung from his inmost soul, " My God, my God, why hast thou forsaken me!" This was the hour of atonement. Then our Lord died, — then the penalty of our sins was visited on Him.

Let your minds dwell upon these words of the sacred writers, as they speak of the sufferings He bore to make atonement for our sins, and you will no longer question the ability of our great High-priest to sympathize with human sorrow in all its degrees and peculiarities, and to its lowest depths. " He was tried in all points like as we are, yet without sin."

This was a necessary part of his fitness to be a High-priest. By his own experience He became one that could " have compassion on the ignorant, and on them that are out of the way." He tasted both the penalty and the fruit of their sins, and knows thus what their sufferings are.

The Scriptures teach us that our Redeemer entered into these human sufferings for the express purpose, among other things, of being prepared by them for his office. " For it became Him for whom are all things, and by whom are all things, in bringing many sons unto glory, to make the captain of their salvation perfect through sufferings." " Wherefore in all things it behooved Him to be made like unto his brethren, that He might be a merciful and faithful High-priest in things pertaining to God, to make reconciliation for the sins of the people. For in that He himself hath suffered, being tempted, He is able to succor them that are tempted."

These were not mere idle words then, nor the utterances of mere poetic fancy, when Watts wrote, —

> " Touched with a sympathy within,
> He knows our feeble frame;
> He knows what sore temptations mean,
> For He has felt the same.
>
> " He in the days of feeble flesh
> Poured out his cries and tears,
> And in his measure feels afresh
> What every member bears."

3. A third answer given to the question of those heart-broken parents was, that Christ cannot but sympathize with us in our trials, because of the intense love He bears to us if we are his people, and because of the deep interest He takes in all that pertains to us, because of his oneness with us. " Of the love of Christ for you," it was said, " you have no doubt." He commended his love toward us in that while we were yet sinners, He died for us ; " and greater love hath no man than this that a man lay down his life for his friends." This Christ did for all his people, and in doing this He revealed a depth of love for them, of which they can form but a very inadequate conception. His love, moreover, is revealed in the representations He gives of it when He speaks of the relation which they bear to Him. They are all members of his body ; He is their living head. He is the vine ; they are the branches. If there is any truth in these representations, and you do not question that they are pure truth, then our great High-priest is not only such an one as can sympathize with his people in all their sorrows, but such an one as cannot but sympathize with them. The head cannot be indifferent to the sufferings of any member ; but on the contrary it counts them its own. The vine cannot be unaffected with an injury done to the smallest of its branches, but it receives it as an injury done to itself.

This deep and tender tone of the Redeemer to all his people, and his oneness with them, are the crowning qualifications for his priesthood. Omniscience might, for aught we know, be to Him all that He needed, to constitute Him a sympathizing friend, and enable Him to enter into the trials of his people, and to feel with them in their sorrows. But before He could be this to our apprehension, personal experience in human woe was needful. We must see Him, as one who had been in our place, and carried our sorrows. Nor would this suffice, if the fact of tenderest love, and an interest in us and in our well-being that was stronger than death, were not present in our minds as the pledge and assurance that nothing of omniscient knowledge, or of human experience, would be lacking in his regard for us. But for this, we might allow to our minds all that is claimed for Christ's ability to sympathize with us, and yet fail of the comfort and support which that ability is intended to give. He might know all our trials; and He might have had deep experience in human sorrow, but how should we know or how could we be assured that this ability to sympathize with men, availed for us, or drew upon us his regards? It does not follow because one has all the qualifications necessary " to feel for others' woes," that he does feel for them. He may nevertheless turn away his eyes from beholding and his mind from thinking upon them. He may be so preoccupied by other thoughts and higher interests, that the suffering ones with whom he might feel a kindred sorrow shall fail to awaken his tenderness. They are bound to him by none but the common ties of humanity, and the fountains of his sympathy may not be unsealed to them. But let the sufferer be one whom you tenderly love, and in whose life and happiness you feel an interest equal to the interest you feel in your own life and happiness, and with whom your life is bound up so that he is, as it were, a part of your very self, — you could not then be regardless of his sufferings. If he were your own child, or your parent, or the companion of your life, then how sure he would be that every tender susceptibility of your nature would be awakened towards him, and flow forth in a full and gushing tide of sympathy.

Christ's love to his people — to you — is represented as greater than the love of a mother to her child. His love is infinite and eternal. It was so great, and so constant, that it followed you, my Christian hearers, into all your guilt and alienation and wickedness, and never rested till it had brought you into his fold. And now it is so strong that an inspired Apostle exclaims in triumphant admiration of it, " I am persuaded that neither death nor life, nor angels, nor principalities, nor powers, nor things present, nor things to come, nor height, nor depth, nor any other creature, shall be able to separate us from the love of God which is in Christ Jesus our Lord." The words of the prophet Isaiah are full of the same sentiment: " Sing, O heavens, and be joyful, O earth, and break forth into singing, O mountains, for the Lord hath comforted his people, and will have mercy upon his afflicted. But Zion said, The Lord hath forsaken me, and my Lord hath forgotten me. Can a woman forget her sucking child, that she should not have compassion on the son of her womb? Yea, they may forget, yet will I not forget thee. I have graven thee upon the palms of my hands."

Shall a mother's love for her children, her interest in them, and her oneness with them, give her access to all their sorrows, so that she shall feel them as her own? then how much more shall the love of Christ, which is so much deeper, his interest, which is so much greater, and his oneness, which is so much more complete and lasting, enable Him to enter more deeply still into our griefs, and feel a more tender and thorough sympathy with us in all our sorrows!

Verily, then, " we have not a High-priest who cannot be touched with the feeling of our infirmities; but was tempted in all points like as we are, yet without sin." May I not, then, brethren, make the Apostolic exhortation my own, and say, " Let us therefore come boldly unto the throne of grace, that we may obtain mercy, and find grace, to help in time of need." May I not say with the Apostle Peter, to every burdened, troubled, and tried soul, " Cast all your care upon Him, for He careth for you."

I cannot close without adding a word, at least, to such of you, my hearers, as have no hope in the Redeemer. This great High-priest has no less of tenderness towards you, than He had towards us, before we sought his mercy. He is even now saying to you, as He once said to us, in all the tenderness of infinite love, "Turn ye, turn ye, for why will ye die? For I have no pleasure in the death of him that dieth, saith the Lord, but that he turn and live." He says to you, as He said to us while we were under sin, — "Come unto me all ye that labor and are heavy laden, and I will give you rest." It is the same tenderness which says to his people, in all their trials and sufferings, Fear not; for I have redeemed thee; I have called thee by thy name; thou art mine. When thou passest through the waters, I will be with thee; and through the rivers, they shall not overflow thee: when thou walkest through the fire, thou shalt not be burned, neither shall the flame kindle upon thee. For I am the Lord thy God, the Holy One of Israel, thy Saviour. The same tenderness that says this to his people, says to you, who are yet unreconciled, and in rebellion against Him, "Seek ye the Lord while He may be found, call ye upon Him while He is near: let the wicked forsake his way and the unrighteous man his thoughts; and let him return unto the Lord, and He will have mercy upon him, and to our God, for He will abundantly pardon."

SERMON XXIII.

THE TRUTH THE INSTRUMENT OF SANCTIFICATION.

John xvii. 17.—*Sanctify them through thy truth; thy word is truth.*

HOLINESS is the great requirement of true religion. "Be ye holy in all manner of conversation," is its law.

Holiness is also its great aim. All its means and agencies are appointed and sustained with the distinct purpose of securing it in the hearts and lives of men. It counts nothing gained, therefore, if this has not been secured, whatever else has been. It counts nothing of any value in one's religious experience or deeds, if holiness has not been its moving spring or its fruit.

Hence the principles and teachings of true religion bar the approach to God of every soul in which unholy purposes and desires bear sway. They deny that it is possible for it to enjoy his favor. They steadily declare that "without holiness no man shall see the Lord." "If I regard iniquity in my heart," says the Psalmist, "the Lord will not hear me." The prophet Habakkuk cries to God, "Thou art of purer eyes than to behold evil, and canst not look on iniquity." And, finally, our Lord Himself declares to all who have sinned, "Except ye repent, ye shall all likewise perish."

The religion of the Bible differs in this respect from all other religions. Of no other is holiness the great and distinguishing requirement. And more than this, just to the extent that those religions which claim to be Scriptural are false in this claim, their demand for holiness becomes less and less stringent, or ceases altogether. They come practically to allow that men may be altogether unholy, both in life and character, and yet be the objects of the divine favor and complacence. Culture, amiability, morality, patriotism, an observance of certain rites, — going through certain exercises of mind or certain processes of feeling, — some one of these, or of a multitude of other assumed excellences, is allowed to come in to balance sin and offset it, and commend the unholy soul to God in all its unholiness.

But it is not so with the religion of the Bible. It encourages no man to think that he is right in the sight of God unless he is holy. It opens the door of heaven to no one unless he is holy. It sees nothing in one who is not holy with which God can be well pleased.

It was natural, then, that our Saviour should set holiness before his disciples as that which ought to be the special object of their desires and endeavors; and that He should, as He has here done, incorporate his own intense desire for them in this particular, into his ever prevailing intercessions. Hence his recorded desire and prayer for all his people is, "Sanctify them through thy truth; thy word is truth."

To sanctify is to make holy. It is to separate the soul from all sin, and consecrate and conform the whole heart and life to the will and service of God. This is the will of the Lord regarding his people. It is the great requirement of his religion. It is the end He has in view in calling them to be his people, and in disciplining them for heaven.

The Saviour's prayer here indicates that the instrument by which this work is to be done is the truth which God has revealed in his Word. And this is in perfect harmony with all the Scriptures. They everywhere teach that the sanctifying agent of men is the Holy Spirit; but that the truth which is contained in the Word of God is alone the instrument. All other things are in vain without this. They may be, and they often are, useful to prepare the mind for the truth to enter, and become saving as it is set home by the Spirit. The providences of God often have this preparative effect. But none of them are, in themselves, saving. The soul is never regenerated, nor made holy by them directly, nor by anything but the truth which is revealed in the Bible.

This, I say, is the uniform teaching of the Scriptures on this subject. Thus, e. g., the Psalmist says, "The law of the Lord is perfect, converting the soul." Our Saviour said to his disciples, "Now ye are clean through the word which I have spoken unto you." The Apostle Paul says to the Ephesians, "Christ loved the Church, and gave Himself for it that He might sanctify and cleanse it with the washing of water by the Word." And the Apostle Peter says to those whom he is addressing in his First Epistle, " Ye have purified your souls in obeying the truth through the Spirit, — being born again, not of corruptible seed, but of incorruptible, by the Word of God, which liveth and abideth forever." Such is the tenor of all Scriptural statements on this point.

The doctrine of the text, then, as of the Bible generally, is that the truth contained in the Word of God is the instrument by which men are made holy.

I invite your attention to one view of the truth which has a manifest adaptation to produce this result. For we ought never to forget that the Spirit of God works not only by means but by appropriate means. There is always a fitness in the instrumentalities that He employs to produce any given result, not less in the spiritual than in the natural world. Omnipotent though He is, there is no evidence that He ever disregards such fitness, or that He ever works a saving change in the heart of a sinner, or sanctification in that of a believer, by means not adapted to produce the renewal and sanctification.

The aspect of the truth to which I wish to direct your attention is that which, for want of a better form of statement, I must call the truthfulness of the truth.

Its sanctifying power is in the fact that it is truth, and not falsehood nor error. Sanctification is a process of making right that which is wrong. The hearts and lives of those who need to be sanctified are influenced by falsehood, and not by truth. If truth governed them they would be right already, and need nothing further in order to holiness. In any department of life, indeed, or in any phase of character, all that is in accordance with truth needs no reforming. All that needs reforming in either heart or life is that which is prompted by error or falsehood. Some false principle, some erroneous idea, or some wrong feeling, is at the root of it, and gives it character. The thing needed is that principles, ideas, and feelings that are right and truthful should displace those that are false, and govern in their stead. In other words, that what is wrong through error and falsehood should be set right by truth. You see this in the business of life. If a man fails of success in his business you at once inquire for the cause of it, and ask what was wrong — *i. e.*, not true — in his plans and calculations and reliances. You assume it as certain that there has been miscalculation, false reasoning, or false trust somewhere. He believed something that was not true, and acted upon it as true, though false. This ruined him. Had he incorporated nothing but the truth into his plans they would not have miscarried. Perhaps he trusted to abilities which he fancied himself possessed of, but which he never had. His self-conceit told him a falsehood about himself, and this wrought his downfall. Perhaps he trusted to a faithfulness which he supposed others whom he depended on possessed, but which they did not. He trusted that which was not true then, and this was the cause of his failure. Perhaps he counted upon prospects of gains which seemed real to him, but which were only imaginary. He reasoned falsely respecting them. He wrought a falsehood into his calculations; failure was the necessary result. In all these cases, truth substituted for whatever was false would have saved him from disaster.

You see the same thing exemplified in individual history, and in social and civil life. Character is ruined, reputation blasted, happiness destroyed simply by individuals acting on falsehoods as though they were truths. It was this, *e. g.*, that blighted the prospects of that young man whom you saw make shipwreck of position, influence, everything indeed that was promising and fair, when he counted upon the supposed advantages of dishonesty, and entered upon a career of pilfering, robbery, gambling, forgery, and ended it with a sentence of fifteen years in the Penitentiary. And what was it but a stupendous untruth, incorporated into the civil and political life of this country, contradicting the opening and self-evident proposition of the Declaration of Independence, that so nearly wrought our ruin as a nation in the demoralizations and disgraces that culminated in the late Rebellion? The truth, as faithfully acted on in our history as it was announced in our Declaration of Independence, would have saved us from the perils and losses and untold sufferings of the past few years.

The course of human life, both private and national, is thus not unlike that of a seaman. If his chart and compass, and all his calculations are true, he sails clear of rocks and breakers and is safe. But admit an untruth into either chart or compass or calculations, and there is no safety for him. He is far more likely to meet with loss and wreck than to prosper. And if he has gone out of his way, nothing but a falling back upon the truth and being governed by it will restore him and make him secure.

It is the same in religion. Whatever there is in the religious life or character that needs to be changed, it will be found, if it is carefully scrutinized, that it is the fruit of an untruth. The beginning of all wrong in this world was such a fruit. Our first mother believed a lie, and acted upon it. This brought death into the world, and all our woe. It is always thus in sinning. The mind accepts something as true which is false, and this turns the life out of its proper course, and makes a deformity in the character. No man can accept as true that which is false in anything that pertains to his moral and religious life, and not be thus injured. And, on the other hand, no man can substitute the opposite truth for this falsehood, and act upon it, without making right that which had been wrong. The truthfulness of the truth will set him right. And if the time shall ever come when truth alone shall have sway over his heart and life, he will then be holy, — made so by the truth.

It is a recognition of this principle that lies at the foundation of all divine exhortations to the study of the Scriptures, and to growth in knowledge, and of all the declarations of evil consequences following unbelief of the truth. Thus Paul says, " If our gospel be hid, it is hid to them that are lost: in whom the god of this world hath blinded the minds of them which believe not, lest the light of the glorious gospel of Christ, who is the image of God, should shine unto them." Again he says of those who perish under the working of Satan " with all power and signs and lying wonders, and with all deceivableness of unrighteousness," that it is " because they receive not the love of the truth, that they might be saved." In other places it is represented as the most fearful of all judicial visitations upon the wicked, that God gives them over to believe falsehoods. It is the surest of all the " tokens of perdition." They have chosen falsehood instead of truth, and clung to it against all the admonitions of conscience, and all the influences of grace; then God gives them over to that which they have chosen. Having hated the truth and persisted in doing it, they are given over to believe a lie.

From this it is evident why the Apostle was so filled with gratitude when he saw the proof that the Thessalonians were truly saved and in the way to heaven. "We are bound," he says, "to give thanks always to God for you, brethren beloved of the Lord, because God hath, from the beginning, chosen you to salvation, through sanctification of the Spirit, and belief of the truth." Hence, also, another Apostle closes his epistle with the exhortation, "Grow in grace, and in the knowledge of our Lord and Saviour Jesus Christ." In Him are all the fullness of the Godhead, and all the perfections of humanity. To know Him is to know both God and man. And herein is the reason of that saying of our Lord in his last prayer for his disciples: "This is life eternal, that they might know thee, the only true God, and Jesus Christ whom thou hast sent."

Remarks. 1. We see the reasonableness and necessity of the demand, which the Word of God everywhere makes, for faith in order to salvation. There must be positive faith — real belief. Disbelief and unbelief are alike ruinous; the soul cannot but be lost by cherishing either. This will become evident by a moment's consideration.

Unbelief is simply want of confidence in the truth. This paralyzes the soul and prevents action in accordance with the truth. We never act in earnest without faith. Unbelief hinders the soul from choosing and walking in the way of life. This is the reason why the "fearful and unbelieving" are grouped by the Spirit with "the abominable, and murderers, and whoremongers, and sorcerers, and idolaters, and all liars, who shall have their part in the lake which burneth with fire and brimstone: which is the second death." Unbelief simply does not choose the way of life, but contentedly remains in the broad way that leads to death, and walks on in it with unconcernedness. It merely neglects the great salvation, and therefore cannot escape ruin.

But disbelief is something more positive. This not only neglects, — it deliberately sets aside the truth as false. It chooses untruth for truth, and with intelligent purpose makes it a guide and principle of action. The disbeliever purposely, and of knowledge, refuses to accept the pointing of the compass as the true indicator of direction; and, accepting his own reason, or feelings, in its stead, calls north south and east west. He calls the broad way the right one, the narrow way wrong: the way to death he calls the way to life. He must, therefore, perish. His disbelief is necessarily his ruin. It could not by any possibility be otherwise. Of such as he the Scriptures declare, " There is a way which seemeth right unto a man, but the end thereof are the ways of death."

It is a necessity, therefore, that faith should be made the condition and the way of salvation for sinners. Sinners have gone out of the way of safety by acting upon falsehood as truth; they can get into that way again only by giving up falsehood, and accepting truth as their guide. To say that a sinner must believe the gospel or be lost, is to say that it is only by accepting and following the guidance of truth that he can escape the consequences of trusting to falsehood, and following it. And to say that without faith it is impossible to please God, is to say that God cannot be pleased to see an intelligent being believing falsehood for truth,— a moral and accountable soul making its way to eternal perdition rather than to eternal blessedness. It is to say, also, that God cannot be pleased that such a moral and intelligent being should make Him a liar. For "he that believeth not God, hath made Him a liar; for he believeth not the record that God gave of his Son." To say that one must believe in Christ or perish, is to say that if he refuses the only Saviour he cannot be saved.

2. That the only safety for Christians, in respect to doctrine or life or experience, is in closely following the Word of God. Turning from this, they are sure to receive for doctrines the commandments of men, human speculations and error, in the place of truth. They will come thus to believe and teach lies, that others, at least, if not themselves, may be damned. This is the fearful tendency of churches and ministers at the present time. They want something " fresher " (?) than the Bible, etc. They have itching ears; turn away their ears from the truth, and turn unto fables; ever learning, never able to come to a knowledge of the truth. Turning from this, their life will be wrong, — offensive to God, because wrong, — barren of good to self or others It becomes sickly and sentimental, a reproach to the name of Christ. Only " thy word, O God, is a lamp unto

my feet, and a light unto my path." Turning from this, religious experience becomes a delusion, an *ignis fatuus*, varying with every varying thing in condition of body or mind or circumstances. Abiding in this, — abide in God, and they are secure as his throne.

SERMON XXIV.

THE FACT OF REGENERATION.

TITUS iii. 5. — *According to his mercy He saved us, by the washing of regeneration, and renewing of the Holy Ghost.*

THERE are certain fundamental doctrines of the gospel which are essential to it, and upon an understanding and reception of which depends the fact whether or not one is a Christian. This is sometimes denied. Indeed it is somewhat fashionable in certain circles, and with certain classes, to scout the idea that a man's Christianity has anything to do with his receiving the doctrines of the gospel; or that his belief or rejection of them has any effect whatever on his character, or is in any manner concerned with his salvation. It is considered more learned, more large-minded, more Christian indeed, and as evincing a richer culture and a finer and more elevated moral sensibility, to count one's religion and his Christianity, if they are esteemed of any value, as something quite apart from and independent of his reception or "belief of the truth." Clothing the word "doctrines" with technical indefiniteness, and dwelling upon it in cant phrases, certain writers and speakers claim to demonstrate that the belief of doctrines is not only of no avail toward the well-being of men, but that it is even injurious to them; tending to make them narrow-minded, heartless, and hypocritical in character, and barren of the fruits of Christianity in their lives.

It is a sufficient antidote and answer to all this to call to mind the fact, that the doctrines of the gospel have no such technical isolation from the matter and substance of it as is here supposed; and that they are not, and they never can become such meaningless formulas as they are claimed to be to any who really believe or thoughtfully consider them. On the contrary, the doctrines of the gospel in the apprehension of such of them as understand and think, are simply and only the teachings of the gospel. They are the statements of truths which God has given us in his Word. These teachings cannot be disregarded, and these statements disbelieved, without disregarding and disbelieving the truths themselves. You might as well talk of disbelieving and casting aside as false the statement of a mathematical principle, or the narrative of a historical fact, and yet claim to accept the principle or believe the fact, as to talk of one's rejecting the doctrines of the gospel, and yet holding to its principles and believing its facts. To reject the statement is to reject the principle; to disbelieve the narrative is to deny the facts. The rejection of the doctrines of the gospel is, therefore, the rejection of the gospel itself, and if the gospel be true, such rejection is necessarily the acceptance of error and falsehood in its place. For it is of revealed truth, as it is of its author: "He that is not for it is against it; he that is not its friend is its enemy." And as a man's character and life are what the principles which he really holds make them, he that rejects the principles, of which the doctrines of Christianity are the declaration, can never have a Christian character, nor live a Christian life. Only by the belief and hearty acceptance of Christian doctrines can either life or character be Christian.

This is in harmony with all the representations of the Scriptures themselves. They know nothing of a piety that is impious toward their own teachings. They know nothing of a reverential spirit toward God, and of faith in Him connected with irreverence toward his Word, and disbelief of its statements. They know nothing of a godly life in conjunction with the rejection of God's Word.

Look at a few passages showing this — fair specimens of many others: " The law," or as it is in the margin of your Bibles, " the doctrine of the Lord, is perfect, converting the soul." " Wherewith shall a young man cleanse his way ? By taking heed thereto according to thy word." " Sanctify them through thy truth; thy word is truth." " If ye continue in my word then are ye my disciples indeed." " If ye abide in me, and my words abide in you, ye shall ask what ye will and it shall be done unto you." " God hath from the beginning chosen you to salvation through sanctification of the Spirit, and belief of the truth." " Ye are born again, not of corruptible seed, but by the word of God." And finally, in almost the closing sentence of the book of Revelation, we have that solemn warning against interference, in any way, with the purity and completeness of the words in which the Holy Ghost has chosen to reveal the mysteries of God: " I testify unto every man that heareth the words of the prophecy of this book. If any man shall add unto these things, God shall add unto him the plagues that are written in this book. And if any man shall take away from the words of the book of this prophecy, God shall take away his part out of the book of life, and out of the holy city, and from the things which are written in this book."

The doctrines then, or, which is the same thing, the teachings of the gospel, can never be given up by those who hold to the gospel itself ; nor can they be neglected and passed over as unworthy of careful and earnest study, and reverent acceptance by those who would know the will of God and be conformed to it. Just to the extent that one holds to these doctrines and lives in accordance with them, he is a Christian ; and on the other hand, just to the extent that he rejects them and fails to live by them, he is not a Christian. He has not the " love of the truth," but abides in darkness and in sin. It was to such as he is that the Lord said, " He that is of God heareth God's words: ye therefore hear them not because ye are not of God." And again, " If a man love me he will keep my words."

Among the doctrines or teachings of Revelation, which are generally esteemed fundamental in the gospel, is one of those which are brought before us in the text: " According to his mercy He saved us, by the washing of regeneration, and renewing of the Holy Ghost."

It is the doctrine of regeneration to which I refer. By the doctrine of regeneration is meant the instruction which the Scriptures contain regarding it. Not what different classes of men have said or written about it; not the speculations in which men have indulged concerning it; nor the theories they have invented for it. The doctrine of regeneration, I repeat, is the teaching of the Word of God on this subject.

1. In the first place the Scriptures teach that there is such a thing as regeneration. This, none who study the Scriptures

can deny or doubt. Allusions to it, and declarations regarding it, abound in every part of the Bible. They are found in the narratives and Psalms and prophetic writings of the Old Testament; and yet more in every part of the New Testament. Samuel said of Saul, that the Spirit of the Lord would come upon him, and that he should be "turned into another man." And it is added, that God gave him "another heart." The Psalmist cries in his prayer, "Create in me a clean heart, O God, and renew a right spirit within me." Through the prophet Ezekiel God said, concerning his people in coming days, " I will give them one heart, and I will put a new spirit within you ; and I will take the stony heart out of their flesh, and will give them a heart of flesh ; that they may walk in my statutes and keep mine ordinances, and do them: and they shall be my people, and I will be their God." This is the most common conception of the doctrine in the Old Testament. " Verily, verily, I say unto thee," said our Lord to Nicodemus, " Except a man be born again, he cannot see the kingdom of God." " That which is born of the flesh is flesh, and that which is born of the Spirit, is spirit." At another time He said in his preaching, " He that heareth my word and believeth on Him that sent me, hath everlasting life, and shall not come into condemnation ; but is passed from death unto life." " Be ye transformed by the renewing of your mind," said the Apostle Paul to the Romans, " that ye may prove what is that good, and acceptable, and perfect will of God." And to the Corinthians he says, " The natural man receiveth not the things of the Spirit of God: for they are foolishness unto him : neither can he know them, because they are spiritually discerned." To the Ephesians he said, " You hath he quickened, who were dead in trespasses and sins." To the Galatians he wrote, " In Christ Jesus neither circumcision availeth anything, nor uncircumcision, but a new creature." Hence of believers it is written, " Ye are created in Christ Jesus unto good works." And, " If any man be in Christ he is a new creature." Believers were born, it is declared, "not of blood, nor of the will of the flesh, nor of the will of man, but of God."

2. Not only do the Scriptures abound thus with passages that distinctly teach the fact of regeneration as a part of the process of the salvation of believers, but their whole theory of

salvation, if we may use such an expression, is based upon and involves it. Take away the fact of regeneration from the religion of the Scriptures, and its character would be wholly changed. It would not be even akin to what it now is. Its very beginning would be left out. Its essential, indispensable, and invariable characteristic would be wanting. It would cease utterly to be the religion of the Bible, and would become that of nature, and of mere speculation and theory. He in whom such a religion alone prevailed would not be a Christian. He would not have put off, as the Christian has by his regeneration, the old man which is corrupt according to the deceitful lusts; and been renewed in the spirit of his mind; and put on the new man, which after God is created in righteousness and true holiness." And being without such a beginning of salvation he would remain still in the "gall of bitterness and in the bonds of iniquity." He would not have been born of the Spirit; and so would not be a spiritual but a natural man. Being only a natural man he would not apprehend the things of the Spirit of God as every Christian does. Having only a carnal and not a spiritual mind, as every truly religious man is, by Scriptures, supposed to have, his mind, would not be as the Christian's is, reconciled to God, but enmity toward him. "For the carnal mind is enmity against God, not subject to the law of God, neither indeed can be." Not being a new creature by regeneration, he would not be in Christ Jesus; none of the old things of sin would have passed away; nothing in his character or in his relations would have become new. And we should find it the same with every great and distinctive element of true religion in the soul of man, as the Scriptures represent it, — it would be wanting in a religion that had not its beginning in regeneration; whereas every such element is by the Scriptures supposed and represented as having its origin and vitality in regeneration alone.

3. Again, the great mass of men who have received their ideas of true religion from the Bible, and have given any evidence that their religion was what the Scriptures represent true religion to be, have always claimed that they had themselves experienced such a change in their characters and relations as that which the Scriptures represent as constituting regeneration. In their own consciousness they are aware of

this change. They have experienced it. From the Apostle Peter, who declared of himself and all whose religion was in accordance with that of the gospel, that God had begotten them again unto a lively hope by the resurrection of Jesus Christ from the dead; and Paul who said of himself and all who stood with Him as the true worshippers of God according to the gospel, " God who commanded the light to shine out of darkness, hath shined in our hearts, to give the light of the knowledge of the glory of God in the face of Jesus Christ;" and John who wrote from his own consciousness and appealed also to the experience of all Christians, " Every one that loveth is born of God and knoweth God;" and, " We know that we have passed from death unto life, because we love the brethren;" from these Apostles down through all the ages of Christianity, it has been a marked feature in the religion of all who have followed the Bible as their guide, and have shown in their spirit and lives that their religion was of the kind described and required by the gospel, that it has acknowledged, nay more, that it has claimed for itself a consciousness of a thorough and radical change of moral and spiritual character. Those in whom it dwelt have, with most remarkable unanimity united in ascribing all that was good in them, and all their hopes of salvation, to the fact that they had passed through this supernatural change, and by it been made new creatures in Christ Jesus. Their innermost life is a constant testimony to themselves that they have been " renewed in the spirit and temper of their minds." They have the witness in themselves that they have been " born of God." And their outward lives have borne testimony that could not be gainsaid that they were men of truth, and terribly in earnest to know the truth.

No man can therefore deny the fact of regeneration, the new birth of the soul, whereby it is changed from enmity to God, to friendship with Him, from a child of wrath to a child of God, from a carnal to a spiritual man in Christ Jesus, without denying the plainest of Scriptural teachings; falsifying the whole theory of religion as it is taught by the sacred writers; and contradicting the concurrent testimony of all the most godly and devoted men that have ever borne the Christian name.

Let me ask each of you, my hearers, if you have experienced this great change in your own souls? If you have, then are you the children of God. You have passed out of death into life. You are among those of whom the Apostle declares they cannot sin. They cannot give themselves to its commission. They cannot get the consent of their hearts to indulge in it. For " why should they that have died to sin, live any longer therein ? " They walk not after the flesh, but after the Spirit. The law of the Spirit of life in Christ Jesus, has made them free from the law of sin and death.

But if you have not had this change in your soul, then are you not spiritual but carnal. You are yet in your sins. You are not the children of God, but his enemies. You are not subject to his law, nor can you be while you remain as you are. You have therefore no fitness for heaven. And if you die as you are, in your sins, where Christ is you never can go. He Himself is saying to you in all tenderness and fidelity, " Except a man be born again, he cannot see the kingdom of God."

SERMON XXV.
THE NATURE OF REGENERATION.

GAL. vi. 15. — *In Christ Jesus neither circumcision availeth anything, nor uncircumcision, but a new creature.*

IT is no uncommon thing for earnest and positive Christians to be thought narrow-minded and illiberal. It is hardly possible that they should not really appear to be so to unchristian men, or to men whose faith in Christian truth is but feeble, and who feel but slightly the importance of it to their wellbeing, or their responsibility in its acceptance or rejection. Truth is one, and not like error, multiform. Therefore he who is earnestly concerned to know the truth, and who clings to it with positiveness when he has attained to it, will always seem narrow in his range of thought and knowledge to those with whom speculations and theories and surmises and guesses are counted of equal value with truth, and perhaps of greater interest. One may watch the ever-varying forms of the clouds with far more interest than the fixed mountain, etc. They will seem to themselves to have a wider and more varied field of thought, and to possess the materials of a profounder and more extended knowledge. They will also seem to themselves to be more unfettered in their spirit, more generous in their culture, and more genial and large-minded in their temper, and in their relations with other men.

It is perfectly natural that it should be so. They are not limited, either in their thoughts or speculations or theories, to the truth. They can go beyond it, or contrary to it, or fall short of it, according as their fancy or their pleasure dictates. Putting the truth upon the same level with mere opinions, notions, impressions, fancies, and going from one to the other with equal facility, and resting in that which is false and unreal as having as substantial a basis of reality as that which is real and true, they cannot but seem to themselves to be wiser, more cultivated, and more intelligent men than he who is so limited as is a simple lover and adherent of the truth.

Being able also to fraternize with so many, and such various classes of men, counting them more or less at one with themselves, since they all hold so much in common with one another, and agree so well in indefiniteness and laxness of views as to all limits of truth and of knowledge, they can hardly help thinking themselves far more liberal in their feelings and character than they suppose he can be who can fraternize with none whom he does not consider as holding the truth; who fears to honor that which is, or perchance may be, false, as though it were true, and who dares not bid a hearty " Godspeed " to those who, he thinks, are, or fears that they may be, followers of error in the place of truth.

By its very nature the truth is limiting in its influence upon the human mind. It restrains its votaries to itself. It cannot admit either fellowship with error or partnership with uncertainties; nor will it allow itself to be put on a level with guesses and speculations and fancies. He who will know the truth, and trust to it, must be willing, not only to accept her teachings, but to swear allegiance to her, and forswear all allegiance to other guides and instructors. Or, to vary the figure, he who would walk in the way that truth marks out, must be willing always to keep to it solely, and to those who also keep to it. He cannot walk in other paths, nor keep company with those who do walk in them. And this is precisely what our Lord teaches us in those momentous words of the Sermon on the Mount, " Enter ye in at the strait gate; for wide is the gate, and broad is the way, that leadeth to destruction, and many there be which go in thereat: because strait is the gate, and narrow is the way, which leadeth unto life, and few there be that find it."

Of the same character are all his teachings. They go to show that they who will be followers of the truth must hold themselves to it, and never allow themselves to wander beyond its limits. He makes the gospel essentially exclusive in its demands upon the confidence of those who accept it. They must accept that and reject as false whatever is not in harmony with it. Nay, more, they must accept it as supreme and sufficient in all the domain over which it presides. It admits no rival, no equal. Its domain is religious truth. This it teaches in fullness and sufficiency. It teaches it as far as the mind of man, in the present life, can be carried, and denounces as false all that is not in accordance with its own utterances. "To the law and to the testimony," it says of all who claim to teach religious truth, "if they speak not according to this Word, it is because there is no light in them." Hence the Apostolic command to the lovers of truth is, " Contend earnestly for the faith which was once delivered to the saints."

This has ever been a marked feature of the worship of the true God among men. Like truth, it has been limiting and exclusive. They who would worship Jehovah must eschew the worship of all other gods. " Thou shalt have no other gods besides me : thou shalt worship Jehovah thy God, and Him only shalt thou serve." This is his law. To this law He has ever held his people ; nor has He counted them his people any further than they have obeyed it.

The worshipper of other gods could, like the advocates of error and falsehood, follow his inclinations and fancies, or even his caprices. There was nothing in his service of one false god that necessarily withheld him from that of other gods. He could be as liberal and catholic in his spirit and in his worship as he chose, or as his friends desired him to be. The Greek could thus go freely from one to another of the thirty thousand gods known and served among his people ; and the Roman could select any one, or go, at his pleasure, from one to another, of the vast concourse who were recognized in the Pantheon — the temple of all the gods. Neither was limited in his range ; neither was an exclusionist. To each, therefore, the worshipper of the one only living and true God always seemed narrow-minded, illiberal, uncharitable, bigoted.

The religion of the New Testament is, in this respect, as in all others that are essential, at one with that of the Old Testament. It is limiting and exclusive. It restricts its followers solely to its own provisions and service, and firmly closes its door against all who would bring to it a divided allegiance. Its whole spirit is that of its Author : He that is not for me is against me ; and he that gathereth not with me scattereth. It claims for itself to be true, and unhesitatingly denounces all others as false. Its very nature is such, moreover, that if it is true all other religions must be false. If the Saviour to whom it points the lost, and in whom it promises them salvation, be a Saviour at all, He is of necessity the only Saviour, and there is "none other name under heaven given among men whereby we must be saved." If its terms of salvation be true, their announcement excludes the possibility of salvation upon any other terms. Its single announcement upon this point is, "He that believeth and is baptized shall be saved; but he that believeth not shall be damned." "For," it is added elsewhere, "without faith it is impossible to please God." If the character which it demands, and declares to be necessary, in order that one should have the favor of God, and enter heaven, be necessary, then it is evident, not only from the declarations of the New Testament, but from the nature of the case itself, that no other character can enjoy the favor of God or dwell in heaven. Heaven is impossible, in the nature of things, to all others.

This was what our Lord taught Nicodemus when He said to him, so solemnly and with so much dignity and self-repose, "Verily, verily, I say unto you, except a man be born again, he cannot see the kingdom of God." This is what is taught throughout the New Testament as often as it makes any reference to the character of the saved in contrast with the character of others, or with that which they themselves possessed while they were in an unsaved state. Their character is unique. That of no other men is like it; nor can it become like it without passing through that change of which the Saviour spake to Nicodemus. It must be a character formed "by the washing of regeneration and renewing of the Holy Ghost."

This is one of the lessons taught us by our text: "In Christ Jesus neither circumcision availeth anything, nor uncircumcision, but a new creature." The Apostle's language is a broad and earnest assertion of the utter inefficacy and uselessness of everything else toward the salvation of the soul, if that change has not passed upon it which is here called a new creation, and in our text of last Sabbath morning,[1] the washing of regeneration. From that text I invited you to consider the fact of regeneration. It is taught as a fact (a) by definite statements

[1] See the preceding Sermon.

in a large number of passages of Scripture. (*b.*) It is involved in the very theory of the religion of the New Testament. That religion cannot have even a beginning without it. (*c.*) And finally, we saw that the fact of regeneration was and ever had been asserted in the religious experiences of the great mass of the lovers of the gospel, from the first announcement of it down to the present moment. Men of unsullied truth and of great righteousness have ever claimed to have experienced this momentous change as the beginning of their religion, and their whole after lives have borne ample testimony that they were men who knew whereof they affirmed, and were incapable of speaking falsely.

I invite your attention now to the nature of regeneration. What, according to the Scriptures, is that change which is set forth under this and kindred terms in the New Testament? It is not to the results of metaphysical or speculative investigation that I wish you to listen; but solely to the teachings of the Word of God.

1. First, it is a change that affects the whole spiritual being. Our Saviour's language is explicit upon this point, as is also that of all the sacred writers. "That which is born of the flesh is flesh; and that which is born of the Spirit is spirit." As the natural birth gives to the being born by it the character of its natural parents, — the only character which they communicate, — that is, one that is carnal or fleshly; so the spiritual birth gives to the soul that is born of the Spirit the character of Him by whom it is wrought. It affects all of one's being that is wrought upon, and from carnal it becomes spiritual. Hence the Apostle Paul uniformly speaks of the two conditions, the one before regeneration and the one that is after it, as fundamentally unlike and directly opposed to each other. "The carnal mind," he says, "is enmity against God; for it is not subject to the law of God, neither indeed can be. So then they that are in the flesh cannot please God." This is the condition of a man in his natural or unregenerated state. He is after the flesh, and he minds the things of the flesh. His whole nature is carnal; he is carnal in all his walk. "But they that are after the Spirit" cease from this, — they "mind the things of the Spirit," or spiritual things. So far as the soul is concerned in becoming spiritual, it has become as unlike what it was before as are two totally diverse natures.

Other representations abound, all of which teach this same lesson, that the regeneration of the soul thoroughly changes the character of that part of our nature which is affected by it. Sometimes, for example, it is spoken of as a new creation: "Ye are created in Christ Jesus unto good works." "If any man be in Christ he is a new creature; old things are passed away; behold all things are become new; and all things are of God." So, too, the Psalmist prays, "Create in me a clean heart, O God, and renew a right spirit within me."

Not unfrequently this great change is represented as a being brought to life from the dead. "You hath he quickened — or made alive — who were dead in trespasses and sins." They who have experienced it are declared to have "passed out of death into life."

Again, we are taught that by the new birth all who pass through the change that constitutes it, are so radically changed that they become pleasing in the sight of God, though they were before this change, like all unregenerate men, displeasing to Him. They become the children of God who were before the children of wrath. "Ye were the children of wrath, even as others," says the Apostle Paul to such as had felt the power of regenerating grace; "but now ye are fellow-citizens with the saints, and of the household of God." And the Apostle John says to all such, "Beloved, now are we the sons of God." And he says again, "Whosoever believeth that Jesus is the Christ is born of God." He thus becomes a child of God. Hence the Apostle Paul says to all believers, "Ye are all the children of God by faith in Christ Jesus." "And because ye are sons God hath sent forth the Spirit of his Son into your hearts, crying, Abba, Father." Hence also it is that John says so confidently of himself and all other believers, contrasting their condition with that of others, "We know that we are of God, and the whole world lieth in wickedness." It is faith in the Son of God that changes the relations of men to God, bringing them from the condition of enemies into that of friends, and from the state of children of the wicked one to be the sons of God; but it is their regeneration alone that brings their natures into harmony with this changed relation, making them inwardly — in heart and character — what faith in the Son of God has made them outwardly.

2. Without dwelling longer upon the general nature of the change which is wrought in the soul by regeneration, let us come to more definite statements.

1. First, it is a change by which spiritual, divine, and eternal things come to be rightly apprehended.

The Word of God teaches nothing more plainly than that the unrenewed soul does not understand, nor rightly conceive of these things. Neither the character of God nor that of his law is truly apprehended; nor is the nature of sin or of holiness, or of heaven or hell, or any of the great mysteries of redemption, nor any of the realities of an eternal and spiritual existence. It is a fundamental tenet of the Scriptures throughout both the Old Testament and the New, that all men are naturally without this discernment and apprehension. By one sweeping and unanswerable statement the great Apostle has combined and set forth the teachings of all the sacred records upon this point: "When they knew God, they glorified Him not as God, neither were thankful; but became vain in their imaginations, and their foolish heart was darkened. Professing themselves to be wise, they became fools. And even as they did not like to retain God in their knowledge, God gave them over to a reprobate mind," that is, as you have it in the margin of your Bibles, "a mind void of judgment." From that time to this it has been true of them that, "the natural man receiveth not the things of the spirit of God: for they are foolishness unto him; neither can he know them, because they are spiritually discerned." Therefore the same Apostle says, "If our gospel be hid, — as to many it is, — it is hid to them that are lost; in whom the god of this world hath blinded the minds of them that believe not, lest the light of the glorious gospel of Christ who is the image of God should shine unto them. For God who commanded the light to shine out of darkness, hath shined in our hearts to give the light of the knowledge of the glory of God in the face of Jesus Christ." It was in recognition of the same truth that the natural mind does not apprehend the things of the spirit of God, but must have the power of discernment given by God Himself, that our Saviour said to his disciples, "It is given unto you to know the mysteries of the kingdom of God, but unto others it is not given." So the Apostle says, "He that is spiritual discerneth[1] all things, yet he himself is discerned[1] of no man." And another Apostle says, " Ye have an unction from the Holy One, and ye know all things."

2. Again, the Scriptures teach us that the regeneration of the soul is a change by which it comes to love spiritual and divine things, — to love God, his law, and his people. The heart is indeed the centre upon which the influences of the new creation are concentrated. It is upon the heart that the great work is wrought. The other parts of our natures are affected but indirectly, and as a consequence of the change which is wrought upon the heart. It is a result of this change alone by which the intellect rightly apprehends spiritual things. Before the new creation the prejudices and disinclinations, and aversion of an unwilling and a hostile heart, hinder a clear perception of the things which are disrelished. They are like the mists and fogs that rise up between one and some object at which he would look, and hinder his vision; and like the miasms that rise with the mists and affect the organ itself with disease, though not with total disorganization. In the words of the prophet Jeremiah is a full and distinct recognition of both this resultant effect of the change in the soul, and of its direct effect on the heart. Pointing forward to the time when the nation and typical Israel should give way, and the true people of God, the spiritual Israel, should be revealed as alone the real Israel, the Lord said, " Behold the days come, that I will make a new covenant with the house of Israel, and with the house of Judah : not according to the covenant that I made with their fathers in the day that I took them by the hand to bring them out of the land of Egypt ; which my covenant they brake, although I was an husband unto them, saith the Lord : but this shall be the covenant that I will make with the house of Israel : After those days, saith the Lord, I will put my law in their inward parts, and write it in their hearts; and will be their God, and they shall be my people. And they shall teach no more every man his neighbor, and every man his brother, saying, Know the Lord: for they shall all know me, from the least of them unto the greatest of them, saith the Lord." The Apostle quotes this very passage, and makes the

[1] Margin.

application of it which we do now, to mark the effect of that spiritual renewing by which sinners become saints, and those who were at enmity with God, and blinded as to his character and law, become his friends, and attain to a saving knowledge of Him and of his character.

There is no need of multiplying quotations upon this point. Every representation which the Scriptures give of the effect of regeneration, is that it changes the heart from enmity to love of God; from disrelish to an affectionate regard for spiritual things; from a spirit of opposition to one of obedience and earnest admiration of the law of God; from dislike and deeply seated hatred of the people of God to tender love for them and oneness with them. So that John boldly declares, "We know that we have passed from death unto life, because we love the brethren. He that loveth not his brother abideth in death." And again, "He that loveth is born of God, and knoweth God."

3. A change by which they come to lead a holy life.

"Whatsoever is born of God overcometh the world. Whosoever is born of God doth not commit sin, for his seed remaineth in him: and he cannot sin because he is born of God."

SERMON XXVI.
THE FRUITS OF REGENERATION.

ROMANS viii. 6, end. — *To be spiritually minded is life and peace.*

EVERY doctrine of the gospel has a direct relation to character and life. Not one of them is merely theoretical and speculative. They were not revealed, nor can they be rightly preached, simply for the intellectual gratification of men; nor merely to satisfy their craving for knowledge; nor alone as mere verbal propositions that men, by the adoption of them, may be brought into the mechanical unity of a soulless orthodoxy; or into outward conformity to some ecclesiastical standard; or into the profession of a heartless and fruitless religion, having, it may be, "the form of godliness, but denying the power thereof."

Much of the reproach that has come upon what are called the doctrines of Christianity, and upon the preaching of them, has come, partly, no doubt, from misapprehension of what Christian doctrines really are; but far more from the misdirected efforts of creed-makers, and preachers who preach creeds rather than the Bible, to compel the intellectual assent of men to bare propositions and formal statements, instead of endeavoring to bring their hearts and consciences under the influence of the truth, and their lives thereby into harmony with the spirit and teachings of Christ. Such preaching, however, is not really the preaching of the doctrines of the gospel. It is so only in name. It has no voice for the soul in its innermost being and wants; and that which does not reach these is no gospel. It has in it no message of good tidings from God. Whatever may be its form of words, there is a something wanting by which all its claim to be the gospel is vitiated unless it has in it words for the heart, and a power to reach and satisfy the wants and cravings of a soul that desires to be at peace with God.

What our Lord said to his disciples when many who had been attending upon his ministry ceased to receive and began to rebel against the moving truths that He taught, and therefore went back and walked no more with Him, " the words that I speak unto you, they are spirit and they are life," is applicable to all the doctrines of Christianity. They are adapted and intended to reach the souls of men, to quicken them into life, and put them upon the securing and working out of a righteous character. A word that is spirit, or spiritual, is one that is suited to the spiritual nature, having power to influence and to sustain it in its being and action. So, too, a word which is life is a word suited to the necessities of a being who has life. Its end and its adaptation is to give life and support, enabling the soul that has been made alive from the dead to continue to live and to bring forth the fruits of life in all its movements and relations. All the doctrines of the gospel are of this character. Rightly preached and rightly received, they always have this power and are followed by these results.

This is, however, in direct and most marked contrast with the effect of all speculative or merely dogmatic preaching or teaching. This accomplishes its whole aim if it has put the learner in possession of certain formal statements and made him apprehend their literal import, considered as verbal propositions, though it has left him without any apprehension whatever of the truth underlying, it may be, those statements, and really entering into and constituting the substance of all Christian doctrine. The Apostle brings out this contrast and impliedly condemns this method of preaching and teaching in that declaration of his to the Corinthians when he was defending his own course as a preacher of the gospel: " Our sufficiency is of God, who hath made us able ministers of the New Testament, not of the letter, but of the spirit: for the letter killeth, but the spirit giveth life." He who is an able minister of the New Testament, or a true minister of it, has always a ministry of this character. He gives the words and forms of sound doctrine indeed, but in doing it he gives also the truth intended by the Holy Ghost in ordering that form of words. They will not therefore be dead words, but words of power, having the truth in them. The truth will be so much more than the mere wording of its utterances, and so fill out and energize the wording, that the ministry of it will no longer be a ministry of the letter but of the spirit. Such a ministry can never come from the mere studying and arranging of words, or manufacturing of propositions. Let those whose power lies in these efforts, and whose highest aims are reached when they have succeeded in them to their own satisfaction and that of their hearers, — let these essay the preaching of the doctrines of Christianity, or let them pass judgment upon the character that such preaching must assume, and you will at once have before you the sad picture which the very phrase doctrinal preaching suggests to so many minds, and which is made the object of denunciation by so many flippant pens and tongues. Doctrines then cease to have any relation to life, or anything to do with the state of the heart, the formation of character, or the movements of conscience. Then the great truths of Revelation are not set forth as truths, every one of which is of God and revealed by Him for the salvation and eternal well-being of men. Then the character of God, his relations to moral beings, the momentous realities of the judgment and eternity, the provisions and offers of the gospel, may indeed be talked about and discussed, as a theorist may discuss anything that has to do with his theory, but with no living interests of any human being; but they will not be so spoken of and so presented as to be real truths for the soul, upon the reception of which, and the manner in which they are treated, hang all the eternal destinies of those who hear. Then the great commands and requirements of the gospel may be mechanically handled and methodically arranged, and unconcernedly disposed of by both preacher and hearer. But they will not be those intensely living and soul stirring commands of which the Psalmist said, "Thy commandment is exceeding broad;" and whose power the Apostle felt when he wrote, "When the commandment came, sin revived, and I died. And the commandment which was ordained to life, I found to be unto death." In like manner, the Scriptural declarations regarding the traits of character that belong to different classes of men, and the fruit which will be brought forth in their lives, these will, in such a ministry, be nominally treated upon, perhaps, and very systematically arranged and classified, as much so, and as heartlessly, as one would arrange and classify the fosils and remains of extinct species of animals. But these traits of character and these fruits of life are not then so presented and urged upon the attention and upon the consciences of men that each one is compelled to know what manner of man he is, and is incited to enter upon the work of making right that which is wrong, and with all earnestness strengthening and perfecting that which is already right. Those doctrines of Christianity which pertain to character and living always have this power upon those who listen to them. They will have either the effect which the Lord's words had upon his disciples when He said, " Verily, verily, I say unto you that one of you shall betray me ; and they all began to inquire, Lord is it I ? Is it I ? " or that Nathan's parable had upon David, and will carry to the consciences of those who heed what they hear, the fearful, or it may be the joyous conviction, " Thou art the man ! "

Such, I think we have seen, is the character of the doctrine of regeneration. The consideration of it as a revealed fact, put us upon the inquiry, — with some of us it was a most anxious inquiry, — whether or not that great fact had been realized in us. The consideration of the nature of regeneration stimulated this inquiry still further, and deepened the anxiety which the consideration of the fact had awakened within us. Considerations of these things have in times past, if they do not now, filled some of us with such thoughts and emotions that as we look back upon them, the words that we sometimes sing are none too strong to express our state of mind, being —

> "My soul in bonds of guilt I found,
> And knew not where to go :
> One solemn truth increased my pain,
> The sinner must be born again,
> Or sink to endless woe."

The passage which I have read for my text, " To be spiritually minded is life and peace," invites our thoughts again to this great doctrine. These words bring before our minds for consideration, the *Fruits of Regeneration.*

The spiritual mind is the regenerated mind, as the carnal or fleshly mind is that which is unregenerated. The one is born of the flesh, and is therefore, as the Saviour Himself declares, flesh. It is not spirit. It is carnal, not spiritual. To be thus minded, the Apostle tells us, in the first clause of the verse, is death. Death is the legitimate fruit which it bears. To be carnally minded is necessarily a state of death, and it can lead to nothing but death in the future. For to be carnally minded is to have a sin-loving heart, a sin-moulded character, and a sin-directed life; and as sin when it is finished is death to the soul in which it has its development, so such a state of mind and heart and life must, of necessity, — it is impossible that it should not, — have death as its ever-springing and ever-ripening fruit.

But the other is born of the Spirit, and is, therefore, according to the same divine Word, spirit. It partakes of the nature of Him by whom it has been begotten, and is spiritual. It is not fleshly. Its desires and movements are all in harmony with its nature, and with the nature of its Renewer. For they that are after the Spirit do mind the things of the Spirit. It is in perfect accordance with their nature to do so. It is thus that they are " spiritually-minded." This is their true state, the real condition into which they have been brought by their new birth. And what the text asserts is, that the natural and necessary result, the legitimate and invariable fruit of being in this state, is life and peace. It is this, and it cannot but be this. To a greater or less extent every regenerate man will have life and peace as the constant and ever-yielded fruit of his regeneration.

1. In the first place, he will have life. He will not be dead. This term life doubtless refers very prominently to the state and relationship of the renewed soul. It is no longer under the displeasure and wrath of God. It is no longer alienated from Him and an enemy to holiness. It is restored to communion and fellowship with God, and to the love of righteousness. This is its condition. It is that of a child of God both in its relations and in its disposition; and this is a condition of life as distinguished from one of deadness in trespasses and sins.

But life is not solely a state or condition and relation of the soul. It is this, but it is something more than this. It is activity. Life is an active principle. It is ever seeking to assert itself in actions. It is so in natural life; the Scriptures teach us that it is so in spiritual life. It will act, and when it acts it will act in accordance with its own nature.

The Word of God does not anywhere countenance the idea that a living soul, or a renewed nature, can be inactive and inoperative. It is a sentiment altogether alien to the Scriptural method of conceiving and representing the regenerate character, that one who has been born of God ever comes into a state that he does not for any great length of time use his regenerated powers, and, feeling the quickening and impelling influences of a new life, seek to give it expression in the conduct. Every attentive reader of the Bible is impressed involuntarily with the incongruity of such a sentiment, or supposition even. It is of spiritual as of animal life, there are always certain and invariable evidences of its presence. The natural heart will beat, the blood will circulate, the lungs will breathe, even if there are no voluntary movements of the body. Sleep itself cannot check these necessary functions of animal life. It is the same with the life of God in the soul. Its heart will beat. Love, however feeble it is, will act, and its throbbings will project the desires and aspirations of the soul towards God and heaven. It will take in to sustain its vitality something, however small it may be, of the love and mercy and grace of God which are diffused around it, as the air is about the breathing body. These things it will do, though it may be greatly depressed, and sadly deficient in the putting forth of direct and conscious energies in doing the good works for which it was created anew in Christ Jesus. As a beating heart and breathing lungs are the necessary accompaniment and evidence of bodily life, so is a loving heart — loving towards God and towards men — and a desiring and aspiring spirit, necessary accompaniments and evidences of the life of the soul. "Every one that loveth," says the beloved disciple, "is born of God and knoweth God. He that loveth not knoweth not God, for God is love." Where there is no love there is no life; and the very nature of love is to desire communion with its object, and to go out from self to be with and enjoy it. Hence the same disciple says unequivocally, "He that loveth not his brother abideth in death." And again, "Whoso hath this world's good, and seeth his brother have need, and shutteth up his bowels of compassion from him, how dwelleth the love of God in him?"

Combining the teachings of the Scriptures upon this subject, they will be found to set forth and maintain as unquestionable, these two principles, namely : first, he that is born of God will love God. His new birth makes him a child of God, — gives him the true spirit of a child towards its father, which is a spirit of reverence, of trust, of love, and of obedience. Love is itself the spirit of obedience. Hence the Saviour says, "If a man love me he will keep my words." It is the nature of love to obey. It cannot but obey. The moment that the soul turns itself to disobedience of God, it is no longer the love of God by which it is moved. Something else, and something antagonistic to love and to God has taken the place of love.

The second principle which a grouping of the teachings of the Bible upon this subject will show, is that he who has been born of God will be a man of righteousness and benevolence towards his fellow men. If he has been born of God he has been born into these traits of the divine character. He cannot love unrighteousness, nor can he get the consent of his will and conscience to practice it towards any with whom he has to do. He cannot be hard-hearted and selfish. The love towards God and towards men which is the very life of a regenerate soul, and the absence of which constitutes in a great measure its carnality and death, and makes its regeneration necessary, this love must act, and acting will, as love always does, draw the soul out from itself, and fill it with kindly desires and merciful feelings and purposes towards others. So far as there is hardness, unkindness, stinginess, unmercifulness, in any man's soul, so far he is carnal and not spiritual. And if these be the prevailing elements of his character, then he is yet in the gall of bitterness and in the bonds of iniquity. The love of God is not in him. He is not born of God. For whatsoever is born of God overcometh the world.

The grand characteristic of regeneration as it affects the life is set forth by the Apostle in his declaration to the converted Ephesians : "Ye are the workmanship of God," — and the Apostle is here speaking of regenerate men, — "created in Christ Jesus unto good works, which God hath before ordained that we should walk in them." "He hath chosen us in Christ, before the foundation of the world, that we should be holy, and without blame before Him in love."

2. Secondly, there is peace. To be spiritually minded is life and peace. This term has direct reference to the condition

of the heart, the disposition and feelings of the soul. It is at peace. This must be the case so far as there is love. The heart that is filled with love is filled with peace. Perfect love casteth out all fear. Perfect love brings the whole soul into conscious reconciliation with God. So far as the love, which regeneration invariably and necessarily begets in the soul, pervades the soul, so far there is peace.

But this term is of wider signification than it has in ordinary discourse. It applies to the whole moral and spiritual being. It indicates that all the faculties of the soul are healthful, and that the whole spiritual nature is acting harmoniously. Nothing in the soul or in its action is working adversely to its own interests or the interests of any other being.

This, too, is a legitimate fruit of love, or, which is the same thing, of regeneration. The regenerate soul is born out of its deadness in trespasses and sins, into the life of holiness, and holiness of necessity brings it into harmony with its own wellbeing and with that of every other creature.

Hence the Apostle Paul, summing up the elements of the spiritual character, says, " The fruit of the Spirit is love, joy, peace, longsuffering, gentleness, goodness, faith, meekness, temperance."

The possession of such a disposition and temper of mind is the possession of peace. And this it is, says the Apostle, to be spiritually minded. This is the fruit of the spiritual mind.

SERMON XXVII.

WHAT IS THE HOLY SPIRIT?

ROMANS xv. 13. — *That ye may abound in hope through the power of the Holy Ghost.*

"THE world by wisdom knew not God." Forty centuries were given it to try the experiment of coming to a knowledge of Him by this means. It made the attempt and failed. During all this time it had made no progress, but had, from generation to generation, become darker and more hopeless.

Yet the human intellect had been cultivated, in some of the choicest natural men of the race, to as high a point as it has ever been carried. Some of the fruits of this cultivation remain, even till now, the masterpieces of thought; and modern education consists in no small degree in the study of them. Some of the men of that experimental period are to-day the guides of the best intellect of the world in some of the darkest, most difficult, and most important fields of thought and inquiry. The profoundest thinkers of modern times gladly sit at their feet, and listen with admiration and reverence to their wisdom. No human thinking has ever yet surpassed theirs for comprehensiveness and subtlety. They were masters both of thought and argument.

It was not for want of intellect, therefore, that the world failed to find out God by its wisdom. It can be safely asserted that if human wisdom, unaided by direct revelation, could attain to the knowledge of God, it would have been done by these men of giant intellect and far reaching thought. No one who knows whereof he affirms would risk the assertion that where they failed in any matter dependent upon the unaided human reason, any who come after them would succeed.

Nor was the world's failure to come to a knowledge of God due alone to the absence of manifestations and proofs of his existence, and some of his attributes. The works of the Creator would have revealed Him with sufficient clearness, in these respects, at least, if any had been found to regard the revelation: "For the invisible things of Him from the creation of the world are clearly seen, being understood by the things that are made, even his eternal power and Godhead."

Indeed, this revelation was so distinct that the blindest could not exclude from their minds all the light that was reflected upon them. The existence and attributes of a Supreme Being were apprehended to some extent, as is seen by their idolatry; but the image of Him which their minds received was so distorted and blurred that it was not an image of the true God. It did not give them a knowledge of Him. They remained in dark and dismal ignorance in the midst of most glorious revelations. And this is the inspired explanation of it: "They did not like to retain the knowledge of God," which even this revelation gave them, "therefore they became vain in their imaginations and their foolish heart was darkened."

But there is much that enters into the true idea of the knowledge of God which the works of creation do not reveal. These cannot reveal in fullness the divine mind and heart. What these are, together with the nature of God and the mode of his existence, must of necessity be made known by direct revelation, or else all our notions regarding them must be speculative only; mere guesses, at best, but not knowledge. The history of the world demonstrates this. Where the Word of God has not been known, there has never been anything like a perfect outline drawn of the divine character and mode of existence as they are set forth by the Scriptures, and as they are almost universally accepted as true wherever the Bible has become the recognized revelation of God to men. And not only so, not only has there been no such distinct outline of his character and the mode of his existence, but there has been no sense of certainty in regard to the notions that were broached or entertained. The few thoughts of the character of God and the mode of his existence that were indulged, were not fixed in the mind and sure, so as to become to it more than speculative and theoretical. They were not knowledge.

Such is the lesson taught us by the history of this world And yet our times are noted for the boldness and assurance with which men decry both the fact and the necessity of a written revelation. It is claimed that the world does, by its wisdom, know God. But when we come to examine the knowledge which these men claim to have attained without the aid of the written Word, two suggestive facts become apparent. In the first place, we find most of the elements of this knowledge manifestly drawn directly from the Bible itself. The speculators have lived under the full blaze of the sun of revealed truth all their lives. They have been taught it at their mother's knees, they have heard it in their father's prayers, and have had all their education where the Bible has infused its influences into every department of government, and of civil and social life. From these sources they have, sensibly or insensibly, imbibed the true ideas of God as his Word reveals them; and then turning their backs upon that Word, and denying its authority and worth, they have set about the work of learning God, and declaring Him, from the results of what they vainly fancy to be independent thought and investigation. Recalling the lessons of earlier years, and acting upon the hints constantly furnished from the Bible in an indirect way through thousands of channels that never can be closed against any class of men in a Christian community, they pride themselves upon these recalled and suggested thoughts as though they were the fruit of thoroughly independent, unaided, and original thinking. The second fact that we find is this: In all the elements of that which these men claim to be a knowledge of God, the moment they depart from the teachings of the Bible we discover a reproduction, not only of the speculations and guesses of the great minds of the past, but of their uncertainty and want of confidence also. That which is taken for truth soon comes to be doubted by the theorizer himself; and is supplemented, if not by himself, certainly by others, with other and equally plausible notions; these to be as soon suspected, and as soon suplemented, by still others of like character and destiny.

The only fair test of the powers of human wisdom to gain a knowledge of God without a written revelation is to take it where no written revelation has ever shed its light. Then the test will be of some value. What you find there will be the real results of this wisdom acting alone. On the other hand it is but fair, nay, you are compelled on every principle of right reasoning, to give the Word of God credit for all that is higher and purer and better in the knowledge of men who have come either directly or indirectly into contact with a written Revelation. They cannot legitimately claim for their own wisdom the origination or discovery of one, not even the least of these higher and better elements. It is a species of dishonorable theft for them to attempt it. In reading or listening to the results of human speculation and reasoning in regard to the being and character of God, or the mode of his existence, this ought to be remembered. Measured by this test, much of what passes for profundity and independent originality will be at once shorn of its glory. Give back to the Bible all that has been surreptitiously taken from it by men claiming to have no need of its teachings in order to the learning of God and divine things, and their nakedness will become pitiable. The sages of the past who knew not, and confessed that they could not know these things, will tower above them in everything that goes to make up manhood and fruitfulness of intellect.

We are brought then to this conclusion, that we are dependent wholly upon the Scriptures for any full and satisfying knowledge of God. From this source alone do we learn what God is, and the method of his existence. And inasmuch as the Scriptures alone teach those things concerning God which make our knowledge of Him different from and better than were the speculations and guesses and unsustained and unsatisfying fancies regarding Him, which were the highest attainments of men who had the highest intellectual life but had no Bible, we are shut up to the necessity of acknowledging it to be a special divine revelation upon this point, and of giving it the place of an infallible teacher and an absolute authority. We cannot, without the grossest inconsistency, either curtail or supplement its instructions. We must take them as they are and accept them in faith whenever they go beyond our present powers of comprehension. When they tell me directly or impliedly what God is, and how He exists, I cannot gainsay what they assert nor correct their statements. I know, indeed, that if they do reveal God to me they must reveal Him in mystery. The revelation of Him must of necessity be a revelation in mystery. Every term which they employ to give me knowledge must contain vastly more that I cannot understand than that I can. To the finite mind God must ever be as the sea is to the natural eye. You can look upon it; it is revealed to you as you stand upon its shore; but how much more of the unknown than of the revealed is suggested to you by the view. Your sight cannot penetrate its mysterious depths, nor take in the immensity of its expanse. That which is seen, while it gives the mind clear and truthful conceptions, as far as it goes, yet suggests and implies infinitely more that cannot be seen, but which must be received on testimony. It is so with the revelations which the Scriptures make of God. They give us clear and truthful views of Him as far as our minds can grasp them; but in giving these they suggest and imply, and, indeed, assert vastly more that must be received on their testimony alone. Anything that claimed to be a revelation of God that did not thus suggest and imply, and assert infinitely more than the human mind could fully comprehend, would by this very failure convict itself of imposture and pretense.

I have been led into this train of reflection, my hearers, by the study of the last few words of our text: "by the power of the Holy Ghost." As we look into the Scriptures we find that the great and fundamental idea which they reveal and constantly insist upon is, that God is One. There is no other God beside Him. This fact Nature herself would doubtless teach, if her laws and phenomena were perfectly understood by men. But so long as they are but partially and imperfectly known, it is by no means clear that the unity of God could be learned from them. As a matter of fact the world never did come to a clear and positive knowledge of this truth from the study of nature alone, or by the exercise of unaided reason. And from the emphasis with which it was asserted to the people chosen to be the depositaries of the oracles of God, and the constant repetition of it, and the sedulous guarding of it lest that people should forget or fail to recognize it, it would seem that God thought the distinct revelation of it to be imperative. Hence from first to last of the volume of Revelation this great truth stands out with special prominence: "There is but one God."

But how does He exist? Here we encounter the mystery necessary in the revelation of the Infinite One. God is one. He is one God. The only living and true God; and besides Him there is no other. But this one God is threefold in his mode of existence. The Scriptures reveal Him to us as the

Father, the Son, and the Holy Ghost, one God. The revelation is distinct and cannot be misunderstood; but the mystery involved in the revelation is deeper than we can fathom, wider than we can measure. The one God, the one only living and true God, is the Father, and the Son, and the Holy Ghost!

In the three sermons on the Sabbath mornings preceding this we have given our attention to the doctrine of Regeneration. Our Saviour calls this a being "born of the Spirit." This has led us to think more or less of this divine agent. My purpose now is to bring before you some of the teachings of the Scripture sconcerning Him. And I do this to help you to realize in yourselves the Apostolic wish, "That ye may abound in hope through the power of the Holy Ghost." As in the sermons on Regeneration so in these, let us lay aside speculation and theory, and give our minds with submissiveness and docility to the revelations of the inspired record itself.

What then do the Scriptures reveal respecting the Holy Spirit?

1. They reveal the fact that there is a Being so named, — there is a Holy Spirit. He is a Being distinct from all other beings. The Scriptures thus speak of Him, using the word Holy Spirit and its equivalents in numerous instances, in such a way as that it cannot by any possibility be made to describe anything but a distinct Being. Their use of the word, in these instances, is not as it is in others, descriptive of the temper or disposition of the mind of an intelligent being, whether God or man. It is impossible to take the word in this sense in many passages of the Scriptures, and retain any intelligible meaning whatever. This will appear as we advance. The passages which we shall quote under another head will be conclusive upon this point, and I need not detain you with a recital of them here.

2. The Holy Spirit is a person. The word *person* is the best word that we have by which to indicate the distinction that the Scriptures make known regarding the Godhead, in teaching us that there is in it the Father, and the Son, and the Holy Ghost. Each of these is spoken of as distinct from the other, and all together constitute the mysterious trinity in unity in the revealed mode of the divine existence.

A person is one who has intelligence, will, affections, and all the qualities necessary to constitute a conscious moral agent. That which has these in himself is a person. It is impossible for us to conceive of it otherwise than as such. If, therefore, the Scriptures represent the Holy Spirit as possessed of these qualities, they intend that we should thus conceive of Him. They do thus represent Him to us. The plain, unforced meaning of very many passages makes this impression upon the mind; and that impression cannot be resisted without doing manifest violence to the words of inspiration. They speak of Him in many relations as thinking, knowing, feeling, acting. He does this independently, as Himself a distinct thinking, knowing, feeling, acting agent.

Let me ask your attention to a few of these passages; and, as I read them, bear it in mind that the Scriptures were given for the express purpose of revealing God to us, and not of misleading us in regard to anything that pertains to Him:[1] "Whosoever speaketh a word against the Son of man, it shall be forgiven him; but whosoever speaketh against the Holy Ghost, it shall not be forgiven him, neither in this world, neither in the world to come." In this passage you perceive that the Holy Ghost is spoken of as a distinct Being, as much so as the Son of man is. He can be spoken against, sinned against, blasphemed. The natural and obvious implication of the words is that as the Son of man is a person of thought, and knowledge, and feeling, and will, so is also the Holy Spirit.

"But when they shall lead you and deliver you up, take no thought beforehand what ye shall speak, neither do ye premeditate: but whatsoever is given you in that hour, that speak ye: for it is not ye that speak but the Holy Ghost." (Mark.)

"The Holy Ghost shall teach you in the same hour what ye ought to say."

"But the Comforter, which is the Holy Ghost, whom the Father will send in my name, He shall teach ye all things and bring all things to your remembrance, whatsoever I have said unto you." (John.) They spake as the Spirit gave them utterance.

"But Peter said, Ananias, why hath Satan filled thine heart

---

[1] I know that it is common with a large class of writers to speak contemptuously of proof texts. Few do this, however, who show reverence for the Bible or bow unquestioningly to its authority.

to lie to the Holy Ghost?" (Acts.) "So they being sent forth by the Holy Ghost." (Acts.) "It seemed good to the Holy Ghost, and to us, to lay upon you no greater burden." (Acts.) They "were forbidden of the Holy Ghost to preach the Word in Asia." (Acts.)

"Take heed, therefore, unto yourselves, and to all the flock over which the Holy Ghost hath made you overseers." (Acts.)

"And grieve not the Holy Spirit of God, whereby [or by whom] ye are sealed unto the day of redemption." (Eph.)

"The Spirit itself [Himself] beareth witness with our spirit that we are the children of God."

"Likewise the Spirit also helpeth our infirmities: for we know not what we should pray for as we ought; but the Spirit itself [Himself] maketh intercession for us, with groanings which cannot be uttered." He maketh intercession for the saints according to the Word of God.

It is needless to multiply quotations, as we might do almost indefinitely. These are fair examples of a multitude of others, — more than enough to teach us that the Scriptures clearly set forth the personality of the Holy Spirit. All the attributes necessary to constitute a person are ascribed to Him. Acts which none but a personal agent could perform are ascribed to Him. Feelings which none but a personal subject could experience are ascribed to Him. He is, therefore, a person.

3. The Holy Spirit is God. The things that are said of Him could be said of no other. The relationship which He is represented as sustaining to the Father shows his deity. He is distinctly called God. On each of these points the light is clear and convincing. Above all difficulties which our minds encounter in endeavoring to comprehend the mystery involved in the revelation of the mode of the divine existence, the revelation itself of the deity of the Spirit comes in and holds us to an acknowledgment of it. We must deny the revelation or admit the deity of the Spirit.

A few passages to sustain each of the points I have specified will suffice.

First, What our Saviour says of the sin against the Holy Ghost could be said of none other than God. To make Him less than God makes the Saviour's words unnatural, and out of harmony with all the teachings of the Scriptures regarding the character of sin and the conditions of forgiveness. The same is true of what the Redeemer said to his Apostles regarding the Comforter, which is the Holy Ghost, who should come and teach them, as He had done, with infallible certainty, all that they would need to know as witnesses of the truth, and the founders of the Church of Christ. The same is true of what He said of the Comforter's remaining forever with his disciples. Wherever they are, that Comforter is with them. He is omnipresent, therefore. He knows all the wants and trials of all the saints in all places. He is therefore omniscient. These things can be said of none other but God Himself.

As to the relation which the Holy Spirit sustains to the Father and the Son, we need notice nothing beyond the baptismal formula and the Apostolic benedictions: "Go ye therefore, and teach all nations, baptizing them in the name of the Father, and of the Son, and of the Holy Ghost."

"The grace of the Lord Jesus Christ, and the love of God, and the communion of the Holy Ghost be with you all."

In this formula and benediction there is a grouping that forbids the thought of inferiority in either the Son or the Spirit. Nothing can justify such grouping, to our apprehension, of the majesty and unapproachableness of God, or harmonize it with the views of the divine glory which the Scriptures so clearly teach, except the recognition of the mystery of the revelation itself that sets before us for our faith to accept, — the trinity in unity.

I add but one other passage, showing that the Holy Spirit is directly and unequivocally called God: "Why hath Satan filled thine heart to lie to the Holy Ghost?" "Thou hast not lied unto men, but unto God."

Remarks. 1. This is the Agent by whom the salvation that Christ came into the world to make possible, is wrought in individual souls. The Holy Spirit alone regenerates them. They are born of the Spirit if they ever pass out of a carnal into a spiritual state. If they are ever saved it is by the washing of water and the renewal of the Holy Ghost.

2. This is the Being that is resisted by wicked men when they refuse to yield to the claims of Christ and the truth upon them.

Hence Stephen's charge against his persecutors was, "Ye stiff-necked and uncircumcised in heart and ears, ye do always resist the Holy Ghost: as your fathers did, so do ye."

This resistance is a most solemn and fearful matter. Carried to a certain pitch, there is no forgiveness, neither in this world nor in the world to come.

Oh, how careful ought those to be in their conduct towards an Agent on whose gracious influences their eternal well-being is solely suspended!

3. This Agent of renewal and Sanctifier and Intercessor of the saints, is sent to men as the Son was sent, in answer to prayer. "If ye then, being evil, know how to give good gifts unto your children, how much more shall your heavenly Father give the Holy Spirit to them that ask Him." "Ask, and ye shall receive."

4. The favor of this Agent, on whom the very life of the soul depends, ought to be carefully cherished by the people of God.

He cannot and will not dwell with cherished sin. He is grieved when his people sin. Their conduct should be a constant utterance of David's prayer, "Take not thy Holy Spirit from me."

SERMON XXVIII.

THE CONVINCING OF THE HOLY SPIRIT.

JOHN xvi. 8, in part. — *He will reprove the world of sin.*

THE person of whom the Saviour here speaks is the Holy Spirit. He was to come into this world under new and peculiar circumstances after Christ should have ascended to heaven. Not that He was ever wholly absent from the earth, or ever ceased to dwell with men. But his being with men before the day of Christ's ascension and his ministering to their holiness and salvation, was with this day in prospect. An atonement was to be made and He who was to make it was to be exalted thereafter a prince and a Saviour, and sit upon the throne of God, and reign over all things for the redemption of his people. In anticipation of this, patriarchs and prophets and all holy men of old lived in the gospel day by faith; and they were dealt with in a measure as though the atonement were already made. For in the mind and purpose of God all was accomplished, and He could in consequence even then be just, justifying the guilty. The way was therefore open for the Holy Spirit to work among men, and He did work in their hearts, so that multitudes were brought "to salvation through sanctification of the Spirit, and belief of the truth."

But when Christ had in fact as well as in purpose finished his work upon the earth, and ascended to the Mediator's throne, it was no longer an atonement to be made that was preached, but an atonement completed. A Saviour was then revealed, not by the dim rays of prophetic light, but by the full shining of historic truth. Men might then hope to be saved, not because they expected a deliverer in coming time, but because a Deliverer had already appeared and was in the full prosecution of his mighty work. It was with this atonement already made, and this Saviour already revealed, that the Holy Spirit was now given. He henceforth wrought among and upon men, by a perfected, and not a prophetic plan of salvation. The means by which He influences the hearts of men since the ascension of Christ are immensely more potent; the way by which He aproaches them far more direct and effective. Hence it was in some sort a new coming of the Spirit, when He began to comfort the people of God in the place of an already manifested Saviour; to take of the things of that Saviour and show them unto his friends, and to make all his influences centre upon Him as the now living, exalted, and reigning Messiah. It was in these circumstances He began, and has ever since been accomplishing the words of Jesus which we are considering, — " He shall reprove the world of sin."

The term " world," in this passage, evidently refers to such as are not the friends of God; the impenitent men of the world. This will be plain if we notice the use of the word in a few other passages. In the seventh verse of the seventh chapter of this book, our Lord says to his unbelieving brethren, " The world cannot hate you; but me it hateth because I testify of it, that the works thereof are evil." In the eighteenth verse of the fifteenth chapter, He says to his disciples, " If the world hate you, ye know that it hated me before it hated you." The same view is sustained by comparing the text with the thirteenth verse of this chapter. In our text Jesus says, " The Holy Spirit will reprove the world of sin;" but, in the thirteenth verse, " He will guide you into all the truth." The disciples of Christ, or the friends of God, are put into contrast with the world. They then are the world who are not the friends of God or the disciples of Christ.

The word " reprove " requires a moment's attention, in order to a proper understanding of the text. Commonly, the word means " to blame, to censure;" but more literally " to manifest a wrong by proof, to convince of wrong." This is, without doubt, its meaning here, — " He will convince the world of sin." The margins of our Bibles give *convince* in the place of *reprove*, and the whole context, and kindred and illustrative portions of the Scriptures, clearly show that convince is the more suitable word to be here employed.

The teaching of the text is then that one of the offices of the Holy Spirit on earth is to convince impenitent men of their sins. Our Lord might have had immediate reference here to something less general than this statement implies. He might have referred specially to the sin of those who had rejected Him during his ministry in the flesh, who were, many of them, convinced of their guilt, in this particular, on the day of Pentecost, when the favor of God towards Jesus was manifested, and He was declared, by his resurrection, to be the Son of God, and by the miraculous powers with which He endowed his disciples was shown to be all that He had claimed for Himself while He was on earth. Men believed not on Him while He was visibly with them; but when they saw, at the coming of the Holy Spirit upon his disciples, such proofs of the divinity of his mission, conviction of their guilt, in disbelieving, was visited upon their minds. The Holy Ghost thus convinced them of sin because of their unbelief.

But whether or not this was the special application of the words, as our Lord uttered them, they yet announce a general and most important truth. They fully imply that, as we have said, it is the office of the Holy Spirit to convince impenitent men of sin while the gospel of a risen and glorified Saviour is preached. It is only by virtue of this his general office that the Saviour makes the special application, if it be such, which some suppose is made in the text. We are safe, therefore, in giving these words their most extended application, to men of all times and all places, who hear of Christ, and are made conscious that they are sinners against God, and need such an one as God has provided in Christ to save them from condemnation.

We are not under the necessity, however, of understanding from the text that every kind and degree of conviction of sin which men have, are from the influence of the Holy Spirit upon them. The conviction here spoken of, let it be remarked, is in view of gospel truth. It is of sin as in some sort committed against the Lord Jesus Christ. For in the following verse it is said by way of explanation, "He shall convince the world of sin because they believe not on me." Evangelical conviction always has in it this element, a reference to Christ. In this, as in everything else, there must be this reference, or there is no gospel, nothing that can save the soul; nothing that leads it to a Saviour; nothing that is radically and permanently beneficial.

But it is for the radical and permanent benefit, even the salvation of lost sinners, that the Holy Ghost moves upon their minds. All that He does is with this end in view. For this He takes of the things of Christ the Saviour, and shows them unto men. For this He opens their understandings that they may understand the Scriptures. For this He came into the world, and for this He remains in it. His great mission is to point to Christ, to testify of Him, and say to every soul thirsting for salvation, " Come, take the water of life freely." Whatever emotions men may experience, therefore, or whatever influences may be upon their minds, unless these emotions and influences lead to Christ, either directly or indirectly, we are not probably justified in ascribing them to the Holy Spirit. He testifies of Christ. He has come in Christ's stead. " He shall not speak of Himself; but whatsoever He shall hear that shall He speak. He shall glorify me."

We are not, therefore, to refer to the Holy Ghost, that conviction of sin which arises simply from the promptings of natural conscience. There is that within men, which is also a part of themselves, by the promptings of which they make a distinction between some things as right, and other things as wrong. There is also inherent in their natures a sense of accountability; a something that makes them feel that they are, in some degree, responsible for their conduct. Their moral standard may be very low, their notions of responsiblity very deficient and the sense of it weak; yet, if they are men, the idea of manhood implies the possession of such a faculty in the soul, and its exercise in distinguishing responsible from irresponsible acts, and pronouncing upon them as morally right, or morally wrong.

Such a faculty implies also some standard of moral conduct; that is, some law which a wrong deed violates; which a deed morally right complies with and honors. Whenever, therefore, that within men which thus distinguishes between the right and wrong of their conduct, pronounces sentence against them as wrong-doers, it convinces them of sin. There is thus conviction simply by the action of natural conscience.

This conviction, however, has not in itself alone necessarily any regard to the gospel, nor is it necessarily and in itself alone connected in any way with means of salvation. It is only the voice of a violated law uttering through natural conscience its sentence of condemnation against the transgressor. Those who never heard of a Saviour feel its power; those who have sinned away the day of grace feel its power; even lost spirits in torment feel its power; and doubtless it is this that points the sting of the second death and fills it with venom, conviction of guilt, ever present, ever haunting the soul; not the conviction of a single transgression, but the combined and concentrated convictions of the transgressions of a life-time. Under the power of natural conscience, these will be, to the lost sinner, a fire that cannot be quenched, a worm that cannot die. These convictions are not therefore necessarily the working of the Holy Spirit on the heart.

Again. We are evidently not required by the text to refer to the Holy Ghost, as his direct and special influence, those convictions of sin that arise simply from the effect of the letter of the Scriptures on the natural conscience. The Scriptures may be read, as any other work is read, with only an intellectual appreciation of their teachings. They will, when thus read, enlighten conscience and greatly quicken its powers. They will bring out, with vastly greater clearness to the mind's apprehension, the distinction between right and wrong, and add proportionably to one's sense of responsibility. The influence of the mere letter of Scripture is so great in this direction, that it would, without doubt, be impossible to find, in those communities where the Bible is known, a single individual over whose conscience it had not a greater or less control. Those who love the Bible and reverence it as the Word of God, those who have little direct knowledge of it, or regard for it, and those who despise it, disbelieve it, and reject it, all feel its power, and in some measure acknowledge its authority. All, even the vilest contemners of it, and those who clamor most loudly against it, boasting of the light of nature within men as all-sufficient for the government of their moral actions, all these are immensely in advance, in this standard of morals, of any who in any age or country have lived where the Bible has not been known. This rule of right and wrong is more clearly defined, and they approach nearer the Scripture standard in their judgments.

It is the letter of Scripture that produces this result, the merely intellectual apprehension of some of the great truths of the Bible. The dictates of natural conscience now become more imperative than they are without the Bible. Its decisions are more distinctly rendered. Its sentences of condemnation are pronounced in a more decided and firmer tone. It therefore more clearly convinces of sin than it does where there is no knowledge of scripturally revealed truth.

But there may be, in all this, no thought of salvation; nothing whose tendency is in itself alone to lead the convicted sinner to seek after a Saviour. He feels himself condemned, but there is nothing that causes him to love sin any the less, nor to recognize, with any less of enmity of heart, the claims of the law which he is conscious of having violated. We have every reason to believe, that not only the spirits of lost men in the world of woe, have all this conviction, but even the devils feel it and are tormented by it. By both, the law of God is clearly known. Its requirements are understood; but the law is nevertheless hated, and its requirements spurned. Sin is loved and cherished, though it has become, by these enlightened convictions, the constant and increasing source of misery. Conviction of this sort has in it no saving element; nothing in the least tending toward salvation. It may exist, therefore, in the minds of men without being produced by the direct agency of the Holy Ghost.

Yet there is a conviction of sin which is the work of the Holy Spirit. And it would be dangerous for any sinner who lives in the enjoyment of the privileges of the gospel, to say of any of his convictions, that the Holy Ghost had no direct agency in their production. We are from our infancy so familiar with the main truths of the gospel, and so little accustomed, and so little able to distinguish the exact character of our mental acts, that we are not always able, indeed, we are generally entirely unable to say with certainty, what portion of our convictions of sin are the promptings of a merely natural conscience, or what are owing to the influence of the mere letter of Scripture. The God who inspired the Bible is ever near those who read it, or who are enlightened by it, and He is not willing that any of them should perish, but that all should come to repentance. When, therefore, we hear any voice of censure from conscience, or when this voice takes its tone from the Word of God, and pronounces our condemnation with more pointed emphasis, let us beware lest we be found resisting the Spirit of God in not heeding such convictions. All conviction obligates to repentance ; it is as much duty to repent without the Spirit as with.

But there is, we say, and our text teaches us to say it, there is a convincing of sin beyond the convictions of the natural conscience, or the simple word which is produced by the direct agency of the Holy Ghost. "He will convince the world of sin because they believe not on me." He acts for Jesus Christ, in this his office work among men. He seeks the salvation of men in all his dealings with them, but it is to the honor of Jesus Christ alone as their Saviour. "He shall glorify me." His mission is from Christ, his agency in the world is for Christ. Whatever convictions he produces must then be gospel convictions. They have reference to Christ, as the Being sinned against, and to Him as the Saviour from sin, both its power and its penalty. The authority of Christ is that which such convictions recognize. Ill-treatment of Christ in not believing on him, and a sense of danger, and of ill-deserving and of self-degradation, because of the rejection of Him by the soul, are some of the elements involved.

Since also the Holy Spirit, while He seeks the glory of Christ in his work among men, seeks also their deliverance from sin, when He convinces them of guilt it is with the purpose of leading them to break off from transgression and seek for pardon. The conviction which He produces has a tendency more or less distinctly felt by the sinner to this end. He may be resisted by the sinner whom He enlightens ; evangelical convictions may be smothered, and fought against, but their tendency nevertheless is, and it is felt to be, to lead him to break off his sins by righteousness and return to God. Unlike the simple conviction of conscience, either natural or enlightened, they are felt in their tender operation, not only in deterring from the commission of sin, but in seeking relief both from the evils it inflicts and its power in the soul. This conviction could not be in the bosom of a hopelessly lost soul. It could not visit the mind of spirits already under the power of the second death. It has in it hope for the sinner. It is therefore the conviction of sinners only who have the gospel offers made to them, and who are within the reach of its remedy. They are, by the

Holy Ghost, convinced of sin with this all-important aim, — that they may be saved. The prompting of the conviction of the Holy Ghost is, " Let the wicked forsake his way, and the unrighteous man his thoughts; and let him return unto the Lord, and He will have mercy upon him ; and to our God for He will abundantly pardon."

The convicted sinner may, we repeat it, resist these influences. He may endeavor to hush the voice of his conscience thus speaking in tones as much clearer than a simply intellectually enlightened conscience, as that is clearer than the mere voice of natural conscience. He may contend with these tendencies in his convictions to lead him to the Saviour, and may still love sin, and desire to live in the indulgence of it ; but the characteristics named mark his conviction to be the work of the Holy Spirit upon his mind by means of the truth of the gospel.

The instances given in the New Testament, of persons who were evidently convinced of sin by the Spirit of God, all bring out clearly this evangelical character of their convictions. When the Holy Ghost was poured out so abundantly on the day of Pentecost, those who had hitherto been hardened and unconcerned notwithstanding all other conviction, — even that which the presence and the discourses and miracles of Jesus wrought in them, — these, now that the Holy Ghost was present to accompany the words of Peter as he preached of a crucified, risen Messiah, were not only convinced of sin in their treatment of Christ, but they were so convinced that " they were pricked in their heart," and yielding to the tendency of their convictions they said unto Peter and to the rest of the Apostles, " Men and brethren, what shall we do ? " There was a regard to Christ in their convictions, a desire for salvation from the guilt of their conduct toward Christ.

Such also was the tendency and the effect of the conviction of sin which the Holy Ghost wrought in the heart of the Philippian jailer. His first impulse was to cry, " Sirs, what must I do to be saved ? " And from that day to the present, the sinner whom the Spirit of God convinces of sin by gospel truth is influenced by that Spirit toward the seeking of his salvation. And though we are not permitted to say, as some do of all conviction of sin, that it is produced by the direct agency of the

Holy Ghost, we are compelled to say of all convictions whose tendency is of this character, which prompt, however feebly, the breaking off from sin and turning to God, are of Him. For the heart of man is naturally depraved. All its imaginings are evil; all its desires are sinful; all its promptings are towards sin. No inclining to holiness ever sprung from a natural heart; for it is evil and only evil continually. But the Spirit lusteth against the flesh. He works upon depraved hearts; and giving new power to conscience, He prompts to the forsaking of sin under its more powerful censures. Because He glorifies Christ in all his work for men, when under their conviction of sin they find themselves urged towards the Saviour, let them know that these workings of their mind come of a higher power than themselves. It is the Holy Spirit who is convincing them of sin, that they may flee to Christ and in Him find eternal salvation.

In conclusion, we remark, from this subject, that it should not be forgotten that conviction of sin is not conversion from it. Conviction — even that which is of the Holy Ghost — may be resisted, and the sinner may turn himself anew to his transgressions. It matters not how clearly convinced he may have been of his sins, nor how much he may have trembled in view of his guilt and condemnation, unless he has followed the prompting of their convictions, and turned to God by faith in Christ and become a child of God, he is yet an heir of wrath, in the gall of bitterness and in the bonds of iniquity. It is not enough that you have found relief from distress of mind in view of your sinfulness. This may have come without your believing in the Lord Jesus Christ, and being saved by his grace. It may have come in ways that shall only enhance your guilt and aggravate your condemnation.

And this leads us to remark, secondly, in the light of our subject, that those who are awakened to a sense of their sins are in most solemn and dangerous circumstances. Is it not a most solemn thought that the Spirit of God is now moving upon your minds; that He is with you; going with you into your retirement; following you into all the walks of life, and constantly saying to you that you are a sinner against God, under his wrath, and at the same time wooing you with the earnestness and love of a parent to seek the salvation of your soul. It is God Himself who is thus convincing you of sin, and urging you to come to Christ that you may have pardon and eternal life. Oh, it is a solemn thing to be thus the subject of the special care and influence of the Holy Ghost! But it is also dangerous. "My Spirit shall not always strive with man," is the emphatic declaration of the Almighty. Every moment you remain in unbelief, not coming to Christ as your Saviour, you are resisting God. He is drawing you from your sins, and urging you to accept the Saviour; but you resist his influence. You still cling to sin and cherish unbelief. You still refuse Jesus Christ. This is nothing short of fighting against God. It is endangering the eternal interest of the soul. There is danger every moment lest God shall say, Let him alone, he is joined to his idols. Do not then, my dear friends, trifle with your convictions of sin. Remember whence they come.

SERMON XXIX.
RESISTING THE HOLY GHOST.

ACTS vii. 51. — *Ye do always resist the Holy Ghost.*

THE doctrines pertaining to the Holy Spirit are among the most solemn and momentous of any found in the Scriptures. They are not, it is true, stated with such directness, nor placed so boldly in the foreground as many other doctrines. Those, for example, pertaining to the Father and the Son, and to the characters and destiny of men. But the doctrines of the Holy Ghost are in the Scriptures. His personality, his distinctive character, the fact that He influences the minds of men towards holiness and salvation, — these and others are clearly taught. Yet they are for the most part rather assumed and implied, or suggested, than formally stated. What is said of Him by the sacred writers is generally said as though his existence and personality and offices among men were already known to those who are addressed, and therefore needed not to be formally declared. What is said of his work is so said as plainly to suggest the great features of his character. At the same time almost everything pertaining to his person, his character, and the method of his work among and upon men is shrouded more or less in darkness, and veiled in mystery. The truth is distinctly seen, but so seen as to suggest far more than is positively manifested.

This is true, not only of the revelation which is made of Him in the Scriptures, but of that which is made by his work upon the hearts of men. It was not possible, for example, for the disciples on the day of Pentecost to doubt the presence, and the mighty power of the Holy Ghost. They knew by his work upon themselves that He was with them, and that He was imbuing their whole souls with holiness and love and faith ; and clothing them with divine energy for the work which the Lord had committed to their hands. Yet there was no visible presence, no audible voice. The revelation, though clear as the sun in the heavens, was yet a revelation involved in impenetrable mystery. More was intimated and suggested than was directly declared, and far more concealed than was brought fully to light.

It is the same with the work of the Holy Spirit among and upon men now. Whether his influences rest upon the mind of a sinner, convincing him of sin and of righteousness, and of judgment, urging him to immediate repentance or wooing him to Christ, — or, on that of a believer, enlightening, comforting. sanctifying, — his influence is in either case a revelation. It makes known his presence, his power, and his deep interest in the well-being of those upon whose minds He moves. But how much more is manifestly kept back than is made known ! They are but the hidings of his presence and his power that are revealed. One becomes sure, it may be, of an unseen presence with Him in such circumstances. If he pause, and reflect and open his mind to the influences that seem to be breathing upon him he will be doubly assured of it. There is no visible and tangible form upon which his eye may look, or of which he may become conscious by his bodily senses ; but that there is an invisible One with him he will not doubt. The invisible presence will impress him with solemn awe, and he will feel that he must walk softly before it, and with most pure and reverent thoughts and aims. He will seem to hear a voice, as Moses did from the burning bush, saying, " The place whereon thou standest is holy ground." He will be ready to exclaim with Jacob at Bethel, " Surely the Lord is in this place." The conviction of his mind will become clear that the invisible and incomprehensible God is present with him — certainly present, — but present in unapproachable mystery; solemnly, earnestly. lovingly present to win him to holiness, to comfort and to save him — but present only to the apprehension of his innermost soul.

In studying what the Scriptures teach regarding the Holy Ghost, this peculiarity in the method and degree of his manifestation must be borne in mind. We can never know Him or his ways but in part. Yet what is revealed, either directly or by implication, is plain, and need never be misunderstood. It is plain although involved in solemn mysteries. But these mysteries do not distract the soul, nor hinder its faith, but fill it with reverence and careful earnestness.

Let us now give our attention to one of the doctrines pertaining to the Holy Spirit. It is involved in these earnest and stinging words of the martyr Stephen to the Jewish Sanhedrim: " Ye do always resist the Holy Ghost." The doctrine is that the Holy Ghost may be, and He is resisted by men. They withstand Him; they oppose his sway; they set themselves against his influences and aim to thwart his purposes. Stephen's murderers were doing this, and as they were doing their fathers had done. " Ye do always resist the Holy Ghost: as your fathers, so ye." It was the constant practice of their lives to do it. Their lives were ordered upon such principles, animated by such a spirit, and aimed at such purposes that they were always resisting the Holy Ghost. It had been the same with their fathers who had persecuted the prophets, and slain those who " had showed before of the coming of the Just One."

By the words immediately following these which we have quoted, it is plain that the resistance to the Holy Ghost of which Stephen speaks was not found alone in their present opposition and murderous purposes towards himself, nor alone in that act of which he now boldly accuses them, — the betrayal and murder of the Just One. It was deeper and more pervasive. It entered into their characters and shaped all their conduct. Their hatred and persecution of him, and their betrayal and murder of the Just One, were but single acts in a whole life of sinning. Stephen therefore sums up the evidence, and gives the essence of their resistance to the Holy Ghost by adding, " who have received the law by the disposition of angels, and have not kept it." This was the root out of which all else had grown. They had the law of God, and yet were living in disobedience to it. Thus they were resisting the Holy Ghost always. The single acts, namely, their hatred and persecution of Stephen, and their betraying and murdering the Just One, were only the more earnest, emphatic, and palpable exhibitions of what was constantly going on in reality though under different and less marked forms. They were always resisting the Holy Ghost because they were living in unchecked and uninterrupted disobedience of the law of God.

This, let me remark in passing, is the Scriptural method of looking at sin. In whatever aggravated forms it may appear in certain deeds, these deeds are but the outgrowths of a common root that is hidden in the heart, and that gives forth the ordinary and less noted deeds of the life, not less than these, the more marked and offensive. There is in them all the spirit of disobedience; and it is essentially the same in one as in another, just as it is the same sap that circulates in every limb and twig of the tree, that circulates in its trunk.

1. In the light of the passage before us then, the first lesson that we learn is, that every one who is living in sin is resisting the Holy Ghost. His life is a life of disobedience to the law of God. He sets himself against that law, and against the divine authority. He has in himself the very principle that gave power and earnestness to the persecutors of Stephen, and to which he traced back, as to its fountain, their resistance of the Holy Ghost. He who is thus living is giving this principle full play in the general ordering of his life. He has in him that germ which bore, as its legitimate fruit, the betrayal and murder of the Just One, and he is bringing forth fruit of the same general character, though not, it may be, of precisely the same species.

How this is resisting the Holy Ghost will be evident if we reflect a moment on what is revealed as the office of the Holy Spirit in the giving of the law of God. The Word of God is from Him. In the writing of it, "holy men of God spake as they were moved by the Holy Ghost." Every command and every precept which a sinner disobeys is the command and precept of the Holy Ghost. It is the expression of his will; and all his authority is in it. It is the Holy Ghost who has spoken in the command and the precept, and it is his voice which the sinner hears, in whatever manner the requirement may reach his ears, or become known to his conscience. To refuse to obey is, then, to resist the Spirit's will; and to disobey is to exalt one's self against the Spirit's authority.

This is the attitude of every one who is living in the commission of sin. Whatever his sin may be, he is setting at naught and trampling upon the commands of the Holy Ghost, opposing his will, and standing out against his authority. This is resisting the Holy Ghost. The Prophet Isaiah so counted it. Speaking of the children of Israel in their wanderings in the wilderness, he says, "the Lord bare them, and carried them all the days of old." "But they rebelled, and vexed his Holy Spirit." Their rebellion was in disobeying his injunctions, refusing to heed his teachings and admonitions. They thus vexed the Holy Spirit. This case is precisely parallel with that of any sinner. He rebels against the authority and resists the will of the Holy Spirit by transgressing the divine law. If he persist in his sinful courses, as the children of Israel did, until God will bear with him no longer, he then, as they did, vexes the Holy Spirit by his rebellion, and he is given over to the evils of the way in which he has chosen to walk, and is left to reap the fruit of the seed he has sown. "My Spirit," says God, "shall not always strive with man." Sooner or later it will be said of each unrepenting sinner, as it was said of Ephraim, "He is joined to his idols: let him alone!"

2. But there are special forms of resisting the Holy Ghost which the Scriptures take cognizance of, and which we may properly consider for a few minutes.

1. One of these was especially in the mind of Stephen when he uttered the words of our text. He had been preaching the gospel of Jesus Christ to his hearers. Like Paul at Thessalonica, he had been "reasoning with them out of the Scriptures, opening and alleging that Christ must needs have suffered, and risen again from the dead; and that this Jesus whom I preach unto you is the Christ." They would not yield to his reasonings, but they set themselves firmly against the truth. Fixed in their unbelief and impenitency and prepossession against Jesus as the Messiah, they could not be induced to heed the message which was addressed to them, nor yield to its claims, or accept its offers of mercy. The gospel was preached to them; they would not obey it. Repentance and remission of sins was proclaimed to them in the name and through the death of the Redeemer; but they turned away from the proclamation as though it were a thing of naught, or something with which they had no concern. In this, especially, was their sin at that moment, and this was the immediate occasion of the withering rebuke that Stephen administered to them. They refused the Lord Jesus Christ as their Redeemer and Saviour. In this they resisted the Holy Ghost. It was

not the manner in which they refused the offered Saviour, nor the angry and bloodthirsty spirit in which they refused Him, that constituted their resistance. These were but incidents. The real act, and that which was lying back of these, and gave them their dark character, was their refusing the Lord Jesus Christ as He was offered to them in the gospel. They, like their fathers, would not endure the showing to them of the coming of the Just One. The essence of their guilt was that they turned away from Him. They said in their hearts and by their lives, "We will not have this man to reign over us."

This, you perceive, is what every sinner does to whom Jesus Christ is preached, and who refuses Him as He is presented in the gospel. To every such sinner repentance and remission of sins is preached, in the name of the crucified but risen Saviour. He is called upon by divine authority to turn to Him in penitence and faith, confessing Him as Lord, bowing to his authority, and humbly accepting his offered mercy. Every exhibition of Christ to lost men, as their Redeemer, is, in the main element, the same exhibition that Stephen was making to his hearers; and every rejection of Christ, when thus exhibited, be the exhibition by whom, or in what manner it may, is essentially the same as that of which they were guilty. In them refusing Christ was resisting the Holy Ghost. It is the same with every one who refuses Christ. For Christ Himself says, "He that is not for me is against me." This places every one who does not receive Christ, among his enemies, and brings rejection of Him by sinners at the present day, upon the same level, and loads it with the same consequences, and with the same guilt, that followed his rejection by those to whom Stephen declared Him. All who refuse the offers of mercy in Christ Jesus now, and will not receive Him as their Redeemer and Lord, — they too are in this resisting the Holy Ghost.

The reason is manifest. The gospel, as the law, is a part of the Word of God. The Holy Spirit Himself has spoken it to men. Holy men, in the writing of the New Testament, not less than in the writing of the Old Testament, "spake as they were moved by the Holy Ghost." Besides, our Lord Himself told his disciples that the special office of the Spirit in the gospel day, would be to guide them into all truth. "He shall glorify me," said the Saviour, "for He shall receive of mine and show it unto you." The Redeemer left his immediate disciples to be thus taught by the Holy Ghost. He revealed unto them new truth,—that which their minds could not grasp until the great atonement had been made,—and He brought all things to their remembrance that the Lord Himself had taught them. These truths, both those that the Apostles were newly taught, and those that they were divinely enabled to remember, were from the Holy Spirit. These truths together constitute the entire gospel of Jesus Christ, and it is this that is preached to sinners when Christ is preached to them, and they are besought to be reconciled to God. It is the message of the Holy Spirit that is then delivered to them. They are his words that are spoken; they are his offers of salvation that are made; it is his exhortation that is then urged upon sinners to exercise repentance towards God and faith toward our Lord Jesus Christ.

Not to obey the gospel is, then, to oppose the will of the Holy Spirit. It is to set at naught his authority, and to go directly counter to his commands and requirements. What is this but resisting the Holy Ghost?

Yet, further, our Lord said to his disciples, " When the Comforter, which is the Holy Ghost, shall come, He will reprove [convince] the world of sin, and of righteousness, and of judgment." This He does not only by the preaching of the gospel, but also by those special influences upon the minds of men by which their attention is aroused, their consciences quickened, and they come into a realization of their sinfulness and guilt, of the righteousness of God, and of their exposure to the fearful condemnation of the judgment of the last day. These awakening influences are from the Holy Spirit. Conviction for sin is awakened directly by his influence upon the mind. Fear of the wrath of a holy God and of coming judgment is thus awakened. It is He who brings into the soul thoughts of these things and by them breaks up, for the time being, the joy and satisfaction which the soul has been wont to have in a worldly and sinful life. It is He who opens eternity and retribution to the view of the soul, and suddenly divests all earthly treasures and pursuits of all value and attractiveness. It is He who meets many a soul Sabbath after Sabbath, and has long been meeting some who are here to-day, now alarming them with thoughts of judgment and fiery indignation, and the wrath to come; now moving them to tenderness and sad unrest and dissatisfaction with themselves; now wooing them by thoughts of heaven, and by the love of Christ, to break off their sins and return to God, and yet they go out into the world each successive week to forget, to become insensible, to drift away again on the current of worldliness and sin towards final perdition.

These influences cannot be disregarded, these experiences driven away by neglect of God and the interests of the soul, all serious feeling continually banished, all convictions of sin smothered, and the Spirit of God not be resisted! He is resisted by all these means, and in all these ways. How long can this course be continued, and He be not vexed and turned to be your enemy, and fight against you? It is fearfully plain by the Scriptures that the Holy Spirit does then turn against the incorrigibly impenitent. I need call your attention to but one passage in proof of this assertion, Proverbs i. 23–31.

2. This brings us to consider another form in which, as the Scriptures teach us, the Holy Spirit is resisted. It is distinctly and formally stated by none but our Saviour. "Wherefore I say unto you, All manner of sin and blasphemy shall be forgiven unto men: but the blasphemy against the Holy Ghost shall not be forgiven unto men. And whosoever speaketh a word against the Son of man, it shall be forgiven him: but whosoever speaketh against the Holy Ghost, it shall not be forgiven him, neither in this world, neither in the world to come." There is no mystery in this. Just let prejudice, selfishness, obstinacy, wickedness, go so far that all argument, proof, even knowledge itself, is trampled under foot, and hatred of Him whom the Holy Ghost presents, and ascribe his deeds to the influence of Satan — and the sin is committed. For the preceding narrative reads thus: "Then was brought unto Him one possessed with a devil, blind and dumb; and He healed him, insomuch that the blind and dumb both spake and saw. And all the people were amazed, and said, Is not this the son of David? But when the Pharisees heard it, they said, This fellow doth not cast out devils, but by Beelzebub the prince of the devils. And Jesus knew their thoughts, and said unto them, Every kingdom divided against itself is brought to desolation; and every city or house divided against itself shall not

stand. And if Satan cast out Satan, he is divided against himself; how shall then his kingdom stand? And if I by Beelzebub cast out devils, by whom do your children cast them out? therefore they shall be your judges. But if I cast out devils by the Spirit of God, then the kingdom of God is come unto you. Or else, how can one enter into a strong man's house, and spoil his goods, except he first bind the strong man? and then he will spoil his house. He that is not with me, is against me: and he that gathereth not with me, scattereth abroad. Wherefore I say unto you, All manner of sin and blasphemy shall be forgiven unto men: but the blasphemy against the Holy Ghost shall not be forgiven unto men. And whosoever speaketh a word against the Son of man, it shall be forgiven him: but whosoever speaketh against the Holy Ghost, it shall not be forgiven him, neither in this world, neither in the world to come."

SERMON XXX.

ON GRIEVING THE HOLY SPIRIT.

Eph. iv. 30. — *Grieve not the Holy Spirit of God, whereby ye are sealed unto the day of redemption.*

I INVITE your attention, in the first place, to the meaning of some of the terms used in this passage.

1. By "the day of redemption" is meant, doubtless, the day of final and full deliverance from all the consequences of sin. That day will be the one on which the Lord comes again to this world. He will come then, "without sin unto salvation," to be glorified in all his saints. Then, but not before, every believer will receive in full the fruits of redemption, and enter fully into all its blessed consequences. Until then he will not be delivered from all the consequences of sin. While he remains in the flesh he is exposed continually to temptations, and always carries about within him that "law in his members that wars against the law of his mind," and brings him to a greater or less extent into "captivity to the law of sin." After his departure from the body he is no longer subject to temptation, indeed, nor to the antagonism of the carnal against the spiritual. Nevertheless, he is not altogether perfected until the coming of the Lord. Till then he is in a state of waiting. For he cannot be wholly glorified individually till the whole Church of the Redeemer is glorified with him. There will be particularly no resurrection, and, therefore, no glorification of his body until then, and hence, until then, his body will not have its redemption. Meanwhile he waits for this, and expects it with strong desire. Therefore the Apostle represents the whole regenerate family as being in this condition of expectancy, — "waiting for the adoption, to wit, the redemption of our body." When this has been raised and made spiritual, and reunited to the soul, then the last and crowning work

of redemption will have been wrought. The purpose of Christ's death respecting believers will have been fully accomplished. Then both soul and body, delivered from all the consequences of sin, will enter on an eternity of perfect holiness.

This will be, emphatically, " the day of redemption."

2. The Apostle says that believers " are sealed unto this day of redemption by the Holy Spirit of God."

This figurative use of the word *to seal* came from the great prevalence and importance of this act among the ancients. Writings were sealed by them more frequently and more sacredly than they are by us, to attest their genuineness and give them binding power and authority. Articles of great value, or of special importance, were solemnly sealed to guard them against interference or intrusion on the part of those who were not authorized to meddle with them. A seal attached to a written instrument was, therefore, a strong testimony that it was genuine, and just what it purported to be. And a seal set on any important or valuable article of property, or of deposit, was a warning to all not to interfere with it, and so it guarded it against intrusion and kept it in safety for its rightful owner.

From these two uses of the seal, namely, to attest the genuineness and authority of written instruments, and to guard important and valuable articles against interference by unauthorized persons, and so preserve them in safety for the use of their rightful owners, — from these two uses of the seal the word came to designate any process by which genuineness was attested, and important articles, or articles of value, were made secure.

Both these meanings of the word enter into its use in this passage. In the first place it is the Holy Spirit who impressed upon the believer's soul those evidences of its new creation in Christ Jesus — of its change from the carnal to the spiritual — that attest the genuineness of its repentance and faith, and the reality of its sonship with God. The Apostle speaks thus of the renewed soul as " an epistle of Christ, written not with ink, but with the Spirit of the living God." All that is Christ-like in such a soul is of the Holy Spirit's producing ; and by producing it within the soul He sets his seal upon it, and makes its genuineness appear clearly and with certainty, not only to the eye of God, but to the believer's own consciousness. It is thus that the Spirit Himself "beareth witness with our spirit that we are the children of God." Hence the Apostle John says so emphatically, "He that believeth on the Son of God hath the witness in himself."

Again, they are the impressions which the Holy Spirit makes upon the believer's soul that guard it against the influences of Satan and of the world, and, by enabling it to endure unto the end, make its ultimate salvation secure. For it is the Holy Spirit of God that evermore is working in us, "the willing and the doing of his good pleasure." It is the Holy Spirit of God who "helps our infirmities" lest we should sink beneath them in despair. It is the Holy Spirit of God who continually "makes intercession for us, with groanings that cannot be uttered," when we "know not what we should pray for as we ought" for ourselves. In this manner, and by these means, it is that the believer's ultimate salvation is made sure. It is thus that he is "sealed by the Holy Spirit of God unto the day of redemption."

3. The next word to which I invite your attention is the central one in the Apostle's command: "Grieve;" "Grieve not the Holy Spirit of God." We have no evidence that the Apostle did not use this word in its common signification. He did not write at random, nor in ignorance, but with intelligence and purpose. To grieve is to cause sorrow and sadness; to give pain and heaviness of heart. As a general rule, he who grieves another does it by disappointing those expectations that rest upon personal love and trust. Love is not responded to and requited where there was good reason to expect it would be; confidence is betrayed, or treated with lightness, when there was good reason to expect it to be held sacred and fully justified by the conduct of the one confided in. When we have neither love for one, nor confidence in him, he cannot grieve us. He may make us sad, he may fill us with sorrow, he may inflict keen mental suffering upon us, but these will not be the sadness and sorrow and suffering that constitute grief. He who inflicts these upon us must be one that we love and trust, and from whom, therefore, we expect something better. It is because the disciples of Christ are loved by the Holy Spirit, and confided in, that they can grieve Him. They can disappoint

Him. They can disregard and abuse his love; they can show themselves unworthy of his confidence. They can therefore grieve Him. The unconverted may strive against Him; they may resist Him; they may provoke Him to anger; but they are never said, in the Scriptures, to grieve Him. His love for them, and confidence in them, are not such as He has towards the children of God. Towards them alone does He have that peculiar love and confidence, whose neglect and disappointment give the peculiar sorrow and sadness and pain of grief.

To say that the Holy Spirit can be grieved, is only saying that He is just such a being as Jesus Christ has revealed God to be. We know nothing of the nature and character of God saving only as they are revealed to us in the person of Jesus Christ. He was "God manifested." As Jesus Christ thought and felt, so God feels and thinks. Jesus Christ was not that emotionless being that speculation and philosophy have held up before our minds as God. On the contrary, He was full of emotion. No being ever manifested deeper feeling, more tender sympathies, more ardent love, more intense desire, or keener susceptibility to pain and mental anguish. When, therefore, the Apostle commands us not to grieve the Holy Spirit of God, he teaches us to think of the Holy Spirit as such a Being as Christ revealed God to be. He is a Being of emotions. He loves; He desires; He trusts; He is deeply interested in the disciples of Christ, and cherishes them with fondness and affection. When they disappoint his trust, and ill-requite his love, He is pained, just as Jesus Christ was pained by these things. They cause Him sorrow and sadness, just as Christ's disciples caused Him sorrow and sadness, when He was on earth, by their unworthy treatment of Him, and this sorrow and sadness and pain are the grief which they are commanded not to inflict on the Holy Spirit of God.

2. This brings us, in the second place, to consider the command itself, and to inquire how it is that believers grieve the Holy Spirit. In general terms, any conduct or any temper of mind that is unholy, must be offensive to such a Being; and this conduct or this temper of mind in those whom He loves and trusts, as He does the disciples of Christ, are an ill-requiting of his love, and an abuse of his confidence. But the verses that stand in immediate connection with the text give us a

more specific answer. When we look at it carefully, we find that this text is the central one of several divine commands. All these other commands sustain a direct and subordinate relation to this one; and each of the others designates a form in which this one is violated. These specific and subordinate commands begin with the twenty-fifth verse, and extend to the end of the chapter. The Apostle had just called the attention of the Ephesian Christians to the fact that they, and all others who had "learned Christ," had put off the old man which is corrupt according to the deceitful lusts, and been renewed in the spirit of their minds, and had put on the new man which after God is created in righteousness and true holiness. In view of this fact he now urges those who have been thus "renewed in the spirit of their minds," to bring their whole being and conduct under the government of this renewed spirit, and to let every feeling and word and deed be an expression of it; and the one great reason why he would have them do it is that they may not grieve the Holy Spirit of God. Hence he says, "Putting away lying,"— the peculiar vice of the old unrenewed spirit, — "speak every man the truth with his neighbor; for we are members one of another. Be ye angry and sin not: let not the sun go down upon your wrath; neither give place to the devil. Let him that stole "— another peculiar vice of the old unrenewed man — "steal no more; but rather let him labor, working with his hands that which is good, that he may have to impart to him that hath need,"— one of the first promptings of a renewed spirit. "Let no corrupt communication proceed out of your mouth," — another special vice of their former state, — "but whatever is good for needful edification, that it may minister grace unto the hearers." Then comes in the text, as the crowning command of all, and the one towards which they all tend: "Grieve not the Holy Spirit of God, whereby ye are sealed unto the day of redemption." Then follows the further specifications: "Let all bitterness, and wrath, and anger, and clamor, and evil speaking, be put away from you, with all malice; and be ye kind one to another, tender-hearted, forgiving one another, even as God for Christ's sake hath forgiven you." The first series pertains mainly to outward life and the great motives of conduct. The second series pertains mainly to the spirit and temper of the mind itself, and the tone of the life. In the centre of these commands, then, you see, midway between those that are prohibitory and those that are positive, stands the command that we are considering. A violation of any one in either of these classes of commands is a violation of this central command. The doing of any one of the specific things that are forbidden, or the not doing of either of the things specifically commanded, is that which grieves the Holy Spirit of God. In other words, the disciples of Christ grieve the Holy Spirit by living a dishonest and immoral life, or indulging in impure and unbecoming words, or cherishing an unkind and unforgiving spirit. For you will see, if you examine the context closely, that these specific prohibitions and injunctions cover just this ground, and that they are a condemnation of just these three classes of sins.

1. First of all, e. g., you have the command against lying and stealing and the indulgence of unholy passion in your dealing with your fellow men. There must be no false dealing, no deception, no defrauding, no taking from any of that which you have no right to take, and no indulgence of an unholy temper towards them, which prompts you to do them injustice or wrong. On the contrary, there must be straightforward truthfulness; downright honesty; an out-and-out Christian fairness and friendliness. Nor is such a command uncalled for even among the professed friends of Christ. For there is many a man among them who will shrink back shocked at the thought, e. g., of uttering a direct and palpable lie, but who will, nevertheless, permit those with whom he is dealing to act under false impressions which he might remove by a single word, and which a thoroughly truth-telling spirit would prompt him at once to utter. The Apostle's injunction covers both sides of the matter. First, you must put away lying; then you must speak truth with your neighbor. You may not deceive him by telling him a falsehood; you may not permit him to rest under a misapprehension by holding your peace, when telling him the truth, as you know it to be, will set him right. Otherwise you violate the obligations of a common brotherhood, for "we are members one of another;" and you give place to the devil to rule your life, instead of bringing your life under the rule, and submitting it to the will of Jesus Christ. Thus you "grieve the Holy Spirit of God," who has

created you anew for Christ, who has pledged you to Him, in all your being, and who seeks constantly to preserve you holy and to perfect you for Him at his coming.

Again, there is many a man who, *e. g.*, would shrink back from the thought of direct and palpable stealing, with the exclamation of Hazael to Elisha, " What, is thy servant a dog, that he should do this great thing?" and yet in many an indirect way he would appropriate to himself that which belonged to another, and have no other misgiving, than a certain indefinite consciousness of meanness and unmanliness. How many are they who, for example, will not shrink from living without labor, if they can, taking, in some form, and enjoying the products of your labor, without rendering you any equivalent! How many are they who would not blush to hold some position of merely nominal service to you, as multitudes hold such positions under our government, and draw the salary and perquisites of office, without rendering the slightest equivalent therefor! But no man, governed by the spirit of Christian honesty, could do any such thing. The Apostle recognizes this in the next verse, as he does also in other passages of his epistles: Let no man steal, that is, appropriate to himself, in any way, that which does not belong to him; but rather let him labor, working with his hands the thing which is good, that he may have means, not only for the supplying of his own wants, but for purposes of benevolence, — without the having and carrying out of which he will fail, not only of the richest Christian experiences, but to give the commonest of all evidences that he is a Christian at all.

This matter of personal labor and its relation to life, which is so mystified among men in civilized society, has no mystification about it in the light of inspired teachings. It is all reduced to a very simple question here. It comes just to this: " If a man will not work, neither shall he eat." If he will not work but half a day, he shall have pay but for half a day. This is the Christian law; and it is a law that governs all classes, and strikes a deadly blow at the root of a very large portion of the practical evils of civilized society. Let the inspired precept have full effect on all classes of people, and instantly the world would be freed from untold amounts of vice and misery. Let it become the inflexible law that the idler shall not eat; let this law govern all public and state charities; let it govern in all benevolent enterprises; let it govern in all families, and in all the relations of each man to every other,— and a temporal and social millenium would dawn in glory upon our poor, deluded, cheated, poverty-stricken world.

But it is not my purpose now to press this Apostolic precept in its general bearings. We have to do with it only in its bearing on our own Christian living, as connected with the command before us, "Grieve not the Holy Spirit of God, by whom ye are sealed unto the day of redemption." And what I say is, that these specific commands for truth-telling and honest living, are not out of place in teaching the disciples of Christ about their relation to the Holy Spirit. No man can live the life of an idler, and be a faithful disciple of Jesus Christ. The very process of making one a disciple of Christ is all in view of a work to which Christ calls him. For he is "created in Christ Jesus unto good works which God hath before ordained that he should walk in them." For him to be an idler is, therefore, to live contrary to, and to thwart, the foreordination of God, and to pervert the whole purpose of Christ in making him a disciple. How is it possible then that he should not by this way of living grieve the Holy Spirit of God, who made him a new creature in Christ Jesus, purposely that he might glorify Christ by doing the works of a faithful disciple?

But if no man can live the life of an idler and be a faithful disciple of Christ, much less can one add to his idleness theft, and be such a disciple. And every one does add theft to idleness, who, having the ability to earn his own bread, eats the bread that another earns. But what a sight this thought brings before our eyes! That great multitude that crowds all our great cities, e. g., doing nothing, because they cannot do what they fancy they want to do, come under this class, and are living in open violation of the divine command. The Apostle's language is very suggestive in its application to this class of idlers: "Let him labor, working with his hands." God has given all men hands to work with. He has given to all men brains enough to guide and direct their hands in work. But he has given very few, comparatively, brains enough to get an honest living with, without the labor of their hands. There are two fundamental and most pernicious errors prevalent in the world on this matter, errors that are most emphatically condemned by the Word of God, and sternly frowned upon by the gospel of Jesus Christ. The first error is, the supposing that manual labor is less respectable, less honorable than other labor; and the other is that other labor is easier than the labor of the hands. Never were greater mistakes made than are made by those who thus judge. Who can tell me in what respect a true man is less honorable when he ploughs the field, or works in a shop with his hands than he is when he stands behind a counter, or sits in a counting-room, or in an office, or in a study, etc. And as to ease, none who have tried brain work after work with the hands will ever commit the mistake of giving the preference to the former. But influenced by these two errors, there are multitudes all around us doing nothing, living the lives of idlers; mere leeches and parasites on society, who ought to be industrious and thrifty citizens. And there is a vast number of others who are trying to do something, it is true; but they accomplish nothing, and are really parasites also on society, because they persist in trying to do that which God never called them to do, and which they have no fitness to do. Looking at both these classes, how many a young man do we see waiting for some place behind a counter, or in an office, who fancies that laboring with his hands would dishonor him, but who feels it no dishonor, no loss of respectability to be living from the industry of his friends. He has always failed, and he will forever fail, in any of the situations which he desires to obtain; but he might easily become a manly and honored member of the community by betaking himself to that calling for which he is fitted by natural gifts and endowments? And how many men do we see in all the professions eking out a miserable subsistence, or starving, unhonored and unfelt in the general interests of society, who might easily make themselves leaders in callings to which their faculties adapt them! Many a doctor, who is thus wasting away his life in waiting for fees which he has no capacity to earn; many a lawyer who pines for cases which he has no skill to manage; many a minister who starves in trying to do that for which God never intended him, might be already on the high road to affluence, and reveling in comforts, the patron of all good enterprises, honored and respected by all in the community whose honor and respect are worth the having, if they had turned their energies to occupations for which they were intended by nature, and been willing to labor, "working with their hands the thing that was good?"

The Apostle comes to the disciples of Christ with a command which, if heeded, will set this matter all right, so far as they are concerned. But in giving this command, he had in view, not so much their material interests,— for these he knew would take care of themselves with such living as he enjoined, — but he had in view the unseemliness and guilt and offensiveness to God's Holy Spirit, of such lives by those whom this Spirit had regenerated, and new created, that they might become men in Christ Jesus, by developing true manliness of character, and living lives of true nobility in carrying out the will of Christ and conforming themselves to his example. This was uppermost in the Apostle's mind; and it was because he saw the matter in this light, that he held up an idle and dishonest life before us as an offense to the Holy Spirit, and warned us not to grieve Him by living such lives.

2. Next after the command touching an unworthy method of life, the Apostle introduces the command against an unbecoming method of speech: "Let no corrupt communication proceed out of your mouth." The word which Paul wrote is very emphatic. "Let no putrid utterance fall from your lips." His reference is to unclean speech of all descriptions, and the word that he has chosen represents it as the vilest and most revolting of all things to the mind of God. Such speech is so utterly abhorrent to all the teachings of the gospel, so utterly at variance with every prompting of the Spirit of Christ, that we cannot conceive of God's Holy Spirit dwelling for a moment in the heart of one who is given to it. Our Lord has told us that it is "that which proceedeth out of the mouth of a man that defiles him;" and the Apostle says of all believers, that they are the temple of God, and that the Spirit of God dwells in them. Then he solemnly declares, "If any man defile the temple of God, him shall God destroy." Such speech is therefore a defilement of God's temple, the dwelling-place of his Holy Spirit.

There is no need of multiplying words upon this point.

Every one who has come to know Jesus Christ, and feel the influence of his life and Spirit,—and every one has who has become his disciple indeed,—has come to feel, by a spiritual instinct, the utter unbecomingness of such language as is here condemned. Every prompting of his renewed nature rises up to rebuke and shame it. The presence of the least spiritual life in him will make him know that such language coming from the lips of a disciple, cannot but be insufferably offensive to the indwelling Spirit of God.

What the Apostle enjoins is, that all such words be eschewed as corrupting and defiling,—corrupting and defiling not only him who utters them, but those also who hear them. On the contrary, let all the words of a disciple of Christ be pure and healthful. If he speaks at all, let him speak that which is good to the use of edifying, that it may minister grace to the hearers. So only can he be pleasing to the Holy Spirit of God, and hope to have his presence and favor.

3. The command that follows our text, as a further specification of the manner in which the Holy Spirit is grieved by the disciples of Christ, is simply a repetition of the command of our Saviour upon which we dwelt a few Sabbaths since. "When ye stand praying, forgive if ye have aught against any, that your Heavenly Father may forgive you." It covers the whole spirit and temper of a disciple of Christ towards all with whom he has to do, and especially towards his fellow disciples: "Let all bitterness, and wrath, and clamor, and evil speaking, be put away from you, with all malice: and be ye kind one to another, tender-hearted, forgiving one another, even as God for Christ's sake hath forgiven you."

Here, as in each of the other commands, there is not only a negative, but a positive side. Not only is the specified evil forbidden, but the opposite virtue is commanded. It is not, as is too often supposed, all of Christian duty to refrain from bitterness of spirit and anger and malice; to be a true Christian one must go further, and be positively kind and sweet-tempered, really and truly tender-hearted, sincerely and cordially forgiving in his spirit towards his brethren. The not doing of the latter, not less than the doing of the former, is an offense to God. The one will check and hinder all growth in grace, and all development of Christian character; the other will exclude grace from the soul, and make the character a moral deformity. In either case the sight becomes offensive to God; and grieves his Holy Spirit. That Spirit has a right to expect the temper and mind of Christ in one whom He has renewed, and sealed for Christ and for heaven. He has a right to expect beauty and loveliness of soul where He has given grace. He cannot but be grieved, therefore, when instead of the spirit and mind of Christ, He beholds the spirit of a demon. Where He looks to find the fruit of grace and of a renewed heart, He finds the outgushing of sin and depravity, and all evil, showing the heart which was once purified, become a cage of unclean birds. He cannot but be grieved. As He loves the believer, as He cherishes him for Christ, as He looks to him as an heir of heaven, He cannot but be saddened and pained.

Such are some of the ways in which the disciples of Christ grieve the Holy Spirit of God. They are the ways which the Apostle himself has clearly pointed out. There is nothing dark and mysterious about them; but they have to do with the commonest concerns of life, and the every-day intercourse of believers with each other and with the world. Everything that is unbecoming in a disciple of Christ while attending to these concerns, or mingling in this intercourse; everything that is wrong and unjust in conduct; everything that is impure in speech; everything that is unchristian, unlovely, ungracious in spirit, is a grief to the Holy Spirit of God.

SERMON XXXI.
DANGER OF FALLING.

———◆———

1 Cor. x. 12. — *Wherefore let him that thinketh he standeth, take heed lest he fall.*

THIS "wherefore" refers to the preceding verse: "Now all these things happened unto them for ensamples: and they are written for our admonition, upon whom the ends of the world are come."

The things that thus happened for examples to us, and that are written for our admonition, were the idolatries, tempting Christ and murmurings of the children of Israel, while they were on their way from Egypt to Canaan. God was displeased with many of them on account of these things, and they were "overthrown" in the wilderness. They were slain by the sword, they were destroyed by serpents, they were carried away by the pestilence.

All these who had thus perished had departed from the land of Egypt full of hope, confidently expecting to be among the number who would enter the land of promise. But they failed of their expectation, their hope was made vain, they perished in the wilderness, because they fell off from their allegiance to God and walked in ways of sin. They thought themselves secure in God's favor. But they forfeited it and were lost. They counted upon an inheritance among the people of God. But they let it slip from their possession while they were grasping for the inheritance of the wicked, and their title was annulled forever.

God has turned their sin and failure into a means of good to us, and a help to our salvation, by setting them before us as examples, and pointing us to them for our admonition. It is in view of them that the Apostle writes the command, "Wherefore let him that thinketh he standeth, take heed lest he fall."

None of us can have a better prospect that his hopes will be realized, none of us can feel himself more secure than did these Israelites. Yet they fell and miserably perished. The argument of the Apostle is that every believer needs to keep a vigilant watch and be constantly on his guard, lest he too fall into sin, and, incurring the divine displeasure, fail of heaven. Here, as elsewhere, the Apostle, like the other sacred writers, recognizes the ever-present liability of all, even the holiest, while they are in a world of temptation and sin, to fall into sin and compass their own ruin. "Let no man be counted happy," says a heathen proverb, "while he lives." The reason is that while he lives he may by some rash or guilty deed bring himself into disgrace and ruin. It is this very thought that is in the Apostle's mind when he is writing the command before us. He had it in mind also when he wrote those remarkable words regarding himself in the chapter preceding this, "I keep under my body, and bring it into subjection lest that by any means, when I have preached to others, I myself should be a castaway." Our Saviour had the same thought and repeatedly impressed it on the minds of his disciples, in those words of warning and of promise, "He that shall endure unto the end, the same shall be saved." And in those other words, "He that putteth his hand to the plough, and looketh back, is not fit for the kingdom of God."

The doctrine of our text, then, like that of all the New Testament and of the Old, is, that no one who is numbered among the people of God is to count himself free from the danger of falling into sin while he remains in this world; nor, if he falls into sin and continues in it, is he to count himself exempt from the liability to suffer its direst consequences. The fall and the ruin of the children of Israel are the example to which God Himself points him, to admonish him of his danger, and arouse him from the indulgence of a false security. As they fell, so may he. As their sin ruined them, so will his ruin him if he clings to it and lives in it. "Wherefore let him that thinketh he standeth, take heed lest he fall."

I invite your attention to a few of the many ways in which the professed friends and followers of Christ are manifestly liable to fall into sin, and continue in it to their own ruin, as reasons why they should take heed as they are commanded to do by our text. I mention these because, though plain, yet they are seldom dwelt upon as sources of danger when the subject is under consideration.

Though they claim to be governed by the truth which Christ has taught, and to be conformed to the righteousness both of heart and life which He requires, they may disobey the truth and become unrighteous, because they have not in them an honest love of truth and righteousness.

It has not required many years of earnest and thoughtful life to convince every candid observer of the working of his own mind, that there is a fearful amount of truth in the words of the prophet Jeremiah when he declares that "The heart is deceitful above all things." Such a man has come to realize that it is not always an easy task to know precisely what the governing motive of his conduct is in very many of the circumstances and relations of his life. He has found that he has oftentimes been taking to himself credit for being actuated by one class of motives, when, as a matter of fact, a class of motives very different and far from praiseworthy, has prompted all that he has done. He has learned that it is no uncommon thing for a man to claim, and perhaps to think with no little certainty, that he really loves some things toward which he is, in truth, indifferent ; and some toward which he has a deep-seated and abiding aversion. To his surprise and chagrin, perhaps, he has discovered, *e. g.*, that he himself has been for a long time mistaking a devotion to his own personal interests as connected with the prosperity of some good cause, for a sincere devotion to that cause itself. He has labored hard for its advancement and success ; all the time supposing that nothing was nearer his heart ; and having the credit of a disinterested advocate and helper of its prosperity. But some change in his circumstances, or in his relation to the cause itself has come. His zeal flags ; his interest ceases ; to his astonishment he discovers that that which has been first and last in his thoughts as the days opened and closed, has dropped out of his mind, and fails any longer to enlist his feelings or his regards. He inquires into the reason of all this, and the truth flashes upon him that the change in his circumstances, or in his relation to the once cherished cause, has made it unnecessary or impracticable for him longer to seek his own personal interests in its prosperity. Here is the secret of his waning zeal and of his indifference

If he is a man that wants to deal honestly with himself he will not stop with this discovery. He will press the matter one step further, at least, and compel himself to confess to his own conscience that he has all the time been imposing upon himself, and acting a most unworthy part in the interests of self, under the pretense of unselfish devotion to that which was good and noble. The selfish motive ceasing to operate, and there being in him no real love to the cause, he will most likely desert it.

Now if one's interest in the cause of Christian truth and Christian living is of this kind, he is in constant danger of falling. Just to the extent that other than motives of sincere devotion to Christ and his cause get possession of the mind, there is increased liability to make shipwreck of all the interest that one has in that cause. If this sincere devotion is wholly wanting in the mind of one who professes to be Christ's, he will be almost certain, sooner or later, to fall openly away from Him. If this devotion exists within him, but is weakened and kept down by the indulgence of selfishness in any form, then there is a constant danger, a fearful liability, of falling into positive and fatal sin. The soul is then all exposed to every form of temptation. Its spiritual vision becomes beclouded; its powers of discernment become blunted; its strength to resist evil is weakened. It will be a miracle of grace if it does not follow the examples by which God has warned it, and bring upon itself irretrievable ruin.

It was in view of such a danger as this that the Apostle wrote, in the chapter following the one that contains our text, "Let a man examine himself;" and again in the Second Epistle to the Corinthians, "Examine yourselves, whether ye be in the faith; prove your own selves." You may profess to be in the faith, and yet be lacking in every quality that makes the character of a genuine believer. You may account yourselves to be something, which the honest proving of yourselves will show you to be utter strangers to.

If the truth regarding many who, professing the love of truth and righteousness, have denied the truth and turned to iniquity, could be known, it would be seen that they never loved the truth, nor ever cherished righteousness in their hearts. Some other motive has influenced them, and while they stood before the world as friends of Christ, they were in reality his enemies.

Thus he is often "wounded in the house of his friends;" but by those who had no right to be in that house. Thus often the cause of truth is made to suffer, and its good name brought into reproach, by those who, though standing before men as its champions, were never in heart loyal to it. They have fallen, and their fall has been counted a fall from the truth when in fact they were always enemies and aliens, though perhaps thinking themselves and others thinking them to be friends.

None of us can be sure that we are not of this number without the most thorough self-searching. Self-deceit is not dislodged by gentle means. Again and again, and with an honesty of purpose that will stand the test of the final judgment, must the soul be brought into the light, and tested by the Word of God before its self-deceivings can all be destroyed, and its sincerity in its attachment to the truth be demonstrated to itself. Let each one of us, then, who thinks himself to be a lover of the truth, and of righteousness, take heed to himself at this point, lest, from a lack of thorough honesty with himself he be found destitute of the love of the truth; and, presuming upon what he does not possess, he fall away from Christ and bring ruin to his soul. Let each one take heed lest through the weakness of his love to that which is right and true, he be taken in the snare of the adversary, and become like those with whom God was not well pleased, and therefore they were overthrown in the wilderness. If, on a searching examination of our own hearts, and a sober and candid judgment upon our lives, we find ourselves to be lacking in whole or in part, in honest devotion to Christ, and obedient submission to his authority, let us not rest until this lack is supplied, and we can each of us say, with the fallen but recovered Peter, "Lord, thou knowest all things; thou knowest that I love thee." There is no other safeguard. It will be in vain that we take heed, if the beginning is not made at this point.

2. Those who profess allegiance to Christ are in constant danger of falling into that which will offend Him and bring ruin upon their souls through the indulgence of a spirit of pride and self-conceit, touching their supposed virtue. The indulgence of such a spirit is of itself most offensive to Him. Scarcely anything else is more severely condemned in the Scriptures. "Pride and arrogancy do I hate," says God. "The proud he

knoweth afar off." And here is the beginning of the danger which comes from the indulgence of such a spirit. He who indulges it is an offense in the sight of God. God removes far from him, and leaves him to himself. There is hardly a possibility, therefore, that he will not fall into temptation, and be carried away by it.

This spirit works insidiously. It puts on deceptive garbs, and reigns supreme in many a heart where its presence is hardly suspected. In those who have any regard to the name and standing of Christian, it is almost always sure to hold its dominion under the form of some Christian virtue. You will therefore see some men, and sometimes really good men, making an idol of their goodness in some one or more of its phases. They lift it up before themselves, and pay it their devout homage. And not only so; they are not satisfied with worshipping it themselves, but they exact homage to it from others also. A man, *e. g.*, fancies himself a paragon of honesty. He takes pride in the thought of his honesty. The more he thinks of it, the more he seems to himself to excel all others in this virtue. He is quite sure that there are few men in the world so honest as he is. Self-conceit begins to work; and, with self-conceit, low and disparaging views of others Like those whom our Saviour rebuked by the parable of the Pharisee and the Publican, he begins to "trust in himself that he is righteous, and despise others." His very honesty thus opens the door to all dishonesty. His pride and self-conceit because of his great honesty have already crowded him into this door, and there can be no certainty that he will not at any moment yield himself unreservedly to some open and disgraceful deed. For he who has come to despise others who are as good, and perhaps better, than himself, because he thinks himself to be better than they, has already begun to treat them dishonestly. He has already begun to trample on their rights. He takes from them, in his thoughts, what belongs to them, and begins to appropriate it wrongly to himself. What but outward restraints will keep him from doing openly and tangibly what he is thus doing secretly, and in his thoughts?

It is the same with every other good quality which is exalted to be an idol, and for the supposed possession of which one begins to take to himself pride, and to indulge in self-conceit.

Self-exaltation becomes the beginning of self-degradation. The soul is deteriorated by it, and soon will come to lose whatever relish or real goodness it had at the start. It becomes hard, censorious, self-flattering. Its moral tone is lost. Its spiritual health is undermined. Its strength to resist evil is weakened; and the words of the inspired writer are almost sure to be verified in its history, " Pride goeth before destruction ; and a haughty spirit before a fall."

We find here an explanation of that strange phenomenon which every observer of men and things as they are, has often noticed, and wondered at, — the fact that so many men fall into the very evils and sins against which they have seemed to be most strenuously opposed; against which they have often inveighed with special vehemence; and for their antagonism to which they have seemed to take to themselves special credit. The most inveterate smokers I have ever known, were men who had been loudest and most bitter in their denunciation of the users of tobacco. In season and out of season they were wont to act the part of censors and denouncers of both the plant and all who used it in any form.

The most disgraceful cases of violation of the seventh commandment that I have ever known, those that were marked by the most degrading and disgusting demoralization, were in men who had made the violation of this command the object of their special denunciation, and had claimed for themselves more than common virtue in its observance.

Some of the most lamentable cases of dishonesty in business that have ever come under my observation have been in men who prided themselves on their integrity, and the possession of so much ability and virtue that they claimed by their whole bearing, if not in so many words, that they could never fail in business, and never forfeit the confidence or ruin the interest of those who trusted them.

But in all these cases, if one observed carefully the spirit of the men, he saw not simply antagonism to the wrongs inveighed against, but a certain air of self-gratulation, self-assumption, and self-conceit, a taking of special pride in their supposed exemption from these particular sins, and an evident purpose to impress him with their superior virtue in these directions, and extort from him homage on account of it.

Like the Pharisee they seemed ever to be saying, "Lord, I thank thee that I am not as other men are," and ever to be wishing to make every one who came into their presence feel that they would not hesitate to finish the Pharisee's prayer, and pointing to the observer, say emphatically and patronizingly, "or even as this publican." His moral strength was thus seen to be impaired. Familiarity with this particular form of sin, when there was either an entire want of love of holiness, or if there was any love of holiness, it was overborne and pushed aside by this spirit of pride and self-conceit, has brought him at last to be on good terms with the very thing that he seemed to hate.

Besides all this, if one is a child of God, though he may not be utterly given over to the consequences of his own folly and wickedness, in indulging such a spirit, yet he is often left to fall into the very sins that he has prided himself in denouncing, that by his fall his pride may be the more effectually crushed, and the soil of his heart be the better prepared for the growth and culture of humility. It is terribly galling to one's good opinion of himself, if he is not lost to all sense of shame, to find himself a victim to the very form of sin which he has made it his special business to denounce, and for being free from which he has often "thanked God that he was not as other men." Men can never come into this wretched condition but through a course of foolish pride, and most offensive self-conceit. It is God's judgment on these when they find themselves there. Let him that thinketh he standeth in any or all virtues, take heed lest through his pride he fall and come into ruin!

3. I notice but one other source of danger which makes the Apostle's exhortation applicable at all times and to all; men are in danger of falling into ways of sin, and of ruining their souls, by making to themselves a false application of the truth. This source of danger has been implied in the other two that we have mentioned. Neither of those, in fact, prevails without more or less aid from this. Yet there is here a special danger which ought to be considered, and carefully guarded against.

The Scriptures are preëminent in their bold and sharp classification of character. They always presuppose a regard to this classification in all they say of privilege or promise or curse or threatening. Every privilege is declared, and every promise is made, with a definite character in view in those for whom the privilege exists, and to whom the promise is given. Those who have not this character have no right to the privilege, nor any inheritance in the promise.

The danger is, that those who lack the character will claim the privilege, and count themselves interested in the promise, and thus, depending for support on that which has no existence for them, fall away and be lost.

A man counts himself one of the elect, and because he counts himself this, takes to himself the privileges which are declared and promises which are made to believers only, — kept by the power of God, through faith. He counts on being kept though destitute of faith. He is sure sooner or later to fall and be lost.

One who rejects Christ as the Lord of his soul, and its Redeemer from sin, reads what is said of those who are in Christ, and though out of Christ, claims for himself all that he reads. Not serving Christ, he does not receive the aid promised to his servants — and falls.

One reads what is said in the one hundred and third Psalm, of the mercy of God to those that fear Him, but passing over the divine limitation, applies all that he reads to himself, though destitute of every characteristic that enters into this limitation. The mercy of God promised and vouchsafed to those who fear Him, fails those who fear Him not.

So one reads what the Apostle says in the eighth of Romans, that "all things work together for good to them that love God," and though utterly devoid of all love to God, says of all that happens to him, "It is for the best." He is ruined through a false application of the truth.

One reads our Saviour's words, "Ye are my friends if ye do whatsoever I command you," and, disregarding entirely the qualifying clause, calls himself a friend of Christ, though his whole life is one of disobedience to Christ's commands; and that too though the Lord has so pointedly asked, "Why called ye me Lord, Lord, and do not the things that I command you?" If such a one does not fall now, yet in the judgment the Lord assures us that He will say to him, "I never knew you. Depart from me."

One reads the Lord's solemn declaration, " No man can serve two masters ; " " ye cannot serve God and mammon," yet makes mammon the god of his heart and life, and stills calls the Lord his God.

One reads, " The friendship of the world is enmity with God ; " " If any man love the world, the love of the Father is not in him," yet claims to be a lover of God, though devoting all his soul to the world, loving it with his whole heart. By a false application of the truth itself, all these fall and perish. Yet the way of safety, and the road to heaven, are so plain, that the wayfaring man, though a fool, need not err therein. Only take heed; but take heed not in your own strength and wisdom. He that trusts in his own heart is a fool. " I am the way, the truth, and the life," says our Saviour. There is safety only in Him — in his wisdom — in his protection. We take heed wisely only by looking unto Jesus.

SERMON XXXII.

THE TWO GREAT CERTAINTIES OF THE GOSPEL.

JOHN vi. 37. — *All that the Father giveth me shall come to me; and him that cometh to me I will in no wise cast out.*

THE circumstances in which these words were spoken give them a peculiar interest. Our Lord had wrought a most impressive miracle in the presence and on behalf of those whom He was addressing. With five barley loaves and two small fishes He had fed them, to the number of about five thousand men, on the eastern shore of the Sea of Galilee. This miracle so affected them that they were ready to lay hands on Him, and by force make Him a king. When He perceived this He left them and went away into a mountain, and when night came He crossed the sea and came to Capernaum. The next day many of those whom He had fed followed Him to this side of the sea. But when they found Him they showed, by the manner in which they accosted Him, and by their whole bearing, that they were under the influence of low and unworthy motives in following Him. They were not elevated, nor earnest and sincere in their spirit. Jesus saw this, and therefore rebuked them, saying, "Ye follow me, not because ye saw the miracles; but ye seek me because ye did eat and were filled." Although they had seen Him do works that no man not sent from God could do; and heard Him speak as never man spake, yet they did not believe in Him. Their minds were so controlled by what was merely temporal and earthly that everything they had seen and heard had failed to arouse them to serious thought, or to awaken within them any appreciation of his true character, or of their own deep spiritual necessities. This failure and their unbelief gave tone to the entire conversation which our Lord held with them. He recognized the fact that nothing He had said to them or done in their pres ence had made any saving impression on their minds; and hence He said to them, in the verse preceding our text, "Ye also have seen me, and believed not."

This is said with manifest sadness. Ye *also*, even ye who have seen and heard so much that ought to have impressed you deeply, and moved you to faith, have seen me, and, like almost all the rest who have seen me and been appealed to by my words and miracles, have not believed. His mission and ministry among men, judged by their results thus far, would be a failure. Almost none of those to whom He ministered believed on Him; almost all turned from Him to perish in their sins. It seemed as though all his labors were to come to naught.

This was the way matters looked, if only present results were regarded, and there was nothing to change the aspect of the case nor awaken hope, unless some other agency should come in than any that had yet been employed. If the issue was to rest solely with men themselves they would certainly all reject Him, and make his great enterprise in their behalf an utter failure. Ye also, like those in Judea and in every other place where I have preached and wrought the signs of a messenger sent from God, have seen me and not believed. What reason was there to suppose that matters would ever be any different?

But there is another view of the case, and in our text the Saviour turns to it; his Father is interested in his great undertaking. All these perishing millions who turn from Him in apathy and stolid unbelief are under his control. He has the right and the power to do with them as He will. All men belong to Him as his creatures, and, as He had the right to do, He has given to his only begotten Son a multitude from among them which no man can number,—and these shall come to Him; these, when they see Him will believe in Him. Millions whom He calls, and whom, if they would come to Him, He would most gladly receive and faithfully save, may turn a deaf ear to his call, and trample all his instructions and offers of mercy under their feet, but they shall not make his mission a failure. Though all these reject Him, and perish because they reject Him; and thus, so far as their salvation is concerned, make his mission a failure; yet there are other millions, even more than can be counted, who will not reject Him. They have been given to Him by his Father; and they will come to Him and be saved. He will not therefore labor in vain, nor spend his strength for naught.

That this is the bearing and spirit of the first clause in our text, becomes still more manifest when we read the two immediately succeeding verses, the thirty-eighth and thirty-ninth: "For I came down from heaven, not to do my own will but the will of Him that sent me. And this is the Father's will which hath sent me, that of all which He hath given me I should lose nothing, but should raise it up again at the last day."

In coming to this world, then, our Saviour did not come alone to save the lost; but He came to do his Father's will in saving them. It is the Father's will that every soul that will look to the Son for help and believe on Him, shall have everlasting life through Him. But multitudes will not look to Him nor believe in Him. In spite of all his tender appeals and faithful warnings, and loving invitations and promises, they will reject Him. But there are some who will not reject Him. There are some who will look to Him for help, and believe on his name. The Father has given Him some, and though all others turn away from Him these will not. The Father has given them to Him to be saved, and it is the Father's will that not one of them shall be lost. The work of saving them will be the joy of the Redeemer's heart; but greater and more absorbing than even this joy is that which comes to Him from doing his Father's will in saving them. They will come to Him,— the gift of his Father makes this sure: and when they come He will save them,— his devotion to his Father's will as well as his own love for them make this sure. This is the meaning of our text: "All that the Father giveth me will come to me; and him that cometh to me I will in no wise cast out."

This text brings before our minds, then, the two great certainties of the gospel. Let us look at them for a moment.

1. Whoever, and how many soever reject Christ, yet enough will come to Him to make the gospel gloriously triumphant in the world. Our Saviour's words were evidently uttered in a spirit of triumph. The words of the previous verse are despondent, but these are not. They were put in as an offset to

what was in itself discouraging and hopeless. He saw all that was of this character clearly, but amid all He saw also the faithfulness of his Father, who had said, "Ask of me and I shall give thee the heathen for thine inheritance, and the uttermost parts of the earth for thy possession." Amid it all, and amid all the darkness and discouragement of his whole career on the earth, even down to the moment when He cried, "It is finished," and gave up the ghost, He was perfectly sure that the prediction of the prophet Isaiah would be fulfilled, "When thou shalt make his soul an offering for sin, He shall see his seed, he shall prolong his days, and the pleasure of the Lord shall prosper in his hands. He shall see of the travail of his soul, and be satisfied. He shall justify many; for He shall bear their iniquities."

This is one of the most encouraging thoughts connected with the mission and work of Christ. He entered upon them in no uncertainty as to the results, and with no possibility of failure. Had success depended solely on those to whom He came, and for whom He suffered and died, there could have been no certainty that any would be saved. Every sinner might have turned away from Him in unbelief, and all his work would have been in vain. Left solely to themselves, it was not possible to know with certainty that one of all the perishing host would turn from his sins and seek the forgiveness that the atonement of Christ would make possible for all. But when the result was assured by the gift of the Father, and success was made certain by his promise and covenant, the case became different. The Father would make his promise good. He would not fail in faithfulness to his covenant. There could be no uncertainty here. When, therefore, the Son of God divested Himself of the glory which He had with the Father from the beginning, and entered on his humiliation and walked in it through a toilsome life, through the agony of the garden, and through the fearful realities of the cross and the grave, He had this to support Him: An innumerable company of the lost of this world have been given me in eternal covenant by my Father. These will come to me. The Father cannot deny Himself; He cannot be untrue to his word; these He has given me; these He has promised to me; these, therefore, will come to me, and I shall look upon their ransomed souls and be satisfied. Though I am rejected by all who see me now though I am mocked by them, and spit upon, and crucified, yet, because the promise and covenant of my Father are sure, these toils, these burdens, these sufferings even unto death, this dwelling among the dead, will not fail of their reward; I shall see of the travail of my soul and be satisfied.

Our Lord often brought out this great truth in his discourses, and especially in his prayer for his disciples. To the obstinate and captious Jews at Jerusalem, who hardened themselves in their unbelief against Him in spite of all that He could do to convince and win them, He said, " Ye believe not, because ye are not of my sheep, as I said unto you. My sheep hear my voice, and I know them, and they follow me ; and I give unto them eternal life ; and they shall never perish, neither shall any pluck them out of my hand. My Father which gave them me, is greater than all, and none is able to pluck them out of my Father's hand." In his prayer, recorded in the seventeenth chapter of this gospel, he says, " Father, the hour is come ; glorify thy Son, that thy Son also may glorify thee ; as thou hast given Him power over all flesh, that He should give eternal life to as many as thou hast given Him." Again He says, " I have manifested thy name unto the men which thou gavest me out of the world : thine they were, and thou gavest them me." And again he says, " I pray for them ; I pray not for the world ; but for them which thou hast given me. . . . . Holy Father, keep through thine own name those whom thou hast given me. While I was with them in the world, I kept them in thy name : those that thou gavest me I have kept, and none of them is lost; but the son of perdition [is lost] ; that the Scriptures might be fulfilled. Father, I will that they also whom thou hast given me, be with me where I am."

And this thought is full of encouragement, not only in its bearing on the mind of our Saviour while He was in the flesh, but to all who desire, and labor for the glory of Christ in the salvation of souls through the gospel. Their desire will not fail of accomplishment; nor will their labors be lost. The gospel is the divinely appointed instrumentality for the salvation of all who will believe, and of the glory of Christ in their salvation. Many will refuse its provisions of mercy, and turn away from its invitations and promises, and perish in their unbelief; but to guard against the possibility of a fruitless atonement, and an unrecompensed redemption, there are vast multitudes among all nations and kindreds and tongues, of whom the Father has made a special gift to his Son, and not one of all these will fail to come to Him. Others may fail, but these will not. Wherever among all the nations of the earth, in separate communities, in congregations, in Sabbath-school classes, these are found, they will give heed to the call of the Saviour to repent and turn to God in faith; and will be saved. These will be made willing in the day of the Almighty's power, and will come to the Saviour.

All others may come if they will. Christ died not alone for those whom the Father gave Him that the success of his great enterprise might not rest in any doubt or uncertainty, but for the world. "God so loved the world that He gave his only begotten Son, that whosoever believeth on Him should not perish, but have everlasting life." And the Apostle John says, " Jesus Christ, the righteous, is the propitiation for our sins ; and not for ours only, but for the sins of the whole world." " We have seen and do testify that the Father sent the Son to be the Saviour of the world."

2. This brings us to the consideration of the second great certainty of the gospel. The first is, that by the gift of a great multitude, which no man could number, of all nations and kindreds and people and tongues, to the Son by the Father, in eternal covenant, it was made certain that He would not suffer and die for a lost world in vain. The second is, that in the gift of his only begotten Son to a lost world, to be the propitiation of its sins, God made it certain that not one sinner in all that world will fail of salvation if he will seek it in the Son of God. This is the truth asserted in the last clause of our text. In the first clause our Saviour takes refuge for Himself in the covenant of his Father, from the depressing and disheartening influence of his rejection by such great numbers of those to whom He was ministering. In the second clause He opens a refuge from despair, and a door of hope to every sinner in the world who desires salvation and is willing to come to Him for it. " I shall not fail of my reward, He says, for those whom the Father giveth me will come to me, if all the world beside turn away from me ;" and then, ever

tenderly mindful of the whole world for which he was about to lay down his life, he adds, " nor shall any one in all this world fail of salvation who comes to me for it."

That this is the exact force of this clause of our text, becomes clear from what the Lord says in the fortieth verse. As we have seen, the thirty-eighth and thirty-ninth verses bring out and reassert the fact that the success of his mission was assured to Him beyond a peradventure in the certainty that all those whom the Father had given Him would come to Him. " For I came down from heaven, not to do mine own will, but the will of Him that sent me. And this is the Father's will which hath sent me, that of all which He hath given me I should lose nothing, but should raise it up again at the last day." This is what He says in the thirty-eighth and thirty-ninth verses, in confirmation and explanation of the first clause of the text. " All that the Father giveth me shall come to me." In the fortieth verse He takes up and expands the idea of the last clause of the text. " And this " — this also — " is the will of Him that sent me, that every one which seeth the Son, and believeth on Him, may have everlasting life ; and I will raise him up at the last day." The word translated *see* in this verse, is not the same as that which is thus translated in the thirty-sixth verse, " Ye also have seen me and not believed." There the word *see* is a merely bodily seeing, without any going out of soul, without any desire or prayer or faith. But in the fortieth verse the word has the sense of looking with the mind ; and implies a voluntary turning of the thoughts to the Redeemer, as the bitten Israelites perishing in the wilderness turned their eyes to the brazen serpent. It is a looking with desire and prayer and faith: " This is the will of Him that sent me, that every one who looketh to the Son, and believeth on Him, may have everlasting life ; and I will raise him up at the last day."

The will of the Father, and the devotion of the Son to the Father's will, extend alike to all who will look and believe. There is no difference. Those who have been given to the Son in covenant, and those who have not been thus given, have but to look and believe, and their salvation is the will of the Father and the purpose of the Son: " Him that cometh to me," — whoever he is, wherever he comes from, — " I will in no wise cast out."

Next to the thought that the triumph and glory of Christ are certain, in that it is certain that a multitude which no man can number from all the nations of the earth will come to Him, and He will look upon them, and feel that in their salvation He has more than a recompense for all his humiliation and death, — next in importance and encouragement to this thought is the certainty that not one sinner of all the millions that are upon the earth can come to Christ for salvation and fail to obtain it. Next to the other truth, this sustains the hearts of those who commend the gospel to the lost, and urge them to turn to God and live. There are no uncertainties; no contingencies; there is not even a doubt. The Word of the Lord Himself has settled the matter, and settled it so plainly, so firmly, so unequivocally, that there can be no misgivings in regard to it. Wherever among all the lost there is a sinner that feels his need of salvation, and is willing to go to Christ for it, that sinner will be received with all tenderness, with infinite love, and made an heir of eternal life. It matters not who the sinner is, nor what his character or deeds, nor what his circumstances; if he wants salvation, and will look to the Son of God, and believe in Him, he cannot be lost.

There are no limitations. Christ feels none. It is true that it is the will of the Father who sent Him that of all which He hath given Him, he should lose nothing; and this will of his Father He will most scrupulously fulfill. Not one of all the mighty host given Him by the Father will fail of eternal life. But then it is equally the will of the Father that sent Him that "every one who looks to the Son and believes in Him, should have everlasting life;" and He will with equal scrupulousness fulfill his Father's will in this particular also. Nothing then in the Father's will puts any limit on the Son that He should not save all them to the uttermost that come unto God by Him. He does not have to ask to what class of sinners any one who comes to Him belongs. It is enough that he comes. This settles the matter. He will be received.

There are no limitations on the ministers of the gospel. They have no bounds that shut them in, and confine their labors to classes of sinners. Their mission is to the lost; and to them because they are are lost. Their commission is unlimited. Their business is to make known the fact that God now commandeth all men, everywhere, to repent; and that He promises salvation to every one who repents and turns to Him by faith in Jesus Christ. As they stand before men in congregations, or deal with them singly as individuals, they are to know them only as sinners for whose sins the Son of God has made propitiation, and for whom the words of Christ stand unrepealed, " Him that cometh to me, I will in no wise cast out."

There are no limitations to the lost who want salvation through Jesus Christ. The fact that any one wants salvation through Him and will come to Him for it, is all-sufficient. It is promised to him, and he cannot fail to obtain it. The Word of God would become untrue if he failed. But God cannot lie. He is not required to ask any question regarding the gift of the Father, nor regarding the class of sinners in relation to that gift to which he belongs. Christ has declared regarding him, whoever he is, whatever his guilt, whatever his relation to the gift of the Father, that if he will come to Him He will receive him. Christ says it. That is enough. If Christ is not to be taken at his word, then there is nothing further to be said. But if He is to be taken at his word, then it is as certain as his throne that no one can come to Him and be lost.

Does it not follow, then, with a logic that will silence every quibble, and set aside every excuse, and cover every one with confusion in the judgment of the great day, who has, on account of any quibble, or any excuse, refused to accept the invitations of the gospel, — does it not follow that all those who will not come to Christ, and believe in Him for the salvation of their souls, are shutting the door of hope against themselves, and bringing on themselves the guilt of those who have trodden under foot the Son of God, and counted the blood of the covenant wherewith He was sanctified, an unholy thing, and done despite to the Spirit of grace.

This is the spirit in which you, Sabbath-school teachers, should go to your classes this afternoon. There are no restraints on you in the offers of salvation which you are to make. There are none on your pupils. All is open, frank, fair, sincere.

Your business is not, as it is not the business of the pulpit, to go outside of what is written, but to deal fairly and earnestly with what is written. The relations of the Infinite to the finite involve mysteries which none but the Infinite can fathom. These are not revealed. He who attempts to deal with them is sure to darken counsel by words without knowledge. Have nothing, therefore, to do with them. Recognize every truth as a truth, and urge its claims.

SERMON XXXIII.

THE PARABLE OF THE POUNDS.

LUKE xix. 11–27. — *And as they heard these things, He added and spake a parable, because He was nigh to Jerusalem, and because they thought that the kingdom of God should immediately appear. He said therefore, a certain nobleman went into a far country to receive for himself a kingdom, and to return. And he called his ten servants, and delivered them ten pounds, and said unto them, Occupy till I come. But his citizens hated him, and sent a message after him, saying, We will not have this man to reign over us. And it came to pass, that when he was returned, having received the kingdom, then he commanded these servants to be called unto him, to whom he had given the money, that he might know how much every man had gained by trading. Then came the first, saying, Lord, thy pound hath gained ten pounds. And he said unto him, Well, thou good servant: because thou hast been faithful in a very little, have thou authority over ten cities. And the second came saying, Lord thy pound hath gained five pounds. And he said likewise to him, Be thou also over five cities. And another came, saying, Lord, behold here is thy pound, which I have kept laid up in a napkin: for I feared thee, because thou art an austere man; thou takest up that thou layedst not down, and reapest that thou didst not sow. And he saith unto him, Out of thine own mouth will I judge thee, thou wicked servant. Thou knewest that I was an austere man, taking up that I laid not down, and reaping that I did not sow: wherefore then gavest thou not my money into the bank, that at my coming I might have required mine own with usury? And he said unto them that stood by, Take from him the pound, and give it to him that hath ten pounds. (And they said unto him, Lord, he hath ten pounds.) For I say unto you, That unto every one which hath shall be given; and from him that hath not, even that he hath shall be taken away from him. But those mine enemies, which would not that I should reign over them, bring hither, and slay them before me.*

THIS parable, though similar, in its main features, to that of the "Talents," recorded in the twenty-fifth chapter of the Gospel by Matthew, is yet very different from it in its details, and in some of the lessons which it was intended to teach. That has to do only with the servants of their Lord, and applies directly only to the professed disciples of Christ. This has to do, not only with servants, but with citizens. It applies not only to the professed disciples of Christ, but to all other men also. That brings to view only the faithfulness and unfaithfulness of servants to their Lord in the use of committed trusts.

This brings these into view, but in addition to them, the allegiance of subjects to their king.

They were uttered by our Lord on different occasions and under different circumstances. The parable of the Talents was spoken on the Mount of Olives, near Jerusalem, and in connection with the prediction of the destruction of Jerusalem. It was spoken to the disciples only, and only in their presence; probably only in the presence of the twelve. This was spoken at Jericho, fifteen miles from Jerusalem, and was addressed, not to the disciples alone, but to a promiscuous company. That was spoken in answer to the disciples' question, which they asked Him privately, saying, "Tell us, when shall these things be? and what shall be the sign of thy coming, and of the end of the world?" This was spoken because He was nigh to Jerusalem; and those about Him, having become deeply impressed with the greatness and power of Jesus, began to think of Him as their Messiah, and to expect that He would immediately reveal Himself in his kingly character: "They thought that the kingdom of God should immediately appear."

The two parables must not be confounded with each other, therefore; nor are they to be looked upon as two versions of the same parable. They are distinct; and each is full of its own special instructions.

Let us now look at the various parts of this parable; and then endeavor to learn some of the lessons it was designed to teach.

"A certain nobleman went into a far country to receive for himself a kingdom, and to return."

To the minds of those who heard our Lord utter these words, "the far country" would be understood to be Rome. Rome at this time was, as she had long been, "the mistress of the world." Her senate, or her emperors, were the king-making power for all the countries within her vast dominions. "Whom she would," says one, "she exalted to a throne; whom she would she deposed." It was customary, therefore, for those who aspired to the government of any country or province, to do just as this nobleman did, go to Rome to receive for himself a kingdom and to return. It was thus that Herod the Great had become king in Judea; and thus also his son Archelaus received the government, in part, in his father's stead, after his death. They went to Rome, and, using such influence as they could command on senate and emperor, they were appointed to the government, and returned to rule over the country in which they had been only subjects, or, at most, rulers of an inferior grade.

"And he called his ten servants and delivered them ten pounds, and said unto them, Occupy till I come."

It is not quite correct to say "his ten servants." This implies that he had but ten servants; and no man with only this number would, in those days, have aspired to be made a king over a province under the Roman dominion. The rich were wont to number their servants, not by tens, but by hundreds, and thousands even. The words should be rendered, "He called unto him ten of his servants." The number ten was a favorite one with the Jews, and was often used, not to designate precisely ten, but any indefinite number. These servants were chosen for the special purpose of being intrusted with their lord's money, and turning it to good account in his absence, that he might not lose the use of it; and, doubtless, with the secret purpose also of testing their ability and faithfulness with a view to their being employed as deputies in the government when he should have received it.

The word "occupy" is not used in this sense now. Except in connection with this parable, this use of it would be almost, if not quite, unintelligible. To "occupy," as here used, means, and this is the meaning of our Lord's word, to carry on business; to traffic. He gave them the money to engage in trade with. It was a small sum compared with the "talents" which were given to the servants by the rich traveller named in the twenty-fifth of Matthew. The talent was worth nearly a thousand dollars; the pound only about fifteen. The traveller moreover gave his money to his servants, in different sums, "according to their several ability." He knew what each one of his servants was able to do, and intrusted him with money accordingly. The nobleman gave his servants all the same amount; and he would judge of their several abilities by the use they made of it. "But his citizens hated him, and sent a message after him, saying, We will not have this man to reign over us."

This nobleman was already in authority over these citizens.

Hence they are called his citizens. He was in an inferior office, but aimed at a higher one. He had a degree of authority over a portion of the country, and its inhabitants were his citizens. It was these who were unwilling to have the nobleman for their king. They therefore sent, not a message, — this is not the meaning of the word which our Lord used, — but an embassy. They sent this embassy, not to the nobleman himself, but to the king-making power to whom he had gone to apply for the government. They represented to the supreme government that they were unwilling to have him appointed to reign over them. They thus attempted to disparage him at the capital and frustrate his plans. This it was that he remembered against them and so severely punished on his return.

Having received the kingdom and returned, he first of all commanded the servants, to whom he had given the money, to be called, "that he might know how much every man had gained by trading." The reports of three only are given. These are given as specimens of all. Some had been faithful; others had been unfaithful; some had shown themselves animated by a spirit of true devotion and allegiance; others had shown themselves destitute of both. Each faithful one had given proof of his capacity for business, and, in doing this, had shown how far his lord could safely trust him to act as a deputy in his government. Each unfaithful one had, in like manner, given convincing proof of his utter unfitness for further trusts, however great might be his abilities. His spirit was not right. He was not true in his heart to his lord. Though numbered among his servants, and treated as a servant, he had the heart of an enemy. "Behold thy pound which I have kept laid up in a napkin."

It is the quaint remark of one of old that the unfaithful servant being too idle to work had no need of his napkin, and therefore could well spare it for the wrapping up of the idle pound. The napkin was the cloth which was carried by those who toiled, and with which they might wipe the sweat from their face; but this servant, not giving himself to work, had no need to carry his napkin.

His spirit of unfaithfulness is revealed, not only by the fact that he did not engage in business with his lord's money, but that he let it lie thus idle. The very least that he could have done was to put it where it would be drawing interest. And the knowledge which he claimed to have of the character of his lord made him without excuse for not making this use, at least, of the money. This was the view that his lord took of the matter, and he dealt with him accordingly. "Take from him the pound, which he is too unfaithful to hold longer, and give it to him who hath ten pounds, who, by having these ten pounds as the increase of the one with which he was first intrusted, has shown himself worthy of being intrusted with more."

The following verse is spoken by our Lord parenthetically, and states a general principle which is acted upon, not less in divine than in human affairs: "For I say unto you, that unto every one that hath shall be given ; and from him that hath not, even that he hath shall be taken away from him." Men are accustomed to treat those in their employ in this manner. The agent who gets with what he has, his principal intrusts with more. The agent who fails to get with what he has, his principal will not intrust with more, but will take away that which he has already given him. It is the same in the sphere of providence and of grace. God deals with men on precisely this principle in his providential appointments. As a rule, he who is faithful with what he has, be it money or mental abilities and acquirements, or social position and influence, he increases in it. The rich man becomes richer, the wise man wiser, the good man better. In grace it is the same. He who improves grace bestowed becomes more and more Christ-like. He who neglects to improve the grace given, sinks back into likeness with the wicked, — dwarfed and deformed in Christian character, and beggared in Christian enjoyments. Having nothing by use and improvement, he loses what he had by gracious gifts.

Having now attended to his own servants, and knowing how he stood among them and in his pecuniary resources, he turns to his citizens: "Those mine enemies which would not that I should reign over them, — who so declared by their embassy at the capital, and thus attempted to bring me into disrepute, and bring my enterprise to failure, — bring them hither and slay them before me."

The power of life and death was almost unlimited in ancient

Eastern governments; and this ending of the parable was in keeping with what those who were listening to the Saviour were familiar. Not only were such kings wont to have their enemies put to death at will, as Herod had put John the Baptist to death, but to have them brought before them and slain in their presence. Thus it was that Joshua treated the five kings whom he had defeated at Gibeon. They were brought forth from the cave into which they had fled for refuge, and brought into Joshua's presence. His men of war were commanded to put their feet on their necks in token of their utter subjection, and then they were pitilessly slain. The principle that seems to have been acted on in such governments, and that is acted on now, is that not only is there no safety to the government if its enemies live, but the enemies of a government are not worthy to live.

Is there not something typical in this almost universal judgment of governments regarding their enemies? An enemy of God's government is unworthy of life. He who continues such an enemy cannot live. For "sin when it is finished bringeth forth death." God counts the enemies to his government unfit to live in it; may He not have given this same idea as a typical one in the constitution of earthly governments.

Let us now give our attention to some of the lessons which this parable was intended to teach.

1. In the first place our Lord taught those who heard Him when He uttered it, and He teaches us that it is not wise to act on the assumption that his coming, or the coming of the kingdom of God, is immediately near. It was because those to whom He spake thought the kingdom of God would immediately appear that He spoke to them as He did. They were to understand, and we are to understand, that the great mass of men will live, and their destiny will be decided in the ordinary way, of acting on committed trusts until their characters are fully developed, and until they can be commended or condemned, on account of the matured fruits of their actions. To the great mass of men there will be no interruption, no sudden breaking off of their duty as it has been assigned to them in providence, by the inauguration of any new method of government in the divine administration. No man is wise who allows himself to be swayed from the plain path of ordinary devotion

to the work of life and service of God, by the idea that he is to be one of the few, and that his life-time is to be the pivotal minute in the lapse of ages, when a new order is to be established by the revelation of the kingdom of God, or the final coming of Christ to judgment. No man knows the day nor the hour of such coming; and if he attempts to decide upon it he is pretty sure to be mistaken. But in the way of simple service of God and the faithful discharge of duty, he cannot be mistaken. In this way he is safe. Out of it he is not safe. Let him give himself to service and duty, and leave God's times in his own hands. Let him toil on patiently, and expect nothing for himself out of the common course of events, as they have fallen to other men, and he may hope for acceptance with God and a gracious reward.

2. But, secondly, the parable teaches that though we are not to assume that our day of service is to be cut short by the coming of the Lord, yet we are to rest assured that the Lord will come to judgment, sooner or later. It is as certain that He will come again as that He has gone away. It is as certain that He will come to judge the world, and his people in it, as that the world and his people are responsible for the use they make of the things with which their Creator has intrusted them: " This same Jesus," said the two heavenly messengers to the wondering disciples as they stood gazing after their ascended Lord, " This same Jesus which is taken up from you into heaven shall so come in like manner as ye have seen Him go into heaven." " Behold He cometh with clouds," says the writer of the Apocalypse ; " and every eye shall see Him, and they also which pierced Him ; and all kindreds of the earth shall wail because of Him." " The Lord Jesus," says Paul, " shall be revealed from heaven with his mighty angels, in flaming fire, taking vengeance on them that know not God, and that obey not the gospel of our Lord Jesus Christ."

But it is not to this coming of our Lord to which we are to give our thoughts, upon which we are to let them dwell, and in anticipation of which we are to spend our time and waste our energies. We are to act on the certainty that He will come, but our thoughts and our energies are to be given to the work that He has assigned us to do. " Blessed are those servants whom their Lord when He cometh "— be it sooner or later : be it at the final day of this world's history, or at the death of the individual servant — " shall find so doing." This blessedness is that which our Saviour Himself pronounces on those who live for duty and faithful service, and not for selfish indulgence and idleness.

3. The third lesson of this parable is, that our Lord regards those who profess to be his disciples as owing Him their undivided service. They are not their own. They belong to Him. They are his servants. What they do, therefore, they are to do, not for themselves, but for Him.

This is the uniform teaching of all the New Testament. Every Christian belongs to Christ, and stands to Him in the relation of servant, having no right to act for himself, as opposed to Christ, nor for his own interests, as independent of those of his Lord. This is the distinction which He makes between his disciples and the unbelieving world. They are his servants; the world are his citizens in rebellion against Him as their rightful king. The world owe to Him the penalty of sin and of rebellion; those who have turned to Him for mercy, and have been received and become his disciples, have not only been restored to citizenship, they have also become his personal servants. Their lives, which were forfeited to divine justice, He saves from death, and then counts them as belonging to Him, not as mere citizens, but nearer, and for grateful and undivided service.

Hence the inference is, — and this is taken for granted by the parable, — that whatever possessions they have they have by his giving; and they are to use them, not as possessions held in their own right, and for themselves; but they are intrusted with them to improve and make the most they can of them for their Lord. Wherever their Lord's interests will be subserved by them, there they are to be used. They may not say of anything they have, " It is mine," any more than one to whom you intrust money or other property to use in your name and solely for your interests, may say that the money or the property is his. It is his only as a trust for which he is solemnly bound, and for faithfulness in the use of which he is held to a strict account. He may not, he cannot, without great wrong, have any interests independent of those of his Lord; much less can he have any that stand in rivalry to those of his Lord. He may not be inactive; much less may he act against his Lord's interests. The servant in the parable was condemned for simple inaction. Christ will not count the disciple innocent who does nothing, even though he claims that he does no harm. He owes Him service. Service he must render, or he is unfaithful and wicked.

4. This brings us to the fourth lesson of the text, that Christ judges all men, not less those who profess to be his, than those who are openly his enemies, by what they have done. What they do shows what they are. This was the criterion by which the nobleman judged both his servants and his citizens. And the nobleman in the parable is the representative of Christ Himself. The faithful servants showed their faithfulness by what they did, each with his pound. They showed it not by the amount that they had made by trading; by this they showed their ability; but the fact that they went to work and did what they could showed that they were true in their hearts to their lord, and that he could continue to trust them, and trust them in matters of graver responsibility.

The fact that the unfaithful servant did not do what he could with his lord's money showed that he was not true in his heart to his lord, and that therefore he could not be trusted longer, and especially that he was not fit to be trusted with graver interests. The citizens showed what their hearts were towards the nobleman by saying, "We will not have this man to reign over us," and by sending the embassy to balk him in his endeavors to get the kingdom. When he slew them, it was for what they thus showed themselves to be, rather than for what they had done; as it was in the case of the servants.

This is the view which the gospel always takes of men's works. They are the evidences of their characters, and of their spirit towards the Lord. It is not that their good or evil deeds can affect his interests, that they are worthy of consideration. Here we find the true explanation of that apparent difficulty which stands in the way of so many when they undertake to harmonize the doctrine of an entirely gracious salvation with the doctrine that each man is to be judged by his deeds at the last day.

Men are saved by the mercy of God, if they are saved at all. He graciously delivers them from their sins, and makes them heirs of heaven. He saves them sovereignly; of his own good will and pleasure. Their song now is, and it will be through eternity, " By grace are we saved. Not by works of righteousness which we have done, but according to his mercy He saved us, by the washing of regeneration, and renewing of the Holy Ghost." At the same time they do and ever will evince the fact that they are saved, by fidelity in life and conduct to the service of Him who has saved them. If they are saved, they have become his servants in their hearts. They will therefore do the work of servants. If they do not the work of his servants, they then show with perfect clearness that their hearts are not right with Him. They are still in rebellion, though they are counted among those that belong to the Lord's people.

Our Lord puts the matter in this light again and again in his teachings. "Why call ye me Lord, Lord," He says, " and do not the things that I command?" "If a man love me, he will keep my words." "A good tree cannot bring forth evil fruit; neither can a corrupt tree bring forth good fruit. Therefore by their fruit shall ye know them. Men do not gather grapes of thorns, nor figs of thistles."

5. A fifth lesson of the parable then is, that at the judgment of the last day there will be but two classes of persons, the approved and the condemned. He who has been reckoned with the servants of God, but has not been a servant of God, will simply be seen by his deeds to be among his enemies, as the unfaithful servant was seen by his deeds to be among the rebellious citizens. Among them he will have his place; and as they are treated, so will he be treated. The enemies of God and righteousness cannot be approved by the judge. They must therefore be condemned. They cannot be treated as righteous, they must therefore be treated as unrighteous. They cannot be treated as the friends of God, because God cannot treat men as being what they are not; therefore they must be treated as his enemies. They cannot enter heaven, because they have no fitness for heaven, they must therefore be excluded from heaven. They cannot be delivered from the penalty of the sins for which they have never repented, but to which they still cling; they must therefore go away into everlasting punishment.

On the other hand, they who have been the friends of God will stand with Him in the judgment. He cannot treat them as being different from what they are. If they love Him, He cannot treat them as his enemies. If they have the hearts of true servants towards Him, He cannot treat them as though they were unfaithful. Their service on earth may have been very small; their pound may have gained but another pound; but this does not matter. In gaining their one pound in humble but faithful service, they served their Lord as truly, honored Him as highly, and developed a character as fit for heaven as they did who with their one pound gained ten pounds. It is not the amount of gain from service to which the Lord looks, but to the fact that the life is a service, and that therefore the heart of a servant is in him who bears the name.

Again, if those who come up to the judgment have lost the spirit of rebels against the law and authority of God, and have in its place the spirit of true allegiance, He cannot then treat them as rebels. They may have gone deeply into rebellion; but now they are loyal; and He will treat them as they are. This is one of the glories of the gospel, that the penitent may not suffer penalty in God's government. God can, through the mediation of Christ, always treat men according to the character in which they appear before Him. It is the gospel — it constitutes a part of its glad tidings — that " the blood of Jesus Christ cleanseth from all sin," before a broken law, and that God hath " set Him forth to be a propitiation through faith in his blood, to declare his righteousness for the remission of sins that are past." The penitent can, through the satisfaction which Christ has made for him to divine justice, be pardoned, and treated through eternity, not as a guilty, but as a pardoned sinner; not as a rebel, but as loyal and true to his God.

Among which of these two companies shall we stand in the day of judgment? Brethren in the Christian profession, as we look over our lives, what do we find? Has our pound been used for the Lord, or has it been hid away in a napkin? As we have acted, so have we been. As we are now dealing with God, so are we in his sight.

You who are not Christ's disciples, will there ever be a fitter time to turn to Him and become such? You do not intend to remain as you are, and in the end be found among those who say, "We will not have this man to reign over us;" but you are now saying it each moment that you continue in sin and unbelief. Have you any reason to suppose that if you refuse submission to Him to-day, you will ever be found among his friends?

SERMON XXXIV.

THE LOST CONDITION OF THE HEATHEN AND GOD'S METHOD OF SAVING THEM.[1]

1 COR. i. 21; ROMANS x. 14, 15. — *After that in the wisdom of God the world by wisdom knew not God, it pleased God by the foolishness of preaching to save them that believe.* [*But*] *How shall they believe in Him of whom they have not heard? And how shall they hear without a preacher? And how shall they preach except they be sent?*

THESE words bring before us the lost condition of the heathen, and God's method of delivering them. I invite your attention to these two thoughts, as they are set forth in the several clauses of this text; and to some of the lessons which they involve.

"After that in the wisdom of God the world by wisdom knew not God." After a period, that is, of at least four thousand years. Before man sinned he was in direct and uninterrupted communion with God, and knew Him through such communion. God talked with him, and he with God. But after the sin of Adam, and his expulsion from Paradise, this kind of intercourse between man and God ceased. A sinful soul could not thus commune with God.

God saw fit to leave the great mass of the human family thereafter to themselves. They had cast Him off and proclaimed themselves independent of Him. The act of sinning was a declaration that they were wiser than God, and able to pursue and find out their chief good independently of Him. He chose to let them try the experiment. He knew that their chief good lay in their knowing and enjoying Him; and He proposed to give them an opportunity to demonstrate for all coming generations, and perhaps for all other moral beings, how powerless are the unaided minds of those who have sinned

[1] Preached before the American Baptist Missionary Union, at the Michigan Avenue Baptist Church, Chicago, Ill., May 21, 1871.

to hold the knowledge of God, or to recover it when once it has been lost.

This experiment was made in the wisdom of God. It was wise in God's sight, the prompting of his wisdom, thus to leave men for ages to the light of Nature, and to their own powers of observation and reasoning, to see if they would come to a knowledge of Him, and make Him their highest good. They were left also amid all the glories of those manifestations of divine power and skill in the creation and government of the world, which reveal the wisdom of God; and which would reveal the Godhead to any human soul that would earnestly and sincerely seek God in these manifestations. Rom. i. 19, 20.

But this experiment resulted, as of course God knew it would, in an utter failure on the part of men. The world, by the exercise of its own wisdom, though flooded with the sunlight of God's presence and power, failed to attain to the knowledge of God. The dislike which they first indulged towards Him remained with them, and gave tone and character to all their searchings after Him. They were through all the ages as unwilling to find such a God as they had rejected, as they were to retain the knowledge of Him in the beginning. Therefore they read nothing aright. All manifestations that revealed God were perverted by them; and the race went on, from age to age, plunging continually deeper and deeper into ignorance and darkness, until the whole world had become utterly hopeless and desperate. The Apostle describes its true condition in one pregnant sentence: "Having no hope and without God." Notwithstanding all its wisdom, and the diligent use of it for ages, the world remained in the godlessness and death into which their first rejection of God had plunged them.

The remainder of this verse brings before us the method by which God proposed now to interpose in their behalf, after they had made their fatal experiment, and demonstrated so thoroughly, for all succeeding times, their own utter hopelessness and folly.

" It pleased God by the foolishness of preaching to save them that believe;" or, more accurately, " by the foolishness of the preaching." He had just said, " Christ sent me to preach the gospel, not with wisdom of words, lest the cross of Christ should be made of none effect. For the preaching of the cross is, to them that perish, foolishness; but unto us who are saved, it is the power of God." What the Apostle asserts is, that this preaching, the preaching of the gospel, the preaching of the cross, which those who reject it and perish count foolishness, was pleasing to God. It was wise in his view, and full of promise and hope; and he appointed it, therefore, to be the great and distinctive instrumentality in saving men, by bringing them to a knowledge of Himself. It was not foolish preaching that pleased God, but that preaching which unbelievers and the enemies of Christ consider foolishness. Its subject-matter does not please them. It is not at all in harmony with their ideas of wisdom.

The form in which the subject-matter is presented does not commend itself to their minds as well adapted to produce the best results. It is too simple; too declarative; not sufficiently speculative and pretentious. Their judgment differs from God's judgment in the matter, because they look upon the character of men, and the object to be accomplished by preaching, in an entirely different light from that in which God views them. They look upon men as needing intellectual entertainment by preaching; and to be put into possession of the results of fine thinking — advanced thinking — or of vigorous speculations, and startling theories or discoveries. But God looks upon men primarily as a guilty race. As has been well said, "Unless the guilt of the pagan world can be proved, the missionary enterprises of the Christian Church, from the days of the Apostles to the present time, have all been a waste of labor. Nay, more, if the sin and ill-desert of the entire human race, in all its generations, cannot be established, then the Christian religion itself, involving the incarnation of God, is an attempt to supply a demand that has no real existence. It is no wonder, therefore, that the Apostle Paul, in opening the most systematic and logical treatise in the New Testament — the Epistle to the Romans, — enters upon a line of argument to demonstrate the ill-desert of every human creature without exception, and to prove that, before an unerring tribunal, and in the final day of adjudication, every mouth must be stopped, and all the world become guilty before God."[1] God thus looks upon men as a guilty race, groping in the ignorance and darkness that sin has

[1] Shedd, *Guilt of the Heathen*, p. 1.

brought upon them, doomed to death, resting under a fearful sentence of condemnation, and therefore needing, first of all, and above all things, forgiveness of sins, and reconciliation with God, and restoration to his favor.

In order to this, it is not amusement that men require. As well might you talk of amusing a criminal, when, from the depths and darkness of his dungeon, he cries for pardon and restoration to the light and privileges of life. It is not speculative thought, nor fine reasoning, nor brilliant speech that they require. You might as well speculate, and reason, and make display of rhetoric for the recovery of men stricken with the plague. Criminals need, and if they are right-minded they intensely long for, a proclamation of mercy, and an offer of pardon. Sick and dying men need to be told of a physician who can heal them. Preaching the gospel is just this. It is a proclamation of mercy, and an offer of pardon to the guilty and condemned. It is the pointing of the sick and dying to a Physician who can heal them. Nothing else is preaching the gospel. This is.

If, therefore, men do not look upon mankind as God looks upon them; if they look upon them not as guilty but as innocent, or but slightly out of the way, and not under a righteous and terrible condemnation; or if they look upon them as naturally pure and right-minded, and not carnal and godless, — "the whole head sick and the whole heart faint," — from the sole of the foot even unto the crown of the head, having no soundness, but wounds and bruises, and putrefying sores, — wounds and sores that all human appliances have never been able to "close, nor bind up, nor mollify with ointment;" if men look upon mankind in this light, then, of course, they will count that preaching to be foolishness which concerns itself wholly with proposing offers and assurances of pardon to the guilty; and proclaiming healing and health, and hopes of life, to the sick and the dying. But because God looks upon men in the other light, and sees them in the other character, therefore such preaching seemed wise to Him. It pleased Him; and He ordained it, and clothed it with honor and dignity, and power to save them that believe.

"But how shall they believe in Him of whom they have not heard?" Glad tidings are nothing to those who do not hear them. The provisions of mercy, and offers of pardon, are nothing to those who have no knowledge of them. They must remain still in ignorance and sorrow and death, notwithstanding all that has been done for them, and all the great and glorious possibilities that have been opened for them. They must be told of these things. They must hear them, if they are to be saved by believing them.

"But how shall they hear without a preacher?" God has chosen to commit the gospel to living men to proclaim. He might have proclaimed it by the trump of the archangel; or He might have emblazoned it in letters of fire on the heavens; and in such characters that every son and daughter of Adam could have read, and not failed to understand it. But He chose to do no such thing. As it pleased Him by the foolishness of preaching, and by nothing else, to save them that believe the tidings He sent them, so it pleased Him that men, and men only, should declare these tidings to those who are to be saved. Unless men preach, the perishing will not hear. If they do not hear, they will never believe. If they do not believe, they will never be saved.

We know not why God does not interpose in some other way. Nor is it necessary for us to know why He does not. It is enough that He does not. The gospel itself assures us that He will not; and the history of the human family is a terrible confirmation of this assurance. The whole world remains in the darkness and desolation of heathenism, saving only those parts of it to which men have preached the gospel of Christ. In these parts there is light and hope. Men have heard, and believed, and been saved. Death reigns unchecked over all the rest. And it is as certain as anything can be that death will continue to reign over them unless, and until, men go and preach to them the cross of Christ.

"But how shall they preach except they be sent?" This is the practical and searching conclusion to which the Apostle's argument has conducted us. It is an appeal to the consciences of those who are addressed; that is, the disciples of Jesus Christ. It will continue to come home to their consciences, so long as his command, "Go ye into all the world and preach the gospel to every creature," demands their obedience.

But, as an appeal to the consciences of those on whom the

authority of the great commission rests, it involves this further question : " Whose duty is it to send men to preach the gospel to the heathen ? " Who is responsible for the sending ? What do the Scriptures teach us on this point ?

In the first place, they make it plain that God must send them. It is his prerogative. If He send them not, they may not go. They have no tidings to carry. No man may take this honor upon himself. No man, no body of men, may thrust it upon him. The Lord has reserved to Himself the sole right to say who shall be the bearer of his messages of pardon and eternal life to the lost, as special ambassadors of Christ. In this day of intense but superficial aggressiveness, this great truth is liable to be overlooked. But the New Testament has made it too plain to be misunderstood. It traces the primary sending of the ministers of the gospel directly to the Lord Himself. When He was upon the earth He Himself called whom He would ; and none entered the sacred inclosure without his bidding. The twelve were called first into the ministry and made candidates for the apostleship. He sent them forth by a special command when He would have them go and preach the kingdom of God. And when the twelve were not enough for the work that He had in hand, and others were needed, He did not throw the ministry open to all of his disciples, and leave it for any, or all, or none of them to go, as it suited their tastes, or convenience, or the wishes of their friends ; but He kept the matter in his own hands ; and by a special call, and a special designation, He " appointed other seventy also." And when the twelve and the seventy combined were still too few, He commanded them to betake themselves to prayer, and beseech " the Lord of the harvest that He would send forth laborers into his harvest." And after our Lord's ascension, and the work of inspired teaching was committed to the Apostles, they inculcated the same great lesson. Every grade of the ministry, from Apostles downward, they teach us, is a direct and special gift of God. " He gave some to the church to be apostles ; and some to be prophets ; and some to be evangelists ; and some to be pastors and teachers." Hence it was that Paul could appeal so solemnly to the elders at Ephesus, when he gave them his farewell charge. " Take heed therefore unto yourselves, and to all the flock, over which the Holy Ghost hath made you overseers." The Holy Ghost; not they themselves; not the church; not councils; not bishops; not these — but the Holy Ghost.

In an important sense, then, it is all God's work, the sending of men to preach the gospel. It rests with Him to convert them. It rests with Him to convince them of their personal duty and special call to become ministers. It rests with Him to follow these convictions with those solemn impressions of which they cannot rid themselves; and which, if resisted, beget within them the painful consciousness, "Woe is unto me if I preach not the gospel!" It rests with God so to order affairs by his providence that these convictions of duty can be carried out; oftentimes so that they cannot but be carried out. It rests with God also to give, not only to these convictions of duty, but to these impressions, which are sometimes far more intense than any mere conviction can be; the special direction which determines the sphere of labor to which the life shall be devoted. To many a called and chosen candidate for the ministry, the Lord speaks as plainly in regard to his field of labor, as he did to Paul, when "essaying to go into Bithynia, the Spirit suffered him not. A vision appeared to him in the night. There stood a man of Macedonia, and prayed him, saying, Come over into Macedonia and help us; and he assuredly gathered that the Lord had called him to preach the gospel unto them." If the experience of many a man, who is now preaching the gospel to the heathen, could be known, it would come out that he had thus been beckoned away from his native land. He could find no rest of soul till he gave heed to the beckoning, and gathered assuredly that the Lord had called him to preach the gospel to the heathen. From the moment that he reached this conclusion, and put himself in the way of obeying the divine call, all was peace. The path of duty became a path of gladness, and prosperity of soul. He was thenceforth sure that God was sending him to preach the gospel to the heathen. He rejoiced in it as a great honor; and it became the one, all-absorbing thought and purpose of his life.

Thus far our way is all clear as to who shall send men to preach the gospel to the heathen. The New Testament is emphatic; it leaves no ground for doubt or hesitation; God must send them.

But as we look into the matter further, we find that this is not all of the answer that the New Testament gives to our inquiry.

All the teachings of the New Testament involve the idea that all the disciples of Christ, though not official ambassadors, are all helpers in the great work of their Lord, and have great and glorious correspondent responsibilities resting upon them. The last commission has this idea plainly on its surface. It was the formal association of the disciples with their Lord, and the laying of their part of the work clearly before them. The division of labor among the disciples themselves, was not definitely stated in the commission; but it was plainly enough involved. In the nature of the case some division of labor must be made. All could not give themselves to the ministry of the Word. Some must "serve tables;" all could not be wholly devoted to ministering in spiritual things. Some must minister in carnal things, that they might have to impart to those whose ministry was solely in the spiritual. Paul often brings out this divine arrangement in the gospel; "They that preach the gospel, must live of the gospel;" and they who are ministered to in spiritual things, must minister carnal things to those who thus minister. This is the constant and emphatic teaching of all the sacred writers; and it is one of the prevailing recognitions of the division of labor involved in the great commission, and contemplated by it.

One very marked example is given in the inspired record, illustrating this division of labor, and showing that the Lord embraced all his disciples in the one command to go into all the world and preach the gospel to every creature. It is found in the thirteenth chapter of the Acts of the Apostles. Paul and Barnabas were living at Antioch. In the church there, there were certain prophets and teachers. While these were ministering unto the Lord and fasting, the Holy Ghost said, in tones that could not be misunderstood, "Separate me Barnabas and Saul for the work whereunto I have called them. And when they had fasted and prayed, and laid their hands on them, they sent them away. So they being sent forth by the Holy Ghost, departed," and went far and near, doing the bidding of the Lord, in preaching the gospel both to Jews and heathen. How long they were gone on this missionary excursion we do not know; but when they returned to Antioch, "they gathered the church together," — the whole church, as being all equally interested, and equally responsible, — "and rehearsed all that God had done with them; and how He had opened the door of faith unto the Gentiles."

This is God's method of carrying forward his kingdom among men. He chooses, calls, designates the men who shall go forth as his ministers; and then He bids others set them apart and send them. This has always been his method. It is the method contemplated in the great commission. It is the only practicable method. It is the only method that has ever availed to bring the heathen to the knowledge of God. As this method has been used, the gospel has been preached to the heathen; the heathen have heard of Jesus Christ; have believed in Him; have called upon Him, and been saved. Just as this method has been neglected, or other methods been used in its stead, the darkness and death and desolations of heathenism have remained unchecked; and the kingdom of Christ has made no advance in the world.

It is thus the spirit and genius of the gospel that all the disciples of Christ be either senders or sent. The Saviour struck the key-note of his dispensation when He said, "As the Father sent me, even so send I you." All are sent of the Lord; some to be senders of others, as Christ Himself was sent to be a sender; others to be sent by the agency of these. Wherever there is a Paul, or a Barnabas, who is called of God to go, there are, as a rule, disciples to whom God says, "Separate me this Paul, or this Barnabas, and send him forth in my name."

But here another question forces itself upon our attention. It grows naturally and necessarily out of those which we have been considering. As the answering of the question, "How shall they preach except they be sent?" compels us to ask, "Who shall send them?" so the answering of this question, compels us to ask, "But how shall they send them?" Let us consider this question a moment in the light of experience and observation. As a matter of fact, how have the disciples of Christ sent men to preach the gospel to the heathen? As a matter of fact, how must they send them, if they send them at all?

1. In the first place, they must do it by bringing moral

power to bear upon them. Every disciple of Christ, who is in sympathy with Him and with his work in this world, — and just to the extent that He is in sympathy with him, — will feel the necessity of giving the gospel to all who are without it. All who thus feel must respond to this necessity in whatever way it is brought before them. They must count it a matter of first and paramount importance that the great commission should be obeyed. Nothing must stand in its way. Obedience to it must have precedence of everything that is worldly, or of minor importance. In this manner a public sentiment must be begotten among the disciples of Christ in favor of this enterprise. It must be made to have a distinct and solemn recognition by every one, when the great question of duty is agitated by him, in deciding upon his calling in life. The tone of the Christian society in which he moves must force him to consider this question of duty in the light of the great commission. Then, if he hears the voice of God calling him to personal service among the heathen, this public sentiment, the tone of the society in which he moves, will give emphasis to this call; and, by the assurance it will give him of sympathy and support, it will remove many of the hinderances that would otherwise lie in his way, and make him hesitate to respond to the divine call, by giving himself heartily to the ministry of the gospel among the heathen.

In this way the disciples of Christ must send forth preachers of the gospel to the uttermost parts of the earth. They must thus bring a moral power upon young converts, and upon young men who are preparing for life, a moral power that they cannot resist when once they have heard the call of God, and listened to the Macedonian plea for help.

2. The disciples of Christ must send men to preach the gospel to the heathen by bringing a spiritual and divine power upon them. "Prayer moves the hand that moves the world." Prayer was ordained of God for this very purpose. "I will be inquired of by the house of Israel, to do this thing for them," is God's interpretation of the doctrine of prayer. He will be moved, and He waits to be moved, by the prayers of those whom He has made workers together with Him in the evangelization of the world.

We have already quoted our Saviour's command to his disciples, "Pray ye the Lord of the harvest that He would send forth laborers into his harvest." This command has never been recalled. The disciples of Christ are to obey it, so long as they see a ripened or a ripening field calling for the reapers to come and harvest it. The very fact of want in any field is an appeal to Christ's disciples to pray that the want may be supplied. Want pleads with them to plead with God.

Again, our Lord has commanded us to pray, in a more general and comprehensive manner, in regard to this matter; and placed it foremost before us as an object of desire and petition in all our prayers: "After this manner pray ye: Our Father who art in heaven; hallowed be thy name; thy kingdom come; thy will be done in earth as it is in heaven." This is to be every disciple's prayer while God's name is profaned in any part of the world, while his kingdom remains unestablished in any land, and while his will is disregarded by any human being.

But God's name will be hallowed among men, only as they come under the saving influences of the gospel; his kingdom will come among men, only as they receive the gospel into their hearts by repentance toward God and faith toward our Lord Jesus Christ; his will will be done among men, only as they make the gospel the rule of their lives, and enthrone its principles and precepts in supreme dominion over their spirit and conduct.

To offer this prayer is, therefore, just to ask that the gospel may reach men, and that they may receive it and be saved by it. But to pray that the gospel may reach men and save them, is praying that the gospel may be preached to them; and praying that the gospel may be preached to them, is praying that preachers of the gospel may be sent to do it.

This prayer, and the one that asks that the Lord of the harvest would send forth laborers into his harvest, come to the same thing, therefore, in their bearing on the matter before us. The disciples of Christ are to pray men into the ministry; and then to send them by the might of their prayers into all the nations of the earth.

3. Finally, the disciples of Christ must send preachers of the gospel to the heathen — with money. However belittling and sordid it may seem to link money thus closely with prayer, and

with moral and spiritual power; however unbecoming it may seem in the view of some men; it nevertheless remains a great and undeniable truth, that God has thus closely and indissolubly joined them, both in his Word, and in his plans for advancing his kingdom among men. He has always recognized the fact that all his servants in this world have bodies, as well as souls. He has recognized the fact that their bodies must be fed and clothed, — gross and unromantic as feeding and clothing may seem; He has recognized the fact that their bodies must be kept healthy, and in good condition for work, — as commonplace and worldly as the doing of this may be. He has always recognized the fact, therefore, that when He calls any disciple to give himself up to the preaching of the gospel, his bodily wants must be looked out for by other disciples; and that, too, not as though he was their hired laborer, but a sharer with them in one common work for the same Lord and Master. The work is as much theirs as it is his; and the responsibility to see it done is as imperative on them as it is on him. The New Testament, therefore, everywhere makes it the duty of those disciples who do not give themselves directly and formally to the preaching of the gospel, to support those who do, with all needed material help; as well as to care for the poor, and to sustain every good and beneficent cause. This is, in fact, what a disciple of Christ is to make money for. Christ redeemed all of each disciple; and the disciple can do nothing less than to consecrate all of what he is or can be to Christ's cause, and the work involved in doing his will.

As a necessary result, the peculiarity of which we speak, the joining of money-giving with praying, must characterize the revelation of God's will in his Word. "Thy prayers and thine alms"—that is, "thy prayers and thy money-giving"—"have come up for a memorial before God," said the angel to Cornelius. God had respect not alone to his prayers, but to his money also, when He came to reward him for his fidelity, and make him the first-fruits of the gospel among the Gentiles. The Bible is full of this peculiarity. Praying and giving, loving God and giving, being loved of God and giving, run all through its pages. Doubtless those who were on the right hand of the Judge in the great day of final reckoning had prayed much, all of them. Prayer is the very life of those who so live that they will have a place at the right hand of the Judge on that day. They could never live nor labor without prayer. "Prayer is their vital breath," all through their lives. Oh yes; they prayed, without doubt; and they doubtless loved God and had his love shed abroad in their hearts. But when the Judge came to receive them, and pass sentence of approval and welcome upon them, He did not say a word about their prayers, or their love or their spiritual enjoyments. There was something that had cost them something, and that had been a measure of the sincerity of their prayers, and of the genuineness of their love and joy. This it was that came up for honorable mention. And what was it? Why, they had given Christ meat when He was hungry, and meat had to be bought with money; they had given Him drink when He was thirsty; they had kindly taken Him into their houses when He was a stranger and in want; they had clothed Him when He was naked; they had visited Him when He was sick; they had gone to Him, and sympathized with Him and helped Him, and borne his reproach, when He was in prison. All this they had done; and all this had taken their money. They had not counted religion so pure, so spiritual, so ethereal, as to be defiled and dishonored by coming in contact with the common bodily wants of Christ, and supplying them by giving Him so gross a thing as money. And when they could not recall the humble, but glorious deeds, for which Christ praised them, He pointed to the redeemed around Him — the saved from all lands, and from among all nations, — to the poor negro slave, to the filthy Karen, to the debased Teloogoo, to the most degraded of the heathen who had been reached by the gospel which their money had sent out; and to all the suffering and needy, who had come up from among the poor and persecuted and ill-treated and neglected, — He pointed to these, and said, "Inasmuch as ye did it unto one of the least of these, my brethren, ye did it unto me."

O my hearers, that religion which Christ has given to man, and which will stand the fearful tests of the Judgment Day, is a religion that concerns itself not alone with loving and praying, but with practical kind-heartedness, with supplying the bodily wants of Christ's servants, — and therefore very, very much with giving money. It has much to do with prayers — and alms.

2. Let me call your attention to a few of the lessons which this subject brings before us.

1. The work of Christian missions is the work of God. It is the great work in which He is engaged in this world. Nothing lies nearer his heart. It is the work that He inaugurated when He sent his only begotten Son into the world to make salvation possible. It is the work for whose sake alone the fires of the last great day are restrained, that they do not burst forth from their hidden chambers, and put an end to all human history. God delays, and is long suffering to usward, because He does not wish that any should perish, but that all should come to repentance and live through an acceptance of the gospel.

The work of missions is the one work by which alone the Eternal Father will make good his covenant with the Son, to give Him the heathen for his inheritance, and the uttermost parts of the earth for his possession. It is the only work by which that great and glorious result can be accomplished which was promised to the Son as a reward for his life of humiliation in the flesh, for the agonies of Gethsemane, and for the fearful death on the cross, — not the death of the body only, but the infinitely more fearful death of his soul, that death which was announced in the startling cry, " My God, my God, why hast thou forsaken me! " The work of missions is the only work by which the promise to this suffering One will ever be fulfilled, " He shall see of the travail of his soul, and be satisfied." The work of missions is the work by which the Almighty Father is now satisfying the infinite heart of the only begotten Son in its longings for the salvation of a multitude that no man can number. It has pleased God by the foolishness of preaching to save them that believe, and his work in behalf of his Son will never be done, saving through the instrumentality of what we call Christian Missions, in sending men to do this preaching.

2. This introduces us to a second lesson. The work of missions is the great work of the disciples of Christ on the earth. In calling them into his kingdom, God has made them workers together with Himself. But if they work with Him, his work must be their work. What He makes of paramount importance, that they also must make of paramount importance. Hence it is that our Saviour now and evermore commands all

his disciples, " Seek ye — whatever others may do — seek ye first the kingdom of God and his righteousness;" and now, and always make it their duty and special privilege to pray, " Thy kingdom come."

3. Genuine sympathy with the work of missions, and interest in it, is one of the characteristics of Christ's friends as distinguished from his enemies. To the unbelieving, and the enemies of Christ it has always appeared foolish to send men to preach the gospel to the heathen. They have always cried out against it as unreasonable. They have scouted it as hopeless and uncalled for. They have ever held the persons of those in great contempt who have gone forth to this work. Sydney Smith spake out the real thought and feeling of unbelief and enmity to the cross of Christ, when he penned those vulgar appeals to the government, in the " Edinburgh Review " in 1809, to " rout out the nest of consecrated cobblers " from the East India Company's possessions; and followed up these appeals with those coarse, though keen and witty invectives against the missionaries and their supporters, for which he so richly merited Robert Hall's famous utterance, that " the writer had the levity of a buffoon, joined to a heart of iron and a face of brass."

The enemies of the gospel have always denounced the raising of money for missionary purposes as a waste, and a burden on the poor. They have set themselves against it as a robbery of the poor and needy. The same witty but godless churchman spoke again for all unbelievers, when he said, in the same article, that " the poor, by their contribution, were pilfered of all their money, shut out from all their dances and country wakes, and are then sent penniless into the fields," etc. In all this the same spirit is manifested that is manifested in denouncing the preaching of the gospel as foolishness. The trouble is the same in one case as it is in the other, namely, this: These men differ with God as to the condition of the lost, and hence as to their wants; and besides this, they have no sympathy with God in his sympathy and love and pity for men. They cannot, therefore, be expected to favor the great work by which God aims to reach men with his sympathy and compassion.

But it is not so with those who have faith in Christ, and are his friends. They are of one mind with God respecting the condition and wants of men. They have not only hearts to feel for the lost, but they have spiritual discernment to see their condition, and the remedy for it.

4. Finally, they who aid in sending men to preach the gospel to the heathen, are, not in word only but in deed, "workers together with God." If the work of missions be the work of God, if it be the work in which He has called the disciples of Christ to labor with Him, then this follows, as a matter of course. And since the work of missions is the work of God; and since it is the work in which He has called his people to labor with Him, therefore, he who aids in carrying it on, is doing the very thing that is hastening forward the fulfillment of God's purposes of mercy and salvation towards a ruined world. He is a sharer with God in bringing about the great result which was promised the Son in covenant: "I will give thee the heathen for thine inheritance, and the uttermost parts of the earth for thy possession." He is lending a hand towards the fulfillment of that promise, so full of hope and glory for man, "He shall see of the travail of his soul, and be satisfied."

SERMON XXXV.

WHAT IS THAT TO THEE?

JOHN xxi. 22. — *Jesus saith unto him, If I will that he tarry till I come, what is that to thee? Follow thou me.*

OUR Lord had been speaking directly to Peter regarding the future of his earthly life, and the service which he was yet to render in the ministry of the gospel. But Peter was not satisfied with knowing what pertained to himself and his own duties. He wanted the Lord to give him an account of the work and future history of the other disciples. He had been commanded to act as a shepherd to Christ's sheep, and to feed his lambs. This was to be the business of his life. He was to give himself to the work of a Christian pastor and teacher. At the same time the Lord forewarned him that in the prosecution of this work he would come to martyrdom. The fate of the Master was awaiting the servant; and he is enjoined not to shrink from it. "Follow me," the Lord said, "even though your following will lead you to the cross where my leadership brought me."

At this point Peter's mind turned suddenly away from himself and his own duties, and looking upon John, he abruptly asked, "Lord, and what shall this man do?"

In his reply to this abrupt and impertinent question the Lord rebuked his meddlesomeness, and called his mind back to his own duty, with the very distinct intimation that this, and not the duty of some one else, was that with which he was to concern himself, and for which alone he was responsible: "If I will that he tarry till I come, what is that to thee? Follow thou me."

He does not tell Peter, not even by implication, what John is to do. He does not say that John shall remain till He comes. But the import of the reply is, that Peter's own work is enough for him to attend to; that he is not responsible for what the Lord requires of John, or any other disciple; and he is not to make it his business to pry into it. Instead of looking after the affairs of others let him attend faithfully to the trust that had been committed to himself; and submit with cheerful acquiescence to the lot that infinite wisdom and love had appointed him. John's duties, and John's destiny, it did not belong to Peter to consider nor to provide for.

This reply of our Lord to the meddlesome question of his disciple involves some important principles touching questions of personal duty.

Let us look at a few of them.

1. In the first place it is implied that every one has a work of some kind to do in this world. This is the general principle underlying all else that is involved in the reply. "If I will that he remain till I come, what is that to thee? Follow thou me." "John has his mission; you have yours." Peter's question, as the Lord's answer, was based on a recognition of this principle. He assumes it as a matter of course upon general principles that John has some work assigned him. "Thou hast designated mine; and now, Lord, what is his? The Lord admits the assumption. He allows that John has a work to do, as a matter of course. But it is not for Peter to concern himself with it.

This principle is everywhere recognized in the Scriptures. Their general teachings and their special doctrines all imply it. Each man was made "for an end." He was endowed with faculties, and placed in a sphere where they could be exercised with a purpose. He is to use his faculties and turn them to good account in the sphere where the providence of God has placed him. Hence the Saviour takes as the starting point of several of his parables the thought that every man has a definite work assigned him to do in the world. He may not be an idler or a drone in society. He may not let his faculties lie dormant. He may not abuse them. He must not repress their activity, but give them lawful scope and exercise; otherwise he is represented as "hiding his talent; as burying it in the earth; as becoming a wicked and unprofitable servant." And Paul wrote to the Thessalonians, "For even when we were with you this we commanded you, that if any would not work, neither should he eat."

And this he commanded, not only on the ground of justice to the rest of the community, whom it would be wrong to tax for the support of an idler; but on the ground of a direct responsibility which the possession of faculties places upon each one to exercise them. The fact that he has ability to work is a clear and unanswerable demonstration that he has a work to do with his powers. God does not act without an end. When He confers on a man capacities for work, the giving of them is a command to make use of them. In giving them He says to the receiver, " Occupy till I come." To receive them and hold them as though they were not thus given is to suppose that God acts without an end. The purpose of the bestowment of capabilities for bodily and mental work is as manifest by the bestowment itself as is the purpose of endowing one with eye-sight. When God gives a man eyes He intends that he shall see. He gives them to him for this purpose. So is it with other capabilities. When He gives him mind or muscle He intends they shall be used.

Accordingly the Scriptures constantly point us forward to a day of final reckoning, when God will call men to an account for the manner in which they have used the powers that He has given them. They are to be judged according to "their works." As they have used their powers well, or ill, or not used them at all, so will be their sentence and their destiny. There will be those who have rightly used the abilities God intrusted to them. These will hear the sentence, " Well done, good and faithful servants." There will be those who have misused their faculties and perverted their powers. These will hear themselves denounced as wicked wasters of their Lord's goods, not only not worthy of any further trust, but worthy of severe condemnation. There will be those who have not used their abilities, but have let them pine away in idleness. With powers to do and golden opportunities for doing, they have done nothing. These shall be rejected from favor, and condemned as slothful and profitless servants, not fit for the trusts they have had, and denied the enjoyment of any others.

2. Again: this work, whatever it is, that every one has to do in the world is his own work. It belongs to him alone to

do it. It does not belong to any other being in the universe. "If I will that he remain till I come, what is that to thee? Follow thou me. Why should you look to John's work? You have not to do that. Look to that which you yourself have to do. It belongs to you to do that. See that you do it." This is the spirit of our Lord's reply to Peter. It is the spirit of the inspired writings as they deal with all men. God has not only given each one a work to do, but He has made that one work his own and not another's. Hence the Apostle says to those whom he is instructing in Christian duty, " Study to do your own business, and to work with your own hands, as we commanded you."

There is no confusion in the divine allotments and purposes. Each object that He calls into being has its specific uses. It is intended to answer a specific end. It is by combining the operations of all that He maintains the harmony of creation and advances toward the accomplishment.of the great purpose for which creation was begun and is perpetuated.

The sun has his work to do ; the moon has hers; the stars have theirs. Each force that is employed in the carrying on of the great processes of nature has its sphere in which to operate, and its own results to produce. There is no confusion. There is no changing of places or of uses. It is not the moon's business, and never becomes her business, to flood the world with light and heat by day. Water does not take the place of fire ; nor does gravity do the work of electricity and of the mind. Each separate tree, each plant, each spear of grass, each leaf, stands in its own place, does its own work, fulfills the specific end of its own existence. Each member of each one's body, each faculty of his mind, has its special purpose. The foot may not do the work of the hand, nor the ear that of the eye. The faculty of reflection may not, — it cannot do the work that belongs to the faculty of perceiving; nor may the thinking and reasoning powers do the work of the affections.

Such is the order, the specificness, and hence the harmony in the works of the Creator. Each thing subserves a definite purpose. Each has something to do, and that something is its own work and belongs to nothing else.

So is it with each individual human being, unless he is out of harmony with everything else that God has made. The work that God expects of him is his own work, and it belongs to no one else to do it. If another attempts to do it he meddles with that which does not concern him.

This, I have said, is the light in which the subject is left by the sacred writers. They enjoin every man to do his own business. They condemn those who meddle with what does not concern them, but belongs to somebody else, as busybodies in other men's matters, and they command all Christians not to suffer themselves to come into the reproach of men by meriting this appellation. Indeed, those who thus go out of their own sphere to meddle with what does not belong to them in the sphere of another, are classed with the worst of characters, and treated as deserving the severest censure. Thus the Apostle Peter says to all believers, "Let none of you suffer as a murderer, or as a thief, or as an evil-doer, or as a busybody in other men's matters," — classing busybodies in other men's matters with the vilest and most reprehensible. And thus the Apostle Paul commands Timothy not to admit a certain class of women into the number who were supported by the church, and were, perhaps, engaged in a kind of local missionary service, for he says they "learn to be idle, wandering about from house to house; and not only idle, but tattlers also and busybodies, speaking things which they ought not."

Then, when the Scriptures come to speak of the final judgment and of the future retribution, they keep the same thought prominent. "Each one," they teach us, "shall give account of himself to God." "Every man shall bear his own burden." "Every man shall receive his own reward according to his own labor." "Behold, I come quickly; and my reward is with me, to give every man according as his work shall be." His work, and not the work of another. If his work is done, he shall have his reward accordingly. If it is undone, his reward shall fail. It matters not what else he has done, if his own work is unfinished, he suffers loss.

This was the view that the Apostle Paul took of the relation of each man to the requirements of God, and to the work given him to do in this world: "I have fought a good fight," he said at the close of his life. "I have finished my course. I have kept the faith; henceforth there is laid up for me a crown of righteousness which the Lord, the righteous judge, shall give me at that day." He looks upon himself as having had a specific work to do, and he rejoices in the fact that he has done just that, and that for doing it he will be rewarded by his righteous judge.

3. This leads me to remark again that each one is responsible for his own work, and not for that of any other. This is the principle to which our Lord appealed when He said to Peter, "What is that to thee?" As though He had said, that lies out of the sphere of the requirements that are made of you. It belongs to another man to look after this, and not to you. The responsibility of it is his and not yours. Why then do you meddle with it?

The fact that each one's work is his own, and not another's, settles the question of responsibility. So also does the fact that the judgment of the last day and the final award are wholly in view of the state in which each one's own work is found. If one's own work has been left undone, and he claims merit and reward for having done the work that belonged to somebody else to do, the question will meet him, "What was that to thee?" "Who required that at your hands? That was not the thing for which you were responsible. This work, that comes up here undone, was all that was required of you. For this only were you responsible. And on the other hand, when the righteous appear before the Judge, it will be their own works alone for which they will be held accountable. Their finished "works will follow them," as the Apostle says, and, being finished, will acquit them of unfaithfulness to their earthly responsibility.

4. No man is responsible for the consequences of the faithful doing of his own work, and he is not to govern himself by any apprehension of what these consequences may be. If he is sure that the work to which he is devoting himself is his work, that he, and he alone, is responsible for the doing of it, and that he alone must answer to God for the faithful performance of it, he is not bound to take heed of anything that may follow the doing of that which is required of him. The consequences of doing what God requires of a man are none of his concern. The servant is responsible only for obedience to his Lord's commands. It matters not on whom these consequences may fall, whether on others, or on himself. They may work

his own death. They did so in the case of Peter. When the Lord gave him his charge to tend his sheep and feed his lambs, He distinctly told him that the work to which he was to devote himself would bring him to a violent death. But that was to have no deterring influence on Peter's mind. He was to go forward regardless of that. If wicked men chose to put him to death in return for his endeavors to do them good in obedience to his Lord's command, they, and not he, were responsible for that. If he was in the way of exact obedience, and of legitimate service, he could not be held answerable for the loss of his life.

It is the same always, and with all men, and with every class of consequences. Let men do the work that God has given them to do, and it is none of their concern what consequences follow. It is not necessary that any man should live; it is necessary that he should do his duty. The preaching of the gospel, for example, will be, it always has been, not only a savor of life unto life to multitudes, but to other multitudes a savor of death unto death. For each consequent alike the faithful administration of the gospel is irresponsible. If men are saved by his ministry, to God is all the glory, as with Him has been all the efficiency. If men are hardened and perish under his ministry, they themselves must bear all the blame. They have had life and death set before them. They have chosen death.

5. No man's life will be a failure who does his own work. He may die without seeing the fruit of his work, as Peter did, yet his work shall abide and accomplish all that God designed it to accomplish in the advancement of his own purpose. When Peter came to the inverted cross he could see but little of the real results of all his labors. The seed that he had sown had borne but little fruit as yet. The great harvest was to linger long before it would be seen. Not until centuries had passed away would it be gathered in. But his life work was done. Like the Apostle Paul, he had finished his course, he had kept the faith. He had given to the great enterprise of saving souls, and elevating a lost race, his toils, and his influence; and now he was giving it his dying testimony. The full result would not be seen till this enterprise was brought to its successful termination. Then, but not before, would his work appear;

and it would be seen that every deed was mighty in its place, and, like a good seed in good soil, under favoring conditions, was ripened into a glorious harvest.

It is the same with all others who go forward in the spirit of obedience to God, and devote themselves to the work that He, by special call, or by his providence, has assigned them. They are, in this thing, " laborers together with God." The great end for which God permits them to labor with Him can no more fail of being reached than the Almighty can fail to bring about his own purposes. The way of obedience to God, in the doing of the work to which He calls men, is the way towards entire success, and a glorious triumph.

Most of those who have been conspicuous as leaders in great and good works have died, as Peter died, while as yet their work was almost without a harvest, — saving a harvest of personal obloquy and misrepresentation and persecution. Good causes come to maturity slowly in this world. Good influences have to struggle long and hard before they can prevail over those influences that oppose them, and secure for men the benign and elevating effects for which they are sent. Truth has to bear long and strive hard before it can gain the ear and the heart of those who cherish error. Everything good is of slow growth in a sinful world. They who toil for that which is good must, therefore, toil not only patiently, but in faith. They cannot walk by sight. One sows, and another reaps; and between the sowing and the reaping the sower is often, generally, indeed, called away, so that he is not permitted to see it. Yet the harvest is sure; and he shall rejoice in it. " His works do follow him " into the revelations and fruitions of the future world.

If any despond because they cannot see their labors for good ripening into rich and abundant harvests under their own immediate inspection, let them remember that the perfecting of results is not their work. They may prepare the soil, they may sow the seed, they may watch and water it with faithfulness, but the bringing forth of the germ, the developing of the stalk, the filling out and ripening of the grain, is not theirs. Paul may plant; Apollos water; but God giveth the increase. If they are sad that they cannot do these things too as well as the first, let them hear the Lord saying to them, " What is that to thee?" That is my business; why do you meddle with it? Be true to me in the doing of that which I have committed to you, and I will see to it that you fail not of your reward, and that your works fail not of grand and satisfying results.

Let this test, "What is that to thee?" be now applied to whatever asks our time and attention, and it will at once set many a perplexing question in a clear light before us. Let the inquiry be heard as from the Lord Himself, and let a conscientious answer be given to one's own heart, and there will remain but little darkness on most questions of duty. No man can do everything, and he is not required to try. Let the question, "What is that to thee?" be put to one's self in the presence of the multitude of claims that clamor for satisfaction at his hands, and it will be like the magnet to the particles of iron amid surrounding dust. All that belongs to him will come forth and fasten itself on his conscience, and commend itself to his judgment, and that which does not belong to him will fall away from his thoughts and from his sphere of activity.

Let this test be applied to most that you, my impenitent and unsaved hearer, are engaged with, and what would be the result? You are in sin; your soul is lost; with a mind that will think, and a heart that will feel forever, either in heaven or in hell; and with God's command and invitation to flee from the wrath to come and lay hold on eternal life, you are going on in steady disobedience to his command and disregard of his invitation, and making your way surely and rapidly to death. Does not the voice of divine love and compassion cry to you as you go from one thing to another, but still leave your eternal well-being uncared for; does it not cry, "What is this to thee?" while heaven is not secured, and your steps are leading down to death? You are like one who is at ease, taking his recreations, seeking his amusements, on board a sinking ship, while the last chance for his escape is passing away from his reach. "What is that to thee?" you would say to such an one; what is that to thee, while your life is in peril, and your only hope of escape is neglected? So our Lord is saying to you, as He looks upon your godless life, and beholds you given wholly to the things of the present world. He cries to you, "Seek first the kingdom of God and his righteousness. What shall it profit a man if he gain the whole world, and lose his own soul?"

What is that to thee? What is anything to thee, while God is crying to you, "Turn ye, turn ye, for why will ye die?"

Let this test be applied to much that Christians themselves are doing, and how great the change that it would work in their manner of life. The occupation of the slanderer, the tattler, the backbiter, the meddler, the busybody in other men's matters, would all be gone in a moment. What a holy calm, what a healthful peace would come over human society. "Where no wood is there the fire goeth out: so where there is no tale bearer the strife ceaseth." How too it would humble the worldly and self-seeking disciple, and infuse into his soul a higher spirituality and nobler consecration! How many schemes of proud and vain ambition would it scatter as the wind drives away the chaff. What is that to thee? heard as from the Lord, and answered as in the presence of the Lord, would soon fill many of our hearts with a peace they have not known for a long time. It would turn away our thoughts from many a vanity, from many a folly, from many a sin, and fix them on eternal realities, and fill them with heaven and God. It would dry up many a fountain of evil and injury to ourselves and others. It would sap the foundations of selfishness and apathy, and open the way speedily to such devotion to the will of the Lord, and the work of glorifying Him in the saving of souls, that there would be little room in our minds, and less disposition, for the indulgence of trifling or meddlesomeness. "What is that to thee?" Hear it from God, dear friends, and answer it in view of the judgment of the great day, respecting every object, and every engagement that claims your time or your attention.

SERMON XXXVI.

MANSIONS IN HEAVEN.

———◆———

JOHN xiv. 2, 3. — *In my Father's house are many mansions: if it were not so, I would have told you. I go to prepare a place for you. And if I go and prepare a place for you, I will come again and receive you unto myself; that where I am, there ye may be also.*

OUR Lord spake these words to reassure and comfort the minds of his disciples. He had just told them that He was about to leave them: " Little children, yet a little while I am with you. Ye shall seek me; and, as I said unto the Jews, Whither I go, ye cannot come, so now I say to you." Besides this He had just announced the startling fact that one of their number was a traitor, and would deliver Him up to his enemies: " He was troubled in spirit, and testified, and said, Verily, verily, I say unto you, that one of you shall betray me." Added yet to this was the announcement that even Peter, who seemed foremost in his devotion, and bravest in his attachment to his master, would, that very night, thrice deny Him.

All these things were disheartening. They were a severe strain upon the courage and faith of the disciples. All their fondest hopes were sadly shaken, if not utterly cast down. They must have been greatly perplexed. Could it be that one of that trusted band was false-hearted, and ready to turn against their Master? Could it be that the very leader of their number, the most forward and daring of them all, was so soon to deny all knowledge of his Master, and all association with Him! They were not prepared for such announcements. If these things were true, what assurance had any of them that their own fidelity would not give way, and they themselves turn against both their Lord and his cause, for whom, and for which, they had supposed themselves ready to lay down their lives? If what they had heard was true, and they were their

Lord's words that they heard, how weak, how dependent, how insufficient of themselves, were they for the work, and the responsibilities, and the realities, to which they had been called, and to which they had supposed themselves unsparingly devoted!

All this weakness and unfaithfulness and unfitness was theirs while their Master was present with them; and would be theirs even if he were to remain with them. But He was not to remain with them. The moment of their realization of their need of Him, and of their helplessness without Him, is the chosen moment to break the unwelcome news that He is soon to leave them, and go where they cannot accompany Him.

If we bring the scene clearly before our minds, I think it will be evident that this must have been one of the darkest and most trying hours in the whole history of their discipleship. Everything seemed lost. They saw themselves homeless, friendless, deserted, and were perplexed and uncertain beyond measure regarding the past, and dispirited, and hopeless, and full of anxious forebodings regarding the future.

It was to sustain them in this hour of depression, and comfort them in the sorrow that was beginning now to come upon them, and to prepare them to meet the stern and trying realities into which they were entering, that He addressed to them the words of our text, and those in immediate connection with it. He leads their minds up to sources of consolation and support which certainly will not fail them, however severe the trials through which they may have to pass. In other words He brings them to exercise that faith which He has implanted in them, by teaching them to look away from the things that are seen and temporal, to those that are unseen and eternal; and to begin to endure as seeing Him who is invisible. "Let not your hearts be troubled. Ye believe in God. Believe also in me. In my Father's house are many mansions. If it had not been so I would have told you. I go to prepare a place for you; and if I go and prepare a place for you, I will come again and receive you unto myself, that where I am, there ye may be also."

1. The first sustaining and comforting thought which He impresses upon their minds is, that there is a home for them in heaven.

This is the exact thought and implication of the words, "In my Father's house are many mansions." It was true that they were to be left desolate in a world that had as sufficient portion for them, no permanent resting-place, no home, no friends. By the failure of their earthly hopes in the swamping of that cause for the sake of which they had abandoned all other causes, He gave them to understand that they saw only their real condition. He did not deny, He did not wish to, that the failure of his own cause, in the light in which they had been accustomed to view it, left them portionless wanderers, and outcasts among men. All this He would not conceal from them; but, on the contrary, He would have them see and understand it yet more clearly. He Himself sees it, and acknowledges it. He has seen it from the first, and He is therefore as calm, as undisturbed in spirit now as He had been at any previous moment of his history. He would have them so too. Hence He says to them, "Let not your heart be troubled. Still have faith in God. Still have faith in me. Your earthly hopes are gone, I know; I have always known that they would fail; they never will be realized. They have never, as a matter of fact, been justified. They never had any foundation in truth. But be not disturbed: there is something higher, more noble, more blessed to which you have been called, and which I have always had in view for you. God has not deceived you: I have not trifled with your feelings, nor abused your confidence. Trust us still; and let your troubled hearts be at rest. Though you are homeless and portionless on earth, there is an inheritance for you in heaven. Though you are destined to bitter disappointment in your expectations of royal favors, and a dwelling-place in the earthly palace of an earthly Messiah, yet in my Father's house are many mansions, dwelling-places, homes. Of these you cannot fail.

Our Lord's allusion here seems to be to what is said to have been the custom of Eastern monarchs of assigning to their courtiers habitations within their immense palaces. Here their friends and servants dwelt and were at home in the sunlight of the royal favor. So heaven, the dwelling-place of God, abounds with homes for his people. There are mansions in the heavenly palace, homes in the temple of the living God.

It was to these our Saviour directed the desponding and

troubled minds of his disciples. To these He would have them look. For these He would have them live. In these He would have them count themselves heirs to an inheritance in comparison with which all the riches of the world are trifles.

2. All this they have and must receive on his simple word; and this is the second sustaining thought that He impresses upon their minds. As in the past, so now they must count that word true, and rest in it as the word of one who was faithful. He could not deal falsely with them. He had not done so in the past. On the contrary, he had dealt in perfectly good faith with them. If all these glorious realities had not been in reserve for them He would have told them so at the first, and not drawn them into discipleship with Him, and into the abandonment of all their earthly hopes to espouse his cause, and link themselves irrevocably with his destiny.

There are few things more comforting and sustaining to a believer than that to which the Saviour here brings the minds of his disciples, namely, his perfect candor and faithfulness. He deals with men fairly. He keeps back from them nothing which it is for their highest interest to know. He reveals the truth to them in no ambiguous terms. He shows them things as they are, and they may rest in them without fear of disappointment or deception. He does not speculate nor theorize, but reveals and declares. Believers must apprehend this as the distinctive feature in their Lord's dealing with them, or they will be often perplexed and disturbed. Their hearts will be troubled. This is true of them in all their relations to the present, and to the future. In hours of present darkness and desolation they must yet trust in his faithfulness not less than when their circumstances were, to their apprehension, more favorable. He foresaw these circumstances when He called them to faith in Him; and these very circumstances are a part of the lot that He has chosen for them, in the midst of which He will be with them, and be all sufficient for them. If anything in all that they are called to endure or encounter could harm them while under his protection and guidance, He would have forewarned them of it that they might not repose any false trust in Him; or He would have led them by another way that they might have escaped. These words, "If it were not so I would have told you," are intended to steady and strengthen the faith which He urges them still, in the most trying and depressing circumstances, to have in his faithfulness.

But they look forward, also, through all that can distress or dishearten, and demand a faith in unseen realities and glories, and a hoping for them, and a trusting in them, solely upon his authoritative declaration. There is a heaven, and there are homes for them in that heaven; and this they must accept, both because if it were not so He would have told them, and also because, since it is so, He has told them. In other words, if the instinctive desires of their souls for a future state, and for a home in heaven and with God, were groundless and destined to disappointment, He would not have left them falsely to indulge these desires. His faithfulness to them and to truth would have undeceived them and saved them from the crushing disappointment that would otherwise have come upon them.

On the other hand, his words of revelation appeal directly to their desires and hopes, and make known the realities of the future beyond this world in clear and unmistakable declarations. In these they must rest, or there will be nothing to allay the anxieties and doubts and fears of a troubled heart.

And here we come to one of those subjects whose contemplation will show us, more perhaps than any other, how utterly and entirely dependent we are upon the teachings of our Saviour for satisfying knowledge. He only has brought life and immortality to light; and has done it only by the gospel. There are times in the history of us all, probably, certainly of most of us, when our whole souls are wrought up into intense thought, and almost an agony of desire to look beyond that deep, dark mystery that we call death, and know what is there. We stand by the form of some dear one who has just entered the dark mystery, and what thoughts come rushing into our minds! Oh, speak to us from that side of the river which you have crossed, we cry; speak but one word, at least one that we may know that that which was most precious to us, and which alone gave preciousness to this now cold, unmoving form, is not like it, cold, unmoving, and unconscious! But the spirit that never before failed to respond to our call is silent. Does it still live; or is it, like the body, dead? If it live, oh where is its abode? What its employments? What its nature and powers? What its relations to God and to those who went before it, and to whom it had been bound in bonds of tenderest oneness and love? But there is no response from the coffin, nor from the grave. Nor is there need that there should be. We have a surer word. To this we do well that we take heed. We have the word of Christ; and to this we are shut up. To faith his word is all sufficient; to unbelief no word could be satisfying. It would still doubt and fear, and be distressed. Stand by the lifeless form of one you love, of one in Christ, and let your soul be harrowed with questionings of what is beyond; be sure that nothing will bring calmness and assurance, until you listen believingly to the quiet but intensely positive words of Christ and his gospel: "In my father's house are many mansions, if it were not so, I would have told you," is the assertion and implication of all you want to know. A mansion is a home for an intelligent, loving, pure-minded social being. It is a place of rest, of refreshment, of peaceful quiet, and of tender and loving converse with those whom we know, who are dear to us, and who are one with us in interest and in aims. Many mansions are many such homes for many such beings. Mansions in the house of God are homes in heaven, homes filled with the light of his favor, and free from all that can harm, or hinder those who dwell in them from the fullest enjoyment and the most unrestrained and satisfying use of all their powers and faculties. It is when we can rise up to the demand made upon us by our Saviour, and truly believe in God and in Him, that our hearts cease to be troubled upon the questions that have agitated and distressed us.

There is a heaven and in it there are many mansions for Christ's people. This we know upon his own testimony. All his ministry for us, and all his dealings with us sustain the argument which He himself here urges in behalf of his faithfulness, "If it were not so I would have told you."

3. The third thought with which He met the troubled hearts of his disciples and comforted them, was that in leaving them He went away to make these mansions secure for them, "I go to prepare a place for you."

Those heavenly mansions had all been forfeited. There was none of all the race of men that had any inheritance in them.

By their sin against God they had alienated their inheritance in them, and the way to heaven was barred forever against them if they were left to themselves. That barrier must be removed by the interposition of the only begotten Son of God, and the forfeited mansions must be recovered for them by his redemption, or there was no hope, no heaven, no home for them.

This was the work for the accomplishment of which He left them. The sins by which they had forfeited their inheritance in heaven must be atoned for. The blood of the Son of God must become their propitiation. Hence it is written, that once in the end of the world He hath appeared to take away sin by the sacrifice of Himself, and his blood cleanseth from all sin. He died to make amends for his people's crimes, and thus to remove the barriers that shut heaven against them, and to bring the mansions of heaven once more within the possibility of possession by them. Hence again it is written, "Christ is not entered into the holy places made with hands, which are the figures of the true; but into heaven itself, now to appear in the presence of God for us." " Now, once in the end of the world hath He appeared to put away sin by the sacrifice of himself."

Thus it was that He prepared a place in heaven for those who believe in Him. For this purpose He left his disciples, and went by a way that they could not go, *i. e.*, by the satisfaction which He himself made to the divine law, unto the Father's presence.

4. But He will come back to his disciples again and take them to Himself. This is the fourth and crowning thought with which He reassures and sustains them in their hour of trial and sorrow: "If I go away," or as surely as I go away, " I will come again and receive you unto myself; that where I am there ye may be also." His interest in them will not cease nor flag. Though absent from them bodily, yet his heart is with them. His going away is purely for their sake. As a father goes before into a distant land and prepares a home that he may return and take his family to it, and that they may then abide with him, so did our Lord go away from his followers only to prepare a place for them, and return and bring them to be with Him forever in his glory.

But when and how does He come and receive his disciples unto Himself?

There is to be a second glorious coming of Christ to raise the bodies of his people from their resting-places in the earth, and transform them into the likeness of his glorious body, by the working of that mighty power whereby He is able even to subdue all things unto Himself. This will be a day of triumph for them, and a day of joyous reunion, not alone of soul and body, but of themselves with each other and with their Lord. It will be a day wherein his words of promise before us will have their perfect fulfillment. But his followers do not remain separated from Him, nor are they till then deprived of communion with Him in his immediate and manifested presence. This is an official coming, if we may use the expression. It is his coming as the Judge of the world and the Head of the Church. It is his coming in final triumph, and for the final perfecting of his Church in the eyes of the intelligent universe. In this coming all believers are equally interested, and it concerns them all alike. It is not individual and special like that coming which is indicated by the text. It is not that coming to them by which He calls them each by name and leads them out.

The teachings of the New Testament leave us in no doubt as to the time and manner of this coming. His own words to the thief on the cross, you know, were, " This day shalt thou be with me in Paradise." That was the day of his death. Our Lord had gone before him; had shed the blood of atonement, had paid the ransom price for the heavenly inheritance, and had begun his all-prevailing intercessions at the throne of once offended but now satisfied justice; this He had done before the penitent and believing suppliant had done with earthly life. The way was therefore open for his departing soul, and the blessed mansions were prepared for his occupancy. The day of his death was the day of the Lord's special coming to him and of his receiving him to Himself, that where He was there he might be also.

Again the great Apostle writes to sustain the Corinthian Christians under their heavy trials and persecutions, and to cheer them to meet death calmly if it comes, " We are always confident, knowing that whilst we are at home in the body we are absent from the Lord; we are confident, I say, and willing rather to be absent from the body and to be present with the Lord." To be absent from the body was to be present with the Lord. At their death, therefore, their Lord returned and received them unto Himself that where He was they might be also.

With this agrees also Paul's own intense desires as he speaks of them to the Philippians: "I am in a strait betwixt two, having a desire to depart and be with Christ, which is far better; nevertheless to abide in the flesh is more needful for you." For him to depart from the flesh was to be with Christ. But to depart from the flesh is to die. To die then is to come into that state which the Lord's words in our text promise to his disciples. In their death He comes and receives them unto Himself, that where He is there they may be also.

This is the individual and special coming which He promises them. It is then He reveals Himself to his people as their present Lord and Redeemer, as He has never revealed Himself to them before. Then their faith in his spiritual presence gives place to positive knowledge and distinct conscious apprehension of his glorious bodily presence, and then they are received in the homes that his atonement and intercession have prepared for them, and they abide with Him thenceforth in unbroken and eternal communion.

In this is the highest bliss of a disciple of Christ, " To be with Him." As his going away from the twelve was, and as his withdrawing the sense of his presence from all believers, is the most saddening of all things to them, that around which all their other causes of sorrow gathered as their centre and support, so his coming and receiving them to Himself to be with Him evermore, is the removal of all their sorrow and sadness and the perfection of all their joy. Thus the Psalmist sung, " In thy presence is fullness of joy ; at thy right hand there are pleasures for evermore."

In the light of this passage of Scripture I remark, —

1. It is right — nay, indeed, it is our duty — to draw comfort and support during the cares and trials, and anxieties and depressing influences of the present life from anticipations of heaven. They who deny this right to the followers of Christ have not rightly apprehended his religion. This is a religion of service, it is true, but it is also a religion of anticipation, of

hope, of joyful expectation. Often did our Saviour, and often did his Apostles, as did the holy men of old, strengthen and refresh their souls by this communion with heaven. "Our conversation," says Paul, "is in heaven, whence also we look for the Lord Jesus Christ. Seek those things which are above where Christ sitteth at the right hand of God."

Present ills and sorrows, cares and toils, are to be counterbalanced by such communion of the soul with the unfading glories and eternal felicities of the home made sure for every friend of Christ in heaven. It is his privilege to sing continually, —

> "When I can read my title clear
> To mansions in the skies,
> I'll bid farewell to every fear,
> And wipe my weeping eyes.
>
> "There shall I bathe my weary soul
> In seas of heavenly rest,
> And not a wave of trouble roll
> Across my peaceful breast."

2. It is right and highly proper that we should think of our believing friends who have departed from us in death and speak of them and comfort ourselves with the assurance, that for them to be absent from the body is to be present with the Lord. They have departed to be with Christ, which is far better for them than to abide in the flesh. We may thus silence every cavilling thought as to their true condition ; we may anticipate the day of blessed reunion with them ; we may rise above that saddening, sickening sense of loss that comes over us in the first dread realization that death has finally done his work upon them, and when we see the grave close over their remains, and when we return to the desolated home that will know their presence no more. Oh, if we can then receive the Saviour's words and rest in them, that sense of loss will depart from us. True we shall miss them, and we shall mourn for them, but we shall not mourn as those who have no hope ; nor shall we miss them as forever lost to us. Our hearts will be cheered and soothed by the sweet influences of the truth respecting their condition, and of the hope which is proffered us of one day joining them in their glorious mansions and in the house of their Father.

We shall cease, then, any longer to think of them as dead or as in the grave. Our Lord's words will come to us with new meaning and power, "He that liveth and believeth in me shall never die." And we shall have a new understanding of the words of the beloved disciple, "I heard a voice from heaven saying unto me, Write, Blessed are the dead who die in the Lord, from henceforth: Yea, saith the Spirit, that they may rest from their labors, and their works do follow them." We shall respond cheerfully to the Apostle's words respecting himself, and true of every believer: "To me to live is Christ, and to die is gain."

To you, then, who mourn the death of your believing friends, let me use the Saviour's language, as I too have heard it by the coffin and the grave: Let not your hearts be troubled. Believe in God. Believe also in his Son. In his Father's house are many mansions. If it were not so He would have told you; and in coming to your friends in death He has come to receive them unto Himself, as the bridegroom receives his bride, that they may be with Him henceforth forever.

SERMON XXXVII.

THE PERPETUITY OF THE SABBATH.

MARK ii. 27, 28.—*And He said unto them, The Sabbath was made for man, and not man for the Sabbath; therefore the Son of man is Lord also of the Sabbath.*

OUR Lord here sets forth the doctrine of the Sabbath. His words distinctly assert three things regarding it, and as distinctly imply three more.

Before we proceed to notice these assertions and implications, it may be well for us to call to mind the fact that the word Sabbath means simply rest; and that the Sabbath day is simply the rest day. In the passage before us, as in every other that contains the word Sabbath, we should only be giving English for Hebrew if we should read rest day instead of Sabbath. "The rest day was made for man."

1. The first assertion of the text is, that the Sabbath was made. The implication is, that it was made by God. It is an institution of God, and not an invention of man.

The question arises, when was the Sabbath instituted? The fact that it was instituted is denied by none who do not reject the truthfulness of the Bible. But there is a strange misapprehension in the public mind as to the time of its institution; and out of this misapprehension have come equally strange reasonings regarding the character and authority of the Sabbath itself. Almost all the objections which are urged against the authority of the Sabbath, and nearly all the reasons given for the non-observance or perversion of it, rest on the assumption that the Sabbath was instituted at the same time with the institution of the ceremonial and ritual service of the Jews on Mount Sinai. The argument drawn from this assumption is that the Sabbath was simply a part of the Jewish Ceremonial Law, and, as such, passed away when that Law was fulfilled in the coming and work of the Messiah. But nothing could be farther from the truth than this assumption is; and nothing could be more erroneous than this reasoning. It is no nearer the truth to say that the worship of the one only living and true God was instituted at the giving of the Law on Sinai, or that the Moral Law was then instituted, than to say that the Sabbath was then instituted. Both the moral law and the Sabbath had existed from the beginning of human history. They were reiterated on Sinai, and enforced with special sanctions. The Sabbath, like some, if not all, the other precepts of the Decalogue, was then invested with certain special and peculiarly Jewish forms of observance. Like every other precept of the Decalogue, the Sabbath was to be observed by the Jews in a certain prescribed form. This form of observance was instituted on Sinai,—but not the Sabbath itself. These forms, both those pertaining to the observance of the moral precepts, and of the Sabbath, came to an end when the object of their institution had been accomplished in the development of Jewish history, but the authority of moral principles did not then come to an end, nor did the institution of the Sabbath then come to an end. Both remained as they were before. All that was ceremonial and Jewish passed away; all that was original and fundamental continued.

All arguments, therefore, that assume that the Sabbath was a Jewish institution, having its origin with other peculiarly Jewish enactments, and passing away when they passed away, are false; and all inferences drawn from them are false.

It requires but a moment's attention to the sacred narrative of the creation, and of the history of the world from that time onward, to the nationalizing of Israel at the foot of Sinai, to correct this false assumption. This narrative brings the institution of the Sabbath before us as the first of all divine appointments for man, as distinguished from the brute creation, and marks the fact of its observance through the intervening centuries with sufficient clearness to be easily traced, although, as was necessary in so condensed a narrative, and as is the case with all other general topics, its mention was rather incidental than direct.

The act of institution itself is, however, stated with explicitness. It took place at the beginning of man's existence. " Thus the heavens and the earth were finished, and all the host of them. And on the seventh day God ended his work which He had made ; and He rested on the seventh day from all his work which He had made. And God blessed the seventh day, and sanctified it: because that in it He had rested from all his work which He had created and made." This was the institution of the Sabbath. It had its beginning with the beginning of the human race.

When the Jewish Law was proclaimed from Sinai, the fact of this original institution of the Sabbath was distinctly brought forward by Jehovah, and given as the reason why the Sabbatic precept was put with the other precepts of the Decalogue. The command is, "Remember"— call to mind and hold in the memory — " the Sabbath day, to keep it holy. Six days shalt thou labor, and do all thy work: but the seventh day is the Sabbath of the Lord thy God: in it thou shalt not do any work, thou, nor thy son, nor thy daughter, thy manservant, nor thy maid-servant, nor thy cattle, nor thy stranger that is within thy gates." This is the command, and a part of its special prescriptive environment. Then follows this declaration as a reason for it all: " For in six days the Lord made heaven and earth, the sea, and all that in them is, and rested the seventh day : wherefore God blessed the Sabbath day and hallowed it." As each of the other precepts was given because the principle which it involved was established in the creation of moral agents, and must ever run parallel with their existence ; so this precept, which sets forth the observance of the Sabbath as a duty, was given at the creation of man, and its obligation runs parallel with his existence on the earth. The " for " in the reason that follows the giving of the fourth commandment, has this force : " Remember the Sabbath day, to keep it holy," — " for its institution runs back to the beginning of human history, and is not only fundamental to the well-being of men, but an expression of the will of their Creator regarding them in all their earthly life."

I have said that the narrative of human history from the creation of man to the nationalizing of Israel before Sinai, showed distinct marks of the observance of the Sabbath during that time. These marks, I repeat, are rather incidental and allusive than direct and primary. Nevertheless, they are suffi cient to show that what God instituted at the creation He did not permit to come to naught, nor be forgotten.

These marks are found in the evident fact that the patriarchs, both before and after the Deluge, were accustomed to a seven days' division of time, and that God regarded it in his dealings with them. Thus we find that seven days was the time that God gave Noah from the going forth of his final command to him to enter the ark, until He brought the waters upon the earth. Seven days was the time that Noah delayed between the first and second sending out of the dove from the ark; and seven days was the time between her return with the olive leaf and her final sending forth. It was "a week" that Jacob was compelled to wait for Rachel after the cruel deception that had been practiced upon him by his father-in-law.

That these seventh day divisions, and the observance of weeks, was in view of the Sabbath, becomes almost if not quite certain, when we find the same division prevailing among the Israelites immediately after their departure from Egypt, and before they came to Sinai. It was before the giving of the Law on that Mount that the manna was furnished for their food. In promising it, and in giving directions concerning it, the Lord addressed them as though they already understood and observed the Sabbath: "Then said the Lord unto Moses, Behold, I will rain bread from heaven for you; and the people shall go out and gather a certain rate every day; and it shall come to pass that on the sixth day they shall prepare that which they bring in, and it shall be twice as much as they gather daily. And it came to pass that on the sixth day they gathered twice as much bread, two omers for one man. And all the rulers of the congregation came and told Moses. And he said unto them, This is that which the Lord hath said, To-morrow is the rest of the holy Sabbath unto the Lord: bake that which ye will bake to-day, and seethe that ye will seethe, and that which remaineth over lay up for you to be kept until the morning." And when the people found that the quantity which was kept over now did not spoil and become corrupt, as it did when they attempted to keep it over on other days, Moses said to them, "Eat that to-day; for to-day is a Sabbath unto the Lord; to-day ye shall not find it in the field. Six days shall ye gather it, but on the seventh day, which is the Sabbath, in it there shall be none."

You perceive then that this whole narrative of the giving of the manna in the wilderness assumes that the children of Israel knew of the Sabbath, and that their division of time into weeks was made by the observance of it. It is seen also by this narrative that God emphasized his claim to this day in his dealings with them before He gave them the Law from the Mount. It is plain, therefore, that the Sabbath existed as an ordinance of God before the giving of the Law, and that the people understood it, and that when they were commanded, soon after, to "Remember it," they were commanded to keep in memory a thing of which they already had knowledge, and not to give heed to a thing then for the first time made known to them. They, as did their fathers, knew of the Sabbath that was instituted at the creation, and by it were accustomed to mark their most common division of time.

These facts establish the truth, then, of what we have said, that the Sabbath was not instituted on Mount Sinai at the giving of the Law. It was there recognized, as the moral principles of the Law were, as already existing; and, as they were, was invested prescriptively with some things peculiarly Jewish. It was, in itself, in all its essential features, instituted at the close of the work of creation, and was never permitted to fall utterly away from the memory of the men to whom God made Himself known by supernatural revelations.

2. This brings us to the second assertion of our text and its second implication: "The Sabbath was made for man." This is the assertion. The implication is that no man, nor any set of men, can rightfully or lawfully deprive any man of the enjoyment of the Sabbath.

The fact that God instituted the Sabbath, and made its observance begin with the beginning of human history, would seem to be enough to establish the fact asserted by our Saviour, even if He had not asserted it. As we have seen, in considering the time of its institution, everything connected with its beginning and history shows that it was made for man,—that is, for mankind. Its institution was for man's sake; and regarded him, not as connected with any age, or any nationality, but as belonging to time, and as a member of the human race. It was not made for the Jews, nor is it in any sense a Jewish institution, any more than the worship and service of God is a Jewish institution. Because, e. g., men, as men, have been endowed with faculties by which they may know God and honor Him, therefore it is their duty and privilege as men to worship and serve Him. Because they have as men been invested by their Creator with the rights and privileges of his Sabbath, therefore it belongs to them as men to observe and enjoy it. There is no more Judaism in the one than in the other. There is no more of the ceremonial and ritual in the one than in the other. The one can no more pass away and become obsolete than the other. The worship and service of God are permitted to man, as man, as his inalienable privilege. The rest of one day in seven, for special devotion to this worship and service, is permitted to man, as man, as his inalienable privilege.

All this is asserted by these words of our Saviour, "The Sabbath was made for man," and he who claims that the Sabbath was made only for the Jews contradicts the words of our Saviour. If the Sabbath was a Jewish institution, having its origin with the ceremonial law that was to be fulfilled and come to an end in Christ; and was, as some claim, abrogated by the coming of Christ, then there is no sense in which our Saviour's words can be maintained. If the Sabbath was made for Jews only, it was not made for man; but it was made for only a small class of men, and for them for only a portion of the time which man has existed and is to exist on the earth. On the contrary, our Lord's word for man is the most general that can be used [διὰ τὸν ἄνθρωπον] and its range of application covers all classes of men, and all time.

The implication, then, is too plain to be denied, that when our Lord says "the Sabbath was made for man," He claims for man as man a privilege and right in the Sabbath of which no man, nor any set of men, may lawfully or rightfully deprive him. It belongs to him because he is a man. God has given it to him. He who deprives him of it sets himself against God, and robs him of that which God has bestowed upon him as his inalienable right and blessing. No one can rightfully take it from him; nor can he rightfully take it from himself. It belongs to him by God's ordination, as his own person and life and as air and food and water belong to him. If he robs himself of his Sabbath he thwarts the ordination of God, throwing away that with which God has invested him and which is, by the ordering of God, inalienable. He, therefore, who refuses to take and enjoy the Sabbath that God has made for him, not only insults God, but he becomes a moral suicide, as clearly and as guiltily as he would become a physical suicide who should refuse to breathe the air that God made for him to breathe, or take the food that he gave Him to eat, or the water He gave him to drink. God made the Sabbath for him as much as He made air, food, and drink for him. It is not only his privilege but his duty to use it, and be blessed by it, as much as it is to use them and live by them so long as God permits him to stay upon the earth.

And the history of the Sabbath shows that God has guarded the Sabbath by constitutional and natural sanctions, just as He has every other ordination which He has made for the good of men as men. They cannot habitually neglect the Sabbath and treat themselves on it as they treat themselves on the other days of the week, and not suffer injury and loss. A man may, *e. g.*, if he chooses, deny himself the food that God has created for him; but if he does, he will become a self-murderer. He may refuse to enjoy the sleep that God has ordained for him; but if he does his constitution will become shattered, and he will perish with the guilt of a suicide on his soul. He may, if he will, violate every moral principle by which God has ordained that a moral agent shall be governed; but if he does he will bring upon himself, not simply the disfavor of God, but the inevitable fruits of vice and immorality. He may thus, if he will disregard God's gift and ordinance of the Sabbath; but if he does, all history shows that he will reap the fruit of self-abuse, and of sinning against the mercy of God.

The Sabbath was made for man. He needs it, and must have it or suffer for want of it.

3. I come now to the third assertion, and the third implication of our text. "The Son of man is Lord also of the Sabbath." This is the assertion. The implication is that any change in the day itself, or in the manner of keeping it which He may sanction, is authorized, and men ought everywhere to conform to it.

The Pharisees complained to Him that his disciples, in following Him through the field of grain, and satisfying their hunger by plucking and eating of it, were breaking the Sabbath. He admitted that their complaint was well grounded so far as the literal application of the merely Jewish precepts regarding the manner of observing the Sabbath was concerned. But he throws Himself back of these precepts upon the great primary and unchanging purpose of the Sabbath itself, irrespective of any prescriptive rules; and asserting the universality of the Sabbath as made for man, and not for the Jews alone, He draws the inference which is contained in this assertion: "Therefore because the Sabbath is of this character, the Son of man is Lord of it." He is man's sovereign and it belongs to Him to rule in all that pertains to man's well-being. Nothing that concerns this is excepted from his Lordship. It is his prerogative to legislate as He will regarding it. No man may call Him to account for what He may enjoin or authorize; and no man may set aside or disallow what He ordains. The Sabbath itself He will not annul, for it was made for man. But the manner in which the Sabbath shall be observed and enjoyed He will Himself prescribe. The Sabbath itself, with all its primary and fundamental purposes, shall go into and become a part of the privileges and blessing of his kingdom; but the manner in which it shall be observed and enjoyed shall be Christian and not Jewish.

All this is clearly contained in the declaration, "The Son of man is Lord also of the Sabbath." Accordingly we find that his disciples immediately after his crucifixion began to act on the principle that He had announced. Their rest and worship day began to be one chosen out of respect to their Lord's resurrection. The manner of observing and enjoying this day was in harmony with Christian rather than Jewish institutions. They denied the authority of all that was Jewish in the Sabbath; and repudiated it as a burden to which a Christian ought not to submit. It had had its day, and, like all the rest that was merely ceremonial in the Mosaic Law, was fulfilled and done away by Christ.

The Apostles, therefore, went boldly forward and took the first day of the week for their Sabbath, and filled this day with services peculiarly Christian in their character. Their rest day became one for the joyous assembling together of those who had hope through the resurrection of Christ, for the preaching and hearing of the word of Christ, and for the breaking of bread in commemoration of the death of Christ.

Here is our authority for the observance of the first day of the week instead of the seventh of the week, and of our giving the day to Christian services. The Lord's Apostles who were commissioned to lay the foundations of the Christian institutions, and who were guided by the unerring Spirit and sustained, for a time, by the weekly visits of their risen Lord, made the first day of the week their special rest and worship day, and invested it with all the characteristics that render it a Christian Sabbath. They acted in Christ's name, and by his authority. Their acts were his, therefore, and his Lordship justified them in doing as they did, and binds us and all men to follow in their footsteps. You must admit this conclusion, or you must deny the authority of Apostolic example in the establishment and observance of Christian institutions. But you do not deny this. You rest upon it as upon the truth itself. You must, therefore, hold to the Christian Sabbath and feel your obligation to remember it and keep it holy as an ordinance of your Lord which no man has the right to annul or neglect.

Remarks. 1. The Sabbath is to the Christian rather a privilege than a law. To observe it is rather freedom than restraint. It is the privilege of resting from toil; the freedom to worship and serve God unmolested by secular cares and occupations. To observe it, in the way that comports with the spirit and teachings of the gospel, is to enjoy the privilege of a nearer and more intimate communion with God and eternal things, and to live, by foretaste, in the glorious freedom of a perfect and sinless service of God in heaven. To the saint it is this. To the sinner it is to embrace and improve God's chosen time for the seeking of salvation, and laying hold of eternal life.

2. They who encourage men to disregard the Sabbath, and give their influence against its divine authority and perpetual obligation, set themselves in opposition to Christ and his teachings, and become the enemies and ill advisers of their fellowmen. Christ declares that the Sabbath was made for man. They deny this, and assert that it was made only for the Jews. His words imply that it was made for the good of man, and that men will be benefited by observing it. They declare that it is not good for men, and that its observance will bring them harm.

With whom will you go, my hearers? Will you take sides with Christ and uphold the institution which He has indorsed, and of which He is sovereign Lord? Or, will you go with those who contradict his words and trample on his authority? Your treatment of the Christian Sabbath will be the answer which you will give to these questions. Go against Christ and you go for the degradation and barbarizing of our land. Go with Christ and you go for the best interests of men in this world and the world to come; for the best interest of your own soul now and hereafter, and, above all, for the honor and authority of the Lord Jesus Christ.

ESSAYS.

THE PENALTY OF SIN.

WE propose to consider the question: "What is the penalty of sin for man in the government of God?"

Penalty has been defined to be "the suffering in person or property, which is annexed by law or judicial decision to the commission of a crime, offense, or trespass, as a punishment." The limitation, "by law or judicial decision," is essential to the correctness of the definition. Sufferings which are not inflicted by law, or judicial decision, are not penalty. It would, perhaps, express more accurately the relation of penalty to law to say, that it is the suffering which is threatened by the law itself, in its penal clause, as the punishment of him who transgresses it. When penalty is inflicted upon the transgressor of any law, it is just that which is thus threatened, and nothing else, judicially visited upon him.

Nothing can be properly named penalty which is not contained in this penal clause of the law, prescribing what shall be the punishment for its transgression. Other evils may be suffered by the transgressor as consequences of his transgression. Inflicted penalty may, also, involve him who suffers it, in a long train of evil consequences from which he can by no means escape. But unless these consequences, whether of transgression or of inflicted penalty, enter into the publication of the law as its penal sanction, and are inflicted by judicial decree, they cannot, in any proper sense of the term, be called penalty. They are only consequences. For example: if a man commits murder in this Commonwealth, the only thing which the law that forbids murder carries with it in its publication, as a penal threatening, is death, — "that intrusive reminiscence of more barbarous times," according to the quiet and very positive assumption of our progressive chief magistrate. Whatever else the murderer may suffer as the consequence of his crime, if he does not suffer death by a judicial sentence, the penalty of his crime is not inflicted upon him. Pangs of conscience, days of anxiety and nights of terror, disgrace to himself and his family, imprisonment and impoverishment, — none of these enter into his penalty, though they are consequences, some of them of his crime, others of his being accused of crime. Again: one who commits forgery may suffer disgrace, may see his family ruined, his prospects in business hopelessly blighted, his property wasted ; not as the immediate consequences of his crime, but of the penalty which the law threatens as the punishment of the forger, and which is inflicted upon him by judicial authority. His confinement to hard labor in the state prison, this, and nothing else, is the penalty of his crime.

Such is penalty, regarded in its relation to law. It is found to be the same when we look at it in its relation to pardon. Pardon, in any given instance, is an exact and full measure of all the decreed penalty that has not been executed upon the transgressor at the time when his pardon takes effect. In the case of the condemned murderer, if executive clemency reaches him in the form of pardon, it simply removes from him the sentence of death. It does nothing more. It removes not one other consequence of his crime. And so, if pardon is extended to the forger, who has been convicted and sentenced for his crime, and is already suffering his punishment, it simply opens his prison door, and bids him go free, without suffering the remainder of his sentence. Not one of the many evils that his penalty has dragged in its train of consequences is removed by his pardon. It does not restore to him, nor to his family, the honor and respect which a convict's doom wrenched from them ; it does not bring back his ruined business nor his wasted property. If he ever regains these he regains them through some other instrumentality than that of pardon. This has taken off from him that, and only that, which was made his punishment by the penal clause of the law which he transgressed.

Penalty is thus limited, whatever be the law for whose violation it is the punishment. All law, to be law, must be sustained by penal sanctions ; and these, to be of effect, must be announced with the law itself in its publication. They are penalty only as they are sanctions, and they are sanctions only as they go forth in the publication of the law to deter those who are subject to it from transgression. We are brought, then, to this conclusion regarding the penalty of sin for man in the government of God; that it is just what the law of God, by its penal clause, announced to man as his punishment if he should transgress. The penal clause in the law of God, like the penal clause in any other law, is properly a judicial threatening of punishment to deter those to whom it is given from transgression, and to uphold its authority. To decide what the penalty of sin is, we have, therefore, only to look at the penal clause of the law of God in the only announcement of it which was ever made to men who had not already sinned. To these only could the penal clause be intended as a deterring threat. To such as have sinned it is the measure of the punishment to which they are already doomed.

We must go back, then, to God's dealings with sinless man, to find by what legal threatening He enforced upon him the authority of his law to deter him from transgressing it. The only instance on record of such dealing is that wherein God forbade the first, the only sinless man, to eat of "the fruit of the tree of knowledge of good and evil." This was an announcement of divine law. The history of the transaction, and other portions of the Scriptures, make it out clearly to have been the formal publishing of the law of God to man. We know not how fully the Lawgiver, in his dealings with Adam, explained the law in its bearings upon moral beings, and upon their relations to each other, and to Himself. But this much is clear, that God invested this single prohibition with all his authority. The whole of the divine law, so far as the authority of God was concerned, was summed up in these simple words: "Of every tree of the garden thou mayest freely eat; but of the tree of knowledge of good and evil, thou shalt not eat of it." This brought the whole of God's authority upon man, and reduced all questions touching the relation which he was to sustain to his Creator to this: whether or not he would be governed by his authority. The prohibition which narrowed the case down to this point, and was thus invested with all the authority of God, was itself the law of God.

Now, what was threatened as the punishment for transgressing this law? For if we examine the prohibition we see that it has its penal clause, a threatening of punishment to deter from transgression. The thing threatened was simply and only death. The only penal clause that went with the law, when it was given, and none was ever added afterward, to deter sinless men from sinning, was this: "for in the day that thou eatest thereof thou shalt surely die." Nothing else was named as a consequence or a punishment. This one clause contained all the penal sanction by which the authority of the law of God was sustained. Nothing else but death was threatened as the punishment for sin. Nothing else, therefore, but death enters into its penalty. Sin may have, and does have, many other consequences besides death following it; and death, the penalty, may, and does, draw after itself many evils which fall upon the sinner; but these do not enter into nor form any part of the penalty. They are not the punishment that the law threatened in its penal clause, nor are they removed, so that they are not still suffered by the penitent sinner, when pardon is vouchsafed to him through the atonement of Christ.

If we abide by these simple principles we shall escape the confusion which is often introduced at this point into the treatment of our subject. It is no uncommon thing to see writers and preachers go directly from the threatening contained in the penal clause of the divine law, to the divine recognition of other consequences of sin and of penalty, and incorporating these into their ideas and definitions of penalty, load it with much that was not threatened, and which pardon never removes. In this way many are brought to treat as penalty all those evils which the Lord named over to our first parents after they had sinned, and already come under the curse of transgression. These evils were dragged in the train of penalty, and had now become the fixed inheritance of man, while he should remain upon the earth; but, we repeat, they cannot be counted the penalty of his sin, because they were not contained in the penal clause of the law to deter from sin, nor are they removed from the lot of men when they are pardoned.

The evils to which we allude are those that are set forth in the third chapter of Genesis: "Unto the woman He said, I will greatly multiply thy sorrow and thy conception; in sorrow shalt thou bring forth children; and thy desire shall be to thy husband, and he shall rule over thee." And unto Adam He said, " Because thou hast hearkened unto the voice of thy wife, and hast eaten of the tree of which I commanded thee, saying, Thou shalt not eat of it; cursed is the ground for thy sake; in sorrow shalt thou eat of it all the days of thy life; and thou shalt eat the herb of the field; in the sweat of thy face shalt thou eat bread, till thou return unto the ground; for out of it wast thou taken: for dust thou art and unto dust shalt thou return."

This passage is often treated, we say, as though it were the penal clause of the divine law. But there is not one word of threatening in it to deter from sin. It holds out no hope of escape from the woes foretold. It was not uttered until after the fatal transgression had been committed, and the divine threatening that contained the penalty had already taken effect upon the guilty pair. The passage was simply the foretelling of those woes which were now unavoidable, whether those to whom it was addressed ever sinned again or not. And, we repeat it, not one of the evils of which the Lord here speaks is ever removed by the pardon which He grants to penitent sinners. They cannot, therefore, be included in the penalty of sin. They do not belong to it, nor form any part of it. If they did, then every pardoned sinner would cease to suffer them the moment he was pardoned, for pardon removes all of penalty. If any of the penalty of sin remains upon a sinner to be suffered by him, he is not pardoned, but is under condemnation still. If, therefore, any one of the evils named in this passage enters into the penalty of sin, there is not a pardoned sinner in the world, and never has been. For it is a contradiction in terms to speak of one's being pardoned, and at the same time suffering penalty. But we see pardoned women, like all others, having their " conception multiplied ; in sorrow they bring forth children," just as other women do. Pardoned men, like all others, find the ground cursed for them ; like others, " they eat of it in sorrow all the days of their life." The earth, therefore, brings forth thorns and thistles for pardoned farmers, just as it does for those who are unpardoned. Moreover, they have to eat their bread in the sweat of their face, just as they did before they were pardoned. Then, at last, both the pardoned and the unpardoned return alike to the dust whence they were taken. In all these respects, "one event happeneth to them all."

It is a curious circumstance that with this last fact standing out so distinctly in all the history of the world, it should have passed into a theological axiom, that "the penalty of sin is death, natural, spiritual, and eternal." But upon what principle can natural death — the separation of the soul from the body — be accounted any part of the penalty of sin? Pardon is the exact measure of penalty, and its mission is to save the guilty, to whom it is granted, from suffering it. But pardon does not save sinners from suffering natural death.

It has been said, indeed, that pardon does not take effect on this part of the penalty of sin until the body is raised from the grave, and that the resurrection is a part of the pardon of sin, as dissolution is a part of its penalty. But this does not relieve us of the difficulty; for, in the first place, the bodies of the unjust are to be raised from the graves as well as those of the just. "There shall be a resurrection of the dead, both of the just and unjust." If, therefore, the resurrection of the body is a part of pardon, or its effect, then the unjust are pardoned not less than the just, and the consequence is that some pardoned sinners are raised to "the resurrection of damnation." Then, secondly, it leaves the pardoned under condemnation until the resurrection, contrary to the express declaration of the Scriptures, that "there is now no condemnation to them that are in Christ Jesus." A partial pardon, the removing of a part of the penalty from a believing penitent, and the leaving of the remainder of it upon him to be suffered, is, happily, an idea foreign to the gospel. In both its letter and its spirit, it repudiates the thought. Nothing could be farther from its teachings than that a child of God is, at the same time, a child of wrath, pardoned, and yet under condemnation; saved and yet punished. God chastens his children; but He does not punish them, visiting upon them the penalty of their sins. From this He wholly saves them by pardon. Otherwise the very naming of pardon would be a mockery.

A fair sample of all the arguments that we have met with for the support of this theological axiom (most writers accepting it as an axiom, and therefore needing no proof), is that very dogmatic one of Turretin (Ques. xii. 5): "Scriptura loquitur in genere de morte, Ergo sub ea complectitur quicquid nomine mortis venit in Scriptura; atque ita non minus mors corporalis, quam eterna intelligenda est." This, though a very poor argument, is, nevertheless, a very good explanation, we apprehend, of the way in which the subject has become so confused in the popular mind. " Scriptura loquitur in genere de morte:" Ergo — without thought or discrimination, and without considering the consequences involved in such an assumption. Death, in every sense in which the Scriptures use the word, is the penalty threatened to Adam in the garden. But if because " Scriptura loquitur in genere de morte, Ergo sub ea complectitur, quicquid nomine mortis venit in Scriptura," then, when our Saviour says, " whosoever liveth and believeth in me shall never die," He means that the believer shall never suffer bodily death ; because, " non minus mors corporalis quam æterna intelligenda est." But the believer does suffer bodily death, just as the unbelievers do. Our Lord had no reference, therefore, to bodily death, when He uttered these cheering words ; and we must not include in the term " death," " quicquid nomine mortis venit in Scriptura ; " nor must we, if we accept our Saviour's declaration as truth, include bodily death in penalty. The death from which He saves the believer is not the death of the body, but it is the death which is the penalty of sin.

We return then to our question : What is the penalty of sin ? We have seen that it is simply and only death ; but that it is not bodily death : that this does not enter into penalty, as one, the least, of its elements. We are led thus to inquire : What is that death which is the penalty of sin ?

The Scriptures alone can guide us in our inquiry. These teach us, in the first place, that death, the penalty of sin, is something that came upon Adam as soon as he sinned. " In the day that thou eatest thereof thou shalt surely die," fixes the time of the execution of the penalty, as clearly as it does the name of the penalty itself. Words could not be combined so as to state with more positiveness, that death should follow at once upon transgression, and at once become the portion of the transgressor. This is so manifest, that men have been compelled, whatever views they have entertained regarding the nature of the death that was threatened, either to admit that it was, in some sense, inflicted immediately upon our first parents when they sinned, or to deny that it was ever inflicted on them. "Adam then became mortal," say some. Others, "he then came under sentence of, and became subject to death." Others have it that Adam then began to die, as we are sometimes told all men do, "as soon as they be born," and that he kept on dying for nine hundred and thirty years, at the end of which he really died — or, more properly, he stopped dying, having been all this time coming to that which Jehovah had solemnly said, in the penal threatening of his law, he should come to the day he sinned. But all these schemes of postponement are very unsatisfactory, as interpretations of the Word of God. They are flatly opposed to the spirit of directness and positiveness which pervades the divine threatening; and, what is worse, if possible, they all leave pardoned sinners to suffer the penalty of their sins during their whole life upon the earth. To be dying for years the death that was threatened as penalty, is to be suffering that penalty for years; and to be subject to that death, and to be awaiting it to the end of earthly life as an inevitable doom, is to be subject to penalty, and awaiting its certain and inexorable infliction. Pardon is thus a nullity. But God does not thus trifle with men. The pardon which He promises to the penitent cannot but be real; and if real, it removes penalty from his lot, and removing this, it removes that which was called death by the penal clause of the law, and which came upon Adam the day he sinned.

We are unable to see why this argument is not a most effectual "short method" with all classes of "Annihilationists," who profess subjection to the authority of the Scriptures. If Adam died the day he sinned, and yet existed as a conscious and accountable being for nine hundred and thirty years thereafter, it is difficult to see that death, the penalty of sin, has anything whatever to do with the mere fact of conscious and accountable existence. It is true that men may come forward and calmly say, as that excessively superficial and illogical writer, Jenkyn, does say in his work on the "Extent of the Atonement," that "the penalty was not executed on man." They may then, as he does, begging the whole question, bring forward their doctrine, and lay it down as in itself an all-sufficient refutation of the declaration of the Almighty. Jenkyn does this when he sustains the above denial by the assertion: "for then there would have been no human race. The first pair would have been destroyed, and mankind would never have come into being." This would be reasoning, if it had been shown that death, the penalty of sin, was annihilation, or the utter ceasing of existence; but inasmuch as this has not been shown, there is no reasoning in it. It is naked assertion; nothing more or less than Jenkyn versus Jehovah. It cannot be that men who reverence the authority of the Bible will be willing long to follow such teachers. But must they not follow them and accept their contradictions of divine assertions so long as they hold that the penalty of sin is extinction of being?

We may add, that the position assumed so confidently by Jenkyn and "Annihilationists" generally, is shown to be altogether untenable, by the same test which we have applied to the teaching of others who put bodily dissolution into the penalty of sin. Penalty is not, in that case, removed by pardon. If bodily death is the penalty of sin, and this is extinction of being, as Jenkyn's words imply, then all the men of past ages, from Adam down to the last generation before the present, saving only Enoch and Elijah, have suffered it. Pardoned and unpardoned have alike been swept away out of being by the fell destroyer, who, though he has seen the " blood on the two side posts, and on the upper door post of the houses" of the penitent and believing, has not " passed over " them. Down to the present hour, the penalty of sin, if this be its penalty, has been executed on man; and if we judge the future by the past, it will continue to be executed on all, without distinction, until the sounding of the last trump. Is it not one of the necessary consequences of extending the real efficacy and highest purpose of the Atonement, as this writer does, that it should thus cease to have any efficacy whatever, and leave the whole race just where it found them? If, then, we assume that death, the penalty of sin, is extinction of being, and that this is accomplished by bodily dissolution, we are compelled, first, to do just as Jenkyn does, deny the truth of the Almighty's threatening, when He declared to Adam, " in the day that thou eatest thereof thou shalt surely die," and, siding with the serpent, say, " nevertheless he did not die;" and then, secondly, the solemn fact which history and observation force upon our attention, that all men do die, compels us to deliver over all classes of men, pardoned and unpardoned, believers in Christ and unbelievers, penitent and impenitent, to the fearful doom of the unsaved; notwithstanding our Lord declares, regarding his people, that they shall never perish, and that none shall pluck them out of his hands.

If we are guided by the Scriptures we shall receive from them further, in answer to our inquiry, that death, the penalty of sin, is something that passed down from Adam upon the human race, and became their inheritance, as it was his: "By one man sin entered into the world, and death by sin; and so death passed upon all men." Through the offense of the one [τοῦ ἑνὸς] the many [οἱ πολλοί] died [ἀπέθανον, aorist] — not became subject to death, or began to die, but died. That death which came upon Adam the day he sinned, went over upon and became the portion of the race. As he was not only the constituted head of the race, but the race, when he sinned, it was the race that sinned when he sinned; and as he was both the constituted head of the race and the race when he died, it was the race that died when he died. Whatever death was to him, the representative of the race, the day that he sinned and all of human nature sinned in him, that death is to that nature, in whatever individual it has its embodiment; and so death, whatever it is, is that which passed down through Adam, even as human nature itself did, to the race, and became their inheritance, as it was his. It is the constant representation, therefore, of the New Testament, that unregenerate men are not simply under condemnation, awaiting the execution of the death penalty, but that it has already taken effect upon them, and they have been devoted to it from the very beginning of their existence. They are born into death, and remain under its power until they are made alive by the energies of the Holy Spirit in their regeneration.

Hence the Scriptures teach us, thirdly, that death, the penalty of sin, is something which is removed from the soul by its regeneration. Those passages of the Word of God which sustain us in making this statement, sustain us also in making the statement immediately preceding it. They all presuppose and recognize the fact, that every unregenerate man is dead, by reason of his unregeneracy. A state of death is natural to

him, as a descendant of Adam. The only living men are those
who have been regenerated. By their regeneration they are
delivered from death, which is theirs by nature, into life, which
men never have but by grace. This is the uniform view of the
New Testament writers, both as to what the salvation of a sinner is, and as to the method of his salvation. Let us look at a
few passages in point: "We know," says the Apostle John,
"that we have passed from death unto life, because we love the
brethren. He that loveth not his brother abideth in death."
But what was the ground of this assertion? Why did he and
those whom he addressed, know that the fact that they loved,
established the fact that they lived? Was it not because it is a
fundamental principle of the gospel, that "love is of God, and
every one that loveth hath been born of God?" To love, with
the love of which the Apostle speaks, is to have been born
again; and, by this birth, to have passed from death into life.
To the same purpose is the declaration of Paul to the Ephesians, in that noted passage which is at once a key to all his
teachings on the subject of life and death, in the higher import
of these terms; and a summary of what, for want of a better
form of expression, we may call his theory of the plan of salvation: "You, who were the children of wrath even as others,
hath God made alive; who were — up to the time of his gracious interposition — dead in trespasses and sins." A little
further on, putting himself among those whom he was addressing, he adds: "Even when we were dead, God, who is rich in
mercy, for his great love wherewith He loved us, hath made us
alive, together with Christ." Nothing, it would seem, could be
more explicit. That process which changes a child of wrath
into a child of God, that is, his being born into the family of
God, his regeneration, makes him alive also from the dead.
Up to the time of his regeneration he is dead; by that act he
is made alive.

Another characteristic passage, which is full of the same
thought, is that one in the eighth of Romans, where Paul
says: "To be carnally minded is death; but to be spiritually
minded is life and peace." The same theory of the method of
salvation is here clearly brought out. On this theory, which,
be it remembered, is the theory of the Holy Ghost, every man
is carnal until he is born again by the Spirit of God. This

birth transforms him from a carnal into a spiritual man, and thus removes death from him, and causes him to live.

These passages are decisive of the point under consideration, even if they are taken by themselves, isolated from the great and fundamental principles involved in the declared necessity of regeneration; but read in the light of these principles, and taken, as they must be if taken rightly, as setting forth the method and kind of salvation necessitated by them, they give us a clearer and more absolute decision, resting on a broader foundation than that of mere proof texts. Thus taken, they cannot be weakened nor explained away, by the pretext that they are only figurative; but they stand forth, the plain and unmistakable recognitions of what is real in the condition of the natural and of the spiritual man.

The Scriptures reply yet further to our inquiry, that death, the penalty of sin, is something from which a believer is saved through faith in the Lord Jesus Christ. The remark made respecting the passages quoted to sustain the preceding proposition, — that they teach also that all natural men are dead — is applicable to the passages which we offer in support of this proposition; they all assume, that is, or plainly declare, that all unbelievers are dead. A few passages will be sufficient, especially as they, too, are not to be regarded as isolated proof texts merely, though decisive of the point if thus taken, but as the unfolding of the method and kind of salvation necessitated by the character of man as an unbeliever, and by his relation to the divine government. Very marked and decided is that passage in the third chapter of John: " He that believeth on the Son hath everlasting life; and he that believeth not the Son shall not see life; but the wrath of God abideth on him." The doctrine here taught cannot be misunderstood. If a man has not life he is dead; but life he has not if he is an unbeliever; and the death in which he lies is penalty, because it is that which rests upon him in the wrath of God. The same Evangelist says again, in his first epistle, " He that hath the Son hath life; and he that hath not the Son of God hath not life." He is dead, therefore, and he can never live, except through that agency by which he comes to " have the Son of God;" that is, as the New Testament always teaches, through the exercise of faith in the Son of God. Hence it is that our Lord

Himself says: "He that believeth in me, though he were dead, yet shall he live; and whosoever liveth and believeth in me shall never die." From that death which holds the unbeliever under its power he is released when he believes. From that moment he lives, and through faith in the Redeemer, he is thenceforth forever exempt from the claims of death, that is, of penalty upon him. We cite but one other passage out of the many which bear directly upon this point: "He that heareth my word, and believeth on Him that sent me, hath everlasting life, and shall not come into condemnation, but has passed from death unto life." That death which came upon him by sentence of condemnation, is removed from him through faith. These, and kindred passages of the Word of God, taken in connection with the constant teaching of the New Testament on the subject of life and death as related to penalty and salvation, leave us no room to doubt that the doom threatened in the penal clause of the law of God, as the punishment of the transgressor, is all removed from him when he believes in Him whom "God hath exalted, a Prince and a Saviour, to give repentance and forgiveness of sins."

Combining now the ideas contained in the two preceding statements, we shall have a direct, positive, and satisfactory answer to our inquiry: What is death the penalty of sin? First, it is that which is removed from the soul by regeneration. The immediate purpose and effect of regeneration is, so to change the sinner's moral nature that he shall cease to be an enemy and become a lover of God. His enmity to God is the special object towards which the energies of the Holy Spirit are directed when he transforms the sinner from a child of wrath into a son of God. Enmity dies away under the Spirit's mighty operation upon the sinner's heart, and love is created in its stead. This is the simple purpose and result of regeneration. When it has accomplished this it has done all its work; for, with love to God come, in their germs at least, every other grace and power of the spiritual man; as enmity to God carries with it every evil tendency, and all the intense selfishness and carnality of natural man. He is then a child of God. All the elements of character that make one a child of God are within him, and they need only the fostering influences of sanctifying grace to develop and perfect them, so that he shall be " perfect man," having attained " unto the measure of the stature of the fullness of Christ." These principles are so obvious to every reader of the New Testament that we need not confirm them by any quotations.

That, then, which regeneration specially and directly removes from the soul of a sinner, is his enmity to God, and alienation of heart from Him and holiness. These filled the soul of Adam, as they would fill the soul of any other hitherto holy moral agent, the day that he sinned. When he chose to disobey the command of God, all holy love died within him, and he found himself in utter alienation from his Maker. His soul had lost all its power and disposition to commune with God, " the fountain of life ; " and his enjoyment of Him and of holiness ceased, as a stream ceases when it is cut off from its fountain. Into this condition of enmity and alienation and godlessness, he came the day that he sinned. He separated himself from God. This was his death. The innermost idea of death is that of separation ; and the innermost idea of the death of the soul is its separation from God. To lose all love for God, and to be cut off, by this want of love, from all communion with and enjoyment of Him and of holiness, and to come thus under the dominion of evil desires, as opposed to those which are good, this is the death which is wrought in the soul " by trespasses and sins." This is the death out of which it is quickened — made alive — by the Holy Spirit in regeneration.

This is death viewed in its effects within the sinner himself: his moral character is such, that, by his very nature, he is not spiritual, but carnal ; not godly, but selfish — incapable of enjoying God or holiness ; separated by an impassable gulf from both. But this is not all. Unsaved sinners are not only enemies of God — God is their enemy. " He is angry with the wicked." As the Executive of a holy but violated law, He holds them under sentence of condemnation. His wrath abides upon them. They are in displeasure, and are not permitted to come into his presence. He thus separates them from Himself, the fountain of life, to be separated from which is to die, whether sinners cut themselves off by the ungodliness and carnality of their own characters, or the Almighty cuts them off in his anger, and by judicial abandonment of them on account of their sins. In either case the separation is death. In the latter it is death viewed as an effect pressing upon the soul from without, and sinking it forever away from all that is desirable in the favor of God, and in the bliss of his presence, into all that is terrible in his wrath and in eternal banishment from his presence.

This is the death which is removed through faith in the Son of God. The immediate purpose and effect of faith is so to change the relation of sinners to God, the Executive of a violated law, that He ceases to hold them under condemnation. Through faith they pass out from the judicial anger of the Lawgiver whom they have offended, and come into his favor. His wrath no longer abides on them; but, from that moment, He bestows on them all the fullness of his love. He no longer separates them from Himself as criminals and enemies, but welcomes them to his presence as his children. Faith thus reunites them with God, the fountain of life; and his "favor which is life," flows forth in streams of infinite love into their souls, and they live forever. Death gives place to life; condemnation and penalty to judicial favor and justification. They have thus "passed from death unto life."

These two things, on the one hand, enmity or godlessness and carnality, separating the soul from God by their very nature; and on the other hand, the wrath of God and judicial abandonment and banishment from God, and from heaven; these, and only these, are removed from the sinner by his regeneration and his faith. These two things fell upon Adam the day that he sinned. They are removed from a sinner when he is pardoned. By their removal the Scriptures declare that he passes from death unto life. Is it not certain that by their coming upon him he passed from life unto death? and that these are the elements of that death which is the penalty of sin?

This has been the state of natural man ever since the fall, and, therefore, he has ever since been under penalty. But though penalty was executed, and man died the day that he sinned, yet the circumstances under which the race was placed were at once modified by mercy. Justice had its course; but mercy was permitted to step in and alleviate the condition of the criminal, to the utmost possible extent consistent with righteousness. The race had had their probation, and lost it, under law. Mercy secured for them a new probation under grace. She was permitted because of "the Lamb slain from the foundation of the world," to carry to the condemned, who were already in penalty, the offer and the terms of pardon. While she waits to see what response men will make to her offers, she is allowed to stay, to a great extent, the fearful train of evils which penalty would otherwise drag after it. She has thus come into our prison-house and filled it with the light of her presence; and she continues to employ all the mighty resources put into her hands by infinite love, in bettering the condition of the already lost, that she may bring them to salvation. The unpardoned are, therefore, in a state of mitigated penalty, while they remain in this world; the pardoned are in a state of disciplinary training for a state where none of the evil consequences of sin will be found.

The probation of grace will end. Then mercy will have nothing further to do with the unpardoned. The dark inheritance of godlessness and carnality, and of banishment from God and heaven, which they have chosen for themselves by transgression, and confirmed and augmented by the rejection of the Son of God, will be entered upon in its unmitigated fearfulness. When this event comes, and penalty is left to do its awful work, without the alleviations which a gracious probation secured for a sinner here; when, that is, the selfishness and carnality of the sinner's heart, his enmity to God and holiness, are left to revel, unchecked by any of the circumstances, or influences for good, that now surround him; when the anger of an offended and insulted God strikes directly upon his soul, without those merciful refractions that now so lessen its consuming power; when mercy, that has held him up hitherto from the lower depths into which unalleviated penalty would have sunk him, holding him that she might offer him pardon and eternal life — when mercy withdraws her hand from beneath him, and her influences from about him, and the sentence comes from the throne of Him who has been waiting to see the result of the probation of grace, "Depart from me, ye cursed, into everlasting fire prepared for the devil and his angels:" then, when death becomes the fixed portion of the soul, and hope of salvation is forever withdrawn, and it is given over, out of the hands of mercy to eternal banishment from God and heaven, after having had the opportunity of coming back to Him, then the sinner enters into the SECOND DEATH, from which even infinite mercy and love cannot deliver him.

GRIFFIN ON DIVINE EFFICIENCY.[1]

THE immediate occasion of this treatise was a review, in the December number of the " Christian Spectator " for 1831, of a sermon by the celebrated Methodist divine, Wilbur Fisk, D. D., on " Predestination and Election." The review was understood to have been written by Professor Eliazar T. Fitch, of New Haven, Conn., and seemed to Dr. Griffin, then President of Williams College, and one of the foremost and most noted champions of Orthodoxy in New England, to be, not what its author claimed for it, a fair statement and defense of Calvinistic, as opposed to Arminian views on these subjects, but a denial of them, and a giving up of all the ground involved in the controversy between Calvinists and Arminians. A more remote occasion of the writing of the work before us was found in a series of articles in the first volume of the " Christian Spectator " (1829), reviewing Dr. Gardiner Spring's dissertation on " The Means of Regeneration." These articles were written by Dr. Nathaniel W. Taylor of New Haven, and seemed to Dr. Griffin, like the article of Dr. Fitch, to teach, not Scriptural Calvinism, but rationalistic Arminianism. Though both of the New Haven professors held firmly to the use of Calvinistic terms throughout their discussions, and in all their writings, yet the explanations of them which they gave, and the uses to which they put them, seemed to Dr. Griffin to justify him in pronouncing some portions of New Haven theology false and dangerous, and in arraigning them before the world for public condemnation.

There was yet another, though much less influential occasion for the writing of this treatise, in the publication, about this time, of a pamphlet, or pamphlets, denying the doctrine of Divine Efficiency, as it was commonly held by Calvinists, but

[1] Read to a Theological Circle, at the United States Hotel, Tuesday after noon, January 10, 1865.

ascribing to God an absolute dominion over the minds of moral beings by mere motives. The authors of these pamphlets fancied that they had relieved the doctrine of divine sovereignty of the most serious, if not of all real objections, when they had transferred its absoluteness from direct influence upon mind by the agency of the Holy Spirit, to an indirect influence through the instrumentality of motives. But their teachings seemed to Dr. Griffin not only not to relieve the doctrine of sovereign efficiency of any difficulties, but to be flatly opposed to the facts of consciousness and to the Word of God.

These various writings indicate to us pretty clearly the class of topics that most occupied the thoughts of New England theologians thirty-five years ago; and at the same time, we think, mark a new era in the history of New England Orthodoxy. All other subjects were thrown into the background by those which pertained to the method and character of God's government of moral agents, and to the nature and grounds of moral obligation. It was around these as centres, and for their elucidation, that the master minds of that day continually moved. With these prominently and mainly in view they were incessantly discussing, and debating upon, " Predestination," " Election," Decrees," " The Permission of Sin," " Human Depravity," " Atonement," " Regeneration," " Perseverance," every subject, indeed, that pertained directly to the relations of God to moral beings, and their relations to his moral government, whether under the law or under the gospel. Herein the treatment of these great subjects differed then from their treatment at other times. Before this they had been discussed rather as isolated truths and for their own sake. Formerly, more than now, it had been counted enough to attack or defend them as true or false in themselves, each by itself an independent centre ; now they must stand or fall just as they could, or could not, be made to harmonize with the assumed principles of moral government and moral agency, considered not so much in the light of the Scriptures, as in that of speculative reasoning, and so-called common sense.

These were the topics discussed with most earnestness. The manner in which they were discussed marked the new era, of which we spoke, in New England Orthodoxy. The stern metaphysical theology of Edwards and Belamy and Hopkins, and their immediate successors, the exponents of New England Orthodoxy in their time, had been, for the most part, made to bow reverently to the teachings of the Bible. The Bible in its plain and obvious sense was the supreme authority. No profundity of thought, or acuteness of reasoning, could place any principle on a basis firm enough to stand for a moment against what was manifestly the general scope of the Scriptures; nor support a speculation that required the wresting of a single text which clearly affirmed a sentiment opposed to it. It was left for avowed Universalists, Unitarians, and Neologists to "explain away" such passages of Scripture as were not in harmony with their opinions; or to set them aside altogether by ingenious glosses, or conjectural emendations of the sacred text. The spirit of all those early fathers of New England Orthodoxy still lived in Dr. Griffin, and often found expression in his writings. Thus, in the work before us, he writes (p. 80): "I believe this because I find it in my Bible: and while it is there, I will lie down upon it and hold it as with the grasp of death, even though as unable to understand it as to understand how God could exist without a beginning or a cause." Again, in the introduction to his work on the Atonement, he says: "In one principle both parties are agreed; that our instructions on this subject are to be drawn from the Scriptures alone, and not from bold and presumptuous speculations. Reason has only to kneel and ask what the oracle says. Her province is to ascertain the meaning of the sacred page by comparing Scripture with Scripture, and, in one description of cases (but not without great caution and humility), with common sense. The test of common sense is to be applied only to distinguish between the figurative and literal meaning of texts which were obviously intended to be subjected to such scrutiny." "To this conclusion," he says, in a note at the close of one of his arguments in the Park Street Lectures,— "To this conclusion, the author has conceived himself driven by the Word of God. Any question connected with the subject which is not decided by that arbiter, he dares not touch."

It was the same with all Dr. Griffin's immediate predecessors in the orthodox churches of New England. They indeed shrunk from the study of no subject however high or recondite or sacred connected with the being and government of God, or the character or interests or destiny of men, considered as immortal and subjects of moral government. They pressed their inquiries on these subjects with the utmost daring, and even with pertinacity. Nothing could daunt them or turn them back ; and, in every department of speculative theology where the Scriptures did not come in to modify or contradict their speculations, after having applied to them the tests of their keen, inexorable logic, they stood by them, defended them, and acted upon them, as, in certainty and authority, second to only the Bible itself. But they were always held, reverently and submissively, second to this.

At the time of which we speak, however, this reverence for the Scriptures had sensibly declined. The leaders of religious thought, especially the two New Haven professors, but most of all Dr. Taylor, who was just then beginning as a young giant to rejoice in his strength, and who, whether right or wrong, has, we think, given direction, more than any other man, to the instructions from New England pulpits for the past thirty years, had begun boldly to invade the domain of Scriptural authority, and while holding the leadership in recognized Orthodoxy, were not only solving all the great questions that had so long taxed the master minds of their fathers, and reducing these questions to place in their systems, without once applying to them the measuring line of the Word of God, but were beginning to apply to the Word of God itself the tests of their own reasonings and boasted common sense, not to learn from it what God had revealed, but what, from *a priori* considerations, He must reveal if He spoke at all on the subjects which were under discussion.

This is the new era in the history of New England theology to which we have referred. It was marked by the inauguration into acknowledged Orthodoxy of what is commonly styled New Haven Divinity. Dr. Nathaniel W. Taylor was its ruling spirit. And yet, this new era with Dr. Taylor, and his semi-rationalistic Orthodoxy, was but the legitimate result and natural outgrowth of the speculative theology of the previous century. That theology, and the character of mind and habit of thought involved in its study, must of necessity develop, first, the rationalistic Orthodoxy of New Haven ; and next, the pure Rationalism of Cambridge, if the minds that are trained under it are not held in check by the gracious teachings and regenerating influences of the Holy Spirit by which the fathers were held back from presuming upon intellectual infallibleness, and kept in humble and willing subjection to the authority of the divine Word. Give to any class of religious thinkers with a New England education the intense mental vigor and activity, and intellectual acumen that these men possessed, and you have only to withhold from them the humility that was so conspicuous a part of their piety, to constitute them thorough rationalists. If these thinkers are the sons of the godly New England divines of the seventeenth and eighteenth centuries, they will, at first, perhaps for a whole generation, be so far under the influence of traditional respect for the Bible as to save them from utterly rejecting it; but yet they will chafe under its authority, and they will strive in all ways but by its open rejection, to emancipate themselves from it. They will, therefore, hold nominally to the Scriptures as a revelation from God, and nominally give them the supremacy over all the reasonings and speculations of the human mind on religious subjects; but where they conflict with these reasonings and speculations, the tendency will be, not any longer as the fathers did, to correct them by the Scriptures, but so to interpret the Scriptures as to bring them into harmony with the reasonings and speculations.

This is incipient Rationalism. Let, now, the traditional reverence for the Bible which these men have inherited from their fathers, be removed, or very materially lessened, and you will have a class of thinkers ready to sit in judgment on the Scriptures themselves, and while, perhaps, not denying to them all authority as a revelation in some sort from God, yet so circumscribing that authority, and handling the Word itself so irreverently, and so exalting their own intellects above it as a revealer of truth and a guide to the soul, that all real authority will be taken from the Bible, and there will no longer be any final appeal to it, and no serious attempts made to cover up the glaring discrepancies between it and their own sentiments. So far as the Scriptures are in harmony with their ways of thinking it is all very well. They are very likely, thus far, to be the Word of God. Whenever, on the other hand, the Scriptures happen to be in conflict with their ways of thinking, it is of little consequence. In that they cannot be the Word of

God. They are thus far entitled to only that measure of respect that is due to any other merely human productions, whose authors were doubtless well-meaning men, and, for the most part, regarded what they wrote as truth ; but being human, and subject to all the ignorance and errors and prejudices of their times, very naturally fell into many and serious mistakes. These are to be corrected by men of a more liberal culture and more comprehensive minds. It is not to be supposed that a book the last pages of which were written nearly two thousand years ago, should be a sufficient treasury of religious truths for an enlightened and scientific age like the present. The progress of society and the elevation of the race will involve and necessitate the discovery of new truths in religion, the correcting of former mistakes, and the doing away of old dogmas. While, therefore, we respect the Bible as having done very well for men of an earlier and less enlightened age, as, indeed, having in it very much that is true and adapted to ourselves, yet our own thinking, or it may be, our own intuitions must supplement what is truth in the Bible, and discriminate between what is truth there, and what is error.

This is New England Rationalism in its second stage of development. You have to carry it but one step farther and its maturity is attained. Let traditional reverence for the Scriptures lose its last hold upon the still earnest and vigorous intellect, let the last traces of the humility of true piety be effaced, and let intellectual pride be advanced to its long coveted supremacy, and the work is done. Theodore Parker then stands before the world the embodiment of perfected New England Rationalism, the legitimate fruit, the necessary result of rationalistic New England Orthodoxy.

It fell to the lot of Dr. Griffin to be associated and to act with men who were in the first of these three stages of rationalistic development, and to witness the acceptance of their sentiments as orthodox by many of the New England churches. He clearly saw the dangerous tendency of these sentiments, if not to Unitarianism and Infidelity, certainly to mislead awakened sinners, and corrupt the ministry of the gospel, and felt himself called upon to put forth every endeavor to correct it, and save to the pulpit, and other methods of religious instruction and address, not only the " form of sound words," but the truthful and saving ideas which those words had from time immemorial conveyed to the Christian mind. This work on divine efficiency was one of the fruits of his labors in this direction. Possessing as he did in so large a degree the piety that can never exalt God too highly, nor too scrupulously guard his throne against the assaults and encroachments of pride, he was shocked at the daring attempts of his brethren to wrench the sceptre of grace from the hand of the Almighty, and give to sinners themselves all the glory of their own salvation by investing them with a self-sovereignty so complete and so independent of God that He stood powerless before the majesty of their lordly wills. He was alarmed to see opinions received as true and evangelical, which, to his view, left the holiness of both saints and angels no securer foundation to rest upon than that which is found in their own feebleness, and liability to temptation. He was pained and saddened to hear men who were counted orthodox, and, as such, had power over the public mind, directing perishing sinners to turn away their eyes from God as their only strength and righteousness, and to find in themselves and their own wills all they needed to transform them from children of wrath into children of God and heirs of heaven. He therefore girded himself to the work of saving his favorite doctrine from the perils into which it had been brought, lest, by its abandonment, the honor of God as the author of salvation and holiness should be tarnished and sinners should go down to death trusting their own works and not submitting themselves to the righteousness of God. That it was his favorite doctrine, and that it was so essential to the honor of God, and the well-being of men, he plainly declares on the first page of his Introduction: "I regard our dependence on divine efficiency," he says, "as one of the sweetest doctrines of the Bible, and know it to be most deeply felt under the special effusions of the Spirit. Take from me my dependence on God, and I must despair. I consider, too, the honor of raising to spiritual life a world dead in trespasses and sins, as one of the brightest glories of the Godhead; and I have been grieved at my very heart to see this honor taken away. This has been the severest cut of all."

The work is divided into an Introduction and ten chapters. In the Introduction he deprecates the tendency of religious controversy to awaken unhallowed passions; but hopes that he shall maintain, throughout this discussion, a kind spirit and good-will towards his brethren, "all of whom," he says, "I respect, and some of whom are my personal friends." Here, also, he defines his meaning of the term "Divine Efficiency," gives the two theories of modern origin that deny it and endeavors, in a few words, to show without entering into details that the one broached and defended by Drs. Taylor and Fitch, is in its most essential points, especially that pertaining to the self-determining power, perfectly at one with Arminianism.

"By divine efficiency," he says, "I mean the effectual power of God immediately applied to the heart to make it holy. This is the meaning which the Calvinistic world have always given to the phrase; and no man has a right to use it in another sense, and set off a contrary doctrine or otherwise. Nor may I be accused of wrongfully charging a denial of divine efficiency, because some may choose to wrap up another doctrine under this name."

The aim of chapter I. is to show, from Dr. Fitch's article itself, that the theory exhibited in his review of Dr. Fisk's sermon, "is," to use Dr. Griffin's own words, "one half the way, pure Arminianism; and the other half, it assumes the high language of Calvinism, with an Arminian meaning two thirds of the way, and for the other third, a Calvinistic meaning wholly at variance with the rest of the system." Dr. Griffin endeavors to show this, first, by spreading out the theory so plainly that "every one can understand it;" and, secondly, by giving "copious extracts" from the "Review" in confirmation of his statements.

The half of Dr. Fitch's theory, which is pronounced "pure Arminianism," is that part of it which pointedly denies the fact of "divine efficiency." In this Dr. Fitch declares that "if God should attempt to make men holy by efficient power, they would not be holy after all, for they would not be moral agents; that all He can do is to throw truth upon their understanding and conscience by his illuminating Spirit, and leave the result to the self-determining power, which is capable of yielding to the motives and capable of resisting any influence which God can bring."

The two thirds of the last half of Dr. Fitch's theory pertain to the doctrines of election and regeneration. Here it is that he uses "the highest Calvinistic language, but with a meaning entirely Arminian." "He says that by the Word and Spirit God insures the regeneration of Peter and John, and, according to an eternal purpose, selects them from the ruins of the Apostacy. He presses the doctrine of election in the strongest possible terms. But how does God insure regeneration? and what is the election contended for? Why, He insures the regeneration of Peter and John by urging upon them motives to which He foresaw that they, by the self-determining power, would yield. His mere determination to do this was the eternal decree of election."

"The other third of the last half of the way," wherein Dr. Fitch is said to use Calvinistic language and support the Calvinistic theory, but with entire inconsistency with the rest of his system, pertains to the doctrine of the perseverance of the regenerate. At this point, Dr. Griffin presses his opponent with his Arminian principles till the certainty of perseverance becomes very dubious. "If God does nothing for Peter but offer motives which the self-determining power is to yield to or reject, there are a million of chances to one that Peter will fall away. Satan fell away from perfect holiness; Adam fell away from perfect holiness: a million to one Peter will fall away from imperfect holiness, in a world full of temptations, with all his appetites and former habits set against him, unless he is kept by the power of God through faith unto salvation.' I beg to know what makes it certain that a single Christian will persevere. God's foreknowledge? That foresees a thing already certain, but does not make it certain." In other parts of the work Dr. Griffin asserts and endeavors to show that foreknowledge is impossible, at least that it is impossible for us to conceive of it as possible, on the principle of the self-determining power, as held by Drs. Taylor and Fitch, and all Arminians. His words are (p. 193), "Indeed, it is an overwhelming argument against this self-determining power, that it would shut out all the actions of creatures from his foresight, and leave the whole moral universe for the future to Him a perfect blank." Again: "As the success or failure [of using means for the salvation of both those who improve them and are saved, and those who neglect them and are lost] must depend on the self-determining power which lies beyond his control, He could not, so far as we can conceive, have foreseen the result." With this in view, the next question which he presses upon Dr. Fitch becomes yet more pointed: "How came it to pass that God, not as a mere prediction of what the self-determining power would do, but as a promise of what He himself would accomplish in reward of Christ, pledged Himself to Him that they all should remain steadfast? The doctrine of perseverance can consist with nothing but God's absolute dominion over mind, either by efficiency or by motives." Dr. Griffin justly adds, in closing his analysis of Dr. Fitch's views on this subject, "if this doctrine is true the rest of Dr. Fitch's theory falls."[1]

Chapter II. is an attempt to show that Dr. Taylor, whom Dr. Griffin counts his chief antagonist, has, in his articles on Regeneration, "exactly revived the old Arminian doctrine that the chief obstruction [to holiness] caused by bad affections lies in their drawing away the *attention* from divine truth; and that nothing is necessary on the part of God but to illumine the understanding by his Spirit." "Dr. Taylor," he says, "everywhere denies divine efficiency, and limits the agency of the Spirit to the mere presentation of motives. Of course he must have the same views of predestination and election (both of which he strenuously maintains) that Dr. Fitch has expressed. Dr. Taylor holds that God can create a being consti-

[1] Assuming that Dr. Griffin has rightly stated the views of Dr. Fitch (p. 13), to pray for the converting influences of the Spirit is an absurdity. If God *has* then done "the best He can by his Spirit for every individual, and therefore as much for one as for another," why pray Him to do yet more? God is asked to do what He can't do, in two respects,—first, because He has already done the best He could—his own resources are exhausted; and, secondly (since the idea of efficiency is discarded), because there is no such thing as absolutely converting or regenerating influence. The man converts and regenerates himself, in view of motives. So to pray that God would convert or regenerate a man is to ask God to do, first, what He can't do; and, secondly, what only the man himself can do.

Assuming, as above, that Dr. Griffin has rightly stated Dr. Fitch's views of election (p. 14), then God elected Peter and John only, because He saw that they would elect themselves; *i. e.* God could not help electing them since He foresaw they would elect themselves. The only election God had in the matter was by creating them to give them a chance to do what they were a mind to regardless of Him, or anything He could do.

Pages 15, 16, top. Nothing could make the salvation of any one certain but efficiency,—God could not foresee or foreknow a thing as certain which was contingent,—and, therefore, could not promise any seed to Christ.

tutionally qualified to act without being acted upon; that the angels are independent for holiness; that man would need no divine interposition but for his obstinate depravity; that this renders necessary a more urgent pressure of motives by the Spirit, to draw his attention from the world and fix it upon divine truth; that there is in man a constitutional susceptibility to the good exhibited in divine truth, founded in self-love or the desire of happiness; that consequently there is in the close consideration of truth a tendency to excite the love of truth; that as the Spirit does nothing but fix the attention upon truths most calculated to persuade, consideration only acts in a line with the Spirit, and has the same tendency in the moment of conversion as before; that consideration produces feeling, and feeling, consideration, while the Spirit by the clear presentation of truth promotes both; that without this consideration God cannot regenerate;" and much more to the same effect.

All the inferences which Dr. Griffin draws from the principles laid down by Dr. Taylor in these articles, are sustained, and all the objections which he urges against Dr. Taylor's views of regeneration, are more than justified by a recipe for regeneration which Dr. Taylor gives in the first number of the "Christian Spectator," and which we do not find that Dr. Griffin has anywhere directly referred to. We commend this recipe to the attention of all who have entered with Dr. Taylor upon the first stage of rationalistic development, and have in consequence become so far free from the trammels of hereditary reverence for the authority of the Bible, as to disbelieve that the regenerate were "born not of blood, nor of the will of the flesh, nor of the will of man, but of God;" and to take issue with our Saviour when He declares that "the wind bloweth where it listeth, and thou hearest the sound thereof, but canst not tell whence it cometh, and whither it goeth; so is every one that is born of the Spirit." Dr. Taylor's recipe for regeneration is this:[1] "Let the sinner then, as a being who loves happiness and desires the highest degree of it, under the influence of such a desire, take into solemn consideration the question whether the highest happiness is to be found in God or in the world; let him pursue this inquiry, if need be, till it result in the conviction that such happiness is to be found in God

[1] *Christian Spectator*, vol. i. pp. 32, sq.

only; and let him follow up this conviction with that intent and engrossing contemplation of the realities which truth discloses, and with that stirring up of his sensibilities in view of them, which shall invest the world, when considered as his only portion, with an aspect of insignificance, of gloom, and even of terror, and which shall chill and suspend his present active love of it; and let the contemplation be persevered in, till it shall discover a reality and an excellence in the objects of holy affection, which shall put him upon direct and desperate efforts to fix his heart upon them; and let this process of thought, of effort, and of action be entered upon as one which is never to be abandoned, until the end proposed by it is accomplished, — until the only living and true God is loved and chosen as his God forever; and we say, that in this way the work of his regeneration, through grace, may be accomplished. In this way he may become a child of God."

There is here no regenerating Spirit; no turning with the cry for mercy to a crucified and risen Saviour; no recognition of the need of pardon; no acknowledgment whatever of God. A sinner whose mind is enmity against God, which is not subject to his law and cannot be; who is a child of wrath, and under righteous condemnation as a transgressor; this one may, without pardon, without the help of God, without even the consent of God, transform himself, by a mere act of thinking, into a child of God, and force himself upon God as such! And all this directly in face of the explicit declaration of the Bible that " the natural man receiveth not the things of the Spirit of God, for they are foolishness unto him; neither can he know them, because they are spiritually discerned;" and all this, moreover, in a series of articles especially intended to show that there is no such thing as a sinner's using this means of salvation. And not only this, not only may the sinner thus regenerate his own soul, but without this process of independent, self-begun, and self-sustained mental exertion, there can be no regeneration. This Dr. Taylor distinctly asserts a few pages further on in his essay: " Regeneration, though always to be ascribed to the grace of God " [out of a lingering respect to the authority of the Bible], " is action on the part of the sinner, and can never take place, unless the objects of holy affection are brought before the mind as objects on which the affections are now to be fixed." Infant regeneration is therefore an impossibility, and never takes place. If death passed upon all men, even upon those who had not sinned after the similitude of Adam's transgression, then, unless they come to years of mature thought, sufficiently mature, at least, to go through this process of comparison and choosing, they never live. These souls cannot be regenerated. They must abide eternally in death!

Among the passages which Dr. Griffin selects from Dr. Taylor's articles to show his views of regeneration, is one which we notice not as a recipe, but rather as giving the rationale of regeneration without divine efficiency: "The sinner desires acceptance with God,—contemplated simply under one relation, namely, as the only means of deliverance from punishment. Nor is this a selfish state of mind [though self-love is supreme! — Dr. G.], but rather a state of mind which is necessarily involved in the mental process of turning from sin to holiness. The supreme affections of his heart being detached from the world, the grand obstacle to his preferring a deliverance from punishment to the only object that can come into competition with it, is removed. And now, according to the laws of voluntary action, nothing is wanting to lead forth the heart in holy affection to God, but clear, just, and vivid views of his glories. Those glories are yet veiled. Still, however, he is willing to fix, and does in fact fix, the eye of contemplation on the object of holy affection, and does, with such glimpses of his glories as he may obtain, feel their attractions and summon his heart to the love of God."

We cannot but agree with our author in the remarks that he subjoins to his review of this process of regeneration: "This is on the whole just such a journey as I should expect a supremely selfish man and totally depraved sinner would make in his own strength from sin to holiness. Treading selfishness under his feet with a heart caring for nothing but himself; panting with 'truly sincere desire, for acceptance with God,' while blind to his excellence, and caring for nothing but to shield himself from punishment; completely detached from the world, and justly prepared to give his heart to God as soon as he can obtain 'clear, just, and vivid views of his glories,' the precise things that never were seen but by holy eyes; put upon using the means of regeneration when the act cannot possibly precede regeneration itself. If this is the road travelled by the self-determining power, surely 'the way of the transgressor is hard.' I should hope that this single attempt might discourage the nations from essaying to go in this new path. Surely it is better to 'go in the strength of the Lord God;' to 'make mention of his righteousness, even of his only.'"

It would seem to be a sufficient refutation of all Dr. Taylor's theory of the process of regeneration to say what Dr. Griffin has not said directly in reply, that if the carnal mind is enmity against God, then the more clearly God is seen the more intensely will He be hated. So that the truth that reveals God, cannot, by any amount of clearness, or power in its presentation, cause an unregenerate man to love God. This cannot be denied unless it can be shown that hate intensified is turned into love by the process of becoming intensified.

Chapter III. is a brief notice of two other writers, one of whom especially had criticised, unfairly, as Dr. Griffin thought, his views of natural ability, and had misrepresented the principles of New England Calvinism respecting this subject. This chapter adds little or nothing to the argument of Dr. Griffin, and is of little importance beyond this one distinct statement: "There is no difference between me and the reviewer about natural ability, except that I place it in the faculties of a mind dependent on God for holiness, and he places it in faculties that move themselves to holy action without divine efficiency." Dr. Griffin had treated this whole subject of "ability" far better, and more satisfactorily, as an answer to his reviewer, in the tenth of his "Park Street Lectures," and might better have left it as it was there, against all that his opponent could have said, than to have brought it into this work.

He then holds that men have all the faculties necessary to make them responsible; that they ought to love God; that the only reason they do not is not the lack of capacity to do it, but of a disposition to do it. The lack, therefore, is moral, not natural. They have a natural ability in the very fact of possessing faculties — and all the faculties needed — to love God; all the faculties that even the regenerate, and the most holy saints in heaven have.

In chapter IV. the author addresses himself directly to the

task of discussing his subject independently, without special reference to opposers, by unfolding "the meaning and origin of corrupt nature." A single paragraph, the second in the chapter, contains the essence of the whole, and puts Dr. Griffin's theory of the origin of sin, and his boldness as a theorizer, before us with very satisfactory distinctness. It shows him as a real descendant of the daring metaphysical speculators that had just passed from the stage of theological discussion,— the Edwardses, Hopkins, Bellamy, Emmons, "et id omne genus."

"Self-love," he begins, "consists in the desire of happiness and aversion to misery, or in loving to gratify our personal tastes and feelings. This is essential to a rational and even to a sensitive nature. This had Adam before the fall; but divine efficiency wrought in him supreme love to God, which kept self-love in due subjection. As soon as God withdrew his sanctifying influence (and that He did sovereignly and not as a punishment), Adam's self-love became supreme (there can be no rivals for supreme affection but God and self), and of course turned to selfishness, and, as soon as God was presented in his law, to 'enmity against God.' For all this no positive act was necessary on the part of God but to uphold Adam's rational existence. If Adam does not love his Maker supremely, he must with supreme desire seek the means of his own personal gratification, or cease to have a rational soul. Now that proneness to gratify himself, growing out of the absence of love to God and the presence of self-love turned to selfishness, or perhaps I may more properly say, that combination of inward circumstances out of which will infallibly arise the exercises of selfishness and enmity against God, constitutes the corrupt nature or temper of which I speak. While his rational existence is continued, and while he does not love God, it must be his nature to be selfish, and to hate God when God sets Himself against him in his law, as much as it is in the nature of the serpent to bite and of the lion to be carnivorous. The difference between the two cases is this: The nature of the serpent and lion depends on their physical formation; the nature of Adam, on the absence of love to God which he ought to exercise. He is to blame for that state of things,— for that nature or aptitude,—and therefore is a moral nature. If one must love his own happiness in case he is even sentient, then a man who does not love God must, anterior in the order of nature to his selfishness, have an infallible aptitude to selfishness. If the soul must have desires after something or cease to be, and must be influenced by the greatest apparent good, then a man who loves himself supremely and God not at all, must have a preparation within him (consisting perhaps in the mere relation of things), to hate God when God comes to be seen arrayed against him in his law. When God reproduced supreme and habitual love to Himself in Adam's heart, that nature or aptitude was changed. It was not the new nature of Adam to seek his own interest supremely and to hate God." A foot-note is added to parry any thrust that might be made at him because of his use of the word nature. " I know," he says, " that the word nature, etymologically considered, belongs exclusively to physics; but for want of another term, and prompted by a strong analogy, men have applied it to our moral constitution. And while it means this, to say that a change of nature must be a physical change, is only a play upon words which involves a serious error." The theory proceeds: " The constitution made with Adam was, that if he continued obedient his posterity should be preserved holy; that if he transgressed they should be abandoned to sin. In consequence of the fall they come into the world without the sanctifying influence of God upon their hearts. The consequence is, they are left under the dominion of selfishness."

Such is Dr. Griffin's view of the "origin of sin" and his meaning of "corrupt nature." The worst that can be said of any part of his theory is that some of it has no direct Scriptural testimony in its favor. But on the other hand it may be said that there is not only no Scripture contradicting it, but that it is, some of it, favored by fair inference from many passages of the Scriptures, and very much of it sustained, and he himself sustains it in a subsequent chapter, by a large array of Scriptural testimony. At all events his theory provides an unquestionable necessity in the nature of moral beings, fallen and unfallen, for divine efficiency in order to their continuing in holiness if they are now holy, or, for their becoming holy, if they are sinful. If any one chooses to deny the need of divine efficiency in order to the restoration of the sinner to a state of holiness it is incumbent upon him to furnish a theory of the origin of sin, and of a corrupt nature, so clearly in harmony with his denial, that it will show that the theory here proposed cannot be true. The difficulty of inventing and defending such a theory on any principles held by his opponents, is well shown, and strength given to his own theory by our author in another part of his work. In the chapter on "Sinless Creatures Dependent for Holiness," he asks, "if sinless creatures are not dependent for holiness [and so do not fall by the withdrawing of that upon which their holiness depends], how will you account for the fall of any? and since some have fallen, what security is there that all will not apostatize? While the heart is right and the mind free, proper motives, set clearly before the understanding, will certainly awaken right affections. And temptations to sin while the heart is right, will instantly be rejected. How then can a holy being apostatize? Not until the heart ceases to be inclined to fall in with the motives which move it before. That cessation cannot be produced by good motives, and before it takes place bad motives cannot operate.

It cannot therefore be the effect of motives. It must result from some influence, or some withdrawment of influence, behind the scene. If it results from a positive influence, God must be the efficient cause of sin; if it results from the withdrawment of an influence, the influence withdrawn was that which before inclined the heart to holy action; and that is the very efficiency for which we plead. A change of heart, or of the causal influence which acts upon the heart, must therefore be the first thing in the fall of a holy being. While the heart is overflowing with supreme love to God, no temptation to transgress can gain the ear; and no delusive speech can gain a moment's credence till faith in God has given way. You seek in vain for the origin of this change in motives bearing upon a heart warm with the love of God. The heart must first degenerate before the motives can touch it. The habit of love itself, or the propensity to love, must fail, before anything in the mind, or in outward temptations, can take hold of the heart to debase it. The first thing to be done is to dry up the fountain of that love, which no mere faculties or motives will ever accomplish. That can be done only by the withdrawment of the influence which produced it. Therefore if God has no efficient influence to withdraw, there is no accounting for the fall of a holy being. The conclusion to which we come is, that the fall of Adam and of the angels furnishes strong proof that a divine influence was withdrawn which had supported their love. But influence or no influence, they fell. And if they had not been kept by divine efficiency, neither are the inhabitants of heaven now kept. And if some fell, thus unsupported, what can prevent them all from falling?"

Chapter V. deals with the doctrine of divine efficiency considered as the cause of all holy exercises, as opposed to the self-determining power claimed by Arminians and not denied by New Haven Calvinists; and shown not to be destructive of the freedom of moral agents, nor inconsistent with its exercise. "The real question lies," Dr. Griffin declares, " between the Calvinistic doctrine of divine efficiency, and the Arminian self-determining power." There is no middle ground between them; unless you claim an absolute dominion in motives, and this was not claimed by those against whom mainly Dr. Griffin was in controversy. Those who did hold to this dominion by motives, then a new system, just beginning to assert itself, are noticed and answered in another part of the volume. So far as all his other opponents were concerned, and, as a moment's consideration will show, so far as these are concerned, the only alternative is, divine efficiency, or the self-determining power, the cause of all holy exercises especially in fallen beings. By the self-determining power, Dr. Griffin says he means " no more than a power that actually turns from sin to God without divine efficiency in view of motives illumined by the Spirit, but not absolutely controlling." If the alternative of the self-determining power be taken to account for the beginning of holy exercises in the mind of the sinner, then one involves himself in the dilemma, and in all the absurdities of asserting an effect without a cause. No man acts unless he is influenced or caused to act. But what causes a mind that hates God to begin to love Him? If you say it causes itself to begin to love, or that it chooses to love, then we ask what causes him to cause himself to do this, or to choose to do it? If you say he chooses to choose, then you have the choice before the first choice, which the self-determining power always involves, and to which it always sooner or later comes, if the attempt is made to account for the origin of holy exercises by it.

If, on the contrary, the alternative of divine efficiency be chosen to account for the cause of holy exercises in a sinner's mind, then it is said that since God, by direct influence on the soul, causes it to act in a particular direction, its freedom is destroyed, and it ceases to be an agent, at least a moral agent. To this it is replied that freedom is not destroyed so long as there is willingness. If a man acts willingly he acts of his own accord, acts freely, and is therefore not only an agent, but a moral agent. Dr. Griffin plants himself firmly on this ground and defies all who deny the doctrine of efficiency to show that because God makes his people willing in the day of his power, He therefore and thereby destroys their power to be willing. But if they are willing then they are free, and the alleged destruction of their freedom, and so of their moral agency, is false. God does not make his own mind, nor his own exercises. Men do not make their own willingness or unwillingness, but if they are willing they act freely, if they are unwilling they freely refuse.

As to sinful exercises, Dr. Griffin claims that we may account for them, and that he does, " by the existence of self-love (essential to every nature above a block), turned into selfishness by the absence of love to God, and moved by motives of which the universe is full, but," he continues, " we cannot account for the holy exercises without going back beyond the motives in view of which they were called forth, to that Power which caused the mind to fall in with the motives: for before holiness is implanted in the heart, there is nothing answering to self-love in the other case, to which the motives are adapted."

Chapter VI. is on the " Importance and Instrumentality of the Truth." The design is to show that those are in error who claim that the only power exerted by God in the regeneration and sanctification of sinners is exerted upon the truth, and not directly on the sinner's heart. Dr. Griffin admits, and glories in the admission, that " the eternal empire of Jehovah over a universe of moral agents, is sustained by nothing but truth, — is nothing but truth illustrated, and applied as motives to obedience, adoration, and praise." He will not be outdone, either in his reverence for the truth, or in exalting it as the great sanctifying instrumentality in the moral government of God.

But as the instrumentality of the truth is solely as motives, and the moral governor acts upon moral agents, as such, only by these, how can Dr. Griffin, who admits and claims all this, escape from what some of his opponents assert, that all the power that God puts forth in regenerating and sanctifying sinners is exerted on the truth as a motive power, and not directly on the sinner's heart. To this, Dr. Griffin, in various places, replies, by bringing forward what plays so conspicuous a part in his "Treatise on the Atonement:" God is not solely a moral governor, though He is this. Men and angels are not solely moral agents, though they are this. Besides moral governor, God is also absolute sovereign, "doing all his pleasure" in the army of heaven and among the inhabitants of the earth, and moral agents are subjects of this sovereign. In this sovereignty, lying back, so to speak, of moral government, and above it; acting in and through, but not disturbing it, is the fountain of all gracious influences, the source of all sanctifying power. From this throne, the throne to which every suppliant looks for mercy, and to which every real prayer is addressed, God as an absolute sovereign graciously dispenses those influences in which is the cause of all holy exercises. These cause the heart to fall in with the truth presented as a motive. But for these the truth, as an instrumentality, would be forever powerless; and the fact that by these God causes all holy exercises — but the agent puts them forth — is in harmony with the teachings of the Scriptures. Does not God give repentance? but the sinner repents. Is not faith the gift of God? but the believer exercises it.

"It is the moral governor alone," says Dr. Griffin in another part of the book, "who says, 'What could have been done more to my vineyard, that I have not done in it?' The sovereign efficient cause says, 'The king's heart is in the hand of the Lord as the rivers of water: He turneth it whithersoever He will.' The moral governor says, 'The Lord is long-suffering, not willing that any should perish, but that all should come to repentance.' The sovereign efficient cause says, 'Therefore hath He mercy on whom He will have mercy, and whom He will He hardeneth.'"

Chapter VII. is the Scriptural argument. In this chapter Dr. Griffin appears in favorable contrast with all his opponents.

While they theorize, and base their theories, for the most part, in all indeed wherein they greatly differ from him, on their own hypotheses, he, having theorized as boldly as they, then brings all his speculations to the test of God's Word, and planting himself there, is not only ready to sacrifice even the evidence of all his senses and his consciousness to its authority, but with calm security bids defiance to all the logic and boasted common sense that a universe can marshal against him. It is this that gives his Essay on the Atonement its greatest charm. And although his array of Scripture is less masterly here than in that work, yet it is sufficient here to place his main principles beyond the reach of all fair question. Under ten different heads he groups together several hundred passages from the Bible, many bearing directly, all fairly, on the side of his doctrine. This marshaling of proof texts, though coming in after the other arguments, in the book, one will not fail to see, was first in the author's mind. He began with the Bible as his centre, and made from it all his excursions into the region of speculation. And there are few of his speculations that do not readily return and link themselves again with this centre.

Chapter VIII. is devoted to the proving that sinless creatures are dependent for holiness. The finest reasoning of the book is in this chapter. He here also presses his opponents most successfully with the consequences of their doctrine of a self-determining power. We have quoted one passage from it, and as there are no new principles brought forward, — none but such as have been stated in the preceding part of the work, — it is not necessary that we should dwell upon it. His opening paragraph will show how he applies these principles, and carries the doctrine of divine efficiency upward and makes it the support and safety of the elect angels. " To me it appears as impossible for God to make a being who shall act independently of Him, as to make a being who for the future shall be self-existent. If God could make a thing, whether a being or a power, that would exist and act, after He had withdrawn, He could make a thing which for the time to come would be self-existent; and yet self-existence would be communicated! A power derived from God to exist without God!"

"The same reasoning will prove that a created mind could not be made to go alone. Without the application of divine efficiency it may be reasonably bound, and therefore may have that power which is the basis of obligation; but nothing can make it independent in its operations: for independent action implies independent attributes, and independent attributes imply independent being, and independent being would be communicated self-existence."

Chapter IX. is on God's power to prevent sin. The question is fairly met, and none of the consequences of the doctrine under discussion are denied. God could have prevented sin. If He had not withdrawn His sanctifying influences from holy angels, and from Adam, they would never have fallen. But these influences were not necessary to constitute them moral agents, nor to make holiness obligatory upon them. They were bound to love God supremely; and in their natural faculties they had all the capacity necessary to do it. The sanctifying influences that insured the continuance of these beings in holiness while they stood, and that now secures the holiness of angels, and all the saints, were purely gracious. They might therefore be withdrawn, and they were withdrawn, as they had been bestowed, sovereignly; and their withdrawal was doing no injustice to those who had previously enjoyed them, because they were fully qualified and so bound to be holy without them.

On the reason for the permission of sin, Dr. Griffin does not pretend to dogmatize. He stands with all true Calvinists, and is satisfied that the glory of God and the best interests of the universe, taken as a whole, are subserved by it. He rests in the words of the Psalmist which furnished Dr. Hopkins with a text for his famous discourses on this subject, and agrees substantially with Dr. Hopkins in the doctrine and inferences which he draws from that text, " the wrath of man shall praise thee, and the remainder of wrath will He restrain."

The tenth chapter is on the " Alleged Dominion of Motives, — a Distinct Theory." " The theory is, that God can mould the heart at pleasure by the mere influence of motives, whether they are adapted to its present temper or not."

It is a sufficient reply to this theory to say that it neither rebuts the Scriptural proofs for divine efficiency, nor sustains itself by the Scriptures, and that it does not relieve the doctrine of sovereign efficiency of any of its difficulties, the purpose for which it was invented. If God can compel by motives, you have the compulsion which you object to as much by these as by efficiency. And if God can thus compel, you are exposed to the same unanswerable question that is urged against efficiency. Why does He not exert his power, and so multiply motives that none will be able to perish? And why did He not so multiply them that none could fall? If continuance in holiness, and salvation from sinfulness, are both alike within the sovereign power of God, so that every holy being will throughout eternity feel and confess in songs of everlasting praises his utter dependence on God for his preservation from falling, he may better stand by the Bible and ascribe his preservation to the direct efficiency of God by gracious influence on his heart, than go beyond the Bible and contrary to it, and ascribe it to absolute and sovereign dominion by motives.

www.ingramcontent.com/pod-product-compliance
Lightning Source LLC
Chambersburg PA
CBHW022149300426
44115CB00006B/408